GREAT
OUTDOOR
ADVENTURES

TOM STIENSTRA'S
ALMANAC

OF THE BAY AREA & NORTHERN CALIFORNIA

SAN FRANCISCO

PUBLISHED BY FOGHORN PRESS

 WRITTEN BY TOM STIENSTRA

Special thanks to Will Hearst and Jim Sevrens
of the San Francisco Examiner.

Book design by Luke Thrasher
Cover design by Karen Schreiber and Camela Curry
Cover photo by Jeffrey Patty. Pictured are Tom Stienstra, Michael Furniss and Bob Stienstra, Jr. on top of Half Dome in Yosemite National Park.

ISBN: 0-935701-05-2
Printed in the United States of America

As with most books, information is subject to the changing times which bring raised fees and altered schedules. We monitor these changes and update as needed, but should we miss anything, we invite your comments and updates on Great Outdoor Adventures. Include your address, and for your efforts, we'll send you our quarterly outdoor newsletter free.
Mail to: Foghorn Press, P.O. Box 77845, San Francisco, CA 94107

"...Out in Luckenbach, Texas, there
ain't nobody feelin' no pain."

-- Waylon Jennings

TABLE

OF

CONTENTS

SAN FRANCISCO

PUBLISHED BY FOGHORN PRESS
WRITTEN BY TOM STIENSTRA

CHAPTER 1

BAY AREA HIKES

WITH

31 ADVENTURES

CONTENTS:—

PUBLISHED BY FOGHORN PRESS

SAN FRANCISCO

QUALITY OUTDOOR BOOKS

BAY AREA HIKES

SOURCES FOR 125 BAY
AREA PARKS

LET YOUR FINGERS DO THE WALKING

G oing for a good walk in a special place is the kind of thing that will never lose its appeal, because it needs no extra pushing. There is no build-up of tension as in a sport, but rather a release from it. Some people have doubted true freedom exists in America, but you can find it on a hike.

That is, providing you have a special place to go. That's the catch for a lot of people.

But in the Bay Area alone, there are thousands of miles of trails to visit, most of them secluded in quiet and beautiful settings. And when the air is clear and clean, the day fresh, it's perfect for a hike.

And of course, the price is right. Access is either free or just a dollar or two.

To find a spot to call your own, here's a capsule listing of sources for maps, information of prime hiking areas:

■ East Bay Regional Park District:

The Regional Park District manages 46 parks that cover 65,000 acres in Alameda and Contra Costa counties. There are more than 500 miles of trails that cut through all kinds of settings, and an additional 100 miles of trails that connect the parklands.

Who to contact: For information and free maps, phone (415) 531-9300, Ext.

2208, or write the Regional Park, 11500 Skyline Boulevard, Oakland, CA 94619.

■ Golden Gate National Recreation Area:

Redwood forests, grassy hillsides, and ocean bluffs make this a spectacular attraction in Marin County. Some of the best spots are Muir Woods, Tennessee Valley, Marin headlands and Mount Tamalpais. A network of trails connects the different parks.

Who to contact: For a free map and brochures, call the GGNRA at (415) 556-0560, or write the National Park Service, Building 201, Fort Mason, San Francisco, CA 94123.

■ Mid-Peninsula Open Space District:

This is one of the best-kept secrets on the San Francisco Peninsula, with 25,000 acres of open land sprawling on 26 preserves -- most of them set along the Peninsula ridgeline at Skyline Boulevard. Access is free.

Who to contact: For maps, phone the District office at (415) 949-5500, or write 201 San Antonio Circle, Building C, Suite 135, Mountain View, CA 94040.

■ Point Reyes National Seashore:

This is a diverse place where you can see tule elks, a waterfall that flows onto the beach, and whale spouts on the ocean, all in one day. The terrain varies from grasslands, chaparral ridges, ocean bluffs, and at the southeast end of the park, forestland.

Who to contact: For information and a free brochure, call (415) 663-1092, or write Point Reyes National Seashore, Point Reyes, CA 94956.

■ California State Parks:

The greater Bay Area has close to 20 state parks that provide hiking opportunities, along with 15 state beaches. The parks range from Angel Island in the center of San Francisco Bay to the redwood forests of Big Basin, Butano, and Henry Cowell parks in the Santa Cruz Mountains.

Who to contact: For a brochure, send $2 for Publications Section, Department of Parks and Recreation, P.O. Box 2390, Sacramento, CA 95811.

■ Other Options:

Many Bay Area counties also manage local-run parks, and information can be obtained by a direct call to them. To pinpoint prime hikes outside of the Bay Area, the best way is to obtain maps from the U.S. Forest Service, which manages 16 National Forests in California. A guide sheet to National Forests is free by writing USDA-Forest Service, Office of Information, Pacific Southwest Region, 630 Sansome Street, San Francisco, CA 94111. Maps of individual forests, which detail all hiking trails and lakes, cost $2 from the same address.

THE BAY AREA'S
TOP 10 HIKES

THE FOOTLOOSE-AND-FANCY-FREE GUIDE

A short drive and two-hour jaunt can take you to waterfalls that resemble murals, dark canyons studded with redwoods, Douglas fir and oak, and mountain peaks where you need a 360-degree swivel on your neck to take in all of the beauty. But where?

Right here in the Bay Area, just over yonder, where the "Quiet America" is out there waiting for you.

All a person usually asks for on a hike is guaranteed solitude and the chance to touch base with thoughts on a personal, gut level. On the Bay Area's Top 10 hikes, as selected by The Examiner, that is precisely what you get -- in addition to stunning panoramas of wilderness settings and the San Francisco Bay alike.

Hiking has always provided a special therapy that can do far more good than an hour on a psychiatrist's couch. In the city, the intrusions of stop lights, traffic jams, horns and jackhammers seem programmed to grind the gears in your head. But on the trail, thoughts suddenly simplify, problems are solved by themselves.

Instead of running down the fast lane with a telescope looking for the horizon, hiking allows you a new perspective, providing you with a first-hand experience of the basic elements of the wild. You may have missed it before. Instead of grappling with a calculator and a bank account, at your grasp are serpentine rock formations, moss-covered firs, or a lavish display of wildflowers.

At the end of the day, you have that good tired feeling and a certain knowledge of accomplishment that isn't measured in dollars and cents. It can tug at your gut -- a profit more real than money. And all you supply is the get-up-and-go.

A few key sources of information can aid your planning. The East Bay Regional Park District, (415) 531-9300, provides free brochures and maps for 600 miles of trails in Alameda and Contra Costa County. California Explorer, 45 Woodside Lane, Mill Valley, CA 94941, publishes eight issues per year ($18) and suggests hikes and trail conditions in Northern California.

For information on the Golden Gate Recreation Area, the book Charette's Maps is available in book stores and mountain shops.

And for a guide to the 200 state parks in California, send $2 to California State Parks & Recreation, Attention: DARC, P.O. Box 2390, Sacramento, CA 95811.

What more can you ask for? Here are

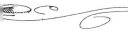

■ 1. Big Basin State Park:

A two-hour hike from park headquarters will take you past awesome native stands of redwoods, along streams in the bottom of canyons filled with an array of flora and fauna -- and ultimately, to a 100-foot waterfall that looks like something out of Yosemite.

And after a wet winter, another series of smaller waterfalls on the same trail cascade down slopes in sheets of bubbling, white water. Trail conditions are good.

How to get there: Big Basin sits off of Highway 236 out of Boulder Creek, a short drive from Santa Cruz.

Who to contact: For more information, call (408) 338-6132.

■ 2. Point Reyes National Seashore:

Rather than a single stunning element of attraction, Point Reyes offers a variety of settings, including freshwater waterfalls tumbling into the ocean and dark canyons shadowed by Douglas firs. And while hiking on ridges, the expanse of the Pacific Ocean sits quietly as a backdrop.

Point Reyes is a geologic phenomenon because the entire peninsula is bordered by the San Andreas Fault and is moving north. In one section, you can view streams sitting on different sides of the fault running in opposite directions.

On weekends, you can expect plenty of company at the Bear Valley Trail, which starts at park headquarters. A better choice would be the Palo Marin Trail,

which enters from Bolinas, which provides expansive views of the ocean and passes by lakes and ponds as well.

How to get there: From Highway 101 in Marin County, take the Highway 1 cutoff at Mill Valley and continue to Point Reyes.

Who to contact: For more information, call (415) 663-1092.

■ 3. Mission Peak:

From the summit of Mission Peak, hikers are offered a panoramic view of the Bay Area -- from Mount Tamalpais in the north to Mount Hamilton to the south. On exceptionally clear days, the snow-covered Sierra crest is visible to the east.

All this for just two hours of hiking about three miles to the top (an elevation gain of 2,500 feet). Other attractions include a resident herd of wild goats, and an ironic combination of flights by both hang gliders and turkey vultures.

Start the hike from the Ohlone College campus off Mission Boulevard near Mission San Jose. The trailhead is above the campus on the road leading past the swimming pool.

How to get there: The most direct route is from Highway 680 in Fremont -- take the Mission Boulevard exit and head north. Turn right on Stanford Avenue and continue until it deadends at the parking lot.

Who to contact: For more information, call (415) 531-9300.

■ 4. Mount Tamalpais:

From the slopes of Mount Tam, you are witness to the spectacular views of the Bay Area and the western section of Marin, which is primarily wilderness.

This is part of your reward for a few hours of hiking. As an added bonus, you will find yourself tucked away in deep canyons on the journey there.

The northern part of the mountain -- where entry can be gained from Marin County's Lake Bon Tempe -- is far less crowded. The geologic composition of Franciscan rock is amazing because the area is part of the Pacific plate that was once under water. Scientists throughout the world come to study it. When Cataract Gulch is flowing and full, it features several waterfalls as well as numerous ferns and wildflowers.

How to get there: From Highway 101, take the Stinson Beach/Highway 1 exit, and continue for five miles. Veer to the right on Panoramic, wind your way up the road and turn right across the Pantoll Ranger Station. When you hit the "T" in the road, keep to the right.

Who to contact: For more information, call (415) 388-2070 or (415) 456-1286.

■ 5. Wildcat Peak:

A hiker perched atop this peak is provided with a 360-degree spectacle of a view at 1,230-foot elevation.

One section especially popular starts at Inspiration Point on Wildcat Canyon Road in Tilden Regional Park. From the parking lot at Inspiration Point, the peak is but two miles distant. The first views are east toward Mount Diablo, but then gradually revealed to the west is San Francisco Bay, its bridges and surrounding cities.

If you want to escape the masses, you can continue on the East Bay Skyline National Recreation Trail, which is ultimately some 31 miles and connects six regional parklands.

How to get there: From the west, take Highway 24 to just east of the Caldecott Tunnel, then take the Fish Ranch Road exit west to Grizzly Peak Boulevard, which leads to the southern entrance of Tilden Park. From the east, San Pablo Dam Road connects to wildcat Canyon Road and continues to the park.

Who to contact: For more information, call (415) 531-9300.

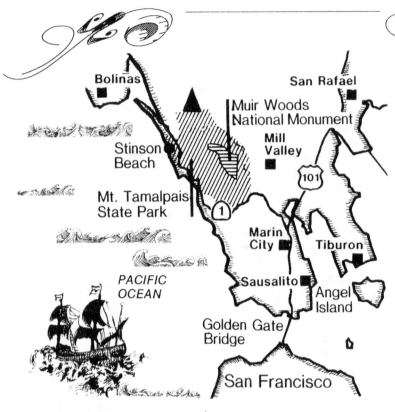

Bolinas

San Rafael

Muir Woods
National Monument

Mill
Valley

Stinson
Beach

101

Mt. Tamalpais
State Park

1

Marin
City

Tiburon

PACIFIC
OCEAN

Sausalito

Angel
Island

Golden Gate
Bridge

San Francisco

■ 6. Muir Woods:

You won't hear any chainsaws out here. Muir Woods is one of the last remaining native stands of redwoods and attracts tourists from throughout the world who have heard about these giant trees, but have never seen one.

It can be quite crowded on weekends, which drops this hike out of the top five, but those who are willing to put in the effort can be surprised at the isolation one can find. No secrets to the trick: Just walk uphill -- immediately, those lacking spirit will drop out and you will find solitude.

You will find yourself enveloped in the redwood environment, replete with ferns, lichen-covered branches and oc-

casional giant banana slugs.

How to get there: Take Highway 101 to the Highway 1 turnoff in Marin and then continue to the Muir Woods cutoff. All turns are well-signed. The park is 17 miles north of San Francisco.

Who to contact: For more information, call (415) 388-2595.

■ 7. Sunol Wilderness:

Tucked away at the south end of Alameda County, this wilderness parkland has cool stream-watered canyons, oak studded hills and a lavish wildflower display during springtime.

Good hikes abound here. One of the best short trips is Canyon View Trail, which winds its way through Jacobs

Valley and leads to Little Yosemite -- a rocky gorge on Alameda Creek. A longer trek will take you to Maguire Peaks, rewarding hikers with vistas toward Mount Diablo and Calaveras Reservoir.

How to get there: Sunol can be reached by taking the Calaveras Road exit south from Highway 680 in Sunol, driving past Welch Creek Road and turning eastward on Geary Road to park headquarters.

Who to contact: For more information, call (415) 531-9300.

■ 8. Redwood Regional Park:

You get a two-for-one here, Stream Trail features thick redwood groves and historic sites, while the East Ridge provides wide-angled views eastward toward Moraga and Mount Diablo. Many people are not aware of redwoods in the East Bay, yet here they are, waiting for you.

For a good loop hike, follow the Stream Trail from the parking lot up to Skyline Gate, a distance of about 2.5 miles, then follow East Ridge Trail and Canyon Trail back to the start. Another prime choice is the French Trail, which traverses the park and offers an experience like being in a deep primordial forest.

How to get there: The park can be reached by driving east on Redwood Road from Highway 13 in Oakland. Cross the intersection with Skyline Boulevard and continue to Redwood Road into the canyon.

Who to contact: For more information, call (415) 531-9300.

■ 9. Butano State Park:

This is a little-known area south of Half Moon Bay in the hills above Pescadero. You can hike along trails decorated by sorrel, larkspur, thumbleberry and trillium, exploring an area boasting 2,200 acres of virgin timber.

At one time, antelope and grizzly bears lived here with the Ohlone Indians. You can turn back the clocks and recreate that setting along the 11-mile loop trail. It's ideal for a spring outing.

How to get there: Take the Highway 1 cutoff to Pescadero and follow the signs to the state park.

Who to contact: For more information, call (408) 335-5858.

■ 10. Mount Diablo Trail:

Ardent backpackers might question the inclusion of this trail, but it is ideal for the person who does not feel up the challenge of a wilderness hike.

The trail starts and ends in rural settings, winding its way on the slopes of Mount Diablo, which has watched over the East Bay for centuries like a silent sentinel. The trail provides easy access as well, in both Walnut Creek and Pleasant Hill. This is a blessing for some, a thorn for others.

How to get there: The starting point is at the Lafayette Ridge Staging Area, located on Pleasant Hill Road just north of Highway 24 in Lafayette. Take the Pleasant Hill Road turnoff from Highway 24.

Who to contact: For more information, call (415) 531-9300.

FIVE GREAT PLACES TO LOOK DOWN
ON THE BAY AREA

ON A CLEAR DAY, YOU CAN PEAK FOREVER

The world ain't such a horrible place after all -- and a trip to a mountaintop on a clear day can make you realize it.

On the crisp, clear days of winter, between storms, you practically need a 360-degree swivel on your neck to take it all in from a mountaintop. You talk about beauty -- the Bay Area has it: Hundreds of square miles of virtual wilderness surrounding the five most prominent peaks. Views of the bay, delta and Pacific Ocean. A sense of peace.

It all comes from the separation from the massive throng scurrying below on the flatlands. And you don't even have to walk to find out.

You can drive to the three highest peaks, Mount Hamilton near San Jose, Mount Diablo near Danville and Mount Tamalpais in Marin. If you want the pure peace and solitude along with the view, get on your boots, start thumpin' and you'll get it. Mission Peak near Fremont and Montara Mountain in Half Moon Bay provide it.

Here's a preview of your trip:

■ Mount Hamilton (4,062 feet):

This is the big daddy, the highest point in the Bay Area. That fact is celebrated by astronomers at Lick Observatory, which is perched on Hamilton's tip top. It's a spectacular but strange lookout. To the west is the massive Santa Clara Valley, the valley floor absolutely packed from end to end with concrete, cars and people. Yet, looking the other way you get a different picture. To the east as far as you can see are hundreds of square miles of rolling, untraveled foothills.

A wandering herd of tule elk live out

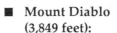

here, one of 15 herds established in California.

Tours of the Lick Observatory are the primary reason people show up here, but they end up remembering two things. One is the view, the other is the drive.

The road up from San Jose is a curious, winding two-laner that seems to take forever to finally reach the top. There's a reason. When the observatory was first constructed, the giant telescope was transported on a flatbed pulled by horses -- in order to keep the upgrade to a minimum, the road has countless switchbacks and turns. It's worth the trip.

How to get there: From the Peninsula, the most direct route is to head south on Highway 101, then take the Alum Rock turnoff and drive east through San Jose. Turn right on Highway 130, also named Mount Hamilton Road, and continue for 22 miles to the peak. An alternate route is available, using Highway 680 to the Alum Rock turnoff, which avoids city congestion.

Who to contact: For more information, call (408) 274-5061 or (408) 429-2513.

■ Mount Diablo (3,849 feet):

Because giant Diablo is surrounded by the San Joaquin Delta to the east and the bay to the west -- both at sea level -- this mountain can provide one of the best lookouts in the Western Hemisphere.

It is no great effort to get here: You can drive right to the top. The best times for your trip are the early morning or late evening.

The air is clearest in the morning and the distances visible are often astounding. To the west, you can spot the Farallon Islands, some 25 miles out to sea. On exceptional days, you can even spot Mount Lassen to the northeast, and the snow-capped crest of the Sierra to the east.

Over the years, several park rangers have told me you can even spot a piece of Half Dome in Yosemite on crystal-clear mornings. I haven't had that view yet, but maybe next time -- with a pair of binoculars.

Evenings are just as spectacular. The distance you can see is much shorter than during the day, but the sunsets are unforgettable. Either way, morning or evening, you can't lose.

How to get there: From Highway 680 in Danville, take Diablo Road and then head east on Black Hawk Road. Then turn left on South Gate Road, which is well signed. A $3 entrance fee is charged per vehicle.

Who to contact: For more information, call (415) 687-1800.

■ Mount Tamalpais (2,571 feet):

The view from the East Peak Lookout on Mount Tam will remind you that the Bay Area is the most beautiful of any metropolitan area in the country.

The sunrises don't come any better. You look down and you see the many little islands that dot theSan Francisco and San Pablo bays, the morning lights ashore, and to the west, miles of Marin wilderness and the Pacific Ocean alive in sunstruck hues of orange.

When John Muir spent his winters in the Bay Area, Mount Tam was the place he kept returning to. You can too, but a paved road makes it an easier trip. At the East Peak, there is a parking lot and visitor center.

There are many good trails on the slopes of Mount Tamalpais. Make a day of it by parlaying a drive to the lookout into one of the prime hikes available. Maps are available at the visitor center.

How to get there: From Highway 101, take the Stinson Beach/Highway 1 exit and continue for five miles. Veer to the right on Panoramic (there are signs), wind your way up the road and turn right across from the Pantoll Ranger Station. When you hit a "T" in the road, keep to the right. Access is free.

Who to contact: For more information,
call (415) 388-2070 or (415) 456-1286.

■ Mission Peak (2,517 feet):

Before you let inspiration get in the way of logic, first make sure you are physically fit before attempting this climb. Right, no roads, just a trail, and a steep one at that -- a 2,100-feet elevation gain in about three miles.

In other words, it is up, up and up. But it's well worth the puffs, the view assures that. In fact, the lookouts get better and better as you rise up, and it makes the climb tolerable once you get in a hiking and breathing rhythm.

Winter and early spring are the best times to go. The air is still cool, the East Bay hills are turning green, and soon the first wildflowers will start blooming. Looking east from the summit at this time and you get a view of miles and miles of hills blossoming in green.

Park rangers have told me that hikers occasionally spot a herd of wild goats from the summit, but it is more common to see hawks and vultures using the rising air currents to float about with scarcely a flap of their wings.

How to get there: You have three options. The most direct is from Highway 680 in Fremont -- take the Mission Boulevard exit and head north. Turn right on Stanford Avenue and continue until it deadends at the parking lot. Access is free.

Who to contact: For more information, call (415) 531-9300. Ask for Public Affairs.

■ Montara Mountain (1,898 feet):

This is the highest point along the Bay Area's southern coast and offers a magnificent lookout that few people have shared.

One reason is that it is a relatively new addition to the state park system and access has only recently been allowed. Another reason is that reaching the top requires a gut-thumper of a hike, nearly a 2,000-foot gain in 3.5 miles. It is enough to keep a lot of folks down at the beach, near where the road and trail start.

I use this mountain to train for Sierra backpack trips, and even though I've climbed Whitney, Shasta, Lassen, Half Dome and completed the John Muir Trail, this peak is right up there as one of my favorites.

To the west are untold miles of ocean which provide an underlying feel of tranquillity as you make the climb. To the north and east is virtual wilderness with Sweeney Ridge, the Crystal Springs Fish and Wildlife Refuge and miles of unexplored foothills.

Hikers in fair shape will take two hours to reach the top, including a 10-minute rest at a saddle/lookout above Pacifica. Figure 90 minutes for the return trip.

How to get there: Take Highway 1 to Montara and park adjacent to the north end of Montara State Beach -- on a small dirt road on the east side of the highway that is blocked by a single pipe gate. That is your access point. A small state park property sign is posted. Access is free.

Who to contact: For more information, call (415) 726-6203.

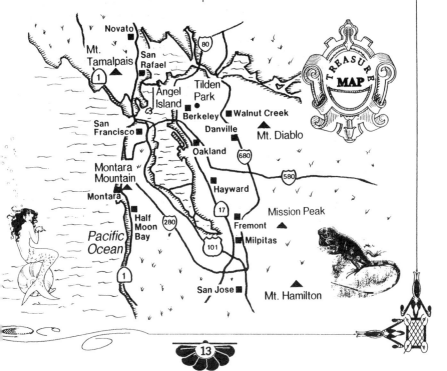

BAY AREA HIKES

FIVE GREAT EAST
BAY HIKES

REDWOODS, STREAMS & LOOKOUTS

S pring is great. The hills are greening up, the first wildflowers of the year are just starting to pop, and the air is clean and cool.

And when was the last time you went for a good walk? For most folks, the answer is way too long ago. But that can be solved on one of the trails in the East Bay Regional Park System.

The Regional Park District manages 46 parks that cover 60,000 acres in Alameda and Contra Costa counties. There are more than 500 miles of trails that cut through all kinds of settings, and an additional 100 miles of trails that connect the parks.

Some of the best include a trail that passes through redwoods and along a trout stream in Redwood Regional Park, a hike to a series of lookouts on the East Bay Skyline National Trail, and a stiff climb to the top of Mission Peak at 2,517 feet.

For additional information or brochures, call the East Bay Regional Park District at (415) 531-9300, Ext. 2200.

A sampling of the best spring hikes in the East Bay:

■ East Bay Skyline National Trail:

This is one of the better hikes in the Bay Area for the views, with great lookouts of the North Bay, and also of Mount Diablo. The trail rolls along the ridgeline and isn't too steep.

The trail starts at Inspiration Point in the Berkeley Hills and then heads northward on the East Bay's ridgeline; a round trip is about eight miles. Two miles in from Inspiration Point is Wildcat Peak, which is one of the highest peaks in the East Bay hills.

How to get there: From Highway 24 just east of the Caldecott Tunnel, take the Fish Ranch Road exit, drive north to the top of the hill and turn right on Grizzly Peak Boulevard. Continue to South Park Drive, make a right, and continue to Wildcat Canyon Road, make another right, and proceed one mile to the parking lot at Inspiration Point.

■ Briones Regional Park:

This is another favorite for its lookout points to the surrounding hills of central Contra Costa County. The park has a network of trails, and with map in hand, you can create your own loop hike.

This is one of the larger parks in the East Bay system with 5,303 acres and 25 trails to choose from. One suggestion is to start at the Alhambra Creek Valley Staging Area off Reliez Valley Road near Martinez. This trail leads to the top of Briones Peak, a distance of only about two miles but more strenuous than most weekend walks.

How to get there: The most direct route is to take Highway 4 to the Alhambra Avenue exit in Martinez, then drive south and bear right on Alhambra

Valley Road. Continue for a mile, then turn left on Reliez Valley Road and watch for the park entrance on the right hand side.

■ Redwood Regional Park:

This is a prime walk that leads through redwoods and along a little-known stream where spawning trout can now be seen. Where? Would you believe in the hills above Oakland? Right.

From the parking lot, you can hike up a valley and alongside Redwood Creek. You can make the hike as long or as short as you want it -- because other trails intersect the stream trail. An option is to make a loop by taking the East Ridge Trail, a round trip distance of just four miles.

How to get there: From Highway 13 in Oakland, take the Redwood Road exit. Drive east over the top of the hill and two miles past Skyline, then look for the park entrance on left side.

■ Morgan Territory Regional Preserve:

This park is located on the more isolated eastern slope of Mount Diablo and has great views of the Central Valley. On a clear day, you can even see the Sierra Nevada.

The trails here follow the ridgelines, and although many do not have names,

most are loop trails. Maps are available at the park's parking lot. Any ridge top is a good destination.

How to get there: From northbound 680 in Concord, take Ignacio Valley Road northeast about six miles to Clayton Road, where you turn right. Just east of the town of Clayton, the road becomes Marsh Creek Road. Continue for a mile and turn right on Morgan Territory Road; head up the twisty road and look for the park entrance on left side.

■ Mission Peak Regional Preserve:

If you don't mind a puffer of a climb, this park should be visited just for the chance to hike to Mission Peak at 2,517 feet -- a three mile climb with 2,100-feet elevation gain from the trailhead just east of Fremont.

Spring is the best time of year to go, when the air is still cool, although it can be a little windy at the top. Occasionally a herd of wild goats can be seen from the summit. It is also common to see sail planes, hang gliders, hawks and vultures circling, as though waiting for each other to make the first mistake.

How to get there: From Highway 680 in Fremont, take the Mission Boulevard exit and head north. Turn right on Stanford Avenue and continue until it deadends at the park entrance.

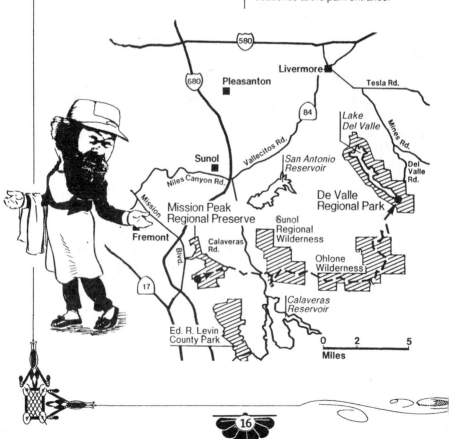

BAY AREA HIKES

WILDLIFE TRAILS WITH NO
HILLS TO CLIMB

EXPLORING THE FLATLANDS

Dear Tom:

My favorite stories are the ones where you tell about secret Bay Area hiking trails, but I've got a problem. My husband won't go unless it's flat, and the walks you describe are usually up.

-- Teri Andrews, San Francisco

Three Bay Area wildlife refuges provide a perfect solution with trails that are close to home, yet secluded; scenic, yet flat. Flat? That's right, there are flat trails in the world. We're talking about the South Bay Wildlife Refuge on the shores of San Francisco Bay in Newark, the Palo Alto Baylands and along the ocean on the San Mateo County coast at Pescadero Marsh. Access to all of these is free.

All three are unique places with flat trails that will take you along some of the Bay Area's premium migratory bird and waterfowl habitats. After an hour or so of walking at any of these spots you will become part of the setting.

■ Palo Alto Baylands:

This is the easiest to reach of the three spots, yet the least known. The trail is set along the South Bay marshlands of Palo Alto, just a few miles from Highway 101.

The tidal marsh is cut by a series of sloughs and filled with plants that support a fantastic diversity of birds. Some 250 different species of migratory birds visit here or call it home. On a recent visit, mallard ducks and white egrets were the most common bird sightings.

You have two options. The most popular is the dirt trail that heads north and winds its way to San Francisquito Creek. At the least, you are likely to see ground squirrels all over the place.

The other choice is the wooden walkway that starts at the Baylands Interpretive Center. The old "catwalk" lifts you just above the soggy marsh and leads to the edge of the Bay. If you want to extend your trip, the walkway also

heads north for a mile along the south bay shoreline, underneath a series of electrical towers.

How to get there: Take Highway 101 to Palo Alto, then take the Embarcadero east exit. Head toward the Bay, past the Palo Alto Airport, Yacht Harbor and park near the Interpretive Center.

Who to contact: Call the Baylands Interpretive Center at (415) 329-2506, or the Palo Alto Recreation Department at (415) 329-2261.

■ South Bay Refuge:

This is a huge area that covers 23,000 acres and is headquartered in Newark near the east end of the Dumbarton Bridge.

It's a major rest stop for the millions of birds on the Pacific Flyway and on a recent visit here, we identified four species of ducks, along with a heron and sandpiper, in about 15 minutes.

The trail is confined to foot traffic only, with no cars, motorcycles or bicycles allowed. It gives it a low-key feel.

The bonus here is that if you bring the family, and the kids would rather fish than walk, this spot is made to order. The old Dumbarton Bridge has been converted into a fishing pier managed by the U.S. Fish and Wildlife Service. Kids can fish for sharks, rays and bullheads nearby.

How to get there: From the Peninsula, take Highway 101 to the Dumbarton Bridge and head for Newark. From Interstate 880 (the Nimitz Freeway, formerly Highway 17), take the Jarvis Road or Thornton Avenue turnoffs to the old Dumbarton. Refuge headquarters is located near the toll plaza.

Who to contact: Call the S.F. Bay Wildlife Refuge at (415) 792-0222, or write P.O. Box 524, Newark, CA 94560.

■ Pescadero Marsh:

This is one of the few remaining natural marsh areas along the entire Central California coast, and offers your best chance of seeing the blue heron -- an impressive creature with a wingspan that can approach seven feet. Pescadero Marsh is a nesting ground for these giant birds.

The marsh is located just northeast of the Pescadero turnoff along Highway 1, 18 miles south of Half Moon Bay. It is the prettiest of the three refuges, bordered by the ocean on one side and open rolling hills on the other. A good footpath takes you along the edge of the marsh.

It's one of the most unusual settings in the Bay Area. With Pescadero Creek at the southern boundary of the marsh, and the ocean just to the west, it attracts birds that live in both freshwater and saltwater habitats.

Although the marsh is just 600 acres, the adjacent miles of open land make it feel much larger.

How to get there: From Interstate 280 or Highways 92 or 84, head west to Highway 1, then turn south and continue past Half Moon Bay. Pescadero Marsh is located across from sand dunes at Pescadero Beach. If you pass the Pescadero Road turnoff, you've gone too far.

Who to call: For general information, call the state park office in Half Moon Bay at (415) 726-6238.

BAY AREA HIKES

FOUR STEEP
THRILLS

GREAT VIEWS AS A REWARD

1st

The Bay Area boasts some steep trails that will make you puff -- and get you ready for the high mountains in the process. Here are four prospects, all with great views.

■ Mount Tamalpais:

Park at the Pantoll Ranger Station and head to the top via the Old State Road and Old Railroad Grade, both old fire roads. The trail starts at 1,400 feet and in four miles climbs to 2,400 feet at the East Peak Lookout. An option is to try the Steep Ravine Trail, which also starts at the ranger station and then drops 1,000 feet to Highway 1 in about three miles.

How to get there: From Highway 101,

take the the Stinson Beach/Highway 1 exit, and continue for five miles. Veer to the right on Panoramic (well-signed), wind your way up the road and turn right across from the Pantoll Ranger Station. When you hit a "T" in the road, keep to the right. Access is free.

Who to contact: Call Mount Tamalpais State Park, (415) 388-2070.

■ Montara Mountain:

This hike climbs from sea level to 2,000 feet in 3.5 miles. It includes a short killer portion, three-quarters of a mile long, that most people won't be able to complete without stopping at least once.

How to get there: Take Highway 1 to Montara and park adjacent to the north end of Montara State Beach -- on a small dirt road on the east side of the highway that is blocked by a single pipe gate. This is your access point. A small state park property sign is posted. Access is free.

Who to contact: Half Moon Bay State Parks, (415) 726-7238.

■ Mission Peak:

From the trailhead near Ohlone College in Fremont, hiking up fire roads will take you from 400 feet to the peak at 2,517 feet in 3.5 miles. It's a real thumper especially because the weather is often hot.

How to get there: There are three options. The most direct is from Highway 680 in Fremont. Take the Mission Boulevard exit and head north. Turn right on Stanford Avenue and continue until it deadends at the parking lot.

Who to contact: Call the East Bay Regional Park District at (415) 531-9300.

■ Rocky Ridge

This is a relatively unknown trail with a wicked climb. The trailhead starts at the Lichen Bark Picnic Area at Del Valle Regional Park near Livermore. In 2.5 miles, it climbs from 700 feet to 2,426 feet. You need a wilderness permit which can be obtained for $1 per person at the park entrance.

How to get there: On Highway 580 east, take the North Livermore exit and go right. Follow North Livermore Avenue to Mines Road. Take a right to the park. On Highway 580 west, take the Vasco Road exit, turning left under the freeway. Follow Vasco to Tesla Road and then turn right. At Mines Road go left to the park.

Who to contact: Call the East Bay Regional Park District at (415) 531-9300.

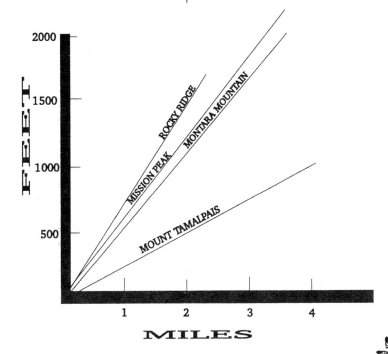

BAY AREA HIKES

POINT REYES

HISTORY, HIKING AND HIDEAWAYS

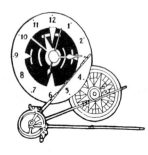

Some places project a special sense of feeling and some places do not. Mount Shasta has it, for instance, but Mount Whitney does not. Lake Tahoe has it, Lake Beryessa does not.

In the Bay Area, Point Reyes has it. Sure, the area offers more recreation potential than anywhere else within 150 miles, but that is not what you remember when you leave the place. What you remember are the feelings you get there.

For one thing, there is a sense of total separation from the Bay Area, even though it's actually very close. For another, there are hundreds of little hideaways to be explored. After awhile some of them start to feel like your own secret spots.

It is a gigantic area, bordered by a wide open ocean to the west, with a unique and varied terrain inland. The coast itself has miles of untouched beach just north of the lighthouse and to the south, it offers miles of little bays, inlets and sea tunnels.

Inland, there is even more diversity. The coastal bluffs are sprinkled with wildflowers and chaparral, the rolling hills with wild grasses and poppies, and the mountain interior is heavily wooded, with little creeks following the earth's fissures.

With that kind of diversity, weekenders are given a huge number of recreation choices. And Point Reyes is one of the few popular

areas able to handle the weekend traffic.

You can pick an easy walk or a rugged stomper, look for a migrating whale or a resident tule elk, stay just a few hours or make an overnight camp of it. You can go canoeing or kayaking, study the geology or simply enjoy the ocean lookouts.

Two things don't fit in, though. The mountain bicycles on the trails seem out of place because any form of mechanization is intrusive to your frame of mind in a place preserved in its natural state. I've done some biking myself, but Wild America and Machine America just don't mix.

The other thing that strikes you are the cows, the good ol' bovines. Nice enough creatures, but there are just plain too many of them. In some areas, you have to remain alert to keep from planting your Vibram soles in the middle of a fresh meadow muffin.

Aside from that, the area is among the best in California for day walks. There are some 30 trails covering 65,000 acres of wildlands. The easier hikes are on the northern end of the parkland, where easy, rolling hills lead to the ocean.

The more rugged trails are in the southern end of the park, in the coastal mountains. The Bear Valley Trail, which extends along much of Coast Creek all the way to the ocean, is one of the better hikes in the park. If you want something more rugged and remote, four other trails intersect the Bear Valley route, all of them with steep climbs.

You know the old adage: If you want to be alone, just start walking up.

If a day hike isn't your game, there are a number of very short walks that can provide excitement. The favorite is at the tip of Point Reyes, where a five to 10-minute walk from the parking lot will take you right to the lighthouse.

The Tomales Peninsula is just as easy to reach, yet far less crowded. It is here that Point Reyes' herd of tule elk roams. The herd, 31 strong, often hangs out near the parking lot. You can take short walks from here, or go for a three-miler out to Tomales Point.

At Tomales Point, there is an area that slid more than 16 feet during the 1906 earthquake, providing a fascinating look into the area's unique geological qualities.

The entire Point Reyes Peninsula is a dislocated land, set just west of

☞ PLANNING A TRIP TO POINT REYES

How to get there: From Highway 101 in Marin County, take the Highway 1 cutoff at Mill Valley and continue to Point Reyes, then take a left and head into the park along the western shore of Tomales Bay.
Trip cost: Access, maps, and camping are free.
Camping: There are four primitive, hike-in campsites. Permits are required but available without charge at Bear Valley Visitor Center.
Who to contact: Call park headquarters at (415) 663-1092. For free maps, write Superintendent, Point Reyes National Seashore, Point Reyes, CA 94956.

This is the best shoreline lookout on the Pacific Coast for spotting migrating whales. Because Point Reyes extends so far west into the sea, the whales often pass within a few hundred yards of the lookout. They can be identified by the telltale spout. Because it is so easy to reach, the lookout is often crowded.

the San Andreas Fault. It's a rift zone and is steadily moving north at an average of three inches per year. The rocks of Point Reyes match those from the Tehachapi Mountains, more than 300 miles to the south.

The area has history and a special feel to it. When you leave, that's what you will remember. The place feels good.

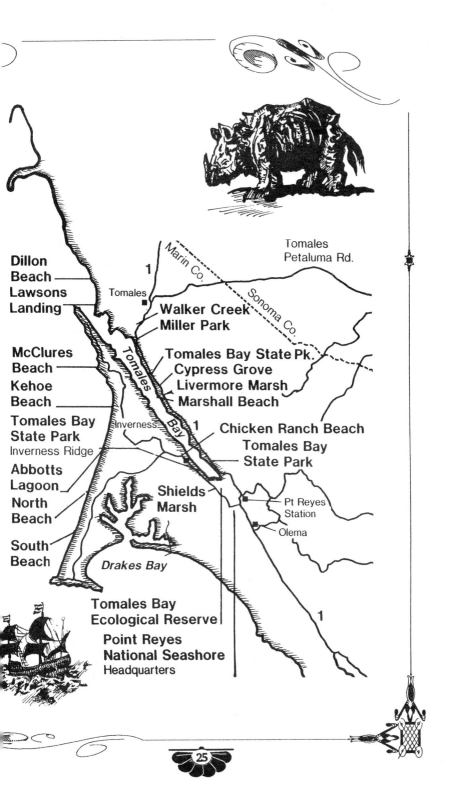

**Dillon
Beach
Lawsons
Landing**

Tomales

1

Marin Co.

Sonoma Co.

Tomales
Petaluma Rd.

**Walker Creek
Miller Park**

**McClures
Beach**

**Kehoe
Beach**

**Tomales Bay
State Park**

Inverness Ridge

**Abbotts
Lagoon**

**North
Beach**

**South
Beach**

Tomales
Bay

Inverness

**Tomales Bay State Pk.
Cypress Grove
Livermore Marsh
Marshall Beach**

1

**Chicken Ranch Beach
Tomales Bay
State Park**

**Shields
Marsh**

Pt Reyes
Station

Olema

Drakes Bay

**Tomales Bay
Ecological Reserve**

**Point Reyes
National Seashore**
Headquarters

1

MARIN'S MOUNT
TAMALPAIS

A HIKER'S HEAVEN

The best place to hike in the Bay Area is on the trails of Mount Tamalpais. It's a trip that everyone should make at least once.

Trails peek in and out of redwoods and tan oak, at times providing the seclusion of forest, at other times guiding you to lookout points with astounding views of the Bay Area and Pacific Ocean.

Mount Tamalpais, of course, is that big mountain you see in Marin County. When John Muir spent his winters in the Bay Area, it was his favorite place to hike. It doesn't take much time here to find out why.

It is one of the few places in the Bay Area that projects a genuine "feel" to it, kind of like sitting in your favorite chair. You might try it on for size and find it fits pretty well. Nowadays, you don't even have to walk to sense this. You can drive to the East Peak Lookout, for instance, which at 2,571 feet provides one of the world's truly spectacular vistas. I've traveled all over the Western Hemisphere and the view from this spot can match just about anything you can drive to, anywhere.

It is a reminder that the Bay Area is a beautiful and special place, just in case you need reminding. I found a clipping dated 1909, author unknown, that described the view here. It reads "Mount Tamalpais -- where 100 points of scenic interest, with San Francisco in the background, unveil to you the diversified lands of sunlit charm beyond the Golden Gate."

You can take it a step further by parking your car, picking a trail and taking a nice walk. Some folks will bring their mountain bikes up here on weekends and cruise the fire roads. Bikes are prohibited on hiking trails, but there are enough fire roads to make it the most popular bike area in the Bay Area.

But you lose much of the intimacy of the adventure on a bike -- or in a car. Try strolling down one of the trails here with a friend. That's when you really can begin to connect with the surroundings.

There are hundreds of miles of hiking trails in the area, crossing land managed by Mount Tamalpais State Park, Marin Water District, Golden Gate National Recreation Area and Muir Woods National Monument. There are several maps and books out as well that detail the area.

With map in hand, you can design your day, whether you want a short stroll, a hike with a picnic or an all-day thumper.

One good spot to start is the Rock Springs Picnic Area, where four trailheads are located.

If you just want to take a 10-minute stroll, the walk to Mountain Theatre is ideal. After parking your car, walk (northeast) up the road for about 100 yards, then take the trail

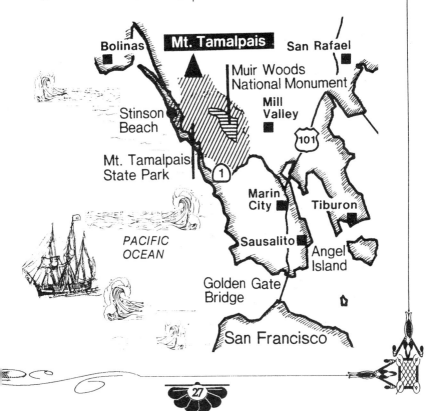

on the right side of the road. Mountain Theatre is a large amphitheater with terraced rows of rocks for seats. At 2,100 feet elevation, you get a good lookout of San Francisco Bay from here.

For a longer walk, with more diverse possibilities, continue on Rock Springs Trail past Mountain Theatre -- for the 2.5-mile hike to the West Point Inn. The trail provides classic lookouts, and in some spots cuts a tunnel through a thick forest canopy. The West Point Inn is a small picnic area that has a limited menu, but the place has a good feel to it. It can also be reached by bicycle via fire roads. On Sundays it is a major destination point for mountain bikers.

There are two other alternate hikes from the Rock Springs Picnic

☞ MOUNT TAM FACTS

How to get there: From Highway 101 in Marin County, take the Stinson Beach/Highway 1 exit. At the first traffic light, go left and continue on Highway 1 as the road climbs and twists. At the top of the ridge, take the Panoramic Highway turnoff to the right. Continue on Panoramic Highway, driving past the turnoff to Muir Woods and eventually turning right at the Pantoll Ranger Station on Ridgecrest Road. The road ends when it hits Ridgecrest Road -- and the adjacent Rock Springs Picnic Area parking area.

Maps: You should get a good map such as the "Trail Map of the Mount Tamalpais Region," available for $3.54 in the mail from Erickson Maps, 337 17th Street, Suite 211, Oakland, CA 94612. A premium color trail map is also available for $6.50 from Olmsted Brothers Maps, (415) 658-4869.

Trip tip: To get to the East Peak lookout from Rock Springs Picnic Area, turn right on Ridgecrest Road -- the road deadends at the East Peak lookout. To see spectacular sunsets, start from Rock Springs Picnic Area, turn left on Ridgecrest Road, which provides lookouts to the Pacific Ocean.

Trip cost: Entry and parking are free.

Who to contact: Call Mount Tamalpais State Park at (415) 388-2070 or Golden Gate National Recreation Area at (415) 331-1540.

Area. One leads southwest, past a grove of big trees and to the hilly grasslands that overlook the Pacific Ocean. This is a popular jumpoff point for hang gliders. Another possibility is the Cataract Trail, which heads north into state parkland. You can continue on the Cataract Trail, an easy walk that laterals the west slope of Mount Tam at 1,850 elevation, or take the cutoff on the Simmons Trail. The latter climbs as high as 2,200 feet, then descends into secluded Barth's Retreat.

Any choice you make will be the right one when you're exploring Mount Tamalpais.

ADVENTURE 9

BAY AREA HIKES

MUIR WOODS

ONLY ONE IS PEACEFUL

There are two Muir Woods and they are about as far apart as the North and South Poles.

One of them seems to have more people than trees. The trail is so heavily used that it is paved with asphalt -- and your chance of seeing a deer is about the same as sighting Bigfoot. The whole place seems about as peaceful as a bowling alley.

The other Muir Woods, however, is a sanctuary, a cathedral of redwoods and ferns. It is a place where people are few and the only sound is that of the light breeze brushing through tree limbs. By the time you leave, the world feels fresh and clean again.

Both of these Muir Woods are in Marin County, set in a canyon on the slopes of Mount Tamalpais. Your approach to the park determines which one you visit.

Take for example my recent visit. When we arrived at noon, the two parking lots were jammed full, in-

cluding four tour buses that were shooting people out like a popcorn machine. The information stand and small store were crowded with visitors. The Bootjack Trail, the paved loop hike that travels along Redwood Creek on the valley floor, was more of a parade than a nature walk.

But then we turned right, taking the Sunset Trail, and in less than a minute, we had entered a different world. This is the Muir Woods where you can find peace and good times.

The Sunset Trail is one of the best-kept secrets in what is one of the West's most popular parklands. It can provide solitude and a good hike. Another option, although better known is the Dipsea Trail and the network of connecting trails on Mount Tamalpais. From the valley floor of Muir Woods, the Sunset Trail veers right and heads up the east side of the canyon. It is a steady grade, just enough to get most hikers puffing in a natural rhythm as you make the climb.

It is three miles before you clear the treetops and get a lookout of the entire valley -- a sea of conifers -- and glimpses of the Pacific Ocean to the southwest. In the meantime, you walk a trail that gets little traffic. Your worries begin to fall away, and no matter what your problems, all seems simple and pure.

There is another attraction as well. When you reach the canyon rim, you can take a quarter-mile detour to the town of Mountain Home, or right turn on the connecting trail that leads to the German House. Both serve ice cold drinks, and nothing tastes better after the three-mile climb to the lookout.

The German House is a premium destination because it has a redwood deck and offers a great view of Marin's wildlands.

The other trail option that provides a degree of solitude to Muir Woods is the Dipsea Trail, although it is a famous route among Bay Area hikers.

This trail runs all the way to Stinson Beach, about four miles, the hiker follows a series of "up and downs." People hiking in teams might consider driving two vehicles, then leaving one at Stinson, one at Muir Woods, in order to hike one way and then shuttle back to the starting point.

August often seems the coldest month of the year here. When the Central Valley burns in 100-degree temperatures, nature's built-in air conditioner will fog in the coast and send chilly breezes eastward.

A unique feature about Muir Woods is that headquarters can be something of a United Nations. Visitors from all over the world touring the Bay Area find the old-growth redwoods a special attraction.

Your options are the quiet of the Sunset or the Dipsea trails.

There are two Muir Woods. You decide which one you want to visit.

☞ FACTS ABOUT MUIR WOODS

How to get there: Muir Woods is reached by taking Highway 101 to the Highway 1 turnoff in Marin, then continuing to the Muir Woods cutoff. All turns are well-signed. The park is 17 miles north of San Francisco.

Trip tip: Hikers only. No mountain bikes, motorcycles, horses or dogs are allowed, except for seeing-eye dogs.

Trip cost: Access and brochures are free, though donations are accepted.

Who to contact: The Muir Woods Ranger Station can be reached at (415) 388-2595, or by writing Muir Woods National Monument, Mill Valley, CA 94941.

ADVENTURE 10

BAY AREA HIKES

MARIN'S HIDDEN ROAD
TO THE OUTDOORS

A JUMPOFF TO 15 TRAILHEADS & THREE LAKES

The Bay Area has plenty of unique, hidden back roads, but the best might just be a little winding two-laner in Marin County.

It's Marin's hidden road to the outdoors -- we're talking about a road that provides access to 15 trailheads for secluded hikes, three lakes, and even a golf course.

The route is called Bolinas-Fairfax Road. It's pretty enough to enjoy just for a Saturday evening drive or a Sunday morning bike cruise, but you can take it one giant step forward by using it as a jumpoff for hiking or fishing trips.

It is located in Marin County west of San Rafael.

To get there is simple enough: From Highway 101, take Sir Francis Drake Boulevard west into Fairfax, then just turn left on Bolinas/Fairfax Road.

That is where your journey starts. After leaving Fairfax, then two miles later passing the Meadow Club Gold Course, the road twists its way up to 600-feet elevation. Another mile and you will start seeing little turnouts spotted on the side of the road. Look closer. Each of those turnouts marks a hiking trail, the trailhead nearby.

Between Fairfax and Bolinas, there are 15 of them. You can either just head down the trail for a little in-and-outer, or manufacture a longer trip by hooking up with the network of trails that are linked in the Marin backcountry.

It can make for very quiet and secluded hiking. If there are no other cars parked on the turnouts, you will know that there is no one else on the trail but you.

Your mission, should you decide to accept it, can be eased by obtaining a detailed map of the area.

Two of the best hikes in the late summer and fall months start on either side of Alpine Lake, which is about a five-mile drive west of Fairfax. You should park at the dam, then take your pick.

The easier hike heads north and follows a gentle grade downhill along the section of Lagunitas Creek that connects Alpine Lake to Kent Lake. Having a picnic at creek side, with the big oaks, you might feel like you're in Tennessee wilderness, not just five miles from the Marin suburbs.

If you want more of a challenge and some good views of Alpine Lake, cross the dam, and right where the road takes a hairpin turn, look for the trailhead for the Cataract Trail. You can self-prescribe a loop trail that zigzags its way to almost 1,700 feet, then drops back down along the southeast shore of Alpine Lake.

In the fall, after the rains come, another good hike can take you to a little-known series of waterfalls. The trail starts about a mile past the golf course at the first large parking area on the left side of the road. The trail begins just across the road, and with map in hand to make the proper turns, can arrive at Carson Falls in an hour's walk.

If hiking is not for you, there are three lakes along Bolinas-Fairfax Road. The most impressive is Al-

pine Lake, a long, deep lake bordered by forest. Fishermen occasionally get some good evening bass fishing here.

The other lakes, which are reached by taking the Sky Oaks Road turnoff, are Bon Tempe and Lagunitas. Bon Tempe is stocked with rainbow trout in the fall and winter and Lagunitas has been drained and converted to a special wild trout lake.

No boats, rafts, float tubes or water contact of any kind are permitted at the lakes, which is something of a ripoff. Marin Water District officials have told fishermen they fear the spread of a water plant called hydrilla, but that is absolute nonsense.

Hydrilla can only be spread by boats if it is somehow stuck on the bottom of somebody's raft or boat, then came off and started growing in the new lake. It's a potential problem at every lake, but the chances are so infinitesimal that other water districts virtually ignore it. At Contra Loma Reservoir near Antioch, which is part of the State Water Project, a sign has simply been posted asking boaters to please clear their boats and propellers of any weeds. That warning has been sufficient since Contra Loma was constructed in 1969. 'Nuf said.

The Marin lakes are all pretty, primarily because they are hidden among forested hillsides. The entire area is like that, hidden and secluded. Driving along the Bolinas-Fairfax Road helps unveil these secrets.

☛ **TRIP NOTE**

How to get there: From Highway 101, take Sir Francis Drake Boulevard west into Fairfax, then just turn left on Bolinas/Fairfax Road.
Maps: The best available map of the area is called Marin Headlands, published by the Olmsted Brothers Map Company, and is available for $5 at P.O. Box 5351, Berkeley, CA 94705. It details all fire roads, trails, creeks, and lakes, and includes contour lines.

BAY AREA HIKES

ANGEL ISLAND

YOUR OWN PRIVATE ISLAND

From atop Angel Island, explorers are offered what may be the most spectacular urban vista in the western hemisphere.

To the west is the golden span at the gateway to the Bay, with the sun sending various hues of red and orange across the Bay to the giant bridge's pillars. Just over yonder are the towering high-risers of The City, while southward, the Bay Bridge stretches out to the banks of Treasure Island. At dusk, it looks like a postcard that tourists buy. But it isn't a postcard, it's real life, and you won't find any tourists here either -- they just plain don't have a clue about this spot.

But then neither do many others. Angel Island is accessible only by ferry boat or private craft, and most people just won't take a few minutes to learn that ferry boats depart for Angel Island several times during the day from Pier 43 in The City, and also from Tiburon. They'll even take you back, that is, if you want to return.

Your reward here is a state park right in the middle of the Bay that offers a day's worth of hiking on the steep trails that lead to the summit of Mount Livermore at 781 feet elevation -- or a unique spot for bicycling, picnicking, overnight camping, or jogging. The latter is particularly popular on the Perimeter Road, a 4.8-mile trek that encircles the island, where you won't have to worry about dodging car drivers of questionable sanity. The road is 75 percent paved, and is well suited for bicycling as well.

Few experiences can match spending a clear night in the middle of the Bay, especially on a warm evening when the stars are shining like diamonds. This is why the primitive campsites on Angel Island are in urgent demand, and that reservations are usually required six to eight weeks in advance of a camping trip.

☞ **ANGEL ISLAND TRIP FACTS**

How to get there: From San Francisco, ferries of the Red and White Fleet depart from Pier 43 at 10 a.m., noon, and 2 p.m. From Tiburon, ferries leave every hour on the hour from 10 a.m. to 4 p.m., with extra boats on weekends. In the winter, trips are offered only on weekends and holidays. Private boats can use the mooring slips at Ayala Cove.

Trip Cost: Round-trip fare on the San Francisco ferries is $6 for adults, $3 for children. Bicycles can travel free. From Tiburon, round-trip cost is $2.75 for adults, $1.50 for children and a 50-cent bonus charge for bikes.

Trip tips: Additional park information is available by calling the ranger station at (415) 435-1915. A park brochure is available for 50 cents, and a guided train ride around the island is available for $2 for adults, $1 for kids 5 to 11, and free for younger children.

SWEENEY RIDGE

THE BAY AREA AT YOUR FEET

You practically need a 360-degree swivel on your neck when perched atop Sweeney Ridge, one of the most spectacular vistas in the Bay Area.

Many Novembers ago, way back in 1769, explorer Gaspar de Portola first viewed San Francisco Bay from this spot, and they say his neck still hurts. Millions of people have since moved to the Peninsula, yet just a few can tell first-hand of the sights from Sweeney Ridge.

It is just a 40-minute walk from the trailhead at the Skyline College campus, located on the ridge which splits San Bruno and Pacifica atop the San Francisco Peninsula. A bonus is that the trail is easily accessible through mass transit, with SamTrans buses providing the connecting link at the Daly City Bart Station. For the future, an access trail from Pacifica has been planned, but when it will be usable by the public is not known.

On clear mornings, when the air

has that special crystal pureness to it, the entire Bay Area seems to be at your feet. With a pair of binoculars or a spotting scope, even the most distant sights seem within your grasp.

Sweeney Ridge provides remarkable glimpses of varied geography, including three of the largest mountains in the Bay Area. To the north is Mount Tamalpais in Marin County, to the east is Mount Diablo, and south is Montara Mountain. You get the proper sense of perspective when you realize how long the mountains have been here -- compared to your own lifespan. Just below is Pacifica, from Mussel Rock to Pedro Point, where the ocean appears like a giant lake lapping at the beach. To the west, the Farallon Islands jut out from the Pacific Ocean, and look within the reach of a short swim -- they are actually 25 miles away. That expanse of curved blue horizon spanning hundred of miles can allow

you to sense that the earth isn't flat after all.

To reach Sweeney Ridge, you hike up a moderate grade that takes you through coastal grasslands, which sprout with green after being watered by the first rains of fall. In the spring, wildflowers explode in color.

The ideal time for a hike here is the morning after a good rain, which leaves the air sparkling fresh and clear. Summer evenings can often be the worst time, because thick fog powered by 25-mph winds can reduce the visibility to zero and make your hike about as cold as an expedition to the Arctic.

Congress once appropriated the money to purchase Sweeney Ridge in order to include it in the Golden Gate Recreation Area, but former Interior Secretary James Watt refused to complete the deal. After Watt was given the boot, residents of Pacifica and San Bruno successfully pressured the Interior Department to purchase Sweeney Ridge.

If Watt had ever walked in Portola's footsteps to this pedestal above the Bay Area, he probably would have signed the papers without hesitation.

☛ SWEENEY RIDGE TRIP FACTS

How to get there: From points south, take Highway 280 to Hickey Boulevard, and head west. Turn left on Highway 35 (Skyline Boulevard), then turn right on College Drive to Skyline College. From the north, take Highway 280 to the Skyline Boulevard exit, and turn left on College Drive.
Mass transit: From the Daly City BART Station or the Serramonte Shopping Center in Colma, SamTrans buses 21B or 20J will take you to the Skyline College campus. From Pacifica or the Tanforan Shopping Center in San Bruno, SamTrans bus 30B will take you there.
Trailhead location: The trail starts on the southeast end of the Skyline College campus, near lot 2. Walk east up past the maintenance yard, and then right to the service road -- a sign marks the trail. An access route from Pacifica is in the planning stages.
Trail time: From the San Bruno entrance, figure about an hour for a round-trip hike, not including viewing and picnic time.

THE SAN ANDREAS
TRAIL

HIKE, BIKE & RUN

Dear Tom,

I'm a runner and hiker, and I would like to know a scenic place on the San Francisco Peninsula that is easy and quick to reach, a place where I can go after I get off work.   --Sue Kusano, Half Moon Bay

Answering Sue's request is the San Andreas Trail. It overlooks Crystal Springs Reservoir and winds its way through wooded foothills. It is minutes away by car for Peninsula residents, can be reached by bus, and provides access to the edge of a special fish and game refuge where eagles still fly. The air is fresh and clean up here, and the wide trail is suited for jogging, hiking, and bicycling.

It sits on the eastern edge of Crystal Springs Reservoir, just off of Skyline Boulevard (Highway 35) in Millbrae. All you have to do is show up, park your car, and go for it. The only irritation is that a few miles of the trail runs fairly adjacent to the road, within earshot of cars. A wall of trees provides refuge in some areas, and south of the access point at Hillcrest Boulevard, the trail meanders away from the road, and cuts along the edge of the south end of the lake.

Whether you run, walk or bike, at some point you will likely come to a complete halt, and just gaze at the wonder of this country. The western slope of Montara Mountain is a true wilderness, untouched by mankind, and the sparkling lake below might trigger visions of giant fish and a special quiet. But don't get any ideas about bringing a fishing rod. Fishing or trespassing on the lake or the wooded refuge to the west, respectively, is illegal and doing so will quickly land you in the pokey. The area is patrolled around the clock.

The San Andreas Trail starts near the northern end of the lake, where a signed trailhead marker sits on

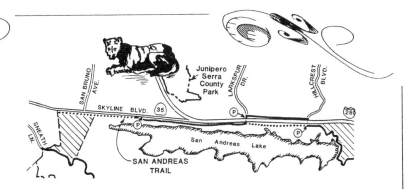

Skyline Boulevard, which runs parallel to the trail. It runs about three miles, fairly level, until the next access point at Hillcrest Boulevard.

A favored option for well-conditioned runners is to start your trip at the Hillcrest Boulevard access point, then head south. The trail connects to the Sawyer Camp Trail, which cuts six miles along the lake, away from the road. It can provide the quiet that you might miss on the San Andreas Trail, but with a longer distance and a steeper grade (a drop of 400 feet), you can plan on some huffing and puffing on your return trip.

During the winter, the area is remarkably cool, green and fresh. Summer evenings can bring the spectacle of rolling fogbanks cresting Montara Mountain to the west.

And regardless of whether you hike, run or bike, this is a magic spot to bust loose -- and it is just minutes from the San Francisco Peninsula.

☞ SAN ANDREAS TRAIL TRIP FACTS

How to get there: From the north, take Highway 280 to the Skyline Boulevard (Highway 35) exit. A signed trail entrance is on the west side of the road. From the south, take Highway 280 to the Millbrae Avenue exit, and head north on what appears a frontage road (Skyline Boulevard) to Hillcrest Boulevard at the trailhead.

Mass transit: SamTrans bus 33B stops at Hillcrest Drive and Skyline Boulevard -- just walk under the freeway to the trailhead. For route information, call SamTrans at (415) 348-8858.

Trip tip: If you plan to run, bring a friend along so you can car shuttle rather than having to double back on the trail.

BAY AREA HIKES

WUNDERLICH
PARK

HIDDEN PENINSULA PARKLAND

The classic Bay Area parkland is one where a hiker feels a distinct sense of remoteness -- without actually being far from home.

Wunderlich Park is such a place, with 25 miles of secluded trails that cut quiet pathways through a wilderness of forest and meadows, yet is located on the nearby San Francisco Peninsula above Woodside.

A good hike can be like taking a shower; it seems to cleanse your mind. Wunderlich Park is one of the best areas for cleaning out the cobwebs, offering a variety of trails from short strolls to an all-day-gut-puffer of a trek. Take your pick. I hiked here with a companion and did not see a single other hiker. That's called solitude. The trails cut through lush ravines to mountainsides studded with redwoods. That's called beauty. It's the combination that you may be looking for.

Your first step should be to obtain a map of the park which details all of the trails. You will discover that because a network of trails intersect at several points, you can self-style your hike to fit the amount of time available as well as your level of ambition.

According to park rangers, a good hike for first timers is a loop trip from the main park entrance to "The Meadows," or to spots such as Alambique Creek or Redwood Flat. If you don't want to spend all day at it, this is a good compromise. It provides a few hours on the trail. But if you want to extend yourself, your goal should be the Skyline Ridge at 2,200 feet elevation.

A 10-mile, five-hour round trip to the ridge is the centerpiece of Wunderlich Park. You gain almost 2,000 feet, which can get you puffing like a locomotive, but most of the grade is a gentle, steady climb, and in the process you cross through a wide variety of plant and tree communities -- and also reach some

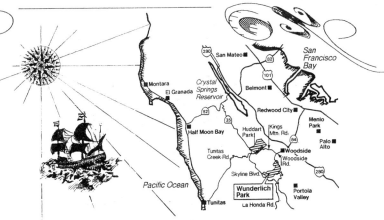

classic vistas of San Francisco Bay and the East Bay hills.

It's at these viewpoints where some of the rewards of hiking become clear. Here you are on the edge of the Bay Area, on the outside looking in. If your typical view of the Bay is from behind a steering wheel, such a vantage point can provide a unique perspective.

A few notes, however. The hiker's motto -- "Leaves of three, let them be" -- should be one of your First Commandments. Poison oak can be quite prevalent in some areas. If you're vulnerable, wear long sleeve shirts, wash your clothes right after your hike, and of course, stay on the trails. The latter can do more than anything to protect you.

No drinking water is available on the trails, so another essential tip is to bring a small day pack with a lunch and drinks, or at least a canteen to slake your thirst.

☞ WUNDERLICH PARK TRIP FACTS

How to get there: The most direct route from Highway 280 is to take the Sand Hill Road exit, then head west to Portola Road. Turn right and continue just past the junction with Highway 84. Park sign is on the left.

Maps: For a free map, send a stamped, self-addressed envelope to the San Mateo County Parks & Recreation Department, 590 Hamilton Street, Redwood City, CA 94063.

Pets: No pets are allowed.

Trip Cost: $2 per car.

Who to contact: Call San Mateo County Parks & Recreation Department at (415) 363-4020, or Wunderlich Park at (415) 851-7570.

ADVENTURE
15

BAY AREA HIKES

M^cNEE RANCH
STATE PARK

PRIME HIKES IN A PRIMITIVE SETTING

L et's get right to the point: You've never heard of McNee Ranch State Park, right?

That's one of the best reasons why this is a place you should visit this weekend. Nobody else seems to know about it either.

McNee is California's newest park, is only 25 miles away from San Francisco, and can provide the Bay Area's best lookouts from the top of Montara Mountain. It's a primitive setting, with no camping or piped water, but it's perfect for short walks or gut thumpers to the ridge -- and you can bring your leashed dog.

And just about nobody's ever here.

McNee Park is located on the San Mateo County coast between Montara and Pacifica.

You'll find it a remarkably peaceful place with many good walks or hikes, and with them comes some of the best coastal views anywhere.

Most of the trails are actually long-abandoned ranch or county roads. They connect to enough footpaths to provide many options for weekend walks.

But no matter how many different routes you take, eventually you will want to bite off the big banana. Head to the top, the peak of Montara Mountain.

It's not far, but it's a challenge, climbing from sea level to 2,100 feet. From the entrance gate at the park to the summit is 3.8 miles. A round trip requires 3.5 to four hours. But in that short time, you can feel all of the elements of a wilderness mountain experience.

The trail follows the ridgeline of San Pedro Mountain until it connects to the Montara Coastal Range, and has three of what hikers call "serious ups." One of the serious ups is three-quarters of a mile, and can get you puffing like a locomotive for two minutes.

Then suddenly, the trail nearly flattens on a short mountain saddle,

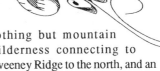

and a 30-yard cutoff on the left provides a perch for a dazzling view of the Pacifica coast, and on clear days, Point Reyes. My dad, Robert G. Stienstra Sr., who's now 63, made the hike to this great lookout. So can you.

Another 45 minutes of "steady up" will take you all the way to the top. You'll start looking around as if you have just discovered the Bay Area for what it is: Miles of open range and mountains, with only the flatlands jammed with people.

On a clear day, the Farallon Islands -- 30 miles away can look close enough to reach out and pluck right out of the ocean, and Mount Diablo to the east, like you could take a giant leap, cross the Bay and land on its peak.

Some 10 miles north and south is nothing but mountain wilderness connecting to Sweeney Ridge to the north, and an off-limits Fish and Game Refuge to the south.

If a highway goes through and cuts the park in two, mitigation for the lost recreation value might be to allow hikers access to the ridgeland, all the way from Sweeney Ridge to Half Moon Bay, and allow low-impact wilderness-style camping of a strict permit system.

More than 150,000 people jam into Half Moon Bay for the annual Pumpkin Festival. Virtually all of them drive right past McNee Park. This weekend if you'd like a nice, quiet walk, stop at McNee and go for it.

☛ MCNEE FACTS

How to get there: Take Highway 1 to Montara, and park at the northern end of Montara State Beach. At the far northern end of the parking lot, cross Highway 1 and you will find a single-pipe gate across a dirt road -- that's the access point. A small state park property sign is posted.

Trip tips: A good idea is to strap on a small daypack in which you can bring lunch and drinks. If you plan to reach the top, it's a good idea to bring a change of shirts so you can stay dry and warm as you enjoy the views. A small stream in the valley is a good watering hole for dogs or horses, but there is no water available at higher elevations -- so bring a quart of water and a small drinking dish for your dog.

Trip Cost: Access is free, including leashed dogs.

Who to contact: Oops, you missed the access gate and you're lost? Call the ranger station in Half Moon Bay at (415) 726-6238.

PACIFICA'S BIG
CANYON TRAIL

A MUST FOR HIKERS

The Bay Area's newest hiking trail is also one of its best.

What you put in is an hour and a half of hiking time, most of it on a calculated, easy grade. What you get out are ocean views, access to true isolated wildlands, and that good feeling that comes with a special walk.

It's close -- and you can get there even if you don't own a car. Rangers call it the Big Canyon Trail, overlooking San Pedro Valley in Pacifica, a 15-mile ride from San Francisco by car or by BART and a SamTrans bus. The trail opened recently and is a 4.5-mile loop hike that is the centerpiece for San Pedro Valley County Park.

There are still places of remote beauty in the Bay Area and this is one of them. The first thing you notice in the park is that it can seem like one of the quietest places you've ever been in the Bay Area. Then you notice the miles and miles of surrounding wildlands that give it this quiet.

Because of that space, the area seems to project a friendly, relaxed feel. There is no litter, the park is sunny and warm compared to the cool, fogged-in coast, and it doesn't take long here and you start feeling pretty darn good.

You might just want to try it on for size some weekend. The few people who know of the place find it fits pretty snug.

After parking, you should head along San Pedro Valley, which opens up into a green meadow bordered by blooming wildflowers. After a mile, it connects to Big Canyon Trail, which rises for two miles along the northern slopes of

Montara Mountain to a series of 1,000-foot elevation lookouts.

On a clear day looking out to sea, you can spot the Farallon Islands, Point Reyes and some memorable sunsets. But even when the coast is fogged in, the views are still prime -- because San Pedro Mountain to the west often diverts the ocean fog. As a result, views of Sweeney Ridge and the surrounding mountains and canyons provide a panoramic setting.

And because of some forethought on the part of rangers, you can enjoy the views without feeling like a juiced orange. The trail up is not steep, but a gentle 10 percent grade for two miles.

"We used a device called a clinometer to keep the slope of the trail at about 10 percent," said ranger Don Curran. "That shouldn't be confused with 10 degrees, which is real steep. Ten percent means it rises one foot every 10 feet of trail."

Because of that, the park attracts hikers of all ages, from kids to seniors, rather than just hard-core foot stompers.

The hike down, returning to park headquarters, is a steep one, having been constructed 10 years ago. Good gripping boots are advised. So which direction you choose to route your trip is a key factor.

"For hikers, we advise walking

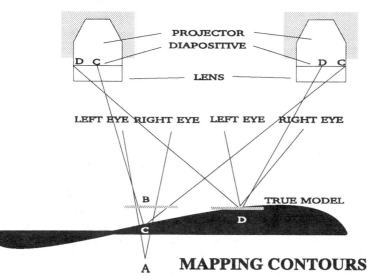

MAPPING CONTOURS FROM AERIAL PHOTOGRAPHS

down the valley, then heading up the Big Canyon Trail," Curran said. "You get the gentle slope up, a flat spot on the top, and a fast trip down." Going the opposite direction would involve a very steep climb.

A sidelight to the park are the frequent wildlife sightings. The park is bordered to the south by land owned by the San Francisco Water District, which in turn adjoins a State Wildlife Refuge. It is common, especially during summer evenings, for animals to venture to the meadow on the valley floor to graze or to get water in San Pedro Creek.

"We see rabbits and deer all the time," Curran said. "I've seem bobcat and coyote, too."

Because of the number of wild animals that move in and out of the park, dogs are prohibited.

The flora varies from chaparral sprinkled with hemlock, nettle and gooseberry to a few thick groves of eucalyptus, and occasional oaks, willows and dogwoods.

☛ SAN PEDRO FACTS

How to get there: Take Highway 1 into Pacifica and turn east on Linda Mar Boulevard, Pacifica's most southerly major intersection. Drive up Linda Mar until it dead ends at Oddstad Boulevard. Turn right, and the park entrance sits 50 yards distant on the left side. It is well signed.

Mass transit: From the BART station in Daly City, take SamTrans Bus No. 1L. For more information on bus routes, call (415) 871-2200.

Pets: Dogs are not allowed.

Trip cost: The entry fee is $2 per vehicle, though the entry way is rarely staffed by park rangers during the week.

Groups: Reservations are required for the Group Picnic Area. Call the County Park Center at (415) 363-4021.

Who to contact: Call San Pedro County Park at (415) 355-8289, where an answering machine will take questions. For more direct information, call the San Mateo County Parks and Recreation Department at (415) 363-4021 or write to Parks, County Government Center, 590 Hamilton Street, Redwood City, CA 94063.

PHOTO
OPPORTUNITY

BAY AREA HIKES

HUDDART PARK

HIDDEN PENINSULA WOODLAND

Huddart Park is a perfect example of an attractive and hidden woodland -- located near thousands of residents -- that seems to go almost unused from October to May. A lot of folks just don't seem to know it's here, even on the crackling fresh weekends of spring.

But it is, some 1,000 acres of redwoods, tan oak and madrones cut by miles of trails that can take you on easy walks, a picnic, or a good puffer of a hike that rises to the 2,000-foot Skyline Ridge.

A bonus is that the Skyline Trail connects Huddart Park to Wunderlich Park, which sits just below the town of Sky Londa. The resulting 20-mile hike provides a good close-to-home weekend backpack trip for Bay Area hikers who don't want to wait until summer for the Sierra

Nevada icebox to defrost. Combined with Wunderlich Park, hikers have access to nearly 2,000 acres of mountain vistas. In all, there are about 45 miles of trails, enough to keep you coming back for more.

Every time you return to Huddart, you can see something different. This factor makes Huddart probably the best hiking park on the Peninsula, and makes it a worthwhile trip for people from all over the Bay Area.

During the summer, Huddart Park is quite popular, especially for family picnics. There are a variety of short, loop trails that are short and match well for little kids and make for a good family trip. One of the best is the Redwood Trail, little more than a half-mile long, that starts from the Redwood Picnic Area. However, because much of it is such an easy walk set amid redwoods, this trail gets heavy use, and by mid-summer is what backpackers call a "highway." For hikers who yearn for a slice of solitude, there are several excellent options, all good half-day hikes.

My favorite is a route that encircles the park, about a five-mile trip that takes you through redwood forests, along stream-bedded canyons to skyline ridges, and eventually back to your starting point. With map in hand, you should start on the Dean Trail from the Werder Picnic Area, and eventually you will connect to Richard Road's Trail, Summit Springs Trail and Archery Fire Trail to complete the circuit. Because several trails intersect at Huddart Park, you can tailor-make your hike to your level of ambition.

Woodside was originally given its name for the stands of native redwoods on the nearby mountain slopes. However, little more than a 100 years ago, there was hardly a redwood tree left. Loggers went wild here after 1849 gold rush, cutting down practically anything in sight. The giant stumps you can see here beckon back to that era -- but the present second-growth forest, now thick and lush, is a testimonial to how man's best work with nature is often just to do nothing.

☞ HUDDART PARK TRIP FACTS

How to get there: From Highway 280, take the Woodside Road exit west, then turn right on King's Mountain Road and drive two miles to the main park entrance.

Backpack camping: Reservations are required through the park office.

Park hours: The park is open from 8 a.m. to 30 minutes after sunset for day visitors, though overnight camping is allowed.

Trip cost: Entrance fee is $2 per car. Camping is $5 per car.

Who to contact: Park headquarters can be reached at (415) 851-0326. At times, the phone is unattended.

BAY AREA HIKES

PORTOLA STATE
PARK

❦   ❦   ❦

ESCAPE FROM SUBURBIA

If explorer Don Gaspar de Portola saw the suburbia of the San Francisco Peninsula today, he'd probably do exactly what thousands of Bay Area residents do every year: Seek the refuge of Portola State Park.

The area from San Francisco to Morgan Hill can seem like one long chain of houses and cars, but just over the Skyline ridge behind the outskirts of Palo Alto there remains this asylum of peace. It looks much as it did when Portola first set foot on the area in 1769. Peters and Pescadero Creeks wind through rugged country studded with redwoods, douglas firs and oak. It's an ideal spot for the weekender who is ready to shed the grip of city life, but who doesn't want to drive far.

Portola State Park is best known for its natural terrain; you'll swear you're in the Sierra Nevada. Hiking, camping, and communing with the quiet are the prime attractions.

Some 14 miles of hiking trails lead through varied terrain and settings. Some hikers head up the ridge through redwoods and into chaparral, while others follow the streams and the forest floor of azaleas and ferns.

Campers have 52 campsites to pick from at Portola, each with a picnic table, barbecue pit, and wood food locker to protect your eats from raccoons during their nightly raids. All of the camping spots are "drive-in" sites, which means a parking space sits adjacent to each spot. Campsites here are usually pretty easy to come by, but during three-day holiday weekends, reservations are a necessity. In order to avoid any frustration caused by competition for camping space, the park system now provides a reservation service through Ticketron outlets for all state parks.

In the spring, a special bonus awaits streamside explorers. Steelhead are spawning in the gravel river beds after a long journey from the ocean to high reaches of the streams. But don't bring your fishing rod. All fishing is illegal all year around here, and has been for a few years. In the winter, the big steelhead are protected so they can spawn, and in the summer, so are the steelhead smolt -- in the past, kids catching those "little trout" in the summer were actually killing baby steelhead, which were trying to grow large enough to head out to sea.

Portola Park is a good destination for a family outing on a weekend or as a place of quiet during the week.

PORTOLA PARK TRIP FACTS

How to get there: From Highway 280 at Redwood City, take State Route 84 to Highway 35 (Skyline). Head south on Skyline for seven miles, and then turn west on Alpine Road. From Palo Alto, the twisty Page Mill Road eventually leads to the park.

Pets: Dogs must be licensed, kept on a leash, and are not allowed on the trails.

Trip Cost: Campsites are $6 per night, day-use fee is $2 per car, and the charge for dogs are $1 per night, and 50 cents per day.

Who to contact: Write Portola State Park, Star Route 2, La Honda, CA 94020, or call (415) 948-9098 for information. For information on campsite reservations (only needed from April to October), call Ticketron for the nearest outlet at (415) 393-6914.

SKYLINE RIDGE

CLASSIC RIDGETOP VISTAS

An ideal hideaway can be the Skyline Ridge Preserve. It is a quiet place that offers not only seclusion, but a trail that winds near both a lake and a pond, as well as along classic ridgetop vistas. The preserve is perched above Palo Alto on Skyline Boulevard, thus it is nearby for thousands of Peninsula residents.

December is one of the best times to visit, since a good Christmas tree farm borders an edge of the preserve, where you can make like Paul Bunyan and cut your own tree. It makes for a good two-for-one offer every December.

As it stands now, this is a good place to go, particularly if you want some peace and quiet. However, the preserve could become one of the best hideaways in the entire Bay Area -- if fishing was allowed in both Horseshoe Lake and the nearby pond. But the Midpeninsula Regional Open Space District currently prohibits fishing here, and that seems a crime by a public agent against the public. Anglers do not have access to a single public lake, reservoir or pond on the Peninsula -- yet here sits Horseshoe Lake, which ranges to 40 feet deep, is lined with tules, and could support an excellent largemouth bass fishery.

Horseshoe Lake is the focal point for the Skyline Ridge Preserve. It is located in the southeastern part of the preserve, and can be reached by a number of trails that connect and then border the western edge of the lake.

Another hike can take you to the highest point in the preserve at 2,493 feet. When you look down from here, the canyon seems to plunge thousands of feet below you. To the east, on a clear day, Mount Diablo rises huge above the East Bay skyline.

Most of the trails are actually more like old dirt roads, but they provide a good walking surface and combined with a network of old paths, can take you to a wide variety of scenic spots. The trails cut through woodlands filled primarily with douglas fir, madrone, and oak, as well as prairie-like grasslands.

In December, you can drive right up to the Christmas tree farm on Skyline Boulevard, and should you decide to cut your tree here, can continue your day by exploring the Skyline Ridge Preserve. In fact, the trail that can take you most quickly to Horseshoe Lake starts at the Christmas tree farm.

Access is free, regardless of whether or not you purchase a tree. The other access point is just south of the intersection of Skyline Boulevard and Page Mill Road.

The Skyline Ridge Preserve spans about 1,100 acres, and is bordered by open space. Visiting here can be a good present for yourself.

☞ SKYLINE RIDGE TRIP FACTS

How to get there: From Highway 280, take Page Mill Road west and continue until you reach the intersection with Skyline Boulevard. It is quite twisty.

Access points: You can gain entry to the preserve at the southeast corner of the Page Mill Road/Skyline Boulevard intersection, or through the Christmas tree farm located two miles south of the intersection.

Trip Cost: Access is free.

Who to contact: For a free map (a photocopy of a topographical map) as well as any other information, contact the Midpeninsula Regional Open Space District at (415) 965-4717.

BAY AREA HIKES

THE BAYLANDS
TRAIL

WHERE SLOWER IS BETTER

If you get a flat tire on the new Baylands Bicycle Trail, it might actually help your trip. The slower you go, the better.

By foot or with two wheels, you have a choice here. Tucked away near the edge of South San Francisco Bay is this sprawling acreage of wild marshlands bridged by a new path. There is no charge to visit and it is just minutes from Highway 101, yet it still retains a spirit independent of the nearby metropolis.

To test it out, I retrieved the old Schwinn one-speeder out of retirement and headed for the Baylands. A friend brought one of these fancy high-tech bikes, you know, gears and such, and did the same.

The opening part of the trail is built from crushed rock, flat and hard, and is bordered by a creek on the left and a golf course on the right. Judging by the golfing ability displayed by the hackers, a football helmet and coat of armor might be suitable apparel. Soon enough the trail turns from rock to hard packed dirt, and you will wind your way past the golf course, past the Palo Alto Airport, and to the marshlands.

Even on a bike, you find yourself intentionally slowing the pace. The air was so clear on our visit that it looked like you could take a running start, clear the Bay, and land on the East Bay hills.

We parked our bikes and decided to hoof it. The tidal marsh here is cut by sloughs and filled with a diversity of bird and marine life, as well as the plants that support it. The food chain that starts in the marshland supports almost all fish and wildlife in the San Francisco Bay and its tidelands. Some 250 species of birds use San Francisco Bay as either a resting spot or home, including birds only rarely seen elsewhere. We counted some 15 snowy egrets.

If you want to extend your visit, you should continue to the Baylands Interpretive Center,

where an old wooden walkway lifts you just above the soggy marsh. It leads to the edge of the Bay. On low tides, the water will roll back and expose bare mudflats for miles. The walkway is accessible to wheelchairs, and for that matter, so is the rock-built portion of the bike trail. The entire trail is not accessible because storms soften the dirt portion.

The marshlands are filled with plants such as pickleweed and cordgrass, and to the developer, may look like a good spot to pave over with concrete and condominiums. However, this is actually one of the most productive chains of life on earth.

When the plants decay, little bits of the decomposed material are carried into the Bay by tidal action and are fed on by small animals such as clams, crabs, snails, and pile worms. The food web is completed when these are eaten by seals, birds, large fish, and other animals. The richness of the area is reflected in the diversity of birdlife and the abundance of ground squirrels.

Yet another option you can take is to follow the bike path across a bridge, then head down the trail behind Palo Alto. It goes practically to the Dumbarton Bridge.

By foot, one to three hours is plenty to allow to see the Palo Alto Baylands Area. Regardless of your physical conditioning or age, it can be enjoyable, because there are no hills at all.

Sure, the rubber on a wheel is quicker than the rubber on a heel, but at the Baylands Bike Trail, you can take your pick.

☞ BAYLANDS TRAIL TRIP FACTS

How to get there: Take Highway 101 to Palo Alto, then take the Embarcadero east exit. At the second light, across from Mings Restaurant, turn left at Geng Street, and continue to its end. The trail begins directly behind the baseball field, and is signed.

Mass transit: SamTrans, (415) 965-3100, does not make trips east of Highway 101 on Embarcadero. It's about a 15-minute walk from the trailhead.

Trip tip: Your best chance of seeing the maximum number of birds and wildlife is in the early morning, when people numbers are lowest.

Pets: Dogs must be leashed.

Trip Cost: Free.

Who to contact: Call the Baylands Interpretive Center at (415) 329-2506, either Wednesday through Friday (2 p.m. to 5 p.m.) or on weekends (1 p.m. to 5 p.m.). The Palo Alto Recreation Department can be reached at (415) 329-2261.

BAY AREA HIKES

SOUTH BAY WILDLIFE
REFUGE

A LOOK AT A DIFFERENT WORLD

How many times have you sped in your car along the shores of San Francisco Bay on Highway 101, 17 or 237, dodging traffic like Mario Andretti at the Indy 500?

It's a common situation, but if you hatch out of that metal cocoon, rub your eyes to a new day and look just over yonder, yea over there, you might get a first look at a far different world. The shores of our bay offer a perfect environment for a diversity of little critters, from tiny crabs to rabbits. And the marshlands also act as one of the major rest stops for millions of birds on the Pacific Flyway.

This all adds up to the San Francisco Bay National Wildlife Refuge, headquartered in Newark near the Dumbarton Bridge, and it spans some 23,000 acres. You can't beat the price, with access, brochures, and regularly scheduled guided walks all free; it's an ideal adventure, especially for families or groups. It can be explored by trail or by boat -- but not by car, motorcycle or bicycle. That means you can go it alone, just your body, and get that special quiet you deserve.

The diversity of wildlife here can be spectacular. First, try to imagine that a handful of bay mud can contain 20,000 tiny living creatures, which key the primary levels of the marine food chain. A good start; then imagine, there are as many different kinds of birds in this area than almost anywhere else in Northern California. In a given year, more than 250 species of birds will find the food, resting space and nesting sites they search for. Bird life, particularly waterfowl, is most abundant in the fall when snow storms across Canada, Montana, and parts of Washington send migratory birds to their wintering sanctuaries by the Bay.

After just 15 minutes and before I lost track, I scoped six different kinds of ducks, along with a pelican, egret, heron, sandpiper and another species I could not readily identify. No problem. A later check at the ranger station provided the answer: A willet, which gets its name from its call during the breeding season, an oft-repeated "pill-will-willet."

On low tides, the Bay will roll back and display miles of tidal flats, often studded with mussels, clams and oysters. Pollution controls since the "Save Our Bay" campaign of the 1960s has been so successful that water is cleaner than it has been in 25 years, and shellfish digging is now permitted in a few areas.

Fishing and hunting (in specified areas) is permitted, and actually can be quite good if you hit the right time and right place. For fishing, the right time is a high incoming tide. The right place is near the Dumbarton Bridge along the main channel of the Bay, a natural fishway. Sharks, rays, perch and an occasional striped bass, jacksmelt and flounder can be caught, according to season.

Most folks, however, go just for the walk, an easy hike along the bay shoreline, a close-to-home spot that you may have driven past thousands of times on a highway, but never taken a good look at.

☞ SOUTH BAY REFUGE TRIP FACTS

How to get there: From the Peninsula, take Highway 101 to the Dumbarton Bridge, then head to Newark. From Highway 17, take the Jarvis Road or Thornton Avenue turnoffs to the Dumbarton. The refuge headquarters is located near the toll plaza.

Mass transit: It's not convenient at the present. The Alameda County bus system schedules a stop about a mile away. For information, call AC Transit at (415) 839-2882.

Trip tip: Bring good walking shoes and binoculars. Leashed dogs are allowed only on the Tidelands Trail.

Trip Cost: Access, brochures and scheduled guided tours are free.

Who to contact: Call Monty Dewey at (415) 792-0222, or write San Francisco Bay National Wildlife Refuge, P.O. Box 524, Newark, CA 94560.

BIG BASIN STATE
PARK

A SCENE OUT OF YOSEMITE

Imagine a short Sunday morning drive from the Bay Area, an hour-and-a-half walk, most of it downhill, then lunch aside a magnificent 70-foot waterfall in a canyon lined with ferns -- a scene that looks like a picture out of Yosemite.

When you visit Big Basin State Park in the Santa Cruz Mountains, you will discover that this image is not the product of your imagination. And unlike a lot of the steep hikes in Yosemite, you won't feel like a juiced orange when you return. Big Basin became California's first state park in 1902, and you have to hike it to understand why. It seems

a place of special calm, with thousands of acres of redwoods, ferns, moss-lined canyons and a series of waterfalls that make prime destinations for hikers.

Time in the mountains here can give you a fresh perspective. A few drops of water caught by a spider web look like crystals in mid-air...a blooming trillium alone in a bed of ferns...huge redwoods, some living for 2,000 years. When you return, you feel like this place has recharged your batteries.

BATTERY

Big Basin is an ideal place for a one-day hike, with some 80 miles of trails to choose from. But many visit the park for weeklong camping trips -- since you won't squander days driving long distances. Some 145 drive-in campsites, and 43 walk-in sites are available, and reservations can be obtained through Ticketron. Each camp is in a redwood setting, and includes a tent site, picnic table, and food locker.

A bonus is that Big Basin also offers unique options for backpackers either in training for a Sierra expedition, or just in need of a good two-day pull. One of the best weekend hikes in the Bay Area can be discovered here. It's part of the Skyline-to-Sea Trail; a 12-miler from headquarters at Big Basin to the Pacific Ocean. A shuttle system by bus allows you to arrive at the trail's end at Highway 1, where you park your vehicle. A small bus then takes you to Santa Cruz, where you transfer and take another bus to the park. I have done this and found it an inexpensive, straight-forward connection.

If you have a little of the wildness in you, then consider the entire Skyline-to-Sea Trail, a 38-mile foot stomper. It starts at Castle Rock State Park on Highway 35, which is perched at 2,700 feet just south of the Highway 9 junction. It's a good three-day jaunt, most of it downhill as the trail descends to the shores of the Pacific. Several backcountry camps are available for overnighters. In order to be certain that wildlife and the forest habitat is not encroached, park rules mandate no fires (use a camp stove), and bedding down only in designated sites.

These strict rules have left most of the native animals as undisturbed tenants. Gone are the grizzly bear, one which killed logger William Waddell in 1875, and the eagle, but remaining are deer, coyote, rac-

coons, bobcats, possums and the like. Also more than 250 species of birds have been observed in Waddell Valley. The most common is the stellar's jay, mistakenly called a blue jay by most; stellar's jay has a crested head, blue jays do not. These birds arrive promptly as your companion when you start eating lunch, hoping for a handout, and leave just as quickly when you are finished.

The centerpiece of Big Basin is Berry Creek Falls. If you have never seen it, then a Sunday drive and hike should be assigned high priority in your schedule. It will make you appreciate the Bay Area as a different and better place than you know it now.

BIG BASIN TRIP FACTS

How to get there: From San Francisco, take Highway 1 south to Santa Cruz, turn east on Highway 9, then turn left on Highway 236 and continue to the park. From the San Francisco Peninsula, from Los Gatos, take Highway 9 over the ridge, then turn right on Highway 236 and continue to the park. Turns are posted.

Trip cost: For day-use, a parking fee of $2 is charged. Campsites are $6 per night.

Camping: Reservations for drive-in campsites should be made through Ticketron. Backpack campsite reservations can be obtained through park headquarters by calling (408) 338-6132.

Shuttle service: For information on the bus shuttle from Big Basin's western boundary at Waddell Beach at Highway 1 to Big Basin headquarters, call the Santa Cruz Transit District at (408) 425-6800.

Maps: Send $1 to Sempervirens Fund, Drawer BE, Los Altos, CA 94022, or call (415) 968-4509.

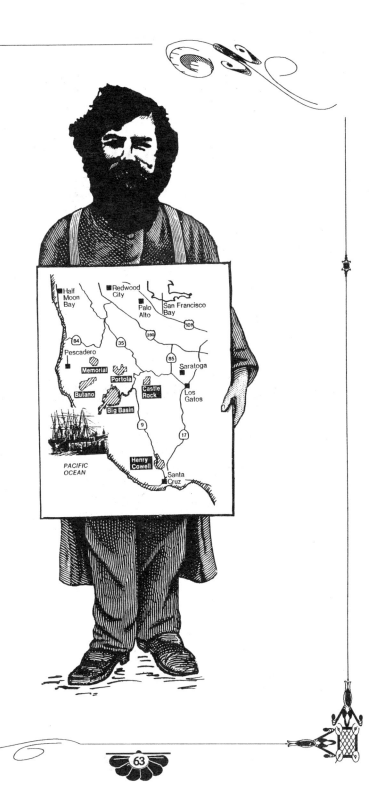

BAY AREA HIKES

PURISIMA CREEK
REDWOODS

An Escape Into The Nearby Woods

Purisima Creek Redwoods is the kind of place many people in the Bay Area constantly yearn for -- but don't even know exists.

This is one of the true great secret spots the Bay Area has to offer. A giant preserve with redwood forests, creeks and glens, and fantastic lookouts, it feels like this spot might be in a secluded Northern California forest, 350 miles away.

But it isn't. It is located on the western slopes of the San Francisco's Peninsula ridgeline, about a 30-minute drive from San Francisco or Hayward, closer for Peninsula residents.

The area offers the opportunity to hike, bike, ride, picnic or just visit by car and enjoy the views. It covers a huge area, some 2,500 acres, starting at the Skyline ridge in the Santa Cruz Mountains overlooking Half Moon Bay. The Skyline entrance is accessible to wheelchairs.

There are three access points, two on Skyline (Highway 35) about 4 miles south of the Highway 92 junction. The other is off Higgins Canyon Road, a four mile drive from Main Street in Half Moon Bay.

Between those points is a vast area that will be preserved forever by the Midpeninsula Regional Open Space District. Because it is a new parkland, having opened in 1988, not many people know about it.

The preserve centers on Purisima Creek Canyon and its classic redwood forests, bedded with ferns, wild berries and wildflowers. There are also great views of the Pacific Ocean and Half Moon Bay to the west, and, from the ridgetop on

Skyline, of San Francisco Bay to the east.

That combination of woods and ocean views makes it feel like Big Sur, Mount Tamalpais and the Humboldt Coast all in one.

This is a do-it-yourself trip. There is no ranger station, park kiosk or information center. If you have a good memory, there are permanent wood trail maps mounted at the trailheads.

A better bet is to obtain the one-page trail map of the park by writing headquarters. The map details 10 miles of trails for hikers along with fire roads for mountain bikes. The southern side of the park is more heavily wooded than that to the north. So if you want views, start from the northern access point on Skyline Boulevard, located near road marker SM 18.36. If you want woods, start at the southern access point near Skyline road marker SM 16.65.

The ideal walk here is to start at the southern Skyline Ridge access point. After parking, you can make the beautiful four mile walk downhill to the western end of the park at Higgins Canyon Road. With a companion, you can park another vehicle at trail's end to use as a shuttle.

That way you can get a one-way hike with almost no uphill walking, perfect for people planning their first walk of the summer. This one is a beauty, the trail following along much of Purisima Creek. At times it is a lush watershed, heavy with redwoods and ferns.

In some of the more open areas,

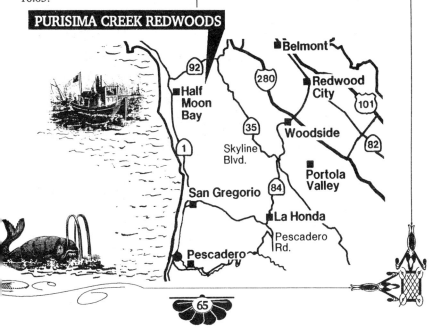

you can spot all kinds of wild-flowers. Large patches of blue Forget-Me-Nots are among those that full bloom.

What you have instead is a big chunk of Bay Area land protected in its natural environment. It is one of the best secrets you will uncover this year.

Like other lands managed by the Midpeninsula Open Space District, this is an open-space preserve, not a developed park. That means there are no barbecues, ball fields, campsites or developed recreation.

☛ PURISIMA TRIP FACTS

How to get there: Access from Skyline: Drive on Highway 92 west toward Half Moon Bay, then turn south on Highway 35 (Skyline Boulevard). There are two access points off of Skyline. The northern access point is a 4.5-mile drive at road marker SM 18.36, the other a 6.5-mile drive at road marker SM 16.65. Parking areas are provided. Access from Half Moon Bay: From Main Street in Half Moon Bay, drive south through town and turn east on Higgins Canyon Road. Continue on the winding road for 4 miles to the park. A small parking lot is on the left side of the road.

Trip Cost: Access and parking are free.

Maps: A one-page trail map of Purisima Creek Redwoods is available by calling (415) 949-5500 or writing Midpeninsula Regional Open Space District, Old Mill Office Center, Building C, Suite 135, 201 San Antonio Circle, Mountain View, CA 94040, or calling (415) 949-5500.

Who to contact: See above for numbers.

PHOTO OPPORTUNITY

BAY AREA HIKES

BUTANO STATE
PARK

WHERE FEW FEET TRAVEL

This rarely-visited park sits just 10 miles south of Pescadero amid a redwood tree and stream setting. It's a year-around facility ideal for either an after work picnic or a weekend hike -- and you can also camp, backpack, run cross-country, or as the park rangers like to joke, just sit down for a communion of thought with a redwood tree.

One of the highlights here is the 11-mile Loop Trail, which is on my list as one of the Bay Area's top 10 hikes. The trail takes you across a broad spectrum of terrain -- and

back to where you started without forcing you to backtrack.

Butano (pronounced Bute-Uh-No) provides an alternative for campers who love redwoods and ferns, but don't have the time for long drives. All of the campsites here are fairly secluded, including 21 with a parking space for a vehicle, and 19 walk-in sites. If you confine your camping to the summer, then file this idea away in your thinking cap. One Memorial Day weekend, when most highways and parks were congested, I headed to Butano and discovered the park quiet, and only half of the campsites being used. For the adventurous, six campsites for backpackers are set on the Loop Trail. Reservations and permits for these few spots are required through park headquarters.

About 80 percent of the park is forested with conifers, with the rest speckled with chaparral, especially along the upper ridges, and wildflowers such as golden poppies and trillium.

A sidelight to the trip, especially for weekend hikers, should be a stop in for dinner at Duarte's Restaurant in Pescadero, a legend on the coastside. Duarte's (pronounced Do-Arts) was constructed in the 1800s -- destroyed in a town-wide fire in 1927 -- and then rebuilt in 1929. It is equipped with gas lanterns, so operations can continue when winter storms batter the coast and knock out power.

If you bring your own food to Butano, you will likely find yourself surrounded by many new friends, especially stellar's jays, looking for a handout. They are among more than a hundred species of birds here. Hawks are common

sightings, and if you're lucky, you might spot an owl at sunset. Squirrels, raccoons, coyotes, foxes, deer and even bobcat make a home on the range at Butano, and on the Loop Trail, it is fairly common to suddenly find yourself practically nose-to-nose with a deer.

That's how it can be when you find a special hideaway -- something that is practically guaranteed at Butano State Park.

← BUTANO PARK TRIP FACTS

How to get there: Take Highway 1 about 15 miles south of Half Moon Bay to Pescadero, and turn left on Pescadero Road. Two miles past Pescadero, turn right on Cloverdale Road and continue for five miles to the park. All turns are well posted.

Pets: Pooches are allowed on leashes in campgrounds, but are not permitted on trails.

Trip Cost: The day use charge is $2 per day per vehicle, and the camping fee is $10 per night per vehicle (up to eight people). The fee for dogs is 50 cents per day, or $1 per night.

Who to contact: Call the Butano State Park at (415) 879-0173, or by writing P.O. Box 9, Pescadero, CA 94060.

WADDELL CREEK

WALK A WILDLIFE SPECTACLE

T he only time most people see wildlife is on television, but there is an easy walk on the outskirts of the Bay Area that can change that for you.

In an evening stroll, we saw seven deer, three rabbits, several squirrels, five quail, a pair of grouse, 10 ducks, a blue heron and baby steelhead feeding on an insect hatch, all in just two hours.

But birds and fish are the centerpiece of this beautiful streamside walk that can take you from lagoon to meadows to redwood forest.

Most hikers call it the Waddell Creek Walk, the trailhead located on Highway 1 just inside the Santa Cruz County line, about 20 miles south of Half Moon Bay. It starts at the Rancho del Oso outpost, the western border for Big Basin State Park. Technically, the trail is the lower portion of the Skyline-to-Sea Trail.

It is an ideal spot to view wildlife and birds in their native habitat. But it is also just a good place to walk, a near-flat trail that plays peek-a-boo with forest and meadow.

An option is to stay overnight. There are secluded hike-in camps available as close as 1.2 miles from the trailhead, with two others within another two miles. Reservations are required. No open fires or barbecues are permitted, so bring a backpacking stove. And camping is

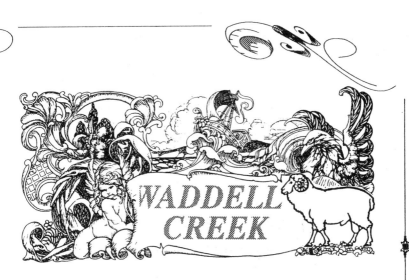

WADDELL CREEK

permitted in designated sites only.

You start the trip with a nice cruise down Highway 1, which provides continual lookouts to the Pacific Ocean. After passing Ano Nuevo and entering Santa Cruz County, be on the lookout for the large sign announcing Big Basin State Park and Rancho del Oso. That's your calling.

The first half-mile of the trail loops around the Waddell Creek Lagoon to the park's outpost headquarters. Maps are available here, along with information about the park.

In the next four miles, you can see as much wildlife as any place in California except the zoo. There are huge meadows on each side of the trail that attract grazing deer, especially during the late afternoon and evening. Photographers with long-range lenses can get classic shots.

In the wooded areas, keep alert for any chattering sound. If you hear it, freeze and scan the woods -- some-

where, likely hopping down the side of a tree and scurrying off to another, will be a gray squirrel.

In areas where the trail is lined with dense bush, walk quietly and keep your eyes looking far ahead. You are apt to see a little brown bush bunny hopping across the trail or playing in the dirt. Often, when they first spot you, the rabbits will freeze in their tracks for 5 or 10 seconds, rather than immediately disappear into the bush. This allows you to watch the little critters closely, and can teach children the merits of quiet in the woods. The deer however seem almost acclimated to the passing of hikers. You also can see a surprising diversity of birds. Because it is close to a freshwater lagoon, ducks and blue heron nest in the watershed. The most com-

mon waterfowl seem to be mallard. The coastal fields, which provide a transition zone between ocean and forest, are perfect for nesting quail. We saw a nice covey, which included some females that were so close to nesting that they were as round as grapefruits.

Waddell Creek itself is a pleasant stream that attracts steelhead in the winter. No fishing is permitted, but you can occasionally spot an adult. It is more common to see the newly hatched smolts, which look like little trout, the three to five-inch steelhead darting to the surface for insects during the evening rise.

The trail is more like an old ranch road and is easy on the feet. It continues like this for 4.5 miles, when it enters the redwood interior of Big Basin State Park. Here, the trail starts to climb. If you have the spirit for it, you can continue up to Berry Creek Falls, and on (and up) farther to the Cascade Falls.

No matter how far you go, it makes for a perfect walk. And it beats going to the zoo by a mile.

FACTS ABOUT THE WADDELL WALK

How to get there: Drive south on Highway 1 about 20 miles past Half Moon Bay, just inside the Santa Cruz County line. After passing Ano Nuevo, look for the signs marking Big Basin State Park/Rancho del Oso.

Maps: For maps of Big Basin, send $1.50 to Sempervirens Fund, Drawer BE, Los Altos, CA 94022; or call (415) 968-4509.

Camping: For reservations to hike-in campsites, phone park headquarters at (408) 338-6132.

Who to contact: For information on Waddell Creek, phone the Rancho del Oso outpost at (408) 425-1218. If the ranger is on patrol, phone headquarters at (408) 338-6132.

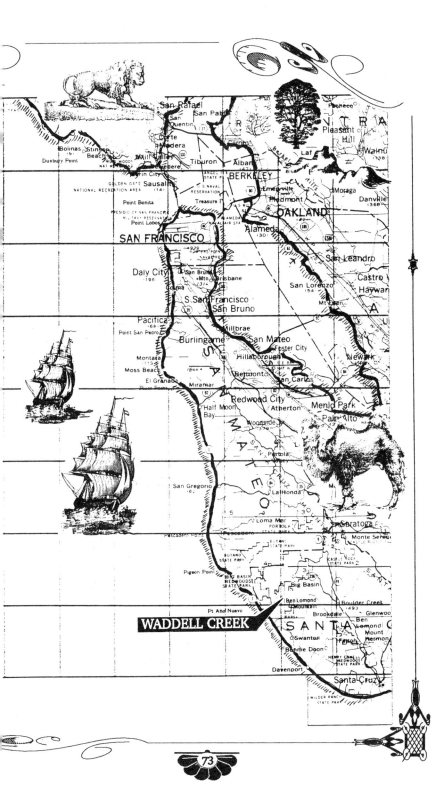

WADDELL CREEK

BAY AREA HIKES

MOUNT MADONNA
PARK

FAMILY FUN IN THE SANTA CRUZ MOUNTAINS

It can be quite a shock to learn of a nearby parkland that provides great scenic beauty, good hiking, camping, horseback riding, and fishing for kids -- that you previously had no idea even existed.

Such is the case for many when they learn of Mount Madonna Park, which is located between Gilroy and Watsonville, and set around the highest peak in the southern range of the Santa Cruz Mountains. A three or four-hour visit here, capped by a dinner at one of nearby Monterey Bay's fine restaurants can make for a classic day.

In late summer, this area can be like a hot volcano, but the temperate days of spring and early summer make for ideal weather for hikes and picnics. Since the hills have yet to get baked, in spring the grasslands explode in color from brilliant wildflower displays.

The park sprawls over more than 3,000 acres, and if you take the time to hike and explore it, you will find a surprisingly diversity. Imagine redwoods near Gilroy. No way? Look closer. The park's major canyons not only shelter redwoods and tanoaks, but are also cut by streams gurgling over rocks and submerged limbs. Redwoods up to 100-feet tall can be found at the top of Mount Madonna, as well as on the west slopes.

Madonna includes a network of 18 miles of trails, which intersect in several spots, allowing you to custom tailor your hike. Be sure to obtain a trail map from park headquarters, since the best hikes are combinations of different trails. My favorites are the Redwood and Blackhawk Canyon Trails. At 1,897 feet, the elevation of the peak of Mount Madonna may not seem like much. But since most of the surrounding land is near sea level, the peak can provide a lookout with impressive views. To the west, you can see the Salinas Valley unfold to Monterey Bay, and to the east, the vast Santa Clara basin.

Some of the better vistas can be seen without even leaving your car, since Pole Line Road and Summit Road rise to near the summit. But don't be content with that. This park has many secrets, none which can be discovered by car. If you don't like to hike, well, there's another way, which may be the most appealing route of all for many. Instead of two legs, use four -- that is, the four legs of a horse.

Mount Madonna Stables on Summit Road is situated perfectly to allow you to play pioneer for a few hours; horses are allowed on almost all of the trails. At times, most often in the early months of the year, the stable closes down its rental busi-

ness, but it is usually open throughout the summer.

On the eastern side of the park, Sprig Lake is available for kids to fish for stocked trout from May through July. It's not much of a lake, and only kids from five to 12 years old are permitted to try their luck.

If Mount Madonna Park sounds like the kind of place where you'd like to spend more than an afternoon, some 115 campsites are available on a first-come, first-serve basis. Unlike state parks, reservations are not necessary. Why? Because most folks have never even heard of this place. For many, it is a well-kept secret.

☞ MOUNT MADONNA TRIP FACTS

How to get there: From either Gilroy or Watsonville, take Highway 152 and then turn north on Pole Line Road. For the slow, winding, scenic route from Gilroy or Watsonville, take the Old Mount Madonna Road to the Summit Road entrance.

Maps: A good map detailing 18 miles of trails can be obtained at park headquarters for free.

Horseback riding: Horse rentals are available usually starting in May or early June from Mount Madonna Stables (408) 847-3793.

Pets: Fido can be brought along for the ride, but is not permitted on trails.

Trip Cost: The entrance fee is $2 per car for day use. Camping is $10 per car.

Camping: Campsites are taken on a first-come, first-serve basis. Group camping reservations can be obtained by phoning (408) 358-3751.

Who to contact: Park headquarters can be reached at (408) 842-2341, though the phone line is sometimes not attended.

SUNOL'S LITTLE
YOSEMITE

❧ ❧ ❧

HIDDEN AWAY IN THE EAST BAY HILLS

little
yosemite

There are unique, hidden places in the Bay Area that can make you feel like you have your own secret spots. That's how Little Yosemite is.

Now wait a minute: "Little Yosemite"? Isn't that the park where three million campers a year look at Half Dome and get their food raided every night by Smokey the Bear? No, that's big Yosemite.

It has a little brother secluded east of Fremont near Highway 680. There is no El Capitan or Cathedral Rocks, but there is also no Curry Village, and that alone is enough to give Little Yosemite a charm all its own.

In other words, there is usually nobody here. Little Yosemite is part of Sunol Regional Preserve, a 6,500-acre wilderness area in the East Bay hills. You say you've never been there? Join the club. On most visits, it can seem like you have the entire world to yourself.

The centerpiece of the park is this hidden and remarkable canyon, named Little Yosemite. It is edged by craggy rock outcrops and cut by a nice little trout stream, now just a trickle. When the rains come, the river makes a nice waterfall around a giant boulder.

It makes for a prime half-day adventure. The park is within short driving range for most Bay Area residents, it only costs $2 per vehicle to enter, and if you have a dog, by all means bring Fido along because this is one of the few places where dogs are allowed on trails.

There are six trails in the Sunol Regional Preserve. For your first trip, the best choice is the Canyon

View Trail, about a 3.5-mile round-trip that sweeps above the valley and to the canyon rim above Little Yosemite. It is best viewed from the top of the cliffs, where you can look down and see the plunging canyon walls. (A wide, flat roadlike trail in the bottom of the valley, makes Little Yosemite wheelchair accessible).

For a good loop hike from the parking area, take the Canyon Rim Trail to the Yosemite Valley Overlook. From there, you will spot a gated cutoff trail that drops down to the floor of Little Yosemite.

Like much of the East Bay hills, Little Yosemite is owned by the San Francisco Water District. In the past year, its officials have shown more regard for non-impact public recreation access than at any time in their history.

The East Bay Regional Park District has taken the lead to work out a few special deals for Water District land -- opening not only Little Yosemite, but the 27-mile Ohlone Wilderness Trail. In the process, it has proved that public recreational access can be provided without impact of any kind.

In fact, the biggest impact to this area is not from people, which are few, but from wild boar, which are many. You can see evidence of rooting and digging, and if you're lucky, might even spot one deep in a shaded canyon. Big Yosemite has bears, this place has boars.

Little Yosemite itself has an ideal habitat for a variety of birds. In a morning, you might spot 20 different species. It's a result of the riparian habitat of the Alameda Creek and canyon setting, which has alder, willow and sycamore.

The rest of Sunol Regional Preserve is made up of rolling hills, a grassland country with a few oak, madrone and digger pine.

Out here you can see redtail hawks cruising for their next meal. In addition to boar, deer sightings are common. There are also a few

skunks in the hills, so if you bring a dog, keep him on a leash -- or it might chase the "black and white cat with the big tail" and end up getting a fresh skunk blast, direct hit.

Regardless of whether you are for an overnighter, or just take the short half-day loop through Little Yosemite, you'll remember this park as a hidden spot -- that you wished you knew about years ago.

☞ PERTINENT FACTS FOR LITTLE YOSEMITE

How to get there: From Highway 680, take the Calaveras Road turnoff just south of the town of Sunol. Turn left at Calaveras Road to Geary Road -- turn left on Geary and follow to park entrance.

Special law: No alcohol permitted in the park.

Trip Cost: A $2 parking fee is charged at the park entrance.

Camping: The few campsites near the parking area are available for $6 per night and includes the parking fee. A backpack camping permit is required by advance registration with a $3 fee, which includes a mile of the Ohlone Wilderness Trail.

Who to contact: For maps or general information, call Ned MacKay at (415) 531-9300, or write the East Bay Regional Park District, 11500 Skyline Boulevard, Oakland, 94619. For trail information, call park headquarters at (415) 862-2244.

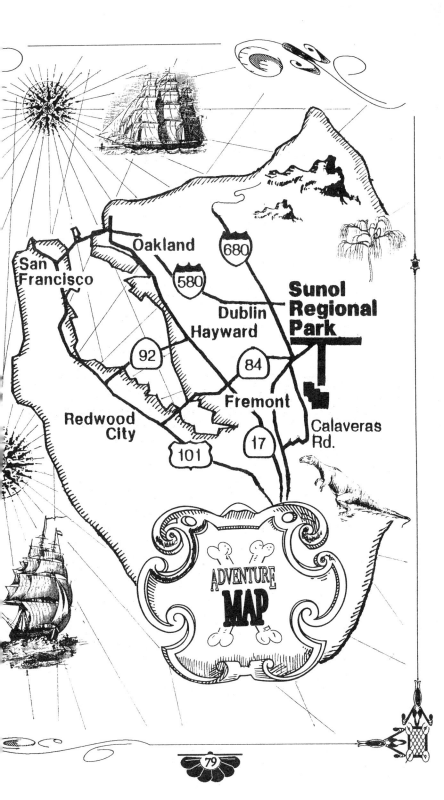

Oakland

San Francisco

680

580

Dublin

Hayward

Sunol Regional Park

92

84

Fremont

Redwood City

Calaveras Rd.

101

17

ADVENTURE
MAP

BAY AREA HIKES

CHABOT REGIONAL PARK

A NEARBY ROMP IN THE GREAT OUTDOORS

Okay, so you don't have anything to do this weekend. Well, if you venture over to Chabot Regional Park, you'll find something better to do than watching a Bonanza rerun.

The park covers 5,000 acres, with 31 miles of hiking trails, and a fish-filled lake with nine miles of shoreline. Want more? There are also horseback riding rentals, boat rentals, camping spots, a marksmanship range, bicycle trails and such picnic activities as horseshoes and volleyball. All you supply is the do.

Chabot is in the East Bay hills above Castro Valley, a few miles east of Highway 580. Some folks pronounce Chabot so it rhymes with habit, but the right way is Shuh-Bowe, named after Anthony Chabot. He was a pioneer California philanthropist who created Lake Chabot in the 1890s by building a dam across San Leandro Creek.

Almost a 100 years later, the lake is still the centerpiece to the park. It provides a close-to-home fishing hole, and receives special stocks of rainbow trout.

You can rent an aluminum boat with electric motor, troll a lure such as a Kastmaster or Super Duper along the west shore near the dam or in Bass Cove and catch some nice rainbow trout. If you want a sure thing, head over to Honker Bay and cast out a white or yellow mini-jig and you can fill up a bucket with five to eight-inch crappie.

If you just want to paddle around the lake, row boats and canoes are available for rent at the marina. If that isn't for you, there are lots of other options.

One of the better deals is the Lakeside Trail, which starts at the marina and traces much of the lake's shoreline. It is paved, so it is accessible to bicyclists and wheelchairs.

If your idea of hiking isn't walking on pavement, then take a look at the Chabot map that details 31 miles of hiking trails. The park is distinguished by a long, grassy valley, bordered both to the east and west by ridges. Select one of the 16 trails, head off up a ridge, and you'll get a workout and some seclusion.

If you want to do some real tromping, the Skyline Trail runs the length of the park and connects northward to a network of six other regional parks. Up along the ridgeline, the chain of cities in the East Bay flats seem quite distant.

If you want to get the same feeling of isolation yet not pay for it in a pair of hiking boots, horse rentals are available for $10 per hour. If you're new to the saddle, don't worry about it. Inexperienced riders will find a lot of these horses are real tame and seem to go on automatic pilot -- and when the hour is almost up, an inner alarm goes off and back they go to the barn. They know where the hay is, and it sure as heck isn't out there on the trail.

Most people who go to Chabot Park do so for an afternoon or evening picnic and will parlay fishing, hiking, or horseback riding into the trip. But you can do it one better,

because Chabot has a nice campground with 75 spacious sites that provide plenty of elbow room, even when it is filled.

At the campground, 62 of the sites are for tents and 12 have full hookups available for motor homes. Piped water, fireplaces and tables are provided at each site, and toilets, showers are available. It's one of the few Bay Area campgrounds that has a lake nearby.

Unexpected things happen at this park. A few years ago, for instance, a 16-pound largemouth bass washed up dead from old age on the lake's shoreline. It was one of the biggest bass in Northern California history.

CHABOT REGIONAL PARK NOTES

How to get there: The key is to get on Highway 580 -- then take 580 to San Leandro and then head east of Fairmont Drive, which goes over a ridge and merges with Lake Chabot Road. A $2 parking fee is charged per vehicle when the park entrance is staffed; otherwise, the fee is $1. Bring four quarters for the machine at the entrance gate.

Fishing: A California fishing license ($18.50) is required, along with a one-day Chabot fishing pass $1.50, which is used entirely for future fish stocks. Kids under age 16 don't need either.

Boat rentals: An aluminum boat with electric motor costs $20 for five hours, or $7 per hour. Row boats cost $4.50 per hour or $13 for five hours. A refundable deposit of $10 is required. Call Lake Chabot Marina, 881-1833.

Hiking: Maps are available at the Lake Chabot Marina Coffee Shop, or you can phone Regional Park Head-quarters at (415) 531-9300.

Camping: There are 75 drive-in campsites available, with reservations through Ticketron. The costs are $6 per night for a tent site, $9 for a motor home site with a hookup.

Horseback riding: Horse rentals are available for $10 per hour for ages 13 and up, $8 per hour for ages 9 through 12. Call Chabot Equestrian Center, (415) 569-4428.

Marksmanship range: Access for shooting sports costs $3.50 for ages 18 and up, $1.25 for ages 17 and under. Call Marksmanship Range, (415) 569-0213.

Who to contact: For general information call East Bay Regional Park District, (415) 531-9300.

BAY AREA HIKES

TILDEN PARK

ADVENTURES TO FIT EVERY STYLE

Indian Summer in the Bay Area can turn your home into a blast furnace. But when you're perched atop Inspiration Point amid the East Bay hills during the early-evening, the cool breezes off the Bay have a way of sweeping away the heat, and with it any of your daily gripes.

This quiet spot is roosted above Berkeley in Tilden Regional Park. What makes this park remarkable is that it offers adventure for a multiplicity of styles, including short hiking, bicycling, horseback riding, weekend backpacking, cross-country jogging -- or even a scenic trail for those who do their walking in a wheelchair. And for a bonus, unlike state-operated parks, you can bring Fido your dog along to join in the adventure.

One of the Bay Area's most dramatic vistas is on the western border of Tilden Park, where the entire Bay and its skyline unfold at your feet. I have seen sunsets here where I shook my head and thought that this certainly must be God's Country -- because nobody else could have thought of it.

A key focal point at Tilden Park is Nimitz Way, a 4.5-mile long trail that winds its way from Inspiration Point to Wildcat Peak. It provides impressive vistas to the east, overlooking San Pablo and Briones Reservoirs. To the west are views of thick, wooded parklands that can stun first-timers whose previous conceptions of the East Bay hills conjure visions of an expanded sweat house. Since this stretch of trail is of gentle terrain and also paved, it is well-suited for wheelchairs, bicycles, or even baby strollers. For the more adventurous, just look over yonder, because it is also the trailhead for the network of hikes that cut through miles of remote and diversified terrain.

Most of the East Bay Regional Park System is joined by the Skyline National Trail, a prime 31-mile hike for backpackers who don't want to drive for hours to find adventure. To the north from Inspiration Point, hikers can extend their walks either into Wildcat Canyon Regional Park, where a gorge has been cut by Wildcat Creek and is lined by riparian vegetation. To the south, you can hike onward through Sibley Volcanic Preserve, Huckleberry Botanic Preserve, Redwood Park and ultimately to Lake Chabot just east of San Leandro, all connected by the Skyline Trail.

Within Tilden Park are two of the highest points in the East Bay hills; Vollmer Peak (1,913 feet elevation)

at the southern tip of the park, and Wildcat Peak (1,250 feet elevation) at the northern end of Tilden. Wildcat Peak is tucked away in an impressive stand of trees, and is a popular two-hour hike from Inspiration Point.

After a day of fighting the inferno of Indian Summer, some folks might yearn for an evening stroll where they can find a cool, gentle breeze along with magnificent views, and perhaps a fairly secluded spot for a quiet picnic at dusk.

At Tilden Park, that is exactly what you can get.

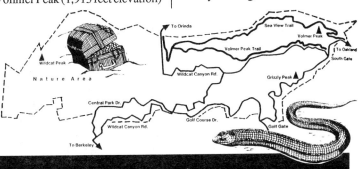

TILDEN PARK TRIP FACTS

How to get there: From the west, take Highway 24 to just east of the Caldecott Tunnel, then take the Fish Ranch Road exit west to Grizzly Peak Boulevard -- which leads to the southern entrance of Tilden Park. From the east, San Pablo Dam Road connects to Wildcat Canyon Road and continues to the park.

Best times: Evenings are prime, especially to cool off after a hot day. Expect company on weekends, although long trails still provide seclusion.

Park hours: Open from 5:30 a.m. to 10 p.m.

Who to contact: For free tips, maps or brochures, call the East Bay Regional Park District at (415) 531-9300.

BAY AREA HIKES

VOLCANIC REGIONAL
PRESERVE

THE MYSTERY OF MOUNT ROUND TOP

Have you ever wanted to walk on the side of a volcano? Well, you don't have to go to Mount Saint Helens in Washington to do so, not with ol' Mount Round Top sitting above Oakland. And you don't have to worry about getting your toes fried either. Round Top is extinct, and is now named the "Volcanic Regional Preserve." It's a unique part of the East Bay Regional Park District.

It's an ideal half-day hike, or evening jaunt, for explorer or geologist alike. From the old quarry site at the eastern border of the park, hikers can get a first-class view of the East Bay hills and Mount Diablo.

Spring is an ideal time to go because the area is fresh with newly sprouted grass and wildflowers, and the park is also cooled by northwesterly breezes off San Francisco Bay. In the summer, particularly in September, it can get so hot here that you might think you could fry an egg on a rock. You'd swear a cauldron of lava was getting ready to blast out of Round Top.

But a close look at the mountain allays those fears. Round Top has already shot its steam. In fact, after it emptied itself of molten lava, the interior of the mountain collapsed into the underlying void left by the outburst. Blocks of volcanic stone are scattered everywhere around the flanks of the peak.

"Some of these have been dated at almost 100 million years old," said Steve Edwards, a geologist at the park. When you pick up a rock that is 10 million years old, it has a way of making our stay on earth seem a little bit short. About a half-mile northwest of Round Top, a quarry operation has made a large cut into the side of the extinct volcano. This allows hikers to view the roots of the volcano, and a major volcanic vent. If you want to explore the unusual geology of the mountain, a tour-guide brochure that marks key spots is provided free by the East

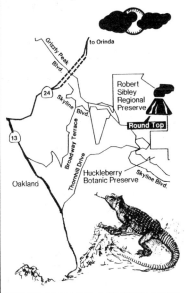

Bay Regional Park District. One sector, located on the northern edge of the park, shows one of the most spectacular volcanic outcrops in the Bay Area.

If geology is not your game, no problem; the park still provides a good half-day hike. Especially if you want to bring Fido. Park rules allow you to let your dog run free in open space and undeveloped areas of parklands, providing your dog remains under your control. Considering that state parks do not even allow leashed dogs on trails, this is quite a bonus for dog owners.

A section of the East Bay Skyline National Recreation Trail cuts across the western border of the park, and connects to a road that circles the park. It makes for a few hours of puffing. For the ambitious, the Skyline Trail can connect you to the town of El Sobrante, 12 miles by trail to the north, or to Castro Valley, 17 miles to the south.

Other volcanic areas in California include the Pinnacles near Hollister, the Sutter Buttes in the Sacramento Valley, and Mount Lassen in the Shasta area. Mount Round Top is right in the backyards of a million East Bay residents, yet is known only to a few.

☛ VOLCANIC PRESERVE TRIP FACTS

How to get there: The easiest way to reach Volcanic Regional Park is from Highway 24. At the eastern end of the Caldecott Tunnel, take Fish Road to Grizzly Peak Boulevard and head south to the park entrance. For additional information, call the East Bay Regional Park District at (415) 531-9300.

Trip tip: If long hikes are not for you, you can drive within a quarter mile of the peak of Mount Round Top for spectacular views of the Bay Area.

Pets: Your dog is allowed to run free in open space and undeveloped areas, but must be under control at all times.

Trip Cost: Access and brochures are free.

BAY AREA HIKES

THE OHLONE WILDERNESS
TRAIL

AN ANSWER TO THE SIERRA

Some of the Bay Area's most unspoiled back country is accessible to hikers along a spectacular 29-mile trail opened in 1985. The trail is set in wilderness in the East Bay between Fremont and Livermore, cutting a path through fields of wildflowers and grasses, forests of oak, and rising to several 3,000-foot lookouts. The latter includes Rose Peak, which provides one of the highest spots in the Bay Area at 3,817 feet.

This hike is called the Ohlone Wilderness Trail and links four parklands in the East Bay Regional Park District. It offers Bay Area hikers a superb close-to-home alternative to Sierra Nevada backpacking -- as well as shorter day hikes that can be taken year around.

A special bonus here is your chance to see rare birds and wildlife. This region is home to bald and golden eagles, as well as a herd of wild goats near the summit of Mission Peak. The rare tule elk might occasionally be spotted along the trail as well.

The Ohlone Wilderness Trail can be an ideal three-day backpack trip, with hikers able to make their trail camps at Sunol and Ohlone Regional Parks. Both are spaced perfectly for a three-day expedition. The opening of the new Ohlone Camp solves what was previously a logistics problem. You can now break the distances down to a 12-mile trip the first day, followed by two days at eight miles each.

Because of the design of the Ohlone Wilderness Trail, portions of it can provide a one-day hike, or what we call "in-and-outers." This seems best for weekenders.

Regardless, if you want to feel the full sense of the victory here, figure a weekend gut-thumper, traveling 12 miles the first day, and 16 the second. It might sound crazy, but you have to have a little of that in you anyway to be a backpacker.

The steepest section of the trail, located near Del Valle Park, has an elevation change of 1,600 feet in just 1.5 miles. If you plan on going up, we're talking serious business, but why kill yourself in the process? By traveling west to east, from Mission Peak Regional Preserve to Del Valle Park, you will be going down, not up, in this steep section of trail.

However, don't expect anything easy. From the western trailhead in Fremont, you will climb from 400 feet to Mission Peak at 2,517-feet elevation in 3.5 miles. If you are not in good physical condition, you will find out quick here. In the spring, this trail is one of the best hikes in the Bay Area. With panoramic vistas of San Francisco, the Santa Cruz Mountains, and on crystal clear days, even the Sierra Nevada, it won't stay a secret for long.

☞ OHLONE TRAIL TRIP FACTS

How to get there: To reach the trailhead at the western end of the Ohlone Wilderness Trail, from Highway 680, take the Mission Boulevard exit -- and turn east on Stanford Avenue. At the end of Stanford Avenue, there is a parking lot, information panel, and the trailhead.

Permits/maps: Since the trail passes through land leased from the San Francisco Water District, a trail permit is required. It can be purchased for $1 by mail by writing Ohlone Wilderness Trail, East Bay Regional Park District, 11500 Skyline Boulevard, Oakland, CA 94619. Include your name, address, and phone number to receive a map and brochure.

Camping: Camping is permitted by reservation only at the Sunol backpack loop; you can book your spot by calling Sunol Park at (415) 862-2244. Reservations are also required at Del Valle Park. Call Ticketron.

Day hikes: For information on one-day hikes, call Sunol Regional Wilderness, (415) 862-2244 or Del Valle Park, (415) 443-4110.

Who to contact: For general information, call the East Bay Regional Park District at (415) 531-9300.

CHAPTER

2

NORTHERN
CALIFORNIA CAMPING
WITH
18 ADVENTURES

CONTENTS:—

PUBLISHED BY FOGHORN PRESS
SAN FRANCISCO
QUALITY OUTDOOR BOOKS

NO. CALIFORNIA CAMPING

10 SECLUDED
SPOTS

SOLITUDE IN THE NORTH

Solitude

I f you want solitude your best bet is getting on Highway 5, kicking it up north for five hours, and settling in at an unimproved forest service campground. In my book, "California Camping, the Complete Guide," we discovered 240 campgrounds in some of the state's most remote areas -- Shasta (56), Siskiyou (42), Trinity (48), Modoc (14), Lassen (19), Tehama (16), and Del Norte (45) counties.

To find a private drive-to spot, these are the areas you are advised to seek out. For details on the north state country, write Shasta Cascade, 1250 Parkview, Redding, CA 96001, or phone (916) 243-2643.

Here are 10 choices to start with.

■ **Shasta:**

1. DEADLUN: Most people have never heard of Iron Canyon Reservoir. Go to Deadlun Camp and you'll get a good taste of it, with good swimming and boating by day and fishing in the early morning and late evening. The campground has 30 spots, with no fee charged. It's located up at 2,750 feet.

How to get there: The camp is seven miles northwest of Big Bend on a Forest Service road. The turnoff is marked on Highway 299.

Who to contact: For more information, call the Shasta Ranger District at (916) 275-1587.

2. MADRONE: This camp is out there in the boondocks, between nothing and nothing, and set in a forest of fir and pine. It's adjacent to Squaw Creek, which is okay for swimming and trout fishing as well if you walk upstream a ways. The camp has 13 campsites and no fee is charged. It is set at a 1,500-foot elevation, located about 50 miles northwest of Redding.

How to get there: Take Highway 299 for 40 miles, then take the Fenders Ferry Road, a gravel road, west for 20 miles.

Who to contact: For more information, call Shasta Ranger District at (916) 275-1587.

■ Siskiyou:

3. TRAIL CREEK: Here's a beautiful spot away from everything. It's set between Callahan and Cecilville near the Salmon River at a 4,700-foot elevation. You can hear the gurgling of Trail Creek nearby as you sleep. The campground has 15 units, each $4 per night, on the honor system.

How to get there: To get there, turn west at Callahan of State Route 3 and drive about 15 miles.

Who to contact: For more information, call Scott River Ranger District at (916) 468-5351.

4. SHADOW CREEK: This is a good option to Trail Creek, located five miles west of the Trail Creek Camp. It has space for 10 campers, and also costs $4 per night, collected on the honor system. It's a peaceful, away-from-everything spot. Good swimming in the south Fork of the Salmon River. The closest amenities are in Cecilville, population 25, about five miles away. For hiking trails, a map of the Klamath Forest details the possibilities.

How to get there: Turn west at Callahan on State Route 3 and drive about 20 miles.

Who to contact: For more information, call Scott River Ranger District at (916) 468-5351.

■ Trinity:

5. JACKASS SPRINGS: Here's an isolated campground that gets very little attention, yet is set right along one of California's favorite reservoirs -- Trinity Lake. The camp has 21 campsites and is free -- just show up with your gear. It is set at a 2,500-foot elevation, beneath the towering Trinity Alps Wilderness. You can camp right along the east shore of Trinity Lake.

How to get there: It is located five miles off Trinity Mountain Road, an unpaved access road.

Who to contact: For more information, call Weaverville Ranger District, (916) 623-2121.

6. BIG FLAT: The South Fork of the Salmon River and Coffee Creek provide a beautiful setting for this little-known spot. It is right on the edge of the Trinity Alps Wilderness, and is a premium jumpoff spot to the Caribou Lakes (a nine mile hike) for a backpacking trip.

How to get there: The camp is at a 5,000-foot elevation, located 20 miles west of Coffee Creek via the Coffee Creek Road off State Route 3.

Who to contact: For more information, call Coffee Creek District at (916) 266-3211.

■ Modoc:

7. CAVE LAKE: Here's a spot way out in the sticks. This lake is located very near the Oregon border in north-eastern California, and adjoins Lily Lake, providing a double-barreled fishing opportunity. Both have eastern brook trout and rainbow trout. The campground has six spots, with no fee charged (heck, if they charged, somebody would have to hang out for a couple of years to collect enough money just to pay for one dinner).

How to get there: The drive includes a nine-mile climb on a gravel road, leaving Highway 395 and taking Pine Creek Road to the lake at a 6,600-foot elevation.

Who to contact: For more information, call Warner Mountain Ranger District at (916) 279-6116.

■ Lassen:

8. CRATER LAKE: And you thought Crater Lake was in Oregon? Well, there's another Crater Lake that nobody's heard of on the eastern side of Mount Lassen. It has pretty good fishing, primarily for rainbow and brook trout, although nothing huge. For a special delight, take a piece of bacon or chicken on a hook and get yourself a pot full of crawdads. There are 16 campsites, each with a $4 per night fee.

How to get there: To get there, drive nine miles east on a dirt road from Bogard Ranger Station, turning off State Route 44.

Who to contact: For more information, call Almanor Ranger District at (916) 258-2141.

■ Tehama:

9. BEEGUM GORGE: Here's a hidden, obscure spot with just three campsites, but it's free, quiet and there's some good evening trout fishing on nearby Beegum Creek. It's set at 2,200 feet and overlooked by Yolla Bolly Mountains. Expect hot weather and bring all of your own supplies.

How to get there: The campground is located 6.5 miles southwest of Platina off State Route 36, west of Red Bluff.

Who to contact: For more information, call Yolla Bolly Ranger District at (916) 352-4211.

■ Del Norte:

10. BIG FLAT: This is a nice little spot set along Hurdy-Gurdy Creek, close to the South Fork of the Smith River. I've had some good trout fishing success here, searching out spots on the river where rapids tumble into pools, and then casting a blue/silver Kastmaster into the white water -- the fish bite when the water flattens out. Like many of the remote forest service camps, there is no reservation and no fee charged. There are 16 campsites and piped water is available.

How to get there: To get there, turn off Highway 199 just east of Gasquet and then turn south on South Fork Road and drive 25 miles.

Who to contact: For more information, call Gasquet Ranger District at (707) 457-3131.

THE CAMP GEAR CHECKLIST

1. COOKING GEAR
- [ ] Matches in different bags
- [ ] Fire-starter cubes or candle
- [ ] Camp stove
- [ ] Camp fuel
- [ ] Pot, pan, cup
- [ ] Pot grabber
- [ ] Knife, fork
- [ ] Dish soap and scrubber
- [ ] Salt, pepper, spices
- [ ] Itemized food
- [ ] Plastic spade

2. CAMPING CLOTHES
- [ ] Polypropylene underwear
- [ ] Cotton shirt
- [ ] Long sleeve cotton/wool shirt
- [ ] Cotton/canvas pants
- [ ] Vest
- [ ] Parka
- [ ] Rain jacket, pants, or poncho
- [ ] Hat
- [ ] Sunglasses
- [ ] Chapstick
- [ ] Sunscreen

3. HIKING LIST
- [ ] Quality hiking boots
- [ ] Backup lightweight shoes
- [ ] Polypropylene socks
- [ ] Thick cotton socks
- [ ] 80 percent wool socks
- [ ] Strong boot laces
- [ ] Innersole or foot cushion
- [ ] Ace bandage
- [ ] Moleskin and medical tape
- [ ] Band-Aids
- [ ] Gaters
- [ ] Water repellent boot treatment

4. SLEEP LIST
- [ ] Sleeping bag
- [ ] Insulite pad or Therm-a-rest
- [ ] Tent
- [ ] Ground tarp

5. FIRST-AID KIT
- [ ] Band-Aids
- [ ] Sterile gauze pads
- [ ] Roller gauze
- [ ] Athletic tape
- [ ] Moleskin
- [ ] Thermometer
- [ ] Aspirin
- [ ] Ace bandage
- [ ] Mosquito repellent
- [ ] After Bite or ammonia
- [ ] Campho-Phenique gel
- [ ] First Aid cream
- [ ] Sunscreen
- [ ] Neosporin Ointment
- [ ] Caladryl
- [ ] Biodegradable soap
- [ ] Towelette

6. RECREATION GEAR
- [ ] Fishing rod
- [ ] Fishing reel with fresh line
- [ ] Small tackle box with lures,
- [ ] Plastic garbage bags
- [ ] Toilet paper
- [ ] Compass
- [ ] Watch
- [ ] Small tackle box with lures, splitshot, and snap swivels
- [ ] Pliers
- [ ] Knife

7. MISCELLANEOUS
- [ ] Maps
- [ ] Flashlight
- [ ] Toilet paper
- [ ] Nylon rope for food hang
- [ ] Handkerchief
- [ ] Camera and film

8. OPTIONAL
- [ ] Axe or hatchet
- [ ] Wood or carccoal for barbecue
- [ ] Ice chest
- [ ] Spatula
- [ ] Grill
- [ ] Tin foil
- [ ] Seam Lock
- [ ] Shorts
- [ ] Swimming suit
- [ ] Gloves
- [ ] Ski cap
- [ ] Air pillow
- [ ] Mosquito netting
- [ ] Foam pad for truck bed
- [ ] Windshield light screen for RV
- [ ] Catalytic heater
- [ ] Water purification system
- [ ] Coins for emergency phone call
- [ ] Tweezers
- [ ] Mirror for sigmaling
- [ ] Stargazing chart
- [ ] Tree identification handbook
- [ ] Deck of cards
- [ ] Backpacking cribbage board
- [ ] Binoculars
- [ ] Notebook and pen
- [ ] Towel

NO. CALIFORNIA CAMPING

SIX BAY AREA LAKES
TO CAMP BY

LITTLE KNOWN LAKES IN YOUR BACKYARD

Most people just plain don't know a good place to go camping that's close to home.

Yet a new study shows that 73 percent of all vacations are for three days or less, 54 percent for weekends only -- which proves the need for quality close-to-home fishing and camping opportunities.

In my book, California Camping, which details 1,500 campgrounds in the state, we found 59 campgrounds in nine Bay Area Counties. But of those, only seven are set beside lakes.

After Lake Berryessa, which is one of the most popular areas in California, most people haven't heard of the other six. Here's a capsule look at them:

■ Spring Lake
(Santa Rosa):

This is Santa Rosa's backyard fishing hole, but is unknown to most others.

The lake has been open for about 10 years, is stocked with rainbow trout and has a resident population of bluegill and largemouth bass.

It's located about five miles outside of Santa Rosa. The campground has 28 sites for tents or motor homes, and three spots for tents only, with no reservations taken. The campgrounds usually have space, and there's good fishing in the morning.

Who to contact: Call Spring Lake Regional Park at (707) 539-8082.

■ Lake Chabot
(Castro Valley):

This is the centerpiece of the East Bay Regional Park District, a pretty lake that is heavily stocked with rainbow trout and also contains hard-to-catch largemouth bass that can reach 10 pounds.

The park has 62 sites for tents and 12 sites for motor homes, with reservations now available through Ticketron. It is set four miles west of Castro Valley.

On warm days, the camp either fills up, or comes close to it (especially on the weekend).

Who to contact: Call either East Bay Regional Park at (415) 531-9300 or Lake Chabot Park at (415) 582-2198.

■ Del Valley Regional Park:

A lot of people have no idea that a big, cool lake is set in the hot golden hills south of Livermore. But there is -- Del Valle Reservoir -- and it is not only stocked weekly with rainbow trout, but supports populations of bluegill and smallmouth bass, and has some big striped bass as well.

The campground has 110 sites for tents or motor homes, and 21 of the sites have full hookups available. Reservations are available through Ticketron. The campground has been full on recent weekends, making reservations a necessity, but space is available during the week.

Who to contact: Call either East Bay Regional Parks at (415) 531-9300 or Del Valle Park at (415) 449-5201.

■ Uvas Reservoir, (Coyote):

Set about 10 miles south of San Jose, this lake provided some of the best largemouth bass and crappie fishing of any Bay Area lake in the spring of 1987. The best strategy has been sneaking up on coves in the lake's backwaters during the evening, then casting a white crappie jig.

The campground has 30 sites for tents and 15 spaces for tents or motor homes. All are provided on a first come, first serve basis. Of the eight lakes in Santa Clara County, this one has provided the best fishing.

Who to contact: Call either Uvas Canyon County Park at (408) 358-3751 or Coyote Discount Bait at (408) 463-0711.

■ Coyote Reservoir (Gilroy):

This is a long, narrow lake set in the oak and grass covered hills east of Gilroy. Fishermen with boats can catch largemouth bass, but primarily during the early morning and late evening.

The park has 74 campsites for tents or motor homes, with no reservations available. A launch ramp for boats is set a quarter-mile from the campground.

Who to contact: Call either Lakeview Coyote Park at (408) 842-7800, or Coyote Discount Bait at (408) 463-0711.

■ Pinto Lake (Watsonville):

You say you never heard of Pinto Lake? Neither have a lot of folks.

The lake is shaped like a horseshoe and it's been good luck for fishing for rainbow trout, bluegill and catfish. In 1985, the summer fishing for crappie was sensational, but it was slow through 1987.

There are two campgrounds; Marmo's Resort has 50 sites and Pinto Lake Park has 33 sites, both areas permitting tents and motor homes.

The lake is full, but the campgrounds are not. They are booked solid only on three-day weekends.

Who to contact: Call Pinto Lake at (408) 722-8129.

NO. CALIFORNIA CAMPING

SIX SANTA CRUZ MOUNTAIN
CAMPGROUNDS

CLOSE TO HOME SECLUSION

Six parks in the Santa Cruz Mountains offer a close-to-home option for campers who want to simplify a weekend vacation.

In the process, you can actually have fun. What? Fun? What's that? Right, you may have forgotten what that's all about. By simplifying your trip, you take out the complications and put back in the fun.

Most weekend trips don't work that way. Frustrating drives in thick traffic can turn many weekend hopes into a long-distance grind. And if you happen to pick a spot where you need a shoehorn to gain entry, well, the whole affair can be about as much fun as waiting in line at the Department of Motor Vehicles. But that's where this story comes in. To reach the Santa Cruz Mountains, there is no long drive. And to find a relatively secluded spot, there is no real problem, although a reservation is advised. There are miles of forest, much of it redwood, and the rangers have placed the campsites with just enough distance between them to retain a sense of privacy.

Each park offers premium hiking opportunities, and most campsites have a tent site, table, barbecue and food locker. The latter is to protect your food from raccoons, the midnight bandits that come in the night wearing masks.

Here's a sketch of each of the six parks:

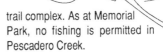

■ Memorial County Park:

This is the closest of the parks available, located between the tiny towns of La Honda and Loma Mar. As in most county parks, campsites are provided on a first come, first serve basis. Memorial has 135 campsites for tent/car campers, with a $10 per night fee. No pets are allowed.

For recreation, Memorial has 50 miles of trails that wind in and out of redwoods and chaparral, eventually heading off to Pescadero Creek and Sam McDonald County Park. Six miles of trails are accessible for the blind or those confined to wheelchairs.

At Pescadero Creek, no fishing is permitted -- the "little trout" are actually steelhead smolts trying to grow large enough to enter the ocean.

Who to contact: Call the Memorial County Park at (415) 879-0212.

■ Portola State Park:

This park is located at the end of a long, winding road that starts at Page Mill Road in Palo Alto, crosses Skyline Boulevard, and eventually drops you in a large forest of conifers.

Campers have 53 sites to choose from, with reservations strongly advised for all weekend trips. They can be made through Mistix, a reservation service, by phoning (800) 444-7275. A $3.75 fee is charged for the reservation service, a separate cost from a $10 campsite fee. Leashed dogs are permitted at campsites for $1, but are not allowed on trails.

This is a good park for hiking, with 14 miles of trails in the park, in addition to a four-hour trip that connects to the nearby Memorial Park and the country trail complex. As at Memorial Park, no fishing is permitted in Pescadero Creek.

Who to contact: Call Portola State Park at (415) 948-9098.

■ Butano State Park:

If you want to parlay a beach trip or drive down Highway 1 to a nice camp in the redwoods, this is the spot. Butano is located about 10 miles south of Pescadero, about a 15-minute drive from the ocean. Most people are surprised when they see the redwood forest at Butano. But the premium hiking is even more surprising. Rangers have designed loop trails so you don't have to backtrack. My favorites are the hike to the Ano Nuevo Lookout, which starts at the park entrance -- and the 11-mile loop trail, which cuts into the park's back country. The latter provides hike-in camp option for a mini-backpack trip. The park has 21 campsites with parking spaces alongside, and an additional 19 that require a very short walk, providing a bit more seclusion. Reservations are provided through the Mistix reservation service at (800) 444-7275.

Who to contact: Call Butano State Park at (415) 879-0173.

■ Castle Rock State Park:

This park is set atop the 2,700-foot ridgeline along Skyline Boulevard, just south of the junction for Skyline and Highway 9. Getting there via either of those roads is a beautiful drive. The park gets its name from a serpentine rock formation. While exploring the immediate area, you can get great lookouts to the west of Monterey Bay and Big Basin. On some fog-bound days, a blanket of the stuff will fill in the basin below, with mountain tops poking through like islands in an ocean of fog. This park acts as the trailhead for the Skyline-to-Sea Trail, a 38-mile hike with a downhill slope that crosses through Big Basin en route to where Waddell Creek enters the Pacific Ocean. Although primarily a day-use facility, Castle Rock has 25 campsites available for hikers at just $1 per night.

Who to contact: Call Castle Rock State Park at (408) 867-2952.

■ Big Basin State Park:

This is the oldest, most famous and favorite of the parks in the Santa Cruz Mountains. It has stands of gigantic redwoods near park headquarters and waterfalls in the back country and, for car campers, campsites set strategically so you don't feel jammed in.

The latter is important because there are 188 campsites at Big Basin State Park, many more than other Bay Area park.

It is a premium place for hiking, either for short days walks or overnighters. Of the 80 miles of trails, my favorite hike here passes by Berry Creek and Silver Falls, although the falls are most impressive after rains, not during the summer. Rangers have set aside seven areas in the back country for backpackers, each with six campsites.

Campsites cost $10 per night. Reservations are advised through Mistix. Call (800) 444-7275. Back country camps cost $1 per night.

Who to contact: Call Big Basin State Park at (408) 338-6132.

■ Henry Cowell State Park:

This is the most distant of Santa Cruz Mountain parks from the Bay Area, set just a few miles inland from Santa Cruz. It is a prime spot whether you visit for just a day or decide to spend the weekend. For the day, you can pick among 20 miles of trails for an adventure, then top it off with a trip to a Santa Cruz restaurant. For the weekend, you can explore an additional 15 miles of trails at adjacent Fall Creek Park.

In the spring, I've camped here when the park has been virtually abandoned. But it's much more crowded in the summer. Even with 113 campsites available at $10 per night, reservations are needed for weekends during summer months. One factor is that tourists from the Southland heading up Highway 1 often use the park as a layover prior to invading the Bay Area. If you have a similar trip planned and are heading south on the coast highway, after staying at Henry Cowell you can hit Big Sur the next night.

Who to contact: Call Henry Cowell State Park at (408) 335-4598.

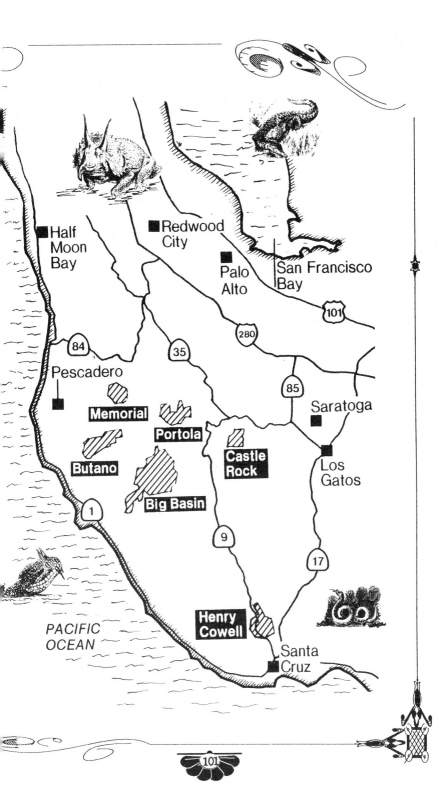

Half
Moon
Bay

Redwood
City

Palo
Alto

San Francisco
Bay

101

84

280

35

85

Saratoga

Pescadero

Memorial

Portola

Castle
Rock

Los
Gatos

Butano

Big Basin

1

9

17

PACIFIC
OCEAN

Henry
Cowell

Santa
Cruz

101

NO. CALIFORNIA CAMPING

UNDER THE SPELL OF
YOSEMITE

※   ※   ※

THE ULTIMATE USER'S GUIDE

Y ou know the stories about Yosemite: Too many people right? Bears raid your food every night, right? A place where a vacation turns into an endurance test called You Against The World.

That's what kept me away for 20 years -- the stories, not the facts. Finally I was forced back. You see, I was hiking the entire John Muir Trail, all 211 miles of it, and from the trailhead at Mount Whitney it eventually pours right smack into Yosemite Valley. You either hit Yosemite or you cancel the hike.

We decided to give it a few shrugs and take our chances. We headed to the park expecting congestion and confusion, just like many Bay Area residents who have delayed or never even made the trip. But it only took five minutes in Yosemite Valley to turn our brains around 180 degrees -- completely under the spell of the world's greatest natural showpiece.

With a little homework, the people and bears can be dealt with easily enough -- that's what this story is all about. But there is no preparation that will get you ready for the first impact of Yosemite Valley.

As you drive into the park, you go through a tunnel and then looking east, suddenly spot sections of high canyon walls. "Is this it?" Just a start, just a start. You go around a bend and suddenly there is El Capitan, the Yosemite monolith, the largest single piece of granite in the world, rising straight up from the valley floor. Then the entire valley comes into view.

It looks as if it has been sculpted and carved. The valley is framed by three-spired Cathedral Rocks and the massive El Capitan, with the awesome Half Dome to the center. There is nothing like this sight anywhere. The canyon walls are crossed by long silver-tassled waterfalls, though sometimes they run a bit thin. On most afternoons, low-hanging "Ansel Adams clouds" will dot the sky from rim to rim.

It's a sight that hits you all at once. If you've forgotten what it feels like, you've been watching too much TV. This is real stuff, no Hollywood needed.

That doesn't mean you should get in your car right now and head off for the park, though you can reach it from the Bay Area in 3 1/2 hours. The ambitious, sudden "Let's go!" is just what causes so many problems for people when they visit Yosemite. After paying the $5 entrance fee, they suddenly find they don't have a campground or place to stay, don't know where to turn -- and are just as likely to wind up spending the night in a Markleeville hotel room as looking into a nice, little campfire along Yosemite lake.

Instead, you should first obtain a good map of Yosemite National Park, then spend a few evenings just gazing at it and envisioning your trip.

The best park map is available for $5, including tax and postage, from Yosemite Association, P.O. Box 230, El Portal, CA 95318; ask for the Yosemite National Park and Vicinity topographic map.

With that in hand, you can plan out your vacation. Where are you sleeping? Available are developed campsites, wilderness camping and tent cabin rentals. Going for a walk? Choose between premium day hikes out of the valley or backpack trails in the high country. Fishing?

The park has 300 lakes, but 60% of them don't even have fish in them. Horseback riding? Where? How much?

Or you could give up and just lay around. In fact, a lot of people do exactly that along the Merced River in Yosemite Valley. But even those folks rest easier if they know where they're spending the night.

The campgrounds in Yosemite Valley are filled by reservation only and are packed during the summer months. You can make reservations up to eight weeks in advance of your stay through Ticketron. Reserved campsites cost $10 per night, which includes a Ticketron Service fee.

Well, the overpeopled valley is a nice place to visit but probably wouldn't want to live there. Options include 11 drive-in camps outside of Yosemite Valley that are filled on a first come, first serve basis. They cost between $3 and $6 per night. The adjacent listing details them.

The largest of the camps is at Tuolumne Meadows, which has 325 campsites available. It is also the farthest camp from the valley, and when all else fails, usually has a space available.

As you enter the park, a sign noting campground availability is posted next to the entrance. It is wise to heed those words, go and secure a spot, then enjoy your trip. On summer weekends, finding a campsite can be an elusive task. Your attempt can be eased greatly by arriving Thursday or by midday Friday.

YOU REALLY CAN GET A CAMPSITE IN THE PARK

Yosemite National Park has 11 campgrounds that do not require reservations. Campsites are filled on a first come, first serve basis. For best success, you should arrive before noon on weekday mornings to secure the best possible spot.

1. Sunnyside Walk-In: Located in Yosemite Valley at 4,000 feet elevation, with 38 spaces available, this campground is a short walk from parking facilities. Fee is $2 per night.

2. Backpackers Walk-In: Located in Yosemite Valley, this campground is expressly for visitors without vehicles, with 25 campsites available and a $2 per night fee.

3. Wawona: Located along Highway 41 in Wawona at the southern end of the park and 27 miles from Yosemite Valley. It has 100 campsites available, $6 per night fee.

4. Bridaveil Creek: Set along Glacier Point Road at 7,200 feet and 27 miles from Yosemite Valley. It has 110 campsites, $6 per night fee.

5. Crane Flat: Located along Highway 120 west near the Tioga Road turnoff at 6,200 feet elevation, 17 miles from Yosemite Valley. It has 169 campsites, $6 per night fee.

6. Tamarack Flat: Set along Highway 120 east at 6,300 feet, 23 miles from Yosemite Valley. It has 52 campsites, $3 per night fee.

7. White Wolf: A major camp along Highway 120 east at 8,000 feet, 31 miles from Yosemite Valley. It has 87 campsites, $6 per night fee.

8. Yosemite Creek: Set four miles from White Wolf, 35 miles from Yosemite Valley. It has 75 campsites and the fee is $3 per night.

9. Porcupine Flat: Also set along Highway 120 east, this one is 38 miles from Yosemite Valley. It has 52 campsites and a $3 per night fee.

10. Tenaya Lake Walk-In: You park in a designated area along Tenaya Lake, then carry your gear in to one of 50 available campsites. Located 46 miles from Yosemite Valley, it has a $6 per night fee.

11. Tuolumne Meadows: A huge drive-in area set at 8,600 elevation, 55 miles from Yosemite Valley. It has 325 campsites and a $6 per night fee.

Another option is reserving a tent cabin or staying at Yosemite Lodge. (See trip facts at end).

Backpackers have an easier and far less expensive time of it. All you need is a free Wilderness Permit, a backpack, and start walking.

To keep people pressure at a minimum, the park has set hiker quotas for each trail head. Half of those quotas are filled by reservation through mail (during the winter and spring) -- the other half are available on a first come, first serve basis. You can pick up your Wilderness Permit at one of four permit stations, located at Yosemite Valley, Tuolumne Meadows, Big Oak Flat, and at Wawona Ranger Station. With camping concerns taken care of, you get on with the business of having a good time. Hiking, fishing, and horseback riding provide the best of Yosemite.

The hikes starting in Yosemite Valley range from an easy half-mile jaunt to the base of Lower Yosemite Falls to the 17-mile grunt to the top of Half Dome with nearly a 5,000 foot climb. Most people want something in between -- an accompanying listing provides 10 prime possibilities.

When it comes to the fishing, most anglers are terribly disappointed with the results. I have a simple rule for Yosemite. If you can drive to it, don't expect to catch anything. The more difficult the access, the better the prospects.

A good primer is the 16-page booklet "Yosemite Trout Fishing," which rates the fishing at the park's 118 lakes that have trout.

You see all kinds of crazy fishing methods being attempted, but for the most part, you need nothing complicated. Just a light spinning rod and reel and small lures such as the gold Z-Ray with red spots, black Panther Martin with yellow spots, blue/silver Kastmaster, and yellow Roostertail.

On my trip last week, my brother and I had a great time of it, catching as many as 30 trout apiece in one evening, with some to 14 inches on another. Like anything, with a little homework, it can be done.

If you don't like to hike in the back country, you can rent a horse to take you there. Stables are located at four locations, Yosemite Valley, Wawona, White Wolf Camp and Tuolumne Meadows.

Of course, you might be perfectly content to sit in a different kind of saddle, the kind on the valley's sightseeing shuttle. To encourage visitors to park their cars, an open-air tour is available -- along with a free valley bus shuttle.

The first explorer to see Yosemite had quite a different vantage point. It was Joe Walker in 1833, whose team reached the valley floor in part by descending the horses by ropes.

Walker is considered by many the West's greatest trailblazer, yet his tombstone at his grave in Martinez reads simply: "Camped in Yosemite, November 13, 1833."

Since that date, millions of people from all over the world have visited the park. Ironically, its popularity is just the thing that keeps many Bay

Area residents -- remember it's only 3 1/2 hours distant -- away from the park.

Haven't been to Yosemite in a while? Maybe not even ever? It's the kind of place too spectacular not to visit.

AVAILABLE HIKING ON EVERY LEVEL

Ten good hikes offer a tour Yosemite Valley:

1. Lower Yosemite Fall: Start at the shuttle stop for Yosemite Falls, and walk a half-mile round trip. Easy.

2. Bridalveil Fall: Start at the Bridalveil Fall parking area, walk a half-mile round trip. Easy.

3. Mirror Lake: Start at the shuttle stop for Mirror Lake and hike one mile to the lake. An option is a three-mile circle around lake. Easy.

4. Upper Yosemite Fall: Start at Sunnyside Campground and hike 3.6 miles one way, with a 2,700 foot elevation gain. Very strenuous, six to eight hours round trip.

5 and 6. Vernal/Nevada Falls: Start at Happy Isles, a trailhead for the Hohn Muir Trail. Vernal Falls is 1.5 miles with a 1,000 foot elevation gain, three-hour round trip. Nevada Falls is 3.4 miles one way with a 1,900 foot elevation gain. Very steep and strenuous, six to eight hours round trip.

7. Half Dome: Start at Happy Isles and hike 17 miles round trip to top, including 500 feet on permanent-mounted cables to make the summit. Very strenuous, 17-mile round trip, 4,800 foot elevation gain, 10 to 12 hours round trip. Plan to drink four quarts of water.

8. Panorama: Start at Glacier Point and hike to Yosemite Valley, 8.5 miles, with a 3,200 foot elevation loss. Moderate, four to five hours one way.

9. Four Mile Trail: Start at Southside Drive, Road Mark V18, and climb to Glacier Point in 4.8 miles, one way, with a 3,200 foot elevation gain. Strenuous, three to four hours one way.

10. Pohono Trail: Start at Glacier Point and hike 13 miles, with moderate downgrade, 1,300 foot elevation loss, six to eight hours one way.

* BARE FACTS TO HELP YOU PLAN YOUR TRIP

How to get there: The fastest route from the Bay Area is to take Highway 580 past Livermore, then take the Highway 205 cutoff to Highway 120. Past Oakdale, take the Yosemite turnoff and continue into the park.

Trip cost: A park entrance fee of $5 per vehicle is collected at entrance points, and includes a map of the park.

Map: Send $5 which includes tax and postage to Yosemite Association, P.O. Box 230, El Portal, CA 95318, and ask for Yosemite National Park and Vicinity topographic map.

Valley tent camping: All campsites are filled by reservation in Yosemite Valley, available through Ticketron for a cost of $10 per night, including a service fee.

Outback tent camping: Eleven campgrounds are filled on a first come, first serve basis and cost from $3 to $6 per night. For campground availability, phone (209) 372-4845 for a recording or the Park Service at (209) 372-0265. Be there before noon. There are no guarantees.

Wilderness camping: A free Wilderness Permit must be in your party's possession. They can be obtained at permit stations located at Yosemite Valley, Tuolumne Meadows, Big Oak Flat and at the Wawona Ranger Station. For more information, phone (209) 372-0265 during business hours or (209) 372-0307 for a recording of conditions.

Tent cabins/lodging: Canvas tent cabins are available for $22 to $26 in Yosemite Valley, Tuolumne Meadows. A room at Yosemite Lodge costs from $33 to $75. A double room at The Ahwahnee, a historic first-class hotel, costs $149.50 per night. For any of the above, call (209) 252-4848. Or write Yosemite Park and Curry Company, Reservations, 5410 E. Home, Fresno, CA 93727.

Fishing: Send $2 to Yosemite Park and Curry Company, Yosemite National Park, CA 95389, and ask for the 16-page booklet, "Yosemite Trout Fishing."

Horseback riding: Horseback riding rentals are available from four locations, Yosemite Valley, Wawona, White Wolf Camp and Tuolumne Meadows. The cost is $20 for two hours, $27 for a half-day, and $45 for a full day. For information, phone (209) 372-1248.

Roads/weather: For recorded information updated daily regarding weather and road closures, call (209) 372-4605.

Who to contact: For general information, phone Yosemite National Park at (209) 372-0298.

NO. CALIFORNIA CAMPING

LASSEN PARK

A NATIONAL PARK THAT GETS MISSED

Lassen Park is Northern California's spectacular national park that you may have always intended to visit. Most folks never quite get around to it.

Sound familiar? To many it does. Lassen has it all too -- great camping, fishing, hiking, lookouts and seclusion, all in one of America's most beautiful parklands. Yet you probably never go.

In my visit, every campground in the park had vacancies. Weekdays are even more sparse. Ask campers where home is and they're as apt to say "Cedar Rapids, Iowa" as they are "Bay Area."

You may have seen Lassen from a distance as you head north on Highway 5. As you get near Red Bluff, look east to the horizon, and spot the old extinct volcano, the one with its top blown off, that rises far above the other mountains. "Oh yeah, that's Lassen."

That's usually as much as the brain gears mesh when you spot Lassen when cruising I-5. But you can get them engaged, and open up a world of adventure at the same time, by turning east on Highway 36 at Red Bluff. In 50 miles, you'll rise above the rock-specked foothills into forest, come around a bend and suddenly enter one of the West's greatest parks.

The old volcano is the centerpiece, of course. Mount Lassen peaks out at 10,457 feet, which you can reach in a 2.5-mile zigzag of a hike. With a quart of water, you can make the climb in less than two hours and not feel like a juiced orange when you get there. The view is remarkable, with Mount Shasta to the north, miles of forest and lakes to the east, and the Sacramento Valley plunging westward.

As you sit on the top of Lassen, you will see why the park is special. For one thing, it doesn't even look like California, but more like Montana, with 80,000 acres of roadless wilderness. You will spot several lakes that look like jewels. And then there is the top itself, a crusty volcanic flume with craters, spires, hardened lava flows and enough hidden trails to spend hours exploring.

The view from the top will likely inspire you to later visit what you can see. And in Lassen Park, that includes 53 lakes. Of those, six can be reached by car, including Manzanita Lake and Summit Lake, where two of Lassen's prettiest campgrounds are located.

Manzanita Lake is set just inside the northwest entrance to the park on Highway 89. It's an idyllic setting and a perfect destination for trout fishermen. The lake is being converted to a natural fishery and a

---

SIX CAMPGROUNDS

Lassen National Park operates six campgrounds with fees ranging from free to $6 per site, per night. All campsites are available on a first come, first serve basis.

Summit Lake: There are actually two campgrounds here, located at each side of the lake. There are 94 campsites, all set near Summit Lake, where you can swim or fish for trout. Many trails begin at this area. The camp is set at 6,695 feet elevation.

Manzanita Lake: The park's largest campground with 179 sites is quite popular because of good fishing and its idyllic setting. Concession services are located nearby. It is located at 5,890 feet near the park's northern entrance on Highway 89.

Southwest Camp: This small camp is set by the Lassen Chalet near the Southwest Entrance Station on Highway 36. It has 21 sites and has full service, plus restaurant and gift shop nearby. Set at 6,700 feet elevation.

Juniper Lake: A good spot for those wanting to "get away from it all." It is located on the east shore of Juniper Lake, one mile from a ranger station on a rough dirt road. There are 18 campsites, no charge for use, but no piped water is available. Set at 6,792 feet elevation.

Butte Lake: A popular lakeside campground with 98 campsites. Many recreational options, with fishing, swimming and good hikes to nearby Cinder Cone and Snag Lake. Set at 6,100 feet elevation.

Warner Valley: A little used spot with 15 campsites, located one mile from Warner Valley Ranger Station. The choice for hikers who like to stream fish. Nearest supplies are in Chester, 17 miles via dirt road. Set at 5,650 feet elevation.

special program is now in effect. Rules mandate lures or flies only with a single, barbless hook -- and a two-fish limit, none longer than 10 inches.

The campground at Manzanita Lake is the park's largest with 179 sites, though being at the park entrance, you may want to push on farther. There are six other campgrounds, including three situated aside lakes -- Summit (94 sites), Juniper (18 sites), and Butte (98 sites). See the adjoining list for a detailed description.

To obtain a lakeside campsite, you might figure you have to book a reservation several months before your visit, right? Wrong. In fact, the park does not even take campsite reservations. It would just confuse things. All campgrounds are filled on a first-come, first-serve basis.

During our visit, we found a fairly secluded spot set on the edge of a meadow, not far from Summit Lake. At dusk, several deer suddenly walked out of the forest and into the meadow, grazing yet keeping ears raised as an intruder alert. We snuck a bit closer undetected and saw a mother with a fawn that hadn't even lost its spots yet.

Along with deer, the park is loaded with ground squirrels, which are always hoping to find a surprise morsel. You'd best not leave anything out for them. That might attract a bear, the masters of the food-raiding business. There are enough bears in the park to cause rangers to advise campers to keep their food in their vehicle at drive-in campsites. Do that and you will have no

---

150 MILES OF HIKING TRAILS

Lassen Park has 150 miles of trails ranging across a great variety of terrain. Here are a few favorite hikes:

Crumbaugh Lake: Three miles of walking with little climb, taking you through meadows and forests to Cold Boiling Lake and on to Crumbaugh Lake.

Paradise: A three-mile round trip with a climb of 600 feet to a beautiful, glacier-carved meadow. It's called Paradise Meadow and contains a great wildflower display.

Mill Creek Falls: This is a four-mile round trip that leads to Mill Creek Falls, which at 70 feet is Lassen Park's highest waterfall.

Devastated Area: This is a one-hour breeze of a walk that tours through the site of a massive mudflow from the 1915 eruption of Lassen Park.

King's Creek Falls: A three-mile round trip with a 700 foot descent that takes you to King's Creek Falls, just 30 feet high but worth seeing. The trail follows a mountain stream that cuts through both meadow and forest.

Sifford Lakes: This is for the adventurous -- four miles round trip, all of it cross-country style. This hike leaves the King's Creek Trail, explores a series of beautiful glacier-carved lakes, and has many great lookouts.

problems.

The park can be toured by car to get an overview of the unique areas. There are signs of the area's latent volcanic underbase -- boiling sulfur vents, huge, hardened mud flows, fields of volcanic lava balls. Lassen blew its top in 1914, then had other eruptions until 1921, so in geological time it's like it happened just yesterday.

You can get an even better look by taking a hike or two. Whether you want an easy stroll or a backpacking trip, there are enough trails to find a perfect match. The adjoining list spots my favorites.

Lassen has more than 150 miles of trails, including 17 miles of the Pacific Crest Trail, which reaches from Mexico to Canada. Habitat varies from forest to alpine tundra, and trails will take you to hidden lakes and streams.

The fishing can give your trip an added piece of sizzle. You can catch brook trout or rainbow trout at most of the lakes.

However, no fishing at all is permitted at Emerald or Helen lakes. One other special rule is that no power boats are permitted on any lake in the park -- but canoes, rafts, row boats or float tubes work perfectly.

The best technique to catch the trout here is to offer what they feed on -- insects. Fly patterns that imitate the insects thus work the best: No. 14 Callibatis, No. 16 Haystack, No. 14/16 Loop Wing, No. 16 Hare's Ear Nymph, No. 6/8/10 olive or brown leach.

Small lures such as the Kastmaster, Z-Ray or Panther Martin can also do the job, but you must approach the lakeshore very quietly. At lakes that permit bait, a good ol' red worm, or cricket, fished with little or no weight, are the preferred entreaties. I personally did not use bait on my trip, but saw some nice stringers of trout of those that did. People from all over America touring California see the big park on the map and head straight for an entrance station. At some point in your travels, so should you.

☞ TRIP FACTS

Maps: A good map of the park can be purchased for $5 and the Lassen Trails Book is available for $2.08. Write Loomis Museum Association, P.O. Box 100, Mineral, CA 96063.

Trip cost: The park entrance fee is $5, and campsites vary from free to a high of $6 per night.

Who to contact: If you have questions about the park, call Shasta Cascade at (916) 243-2643 and ask for Johnathan Reginato, who provides a free information service, or call the park at (916) 595-4444.

NO. CALIFORNIA CAMPING

PLUMAS WONDERLAND

MORE DEER THAN PEOPLE

Plumas County is one of the great undiscovered treasures of Northern California.

A lot of people miss it because Plumas is located between Tahoe and Shasta, the top two vacation spots in the state. Those who take the inbetween route will find a huge variety of lakes, streams, mountains and meadows to self-style virtually any kind of outdoor vacation.

Plumas is set at the northern end of the Sierra Nevada, 200 miles from San Francisco -- and has more than 60 campgrounds, 100 lakes and 1,000 miles of streams. Yet the county population is only 15,000 in an area of 2,500 square miles.

If you get the idea that there is plenty of room, you are right. The deer outnumber the people by far.

The best place for newcomers in search of solitude and good fishing is Plumas National Forest. The mountains here are filled with pines, firs and cedars. You can reach 42 campgrounds by car, including many small, hidden spots accessible by forest service roads.

A map of Plumas National Forest can help you find your own, secret camp. Forest service maps detail all back roads, lakes, streams and hiking trails.

The best camping spots are those adjacent to streams and lakes. The Middle Fork of the Feather River has the most idyllic spots and best trout fishing, but to reach the river usually requires some hiking. It is regarded by most well-traveled outdoorsmen as one of the state's top five trout streams.

The North Fork of the Feather is more accessible, with Highway 70 running alongside much of it. The trout fishing is decent, primarily for 9 to 11 inch rainbow trout.

Other streams that provide good trout fishing include Indian Creek, Yellow Creek and Nelson Creek.

If you prefer lake settings, the Plumas country offers many opportunities. The most famous are Lake

Almanor and Davis Lake. Almanor, a big lake set near Chester, is the best for power boaters. Davis offers fishing for big rainbow trout.

But there are many other choices. Butte Lake, set a few miles from Almanor, has some of the largest rainbow trout in California. Bucks Lake, a short drive from Quincy, provides some of the most consistent trouting for 9 to 12-inchers in the county.

The best source for fishing information up here is Allan Bruzza at the Sportsmen's Den in Quincy, who knows every inch of this country. He can be reached by phoning (916) 283-2733.

A good spot for a first trip is the Plumas Eureka State Park. It is set just west of the intersection of Highways 70 and 89 in the historic goldmining area of Johnsville. You can either hunker down here, playing at Eureka Lake or taking day hikes in the forest, or set out for something more ambitious.

Also, Gold Lakes Basin borders to the southeast. This is for backpackers only though. For those who want to get off the beaten path, there are more than 50 lakes to choose from. The area is similar to the famous Desolation Wilderness near Tahoe, but gets about one-tenth the use.

It is primarily granite basin terrain, with a few stands of sugar pine and the lakes like deep bowls of water. Since they are natural lakes, they are full, unlike California's reservoirs that are being drained for agricultural use.

Many side trips can be parlayed along with your base trips here. You can visit the state's second-highest waterfall, Feather Falls, at 640 feet. The streams here are in the heart of the gold country, and you could get lucky and pay for the trip with a few hours of panning. If you don't like to hike, you might consider a stable that provides horse rentals and visit the back country.

Remember it's Feather River country -- a hundred lakes and a thousand miles of streams, enough adventures to fill every day of the summer with a unique adventure.

☞ Trip facts:

How to get there: There are two routes. From the Central Valley, take Highway 70 up the Feather River Canyon, or from Highway 80, turn north at Truckee on Highway 89 and cruise through the forest country.

Maps: A map of Plumas National Forest can help you find your own, secret camp. It costs $1 and can be obtained by writing Maps, U.S. Forest Service, 630 Sansome Street, San Francisco, CA 94111.

Who to contact: For a free recreation map and brochure, write Plumas County Chamber of Commerce at Box 11018, Quincy, CA 95971, or phone (916) 283-2045.

NO. CALIFORNIA CAMPING

PRAIRIE CREEK
REDWOODS

WHERE THE ELK ARE AS BIG AS ALL OUTDOORS

The first time you stare a giant animal eye-to-eye, it can make your eyebrows tingle. It doesn't have to be something that can eat you -- it just has to be big.

There is a sudden reckoning in your brain that the critter standing in front of you is one huge fellow, and whether he knows it or not, he could do the Bigfoot Stomp all over your body. The funny thing is, though, he usually doesn't seem to know it.

This is how it is with Roosevelt Elk, a monstrous-sized critter that stands five feet at the shoulder. The bulls have long pointed antlers that look like they could turn you into an instant shishkabob. But unless you try to pet one on the nose and say, "Nice elky," this animal prefers to maintain a demeanor that suggests a degree of royalty, rather than that of a Doberman attack dog.

Visitors at Prairie Creek Redwoods State Park on California's northern coast get a quick understanding of this, even after the initial shock of seeing something so huge, so close. The elk here are wild, not tame, but are domesticated to the point they will allow various forms of humanoids, even Southern Californians, to view them from a certain distance.

When the big bulls look up and freeze you with a stare, that means "close enough, buddy." Most people seem to understand this language.

If you have never seen a huge elk in its native habitat, Prairie Creek Redwoods is the spot. The park is located about 50 miles north of Eureka, where the two-lane Highway 101 cuts right through the park.

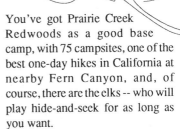

Often enough, the elk will herd up just beyond the old wooden rails that line each side of the road.

Sometimes all you have to do is pull over on the road's shoulder, which has been enlarged for parking, for what may be your first significant wildlife sighting not made in a zoo. As many as 50 to 75 elk will mill around in the large meadow right along the highway. It can make for remarkable photographs.

One time while studying a big bull through a pair of binoculars, I saw a family of tourists in a motor home cruising by, when the driver accidentally turned his head and spotted all the elk in the adjacent meadow. He suddenly braked hard, jerked the RV over to the side of the road, and jumped out. "Look at that! Look at that!" he shouted to his family.

Ten minutes later, as he was calming down, he said to his wife, "Wendy, those are the biggest deer I've ever seen in my life. We sure don't have anything like that in Oklahoma. Did you get a picture? Howie back home won't believe this."

If you've never ventured up here, there's a lot of other things you and Howie won't believe.

Like the cathedral-like redwood forests, the secluded campgrounds, scenic drives and some of the prettiest day hikes in the country.

You've got Prairie Creek Redwoods as a good base camp, with 75 campsites, one of the best one-day hikes in California at nearby Fern Canyon, and, of course, there are the elks -- who will play hide-and-seek for as long as you want.

The redwoods here average more than 200 feet tall and 12 to 13 feet in diameter. They aren't as big around as the Sequoias in Yosemite, but they are taller. Put thousands of them together, most 1,000 years or older, and you get the feeling this place has been here awhile without anybody fooling with it.

It's even more special in Fern Canyon. This canyon has 50-foot high walls that are masses of ferns and flora, and the redwoods tower above. Most people have never seen anything like it.

The walks are not difficult, with little elevation gain and loss. There are many shorter options to the Fern Canyon Trail available right from the parking lot at Prairie Creek Redwoods. A good trail map is available at park headquarters for 75 cents.

Prairie Creek is one of four contiguous parklands on California's North Coast that stretches for miles and miles. That provides camping options and plenty of alternatives if you want to extend your stay. If the 75-site campground is full at Prairie Creek, you can camp at Gold Bluff Beach (27 campsites), Del Norte State Park (108), or in adjacent Six

Rivers National Forest.

But if you want to see elk, Prairie Creek is the spot.

Two years ago, a fellow decided he wanted a special picture of an elk, that is a close-up head shot. Well, the ambitious photographer did not have a zoom lens, so he innocently walked right up in front of an elk to take a picture.

Well, Mr. Elk did not like that. In fact, Mr. Elk snorted and chased that fellow right up a tree. At last look, the fellow was perched on a limb, the elk standing below, looking up at him.

As far as I know, he's still there and with pictures to be produced far more interesting than he first thought.

☞ ELK COUNTRY TRIP FACTS

How to get there: Take Highway 101 straight norht. The highway splits the park, which is about 50 miles north of Eureka.

Camping: Campsites are $10 per night. Reservations may be made through Mistix at (800) 446-7275.

Camping Options: Options include Gold Bluff near Fern Canyon; Del Norte State Redwoods, north of Klamath (707) 458-3115; Jed Smith Redwoods, east of Crescent City (707) 464-9533; Six Rivers National Forest, north and east of the park (707)442-1721.

Nearby trips: Two suggestions, both are well signed. To get to Fern Canyon Trail, take Davison Road off Highway 101. To get to Lady Bird John Redwood Grove, take Bald Hill Road off Highway 101.

Who to contact: Call Prarie Creek Redwoods State Park at (707) 488-2171.

PHOTO OPPORTUNITY

NO. CALIFORNIA CAMPING

JEDEDIAH SMITH
STATE PARK

BIG TREES & BIG FISH

Disneyland, San Francisco, and the North Coast redwoods are California's primary tourist draws, but it is only in the sanctuary of our forests of giant trees, where you can find peace as well as adventure.

Jedediah Smith State Park is the northernmost of 30 redwood state parks that are set along the coast from Monterey to the Oregon border, and is my favorite because of the variety of adventures that await explorers. The kicker is that the summer climate is far warmer here than most areas that harbor coastal redwoods.

The park is set in the northwest corner of California off Highway 199, just on the edge of the Smith River, California's largest undammed river. In the spring and summer, the South Fork provides good fishing for rainbow and cutthroat trout -- and in the fall and winter, the main Smith draws runs of giant salmon and steelhead, although they can prove quite elusive.

Regardless, many are caught. One fall at the California border patrol station, a gent got out of his car and told a patrolman: "Well, I didn't bring anything in, but I am taking something out." He opened the trunk of his car and showed a 68-pound salmon, which measured about 4.5 feet long.

In early summer, anglers can often catch two or three trout out of each hole, simply by casting a small lure in stretches of white water, and letting it tumble downstream into the holes.

Jed Smith Park is an ideal base station for your fishing adventures on the nearby river, and a good stopover for vacationers heading northward as well. For hikers, the park has 23 miles of trails that wind through a countryside studded with redwoods, and is located on the edge of the vast Six Rivers National Forest -- which contains more than one million acres of relative wildlands.

This nearby diversity magnifies the appeal of the park, so even with 108 campsites, you can expect reservations to be necessary, particularly during the summer.

The trails at Jed Smith State Park vary enough so you can match your like to your physical condition. Of the 11 trails, six are rated "easy" and follow relatively flat terrain. A good example is the Stout Grove Trail, where you cross the Smith River by footbridge, and walk a half-mile to reach the awesome Stout Tree, which measures 340-feet tall and 20-feet in diameter.

A good two-hour hike, rated "moderate", is the Hiouchi Trail, which takes you along the west bank of the Smith River, and even right through a hole in a giant burned-out redwood.

For people who hear the call of giant trees, it beats Disneyland by a mile.

☞ JED SMITH PARK TRIP FACTS

How to get there: Take Highway 101 north through Crescent City, then take the Highway 199 turnoff and continue for 10 miles. The park is well-signed and located on the right side of the road.

Trip Cost: Campsites cost $10 per night per vehicle. Reservations are strongly advised in the summer.

Campsites: Each campsite has a table, stove and cupboard. Restrooms with hot showers are nearby. No trailer hookups are available. If you want a more remote campsite, you should contact the Gasquet Ranger Station, (707) 457-3131, for camping areas in the Six Rivers National Forest.

Reservations: Camping reservations at Jed Smith Park can be made through Mistix at (800) 444-7275.

Other overnight options: If you want to explore the area, but not camp, Trapper Joe's, (707) 457-3475, in Gasquet provides cabins and a first-class restaurant.

Who to contact: Call Jed Smith State Park at (707) 464-9533, or write P.O. Drawer J, Crescent City, CA 95531.

NO. CALIFORNIA CAMPING

SHASTA GETAWAY

ADVENTURE AT THE FOOT OF A GREAT TEPEE

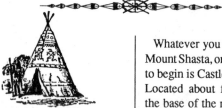

Indian legend has it that Mount Shasta was formed when the Great Spirit poked a hole in the sky and shaped a tepee with the fallen pieces. From afar it's almost possible to believe it. The great snow-capped volcano is sometimes visible from as far as 150 miles away, rising 14,162 feet above the lowlands.

But Mount Shasta is more than just an imposing silhouette that casts its shadow over Interstate 5. It's also the centerpiece for one of the West's great lands of adventure. Name the activity, and the 25-square mile area that encircles Mount Shasta has it: quality stream and lake fishing, boating, hiking, rafting, camping, backpacking and, in the winter, both alpine and Nordic skiing.

Whatever you want to do around Mount Shasta, one of the best places to begin is Castle Crags State Park. Located about fifteen miles from the base of the mountain, the park offers an awe-inspiring view of Shasta, along with many "crags" -- tall spires of ancient granite -- that sometimes seem to lift above even Shasta's peak. Castle Crags Park offers 64 well-spaced campsites; as at most California state parks, each comes with a table, barbecue stove and storage locker, plus nearby restroom/shower.

Fishing aficionados won't want to wait for a night of rest before grabbing a fishing rod. The rainbow trout fishing at Castle Creek offers some of the best and most dramatic in the world: Giant rock clusters jut thousands of feet above the river in shapes that look like something out of a prehistoric movie. Sometimes it takes a sudden jolt on your fishing rod to bring you back to reality.

Castle Crags is only one of about

50 campgrounds that ring the Mount Shasta area, ranging from areas that offer full hookup facilities for motor homes to primitive sites in the Klamath and Shasta National Forests. If you carry a cartop boat or trailer, then head to Lake Siskiyou, Lake Shastina or Lake McCloud for a prime camping/fishing experience.

Siskiyou, a small jewel of a lake, glistens in the very shadow of Mount Shasta. The lake's western shore features both campsites and a swimming area, and the lake has plenty of trout and bass. You can rent boats and motors at the Lake Siskiyou Marina.

The Siskiyou Campground is an ideal base camp for exploring a network of relatively untraveled back country roads and trails. Nearby Gumboot Lake, for example, which is one of the 58 alpine lakes in the Trinity Divide country, is located in an area that's largely national forest land. Some of the best fishing around Mount Shasta can be found at Lake Shastina and Lake McCloud, which offer good hopes for rainbow trout and the occasional large brown trout.

If you yearn for a more remote setting, then take the winding, gravel forest service road into the canyon past Lake McCloud, where you can find the McCloud River. Deer roam this area without fear, old trees are left standing, and rainbow and brown trout are the kings of the stream. Relatively little has changed here over the past 200 years. And it won't change much

more, since the Nature Conservancy, a national organization dedicated to purchasing unique wildlands, manages more than six miles of the McCloud watershed. Fishing access is free, but restricted to no more than ten rods on the river. All trout hooked here must be released, and you must use single barbless hooks on flies or lures.

According to a Nature Conservancy logbook, the average catch is four or five rainbow trout per angler. Experienced anglers do better, especially for larger trout. Because all are released, that means they are still out there, waiting for you.

Drive-in campsites are available near the McCloud River at the Ah-Di-Na Campground. It is first come, first serve with no reservations. If you prefer a closer-to-blacktop approach to stream fishing, there are a number of options. One of them is the Upper Sacramento River, a gentle, tumbling stream that provides good trout fishing from above Shasta Lake to Bos Canyon Dam. Because Interstate 5 runs adjacent to the stream, access is quite good, especially through small

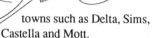

towns such as Delta, Sims, Castella and Mott.

For some people, fishing is an exciting battle with Mother Nature, however if you'd rather simply commune with her, consider spending a few days hiking, rafting or houseboating.

A network of trails crosses the mountain country, and you can tailor your walk to your level of ambition. One of the best hikes is the Pacific Crest Trail, which cuts across the southern slope of Mount Shasta, running past Castle Crags State Park, the Sacramento River and McCloud River.

Another option for well-conditioned hikers with the proper equipment is to climb to the top of Mount Shasta itself. You need crampons, an ice axe and good boots and spirit. Even though the climb is a steep

one, the panoramic lookouts will do wonders for your resolve. The old mountain provides magic inspiration.

You say you don't want to sweat on a trail, that vacations aren't meant for work? Then consider some white-water excitement. The gurgling of streams is the mountain symphony, and riding a raft down the untamed stretches of the Sacramento or Klamath Rivers can be a wild but relatively easy way to spend a day or two. Wilderness Adventures is one of many companies in the area offering one-day trips for about $55 and two-day trips for

$190 per person. The fee includes all meals.

The laziest vacation of all could be renting a houseboat on massive Shasta Lake, the largest reservoir in California. Though two million people venture to this lake every year, it has the space to handle them: 365 miles of shoreline, 1,200 campsites, fifteen boat launches, 22 resorts and twelve marinas to rent houseboats. Figuring you'll need a week on a houseboat to do it right, you can rent one that sleeps six to fourteen people for $900 to $1,895. While you're motoring about, you might pick up a fishing rod. Some 22 species of fish live in the lake.

In the winter, skiing down the side of Mount Shasta can beat the heavily used slopes of the Sierra Nevada. Because the skiing operation here was built in 1985, the public has not yet discovered how good it is. You'll find short lines at the three lifts and lots of room on the slopes. For cross-country skiing, Bunny Flat is the top spot.

Whether or not you believe the Indian legend, it's a fact that Shasta has become a happy hunting ground for people who love the outdoors.

☞ MOUNT SHASTA ADVENTURE TRIP FACTS

Sacramento River: For fishing information, call guide Joe Kimsey at (916) 235-2969. Access is free.

McCloud River: For reservations to the prime fishing area, call the Nature Conservancy at (415) 777-0541. Access is free. For the latest on insect hatches, call the Fly Shop at (916) 222-3555.

McCloud Reservoir: A good boat ramp is available, and shore fishing can also be good. Access is free. You can get fishing tips from Shasta Cascade at (916) 243-2643.

Lake Siskiyou: For fishing tips, call Don Moore at (916) 926-2618. Boat rentals, camping, and boat launch are all available.

Hiking: The Sisson-Callahan Trail is one of the best on the west side of Mount Shasta. For map of trails on Forest Service land, write Shasta Cascade at 1250 Parkview, Redding, CA 96001.

Lodging: At Mount Shasta, the Best Western Treehouse (916) 926-3101 is one quality motel with all the amenities provided.

Who to contact: Call Shasta Cascade at (916) 243-2643 for information on the entire area, free maps, and brochures.

CASTLE CRAGS
STATE PARK

AWESOME GRANITE SPIRES

One of the truly awe-inspiring views of the world can be seen at Castle Crags State Park, where soaring spires of ancient granite seem to lift above even the giant Mount Shasta. At the base of the Crags tumbles Castle Creek, a classic babbling brook, where fishermen catch rainbow trout as well as a great view. All is surrounded by miles of forested mountain wildlands, just 25 miles north of Shasta Lake.

Many people have eyed glimpses of Castle Crags while heading up Highway 5; the ridge sits just west of the highway. But by driving on, they are missing what is one of California's geologic wonders, as well as just a darn good place to spend a weekend. You can camp, fish, hike, picnic -- and for the inspired, backpack into adjoining wild country to find a series of hidden lakes that provide more good trout fishing.

For car campers, there are 64 well-spaced campsites, with most of them large enough to accommodate trailers -- though no hookups are provided. As at most state parks, each campsite comes with a table, barbecue stove, and storage locker, with a nearby restroom/shower available.

Elevations range from 2,000 feet at the campsites to 6,000 feet at the top of the crags, so although quite warm in the day, the temperature can be downright chilly at night, unexpectedly so in spring and autumn. Campers should come prepared for both.

Although the trout tend to be on the small side in Castle Creek, every angler should try fishing here at least once; the setting below the awesome crags is that remarkable. The fishing is best by far during the early morning and late evening, using flies. The nearby Upper

Sacramento River can provide an alternative.

Castle Crags sits on the edge of wildlands studded with pines, firs, cedars, along with a number of alders, maples and oaks. Do not be surprised if you see wildlife, particularly if you come late in the year. Tourist numbers are far fewer than in the summer months, so deer and bear are less apt to be spooked. Year around, however, the park attracts squirrels, chipmunks, raccoons and countless lizards; all seem to be looking for a handout.

No matter where you go here, you are always in the shadow of the dramatic features of the land. To the north, dominating the countryside for a hundred miles, is the 14,162-foot Mount Shasta, always huge, always covered with snow.

But the crags themselves provide a more fascinating attraction. The giant rock chutes and clusters jut high for thousands of feet. They look like something out of a prehistoric science fiction movie, but unlike a movie, Castle Crags is real, not make believe.

☞ CASTLE CRAGS PARK TRIP FACTS

How to get there: Head straight up Highway 5 past Redding, and continue about 25 miles north of Shasta Lake near Castella. The turn-off is well signed, and the crags can be seen from Highway 5.

Trip cost: Campsites are $10 per night.

Driving time: If you leave at 6 a.m. from San Francisco, you should arrive by noon, about a five to six-hour cruise (270 miles).

Camping: Call Mistix for reservations at (800) 444-7275.

Lodging: If you do not wish to camp, write Shasta Cascade, 1250 Parkview Avenue, Redding, CA 96001, for a list of available lodging, and any information about Siskiyou, Shasta, Trinity, Lassen, Modoc, and Tehama Counties.

Who to contact: Castle Crags State Park can be reached by calling (916) 235-2684. Shasta Cascade Wonderland Association can be reached at (916) 243-2643.

NO. CALIFORNIA CAMPING

HOPE VALLEY

MOUNTAINS, CABINS & TROUT STREAMS

The early pioneers traveled more than 2,000 miles to face the Sierra Nevada, their last barrier to the land of golden dreams in the Sacramento Valley. In the 1980s, "pioneers" from the Bay Area head to South Tahoe with golden dreams in the casinos. As with the 49ers, a day or two here in nearby Hope Valley can add a degree of reality to your trip.

The remnants and scars of the westward migration of gold seekers can still be seen in Hope Valley, a territory known for its natural beauty, historic character, hiking and trout fishing. Campgrounds set alongside the Carson River, along with cabins at Sorenson's Resort can provide a temporary home, and many folks venture to this area for the hot springs in nearby Markleeville.

Hope Valley is located about 20 miles south of Lake Tahoe. The valley is divided by Highway 88, a quiet two-laner. Access to the campgrounds and river is easy.

A good day hike, which most people will find quite easy, is to retrace some of the same steps taken by the pioneers on the Immigrant Trail. Sorenson's Resort, which is more of an assemblage of cabins than a resort, offers a guided tour of this trail. Jess Machado of Stockton is the lead tour guide. In 1929, he was the first person to make lasting markers of the trail, and has discovered hundreds of artifacts in the area. Much of this route, which continues over Carson Pass, was used as a Pony Express route.

Come evening and it's time to pull out your fishing rod. The trout fishing on the Carson River provides the classic "babbling brook" setting that armchair fishermen like to imagine. However, the trout are real, not imaginary, and that means a de-

gree of smarts is necessary to hook them. Because access to the river is so easy, the fish can be spooked by folks who approach without care. The trout should be stalked. Regardless of your experience, you should move to a new spot after just a few casts. The best fishing here in late summer is usually from 7 p.m. to dusk, with carefully presented fly patterns. The mosquito, abundant here, is a favorite.

Summer is the most popular time to visit, but my favorite period is in the fall, after Labor Day weekend has passed. Most of the summer vacationers are back home, the road is no longer clogged up with Winnebagos, and you can see the remarkable change in seasons, from summer to fall. In the Sierra Nevada, the Aspens explode in color, and being here in the center of it, can make you feel much as the pioneers did 130 years ago.

☛ HOPE VALLEY TRIP FACTS

How to get there: From the Bay Area, take Highway 80 to Sacramento, then turn on Highway 50 and continue to Highway 88 near the crest. Turn east and Hope Valley waits just 15 miles distant.

Log cabins: Log cabins at Sorensen's Resort include two beds and a kitchen and start at $45 per night.

Tour guide: Sorensen's is offering two nights of lodging, four meals, and a tour guide for the Emigrant Trail for $98 per person.

Camping: Campsites are free on a first come, first serve basis. Campgrounds operated by the Forest Service sit at river's edge and are quite popular during the summer.

Who to contact: For information regarding fishing tips, tour guides, cabin reservations or camping availability, contact Sorensen's at (916) 694-2203. For a brochure on the Immigrant Trail tour, write Sorensen's, Hope Valley, CA 96120.

NO. CALIFORNIA CAMPING

BOTHE-NAPA
STATE PARK

A REDWOOD OPTION TO NAPA VALLEY

Most people think of the Napa Valley as a 20-mile stretch of wineries and tourists, but nearby Bothe-Napa State Park offers a relatively unknown spot for camping, picnicking, and hiking trails that wind their way through the most easterly stands of coastal redwoods.

Now wait a minute, redwoods in the Napa Valley, you say? That's right, and that's not all that will surprise Bay Area residents who are more accustomed to driving past this area rather than walking through it. Bothe-Napa State Park is cut by Ritchey Creek at the bottom of a canyon, and bordered by rugged mountains that climb from 300 to 2,000 feet. It provides habitat for squirrels, foxes, deer, raccoons and coyote.

One critical tip is to be sure to get a reservation if you plan on camping, because the park has just 50 campsites, including 10 walk-in sites. Reservations can be made through Ticketron as far as eight weeks in advance of your stay, and rangers advise allowing a minimum of two weeks for lead time. Each campsite offers a table, cupboard, and barbecue stove. Rangers ask that no downed wood be used for fires. They sell firewood at the park entrance if you do not bring your own. Barbecue chips are advised for cooking.

Many of the park's visitors are folks who have just taken a tour at one of the Napa Valley wineries. They're just looking for the shade of a tree to sit down and sample the contents of a recent purchase, and usually find the park by accident. However, on the return trip most make it no chance occurrence. Not with walks available that span from an easy stroll on the loop trail to a rugged hike that will take you up to ridges for panoramic views. The best of the latter is the Coyote Peak Trail, an hour-long jaunt that climbs to a vista offering views of the park's back canyon and scenic glimpses of the Napa Valley.

One of the most popular hikes at Bothe-Napa Park is the Ritchey Canyon Trail, an easy walk that borders Ritchey Creek, a year-around stream, and is hidden by redwoods, firs, and ferns. This cool hideaway is a special refuge during the summer, when temperatures often reach 90 to 100 degrees.

One key tip is to stay on the trail. The climate here is suited perfectly for poison oak, and the park is loaded with it. Remember that poison oak always grows in clumps of three leaves, and turns from a shiny green in the spring to rich orange and red in the summer and fall.

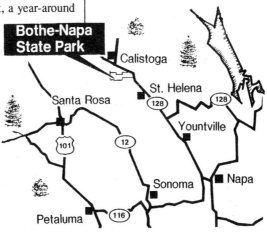

BOTHE-NAPA PARK TRIP FACTS

How to get there: From Napa, take Highway 29 north through Napa Wine Valley, past Saint Helena, and turn left at the park, just past Bale Lane.

Trip cost: Campsites cost $10 per night per vehicle, day-use is $2 per vehicle. A swimming pool is available at park headquarters, with an access fee of $1.

Reservations: Camping reservations can be made through Ticketron, and are recommended at least a minimum of two weeks in advance of your trip, or call Mistix at (800) 444-7275.

Pets: Fido the dog must be kept on a leash and have proof of rabies vaccinations. Dogs are not allowed on the trails.

Who to contact: Call the Bothe-Napa State Park at (707) 942-4575, or write at 3801 Saint Helena Highway North, Calistoga, CA 94515.

NO. CALIFORNIA CAMPING

ANNADEL STATE PARK

WHERE THE MASSES RARELY VENTURE

An example of an ideal spot rarely visited by the masses, especially in the fall, is Annadel State Park. It offers a 35-mile network of trails for hikers or horsemen, good black bass fishing, yet sits just an hour's drive north of San Francisco, just east of Santa Rosa. The rangers here call Annadel a "wilderness at your doorstep."

The park spans almost 5,000 acres of rolling hills, meadow and woodlands, and is cut by several creeks. A secret is that two miles inside the park borders is Lake Ilsnajo, a good bass and bluegill fishing lake that will always remain that way because you have to hike for an hour to reach it. Most people are not willing to hike to fish. That's fine for those who do. They know that the lake record here for bass is a nine pounder, and that every fall and spring, others of similar proportions are tangled with.

If you like to explore by foot or horseback, then Annadel Park is your match. My favorite hike here is taking the Lake Trail to Lake Ilsnajo (2.5 miles), stopping to fish, then returning via the steep Steve's Trail (three miles). Horses are allowed on the trails, and although the creeks do not flow year around, there is almost always plenty of water available for Old Paint. For yourself, be sure to carry a canteen. While camping is not allowed in Annadel State Park, if you want to make a weekend out of your trip, there are some nearby spots to put up a tent. The western edge of Annadel is bordered by Spring Lake (which is stocked with trout) and its 31-site campground. It is first come, first serve.

The rangers at Annadel say that a few herds of wild pigs run loose at the park, rooting, snorting, and doing what wild pigs do. Their reputations as fighters is overblown; I've been face-to-face with

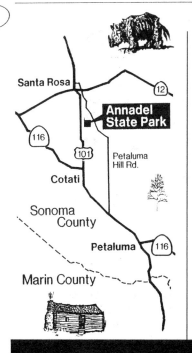

several wild boars, and given a choice, they will always run. Just don't box them in. This wild country is also home for deer and fox, although sightings seem to be infrequent.

The terrain varies, so use care in selecting a hike. How much sun each respective area receives determines the kind of plant and tree growth it can sustain -- so in just a few hours, you can hike through forests of Douglas Fir to meadows and on to chaparral areas. A dozen different plant communities thrive here. And so do the bass in the lake. Arriving here by foot after a hike on a fall morning seems like a perfect way to start a day.

☞ ANNADEL PARK TRIP FACTS

How to get there: Take Highway 101 to Santa Rosa, and head east on Highway 12. Veer right on Montgomery Drive, then turn right again on Channel Drive and continue to the park.

Trip cost: Access is free; trail maps at the park are available for 75 cents.

Horses and dogs: Horses are allowed on trails, but dogs are not.

Fishing tip: Purple plastic worms are tops for the bass at Lake Ilsanjo, and bluegill prefer small baits like meal worms or red worms.

Hours: Annadel is open from sunrise to sunset.

Camping: Thirty-one campsites are available at the adjacent Spring Lake Park Campground on a first-come, first-served basis at $6 per vehicle. For information call (707) 539-8092.

Who to contact: Call Annadel State Park at (707) 539-3911, or (707) 938-1519, or write at 6201 Channel Drive, Santa Rosa, CA 95405.

NO. CALIFORNIA CAMPING

WOODSON BRIDGE
STATE PARK

ROLLING DOWN THE RIVER

Days of Huck Finn, Tom Sawyer and the Mississippi River come to mind at Woodson Bridge State Park. Hot weather, good fishing, and perhaps a raft trip down the ol' Sacramento make for a classic autumn day. And come nightfall, you can just roll your sleeping bag out on the banks of the Sacramento, or set up camp at one of the 46 sites at Woodson Bridge Park.

The Sacramento River rolls its way some 450 river miles from the base of Mount Shasta to San Francisco Bay, but no stretch is more

alive with fish and wildlife than from Red Bluff to Chico. Woodson Bridge Park, tucked away on the river bank east of Corning, is centered on this prime stretch of river. Canoeists, rafters and inner-tubers alike will plunk in upstream at Los Molino or Red Bluff, and lollygag their way down the river, the sun blazing but the stream cool. Woodson Bridge is the destination.

Campsites here are set under huge oaks, and like most state parks, each comes with a table, barbecue stove, and cupboard. For the more adventurous, a boat-in camp is located on nearby Kopta Slough, a secluded area still in its native state.

Woodson Bridge has become a center for fishing, both for anglers with and without boats. Salmon, shad, and catfish are the primary attractions. For power boaters, a good ramp is set right next to the bridge itself, on the eastern side of the river. From here you can zip upriver to the mouth of Deer Creek, the top spot within miles for salmon from August through October.

For those without boats, the Woodson Bridge area is considered one of the best stretches in California for shad. In July and August, anglers will wade out and then cast

upriver with a T-Killer, Fle-Fly, or Shad Dart, allowing the lure to drift downriver with the current, retrieving line as it goes. Most anglers here catch three or four shad per hour, but the "know-hows" can catch one every five to 10 minutes, and in an evening sometimes catch-and-release a 25-fish limit.

If you prefer to relax when you

fish, then instead head to Kopta Slough and try some bait dunking. Its calm, warm waters hold catfish, along with bluegill and a few black bass.

Even though the park is centered in the hot north valley, the river provides the lifeblood for an array of birds and wildlife. Herons, geese, ducks, hawks...the list is quite surprising. You also might see beaver, squirrels, and deer, with a remote chance of getting a visit from an opossum, raccoon or skunk.

But beyond that, the Sacramento River itself provides a way to turn back the clock to a time when priorities were reversed for many. Whether or not you got a catfish last night was as important as if you got a paycheck.

Just ask Huck Finn.

☞ WOODSON BRIDGE TRIP FACTS

How to get there: Drive on Interstate 5 to Corning, and turn east on the South Avenue exit -- and take that road all the way to the river. The park sits on eastern shoreline, just next to the bridge.

Trip cost: Campsites are $10 per night, with reservations available through Mistix at 800-444-7275.

Who to contact: Call Woodson Bridge State Park at (916) 824-4107, or call Shasta Cascade at (916) 243-2643.

NO. CALIFORNIA CAMPING

ARMSTRONG
REDWOODS

A RETREAT FROM INDIAN SUMMER

The blast furnace heat of the Bay Area's Indian Summer might make you wish you were seated in the middle of a cool redwood forest, sipping on a drink. If you're willing to make a 90-minute drive north of San Francisco, you can get exactly that.

Armstrong Redwoods State Reserve is the answer, a jungle of some of the tallest trees remaining in California, including several that have lived for more than a thousand years. The reserve sits adjacent to the Austin Creek Recreation Area, so you can turn your sojourn into a full-scale camping, hiking expedition. And if you plan on heading up during the fall or winter, bring your fishing rod as well. The Russian River borders Highway 116, and one of the best spots on the river for steelhead is at the mouth of Austin Creek -- just a short distance from the Armstrong Redwoods.

This is all tucked away just northwest of Santa Rosa, a short and easy distance from The City. Yet despite the relative ease in getting here, you can still capture a sense of total privacy that comes when in the midst of giant redwood trees. Some 5,000 acres of wildland, studded primarily with redwoods, tanoaks, and madrone, provide just that.

This area was set aside as a redwood reserve way back in the 1870s by a logger, of all people. While other timber interests were cutting wide swaths through California's giant redwoods, logger James Armstrong set this area aside. Armstrong was one of the few loggers who recognized the beauty and value of the forests, as well as the lumber value, and this reserve bears his name because of it.

Campers will find two alternatives: 24 drive-in sites awaiting at tiny Redwood Lake, or three prime hike-in areas. The drive-in family campground near the lake sits at the end of a steep, winding two-laner that climbs a thousand feet and can-

not be negotiated by trailers or motor homes. Another choice is to head to the primitive campsites at Gilliam Creek, Mannings Flat, and Tom King campground, short hikes on the park's trail system.

A bonus here is that the trails follow the streams that cut through the park. Austin Creek, Gilliam Creek, Schoolhouse Creek, and Fife Creek provide a water source (boil or filter before drinking) for backpackers. In addition, horses are allowed on the trails so equestrians can share in the redwood beauty with Old Paint having to do all the puffing. Austin Creek, a tributary to the Russian River, is home to a wide variety of animals and birds. In the fall, when water is a bit scarce, deer, raccoons, squirrels are more likely to be seen near the watersheds. On rare occasions, the park rangers say bobcats and wild pigs can even be spotted.

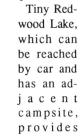

Tiny Redwood Lake, which can be reached by car and has an adjacent campsite, provides bass and bluegill fishing, but the fish tend to be on the small side.

Not the trees. You can drive all over the world and not see taller trees than are hidden in the Armstrong Reserve. You can also search for a long time for a better refuge during Indian Summer, and not find it.

☛ ARMSTRONG REDWOODS TRIP FACTS

How to get there: The easiest route from The City is to head north on Highway 101, and take River Road (located five miles north of Santa Rosa). Head west on River Road for 20 miles to Guerneville -- and take a right on Armstrong Woods Road.

Trip Cost: Drive-in camps are $10 per night, and backpacking campsites cost $3 per night.

Dogs: Dogs are permitted only in Armstrong Redwoods, and not on the trails in the Austin Creek Recreation Area.

Supplies: Last-minute shopping can be done in nearby Guerneville.

Who to contact: Call Armstrong Redwoods at (707) 869-2156 or (707) 865-2391, or write at 17000 Armstrong Woods Road, Guerneville, CA 95446.

MOUNT DIABLO
STATE PARK

STUNNING VISTAS

As real mountains go, Mount Diablo isn't so tall at 3,849 feet, but since it is surrounded by the Bay Area and Delta -- virtually at sea level -- hikers have one of the best lookouts in the Bay Area from its peak. It is best known for dramatic panorama views on clear days -- as well as being uninhabitable on hot ones during the summer.

Once camp is set you should do some thumping and hike your way from the campground up to the summit, about a one-mile walk. Providing a clear day, you will likely be stunned at how far you can see.

You can look west to the Golden Gate (remarkable sunsets) and on sparkling clear days, even spot the Farallon Islands about 25 miles out to sea. On exceptional days, you can even see Mount Lassen and the snow-capped crest of the Sierra Nevada, as well as a piece of Half Dome at Yosemite. You can travel around the world and not match a view like this.

Just don't expect to show up with your car at sunset for the jaunt up Mount Diablo. With the exception of campers, the park closes to visitors at sunset, and the gates will be locked one hour after that. Mount Diablo is open at night only for campers.

The park itself is a sprawling 10,000 acres that is home for deer, squirrel, skunks, rabbits, and even mountain lions and other rarely seen creatures. Because of its native grass and oak woodlands, fire danger can be so extreme in the summer that the park is occasionally closed on a day-to-day basis.

☞ MOUNT DIABLO PARK TRIP FACTS

How to get there: From Danville (Highway 680), take Diablo Road and head east on Black Hawk Road -- then turn left on South Gate Road.

Trip Cost: Campsites cost $10 per night for the first vehicle. Additional vehicles will be charged $3.

Reservations: During the summer, camping reservations are on a first come, first serve basis. During the winter months, reservations can be made through Mistix at (800) 444-7275.

Campfires: Use of fire is often prohibited in July and August, due to fire danger. In any case, gas burning stoves are recommended.

Who to contact: For park information, write Mount Diablo State Park at P.O. Box 250, Diablo, CA 94528, or call at (415) 837-2525.

NO. CALIFORNIA CAMPING

PINNACLES NATIONAL MONUMENT

JUMPING OFF INTO A DIFFERENT WORLD

If you ever have wanted to stop the world and jump off, Pinnacles National Monument is a good place to do it, at least for a weekend.

For one thing, it actually looks like a different planet. So, in a way, you really are stopping the world and jumping off.

For another, it is a totally out-of-the-way place, located in obscure San Benito County, about an hour's drive south of Hollister. Nobody comes here by accident.

You add those factors together and it makes an ideal hideaway for an overnighter, whether you just want to get away from it all or want the chance to explore the strange caves and huge volcanic clusters that cover much of the 16,000-acre park.

Winter and early spring are the only times to make a trip. In the summer and fall, it's hot, dry and sticky down here. You might as well plan a trip to Mercury. "It can get extremely hot, like in the 90s and 100s just about every day of the summer," said ranger Augusto Conde. "Spring is the time to come."

This is a place of secrets, and the two extensive cave systems hold many of them. The Bear Gulch Cave is approximately four-tenths of a mile long and the Balconies Cave extends about three-tenths of a mile.

They are not subterranean tunnels, like the old gold mines of the Sierra Nevada, but talus caves. They were created over time in canyons and crevices where rocks have slipped or fallen, and where storm runoff has removed the softer volcanic material. The result is a unique series of connected spaces within a rocky canopy.

The only thing I've seen quite like it are the Oregon Caves, located just across the California border off Highway 199.

Once you enter the cave system, you feel like you are entering a new world. If you turn your flashlight off, it gets as dark as the eyeholes of a skull. You wave your hand in front of your face and you can't see it. Hey, turn the light back on, it's spooky in here!

As you probe on, you need to keep the light roaming the darkness, not just when you're walking. Do the latter and you are liable to ram your head into a stalactite, which is a different way of adjusting your thought pattern than you had originally planned with this trip.

All the cave walks are self-guided, which adds a lot to the adventure. (At the Oregon Caves, only guided group tours are permitted.) If you forget your flashlight, rangers sell them. If you remember to bring your own, be certain your batteries and bulb are fresh.

The caves are subject to closure if there are earthquakes or heavy rains, either of which can loosen material. What the heck, closing it is better than having a five-ton vol-canic block fall on your foot. However, when rain is light, the caves can be open all winter without closure.

The rest of the park is as unique as the cave system. The Pinnacles consist of a huge rock mass that suddenly rises in chutes from the valley floor. It was created from a volcanic blast, similar to the one that formed the Sutter Buttes north of Sacramento. Hawkins Peaks, a vertical and barren spire at 2,720 feet, is what remains of the volcano's flume.

The trails can take you to the canyon ridges, which provide great lookouts onto the surrounding valley. One of the best is the High Peaks Trail. Because it is a primitive area with no piped water, be certain to bring a filled canteen or a day pack with your favorite liquid refreshment.

Two campgrounds are available, one primitive and isolated (located on the west side of the park), the other privately developed with full facilities (located on the east side of the park). Because no road extends through the park, you can't just hop over to the other if your first choice is filled. It is strongly advised to phone ahead for space availability. Recent weekends have been crowded, particularly on the east side.

The primitive camp is located on the western side of Pinnacles National Monument. You reach it by driving south on Highway 101, then turning east on Highway 146. The

road narrows and leads to a small campground with 24 sites, with water and toilet facilities available nearby.

The east side gets more visitation because it has a better access road and full facilities, and is closer to the Bear Gulch Caves. The camp here is called Pinnacles Campground Inc. and is privately operated. It includes space for motor homes.

It can fill up on weekends. To assist with the growing number of visitors, rangers have arranged a shuttle system to carry day visitors from a parking area to the caves.

A good time to plan a trip is for March or early April. That is when the valley's wildflowers begin to bloom, and with the greened-up hills as a backdrop, they provide the most colorful scenes of the year here.

It's one of the few places where you can stop the world and jump off. At least for a weekend.

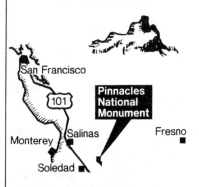

 PINNACLES MONUMENT TRIP FACTS

How to get there: Most people enter from the east side. From Hollister, head south on Highway 25 for about 30 miles, then take the signed Pinnacles cutoff west on Highway 146. From the west, the road is narrow and winding. Take Highway 101 south of Salinas to Soledad, then take Highway 146 east to the primitive camp.

Developed camp: Pinnacles Campground Inc. is a privately operated campground with full facilities, located on the east side. Often at capacity on winter and spring weekends. For more information: (408) 389-4462.

Primitive camp: The primitive camp is located on the west side and has 24 campsites, with water and toilet facilities available. Rangers can be reached at (408) 389-4526.

Who to contact: Rangers at headquarters can be reached by phoning (408) 389-4578 during the day or (408) 389-4520 after 5 p.m.

NO. CALIFORNIA CAMPING

BIG SUR
STATE PARK

WHERE THE WORLD SLOWS

Big Sur State Park is just far enough away -- about 150 miles south of San Francisco -- to give the weekend explorer that distinct feeling of total separation from the routine of the Bay Area.

When was the last time you had such an experience? The world passes quite a bit slower when you're in the midst of the big redwood trees at Big Sur. You will find it to your liking. Winter, spring and fall are the best times to visit, since the summer brings a hamster-run of tourists up Highway 1 from Los Angeles this way, something worth steering clear of.

The park offers 218 campsites, steelhead fishing in the Big Sur River, an extensive network of hiking trails, and being located south of Monterey, quite warm weather.

The hiking is a primary attraction. You can take a short walk to one of the nearby overlooks, or hike off on an overnighter into the giant and rugged Ventana Wilderness of Los Padres National Forest, which adjoins the park. If you go, be sure to see Pfeiffer Falls, which tumbles in the center of a dark, fern-lined canyon. Since elevations range from about sea level to 3,000 feet, some trails can get you puffing pretty good.

This is the southernmost of the redwood ranges, hence the heavy Los Angeles traffic in the summer. But like other coastal redwood parks, the south facing slopes are filled with a chaparral-type community, with tan oak, manzanita, and the lake. It means a hike here can take you in and out varied habitat areas. And with it, comes a variety of wildlife. Squirrels, raccoons, deer, along with stellar's jays, hawks, and turkey vultures are the most common sightings. How-

ever, in the canyons of the adjoining Ventana Wilderness, wild boar are known to root about, though I have never seen one here. (Hunting is permitted outside of park boundaries, in the national forest.)

Steelhead fishing in Big Sur River from January to early March attracts quite a few weekend anglers from the Monterey area. While the angling cannot compare with even the Russian River, it does provide a good combination camping/steelheading trip. The steelhead wait in the ocean, waiting for rain, and the resulting higher river flows, before completing their migratory trip. Given a moderate rainfall, which will freshen up the river, the angling should kick in.

With 218 campsites, there is no shortage of spots to stake a tent during most of the year. However, during the tourist season, from June through Labor Day, a reservation through Ticketron is a must. Remember that Highway 1 is considered one of the classic drives in America; folks from everywhere see Big Sur on the map; and it looks like the ideal stopover on a vacation. Well, in many ways it is, so you can't really blame them.

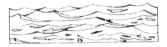

On one side is a forest studded with coastal redwoods, the tallest trees in the world. On the other is the Pacific Ocean, which seems to just lap at the beach here on calm days. Add in an ideal climate, much warmer than the Bay Area, and you have Big Sur State Park.

☞ BIG SUR STATE PARK TRIP FACTS

How to get there: From Monterey, simply head south on Highway 1 for 31 miles, where the entrance is well-signed.
Trip Cost: Day-use fee is $2 per vehicle. Campsites are $10 per night.
Motor homes: RV's up to 27 feet long can use the regular drive-in campsites.
Reservations: From Memorial Day through Labor Day, reservations are necessary through Ticketron.
Brochure: You can obtain a brochure by sending 25 cents to Pfeiffer Big Sur State Park, P.O. Box A, Big Sur, CA 93920.
Who to contact: For up-to-the-minute information, call the Big Sur ranger station at (408) 667-2315.

CHAPTER 3

COASTAL FUN

WITH

11 ADVENTURES

CONTENTS:—

PUBLISHED BY FOGHORN PRESS
SAN FRANCISCO
QUALITY OUTDOOR BOOKS

COASTAL FUN

10 FAVORITE SPOTS ON THE
BAY AREA COAST

DAYTRIPPING BY THE SEA

What to do? Here are the requirements: 1. Close to home. 2. Unique adventure. 3. Okay for anybody. 4. Inexpensive. 5. Easy.

There's not just one answer, but 10 of them on the coast from San Francisco to Santa Cruz. From an easy walk overlooking the Golden Gate, to horseback riding on the beach, to looking for abalone shells near a genuine lighthouse, to just hunkering down with a fishing rod for perch. Any way it might come into focus for you, a Pacific seashore adventure can provide the number one answer.

Your options include:

■ **1. Cliff House Hike:**
Here's a walk with classic vistas that tourists don't know about, and many locals take for granted and therefore don't go. It starts at the Cliff House, the historic restaurant perched at the entrance of San Francisco Bay, then leads along the bluffs west of the Golden Gate Bridge. The trail plays hide and seek among cypress trees, providing several great lookouts on the Golden Gate along the way. Circle back and you can end the trip with liquid refreshment at the Cliff House's Phineas T. Barnacle bar.

How to get there: From the interior of The City, hop on Geary Boulevard and follow it west. It turns into Point Lobos and the Cliff House will appear in front of you. From Highway 1 or 280, take Skyline Drive (Highway 35) north to the Great Highway. Two large parking areas are available.

■ **2. Pacifica Pier Fishing:**
Many species of fish, primarily perch, rockfish and lingcod, take advantage of

autumn by moving into the inshore shallows along Pacifica's rocky coast.

It is one of the few times of the year when abundant numbers of fish are within range of fishermen without boats. The perch fishing is particularly good along several Pacifica beaches, the rockfish good at Pedro Point, and a little of everything at Pacifica Pier.

How to get there: To reach Pacifica Pier, take Highway 1 into Pacifica and take the Sharp Park exit. Head west for a half-mile and you will see the pier, which extends past the ocean breakers.

Who to contact: For more information, call Coastside No. 2 at (415) 355-9901 or the Pacifica Pier at (415) 355-0690.

■ 3. Tidepool Hopping:

Low tides roll the ocean back and unveil the coast's rock tidal basins, where marine life thrives in little pockets of sea water. One of the best is at Fitzgerald Marine Reserve in Moss Beach.

You can spend several hours rock-hopping your way along the exposed reef, find all kinds of little sea critters.

This is one of the finest tide pool habitats in Northern California.

How to get there: You can reach it by taking Highway 1 into Moss Beach, which is located between Half Moon Bay and Pacifica, then turning west on California Street. A small sign on Highway 1 marks the turnoff.

Who to contact: Call the Fitzgerald

Reserve at (415) 728-3584 or San Mateo County Parks at (415) 363-4020.

■ 4. Princeton Harbor:

A rejuvenation project has brought new life to Princeton, the centerpiece of Half Moon Bay. It's been cleaned up, rebuilt, and now has more the feel of Monterey. You get the classic wharf setting and restaurants with harbor views. You can take it a step further, beachcombing the quiet northwest end of the harbor, fishing from the Princeton jetty or even boarding a boat for deep sea fishing.

How to get there: Getting there is easy. Take Highway 1 to Princeton, where you'll find one of the few stoplights on the entire San Mateo County coast. Turn west and you're there.

Who to contact: Call Huck Finn Sportfishing at (415) 726-7133 or Shorebird Restaurant at (415) 728-5541.

■ 5. Beach Horseback Riding:

The San Mateo County coast is something of an anachronism in the Bay Area. There are still dirt roads, farms, hometown post offices -- and people riding horses.

You can join in by renting a horse for an hour or more and taking a ride on the ocean bluffs or along the beach. It's a particularly unique setting, with the wide open expanse of the ocean on one side and the untouched Montara Mountain ridgeline on the other.

In Half Moon Bay, two stables rent horses to the public. The cost is $10 per hour. At Friendly Acres, 15-minute pony

rides are available for kids.

Who to contact: Call Friendly Acres at (415) 726-9871 or Seahorse Ranch at (415) 726-2362.

■ 6. Pescadero Marsh:

This is one of the Bay Area's great unknown wonders. A 600-acre natural marsh provides perfect habitat for some 250 species of birds, including blue herons with seven-foot wingspans. It's an ideal walk for anybody, with a nearly flat dirt trail circling the marsh.

How to get there: It is located just east of Highway 1, 18 miles south of Half Moon Bay near the Pescadero Road turnoff. The Highway 1 shoulder has been widened here to allow parking.

Who to contact: Call Half Moon Bay State Parks at (415) 726-6238 or Duarte's at (415) 879-0464.

■ 7. Pigeon Point Lighthouse:

This may be the most photographed lighthouse in North America. When you get there, everyone will have a camera out.

There's a reason. It's one of the classic ocean settings on the Pacific Coast. The lighthouse is a beacon to ships, protecting them from the shallow reef that extends southward to Franklin Point. After you take the obligatory picture, explore the tidal basin in Whaler's

Cove or beachcomb for abalone shells. Highway 1 bike riders can spend the night at the lighthouse, which has hostel facilities.

How to get there: At Pigeon Point, the lighthouse sticks out like a, well, lighthouse, just east of the highway about six miles south of the Pescadero Road turnoff. As you're cruising Highway 1, when you see it, just follow your nose.

■ 8. Ano Nuevo Reserve:

This is the most popular wildlife reserve on the Pacific Coast -- and not just for people. The beachhead and neighboring Ano Nuevo Island attract thousands of elephant seals every winter.

The first few usually start arriving in late October or early November, and stick around through March. In the span between, visitors have a rare chance to stare a three-ton sea creature right in the eye. Guided tours of small groups start in December, reservations necessary, with 45,000 people taking the trip each winter. In the fall, people are few and the area is quiet.

How to get there: The reserve sits just west of Highway 1, the turnoff is well signed, about 10 miles south of Pescadero.

Who to contact: Call Ano Nuevo Reserve at (415) 879-0595.

■ 9. Waddell Creek Walk:

Ol' logger Bill Waddell got killed by a grizzly bear here in 1875, and that helped get a creek named after him. While you won't find any grizzlies, much of the natural and historic feel of 100 years ago remains.

The trail starts at the Pacific Ocean, cuts past a natural marsh, then heads

into the forest interior, running adjacent to Waddell Creek. It is the western apex of Big Basin State Park, part of the 38-mile Skyline-to-Sea Trail. The trail is near level for several miles.

If you are ambitious, you can cross the creek and continue on to Berry Creek Falls, a full-day trip.

How to get there: The trailhead is located about a mile south of the border dividing Santa Cruz and San Mateo counties, with a large sign noting an entrance to Big Basin State Park.

Who to contact: Call Big Basin at (408) 338-6132.

■ Santa Cruz Wharf

This area gets its best deep-sea fishing of the year in the fall. The large sportfishing vessels have the choice of many prime areas, including the underwater Monterey Canyon, and reefs off of Davenport and Ano Nuevo Island. Trip cost is $23.

An option is to rent a 16-foot skiff equipped with a 6-horsepower engine. The cost is $25 per boat, plus $5 per person. Rod rentals and tackle are also available.

How to get there: Drive south on Highway 1 into Santa Cruz, then turn west on Bay Street and continue until it ends. From there, turn left at the Dream Inn, and drive down the hill to the foot of the wharf.

Who to contact: Call Deep sea charters at (408) 425-7003, Santa Cruz Boat Rental at (408) 423-1739, or Stagnaro's Restaurant, (408) 423-1188.

NORTH TO SOUTH, PACIFIC SEASHORE ADVENTURING

1. Cliff House hike, San Francisco 2. Pacifica Pier perch fishing 3. Tidepool hopping at Fitzgerald Marine Reserve, Moss Beach 4. Princeton Harbor 5. Horseback riding on the beach, Half Moon Bay 6. Pescadero Marsh 7. Pigeon Point Lighthouse 8. Ano Nuevo State Reserve 9. Waddell Creek walk, western boundary of Big Basin State Park 10. Santa Cruz Wharf

FIVE GREAT SPOTS
FOR BEACH CAMPING

SUN, SAND & THE TIME OF YOUR LIFE

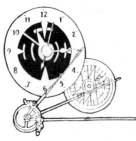

It can add up to the time of your life: the cruise down the coastal highway, ocean sunsets, fishing practically at the threshold of your tent and playing hide-and-seek with all the little tide-pool creatures. It goes on: waking up to the sound of the sea, playing tag with the waves, beachcombing at low tide and going for long walks with someone special.

But alas, if you are unprepared, just making it through a weekend can turn into an endurance test -- and you have about as much chance at winning as trying to fight an earthquake.

My first beach camping trip long ago was like this. I arrived late one evening at a state beach in Monterey, with no reservations, and found the campground full. So I had to strike out on my own, laying my sleeping bag down on a piece of secluded beach and going to sleep with the sound of waves in my ears.

Everything seemed great, right? Hey, the ocean was just waiting for me to pass into slumberland.

At about 4 a.m. a single thunderous wave cascaded over me. It was a shock, like sticking your finger in a light socket.

The following 10 hours were a disaster: turning into a human icicle in a wet sleeping bag, then trying to sleep in the truck...a cold, foggy morning making the beach feel like the North Pole...breakfast marinated in sand...getting hit in the arm with a sea gull dropping...snagging up on every cast while trying to fish. By noon it was time to surrender.

Well, that was more than 15 years ago. But you might have the same experience today if you head off unprepared.

For starters, camping reservations are a necessity; coastal state beaches are among the most popular campgrounds in the world, especially in the summer.

It is recommended you call the campground of your choice to learn of projected availability, then call the toll-free reservation line for Mistix to lock up a spot. The number is (800) 444-7275. Most state parks set at a beach frontage charge around $10 per night for a campsite.

The next step is getting your gear together. Make a list or see the appendix for my list -- at the minimum, the list will keep you from forgetting the toilet paper. At the maximum, it will put a lot of fun back into your vacation by taking out the futility.

You can add to that fun by being prepared to deal with two key elements: the weather and the sand.

When many people across the country envision this coast, they think of warm, sun-swept days. The truth is that at Northern California beaches, about half the days are foggy and cold.

Even on warm days, it is common for damp fog to cloak the coast during the night -- then break up by midmorning. This fog brings with it a penetrating cold, the kind that goes to the bones.

Thus, a tent is mandatory. And if you plan to camp on sand, make sure you have the kind of tent that doesn't need stakes.

Also make certain that you have a warm sleeping bag, and with it, some kind of ground pad, either a lightweight Ensolite pad or a more expensive Therm-A-Rest, to provide insulation. If you lay a sleeping bag directly on the ground or beach, the coldness of the ground will suck the warmth right out of you. By 2 a.m. you will feel like you are sleeping in a freezer, even in moderate temperatures.

Another key factor to an enjoyable trip is to play on the beach, rather than eat a good portion of it with every meal.

At state park beaches, picnic tables and food lockers are provided, so that task is easier. If you are freelancing it in a remote area, it becomes more difficult.

The answer is to have all food in separate, air-tight containers. This will allow you to set your food down at your picnic site without worrying about it tipping over and filling with sand.

Of course, sometimes disaster seems fated. One time I dropped a roasted hot dog on the beach, and it was so completely coated with sand that even my dog wouldn't eat it.

For the most part, however, beach camping is a unique and fun experience. But do remember a tide book. It might just keep you from getting a surprise dunking some night.

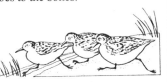

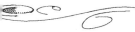

■ 1. Sunset State Beach (Monterey Bay):

Sunsets often look like they are imported from Hawaii at this park, a favorite for vacationers and a good alternative to Big Sur to the south. There are several good trails for short walks, and clamming can be good during low tides.

There are 90 spaces for tents or motor homes up to 35 feet long, each which comes with a picnic table.

Who to contact: For information, call Sunset State Beach at (408) 688-3241.

■ 2. Half Moon Bay State Beach (San Mateo County):

A pretty and popular spot, with tent campsites available on a grassy area instead of sand. It is a prime spot for a long beach walk, especially during low tides. A bonus is the nearby Pillar Point Harbor, located seven miles to the north, with a boat launch, sportfishing operations and quality restaurants.

The park has 51 sites for tents or motor homes, with piped water and restrooms provided.

Who to contact: Call Half Moon Bay State Beach at (415) 726-6238.

■ 3. Salt Point State Park (Sonoma County):

This is just far enough away from the Bay Area to give visitors a feeling of total separation from mass humanity. It is a great spot for abalone diving in season, beachcombing and quiet walks. Horseback riding rentals are available nearby.

The park has 40 tent sites, 30 motor home spaces, and 108 campsites for tents or motor homes, with all facilities provided at the park or nearby.

Who to contact: Call Salt Point State Park in Jenner at (707) 847-3221.

■ 4. Van Damme State Park (Mendocino County):

This park is at an ideal location for year-around adventures. You get an ocean frontage on one side and a forest on the other. Little River cuts through the park. In the winter, the nearby Noyo and Navarro can provide steelhead fishing.

The park has 71 campsites for tents or motor homes up to 35 feet long, with all facilities available at the park or nearby.

Who to contact: Call Van Damme State Park in Mendocino at (707) 937-5804.

■ 5. Patrick's Point State Park (Humboldt County):

This is a real favorite, with campsites set amid Sitka spruce, trails that tunnel through thick fern vegetation, and an agate beach, There are several ocean lookouts where visitors can spot migrating whales. It's often foggy and damp here, but always beautiful.

There are 123 campsites for tents or motor homes up to 31 feet long, with picnic tables, fireplaces, and piped water provided. Restrooms are also available.

Who to contact: Call Patrick's Point State Park in Trinidad at (707) 677-3570.

PHOTO
OPPORTUNITY

FITZGERALD MARINE
RESERVE

A POPULAR OUTDOOR CLASSROOM

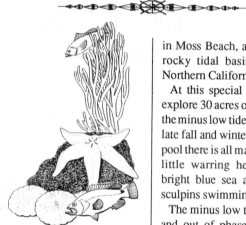

The closer you look, the better it gets. The problem is most people don't look close enough.

When you go tide-pool hopping, you either look close enough to see all the little sea critters playing their wars and games, or you see nothing. Most people take just the opposite perspective - - gazing off into the distant future. Along the Pacific Coast, you must instead focus on the moment or miss it forever.

There is no better place to do that than at Fitzgerald Marine Reserve in Moss Beach, although there are rocky tidal basins all along the Northern California coast.

At this special reserve, you can explore 30 acres of tidal reef during the minus low tides that arrive every late fall and winter. In almost every pool there is all manner of life, from little warring hermit crabs to a bright blue sea anemone to little sculpins swimming about.

The minus low tides will cycle in and out of phase on a two-week basis.

During a minus tide at Fitzgerald Marine Reserve, the Pacific Ocean will roll back, leaving pools, cuts and crevices filled with a few feet of sea water. You can walk on the exposed rock, probing the tide waters below as you go.

You don't have to worry about a sudden, giant wave hammering you from behind. On the outside edge of the tidal area, about 50 yards from the beach, there is a natural rock terrace that blunts attacks from

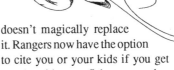

waves. So you don't have to worry about getting swept away. Neither do the critters that live here, all of them are protected from heavy ocean surge.

This is one of the most abundant and diverse regions of any kind in California. The ranger here says there are 200 species of marine animals, 150 of plants and 125 of gastropods, or mollusks. Just take a close look.

You don't need to be an oceanographer to enjoy it. The easiest critters to recognize are starfish, hermit crabs, rock crabs, sea anemones, sea urchins and zillions of different kinds of snails. For instance in one pool, we saw two hermit crabs trying to pick food from the edge of a giant aqua-colored sea anemone. The anemone just flinched its rubber-like tentacles, sending the hermit crabs on their way. It's all a lesson in detail, to see the world as a connection of many small living things, rather than just one, giant blob.

That's why 20,000 kids visit the marine reserve every year. It's become the most popular outdoor classroom in the Bay Area.

One lesson the rangers teach quickly here is to look, but not touch. That's hard for kids, particularly when they find a large starfish. The problem is that adult starfish average 15 to 25 years old, and when one is taken, another

doesn't magically replace it. Rangers now have the option to cite you or your kids if you get caught with a starfish or any other marine creature.

But hook-and-line fishing is permitted because studies have demonstrated that sportfishing has no impact on fish populations here. Part of that is because of the difficulty of the sport.

If you show up with your fishing rod and cast out a bait, you will inevitably find yourself snagging on the reef and every single cast, losing your gear and wanting to quit the sport forever.

A better technique is called "poke-poling." You use a long calcutta pole or its equivalent, like a worn-out CB antenna, and tie a three-inch piece of wire and a 2/0 hook on the end. Then place a small piece of squid bait on the hook, and poke the pole in crevices, under ledges and in any deep holes on the outer edge of the tidal basin.

While other people are snagging, you can catch sea trout, cabezone, lingcod, and eels with this unique method. As in tidepooling, the best fishing is during the minus low tides.

This area is also a favorite for scuba divers, abalone pickers, and plain ol' beach-walkers.

Just remember to look close -- you don't want to miss it.

HINTS FOR GREAT TIDE-POOL HOPPING

How to get there: From the north, take Highway 280 or Highway 101 to Highway 1, and continue on through Pacifica over Devil's Slide and into Moss Beach. The turnoff is well signed. From the East Bay, Peninsula and south, take Highway 92 into Half Moon Bay, then head north on Highway 1 seven miles to Moss Beach.

Trip Cost: Entry is free.

Best times: Prime times are during the minus low tides throughout the year.

Tips: Dogs are prohibited. Wear good-gripping rubber-soled shoes.

Who to contact: For information, call the Fitzgerald Marine Reserve at (415) 728-3584, or contact the San Mateo County Parks & Recreation Department at (415) 363-4020.

COASTAL FUN

ANO NUEVO
STATE PARK

THE LIFE OF AN ELEPHANT SEAL

It's not easy being an elephant seal these days, not even during the annual migration to Ano Nuevo State Reserve south of Pescadero.

For one thing, a fella has about a one-in-three chance of going through life without making love even once. You can get so lonely. Then, just when you spotted lovely Brunhilda lying on the beach, and she wiggled her cute whiskers at you, some big ol' 5,000-pound lummox comes along and bites you in the neck.

And you never know what those female elephant seals are really thinking. Why just the other day, lovely Brunhilda, that 1,800-pound, slug-like mass of beauty, had to be thrown down, bitten in the neck, then held down with a flipper when all you wanted was just to talk to her.

But look at it from the other side. It's no easy thing being a lady elephant seal, either. Why it's so hard to keep from getting skinny after childbirth -- you lose two pounds for every pound little Henry gains. And it is so embarrassing being on the beach in front of all the guys, you know, being so skinny.

And those male seals never know what they want. Why just a day after Brunhilda let Albert bite her, she saw him giving several other younger female elephant seals the flipper treatment. And they were so ugly, so skinny. But they were just lying there on the beach like they were dead and Albert couldn't resist them.

Then there's Junior. He's so darn hungry all the time, he might eat you right out of your own beach. Of course, he was a big baby, a 75-pounder, and it looks like he'll

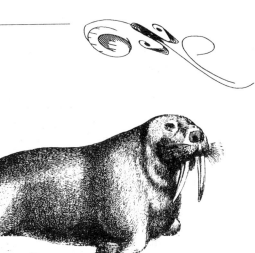

make 300 pounds as a 4-week-old. After that, it's adios, time to head out and get squid on his own.

See you next winter, that is, unless you get eaten. You heard, eh? Right, good ol' Wendy, that beautiful mass of flesh, ended up in the stomach of a Great White shark last summer. Oooh, she used to drive the guys crazy, the way she'd flip sand on her back. Oh well, win some, lose some.

What the heck, there are better things to think about. Like the annual winter get together at Ano Nuevo State Reserve. Last year thousands of elephant seals showed up and it was a wild one. It's hard to forget how Brunhilda went crazy when Big Mike picked her out and then just about crushed her to death -- right on the beach in front of everybody.

You know Big Mike, he's just under 20 feet long and leaves the biggest trail in the sand of any elephant seal in Northern California. He's also got the biggest nose in the state and it drives the women insane.

Ano Nuevo is about 20 miles south of Pescadero, just off Highway 1, about a 45-minute drive from San Francisco. Of course, elephant seals take the sea route to get there every winter. They start arriving in December. Then the beach starts to get crowded and the fights get pretty good. But the wise few know that the real big and tough old-timers, like Big Mike and Albert, arrive then and take charge. One of their favorite tactics is to

wait until the younger guys bite each other to bloodied pulps, then move in and trounce the young upstarts in their weakened state and steal their women.

Everybody knows you can get bigger harems that way. Heck, Big Mike had about 50 last year in his.

Watching the people is another hobby. What the people do is walk in small groups on a roped-off path through the animals.

But any elephant seal knows the old "play dead" trick. You see, a lot of these people will try to take close-up pictures, but they forget to bring a telephoto lens. So the strategy is to lie there, pretending you're asleep, and let the person get pretty close to you for the picture. Right when they start to relax, you suddenly raise up in a mass of blubber, let out a funny noise, and then make a few quick squirms toward them.

They'll run away like they were wearing pork chop underwear and were being chased by a pit bull.

But that's about as exciting as it gets for an elephant seal, that and wondering if it was really you that Brunhilda wiggled her whiskers at.

After all, being a sea elephant isn't all fun and games. There's a serious side to it.

☛ ANO NUEVO TRIP NOTES

How to get there: Ano Nuevo State Reserve is located just west of Highway 1, about a 45-minute drive from San Francisco.

SamTrans buses: SamTrans offers Saturday and Sunday tour packages. Advance reservations are required. Call (415) 348-SEAL for information.

Trip cost: Tickets for the guided tours are $4, and a parking fee of $3 per car is also charged.

Ticketron: Reservations are required through Ticketron outlets. For information on the nearest outlet, phone (415) 546-9400. No self-guided tours are permitted until May, when most of the elephant seals have departed.

Length of walk: The tour is about three miles long. A shorter route is wheelchair accessible.

Who to contact: Call Ano Nuevo State Reserve at (415) 879-0454.

COASTAL FUN

PESCADERO
MARSH

BRAKING FOR WILDLIFE

Zillions of folks speed down Highway 1 on weekend drives to Santa Cruz, but only a wise few put their foot to the brakes instead of the gas peddle when they reach Pescadero. Those few have a secret. If you listen close, you can learn about it.

Sitting just east of the highway is a vast natural marsh area, 600 acres in all, which has a quiet trail winding its way around it. It may provide the best area in Northern California to see the great blue heron. It is hikable by almost anybody. And its is one of the most overlooked wildlife areas in the Bay Area. The kicker is that after your walk, you can put on the feed bag at Duarte's Restaurant, which can just about match anything Santa Cruz has to offer.

State rangers say that the Pescadero Marsh is one of the few remaining natural marsh areas on the entire central California coast. For that reason, it is critical that you not wander off the trail and unknowingly let your feet destroy any of this classic habitat. The trail is almost flat, which makes it an easy walk for almost anyone of any age. It routes you amid pampas grass, pickleweed, bogs, and almost all the while, birds of a surprising variety. It is the main stopover for the birds of the Pacific coastal flyway, as well as home for a good population of year-round residents.

You do not need to be a "bird watcher" to enjoy the scene. However, if you have binoculars, bring them. During the year some 250 different species of birds use the marsh. The most impressive is the blue heron, a magnificent creature that stands almost four feet tall with a wingspan of seven feet. The sight of a few of them lifting off is a classic picture. They fly with labored wing beats, which makes them appear even bigger. Pescadero Marsh is one of the prime nesting grounds for the blue heron.

Other unique birds sighted here include the snowy egret, a pure white, frail-looking fellow that seems to spook easily, and the night heron, a bird that seems to have all its features squeezed together; short necked, short legs, short bill. The distinct appearances of these coastal birds seems to give them a personable character, especially in the case of the night heron. After awhile, they seem like old friends.

The marsh is bordered by the Pacific Ocean on one side, and Pescadero Creek on another, so the result is a unique setting that can attract birds that live in both saltwater and freshwater environments.

And after your walk, there is no reason to get back on the Highway 1 treadmill and hightail it to Santa Cruz for eats. Not with Pescadero's historic Duarte's Restaurant, a place ingrained with a coastal tradition that offers outstanding homemade bread, artichoke soup and full dinners. Those "in the know" have learned that

makes for memorable moments.

Most people believe you have to put your foot to the gas peddle and keep it there to find a secret spot. In the case of the Pescadero Marsh, however, it is a matter of putting your foot to the brakes.

☛ PESCADERO MARSH TRIP FACTS

How to get there: From Highway 280, 92, or 84, head west to Highway 1, then turn south and continue past Half Moon Bay. Pescadero Marsh is located just northeast of the Pescadero turnoff, 18 miles south of Half Moon Bay.
Trip Cost: Access is free.
Duarte's: For reservations to Duarte's Restaurant in Pescadero, call (415) 879-0464.
Who to call: For general information, call the state park office in Half Moon Bay at (415) 726-6238.

COASTAL FUN

THREE WAYS TO WATCH WHALES

LAND, SEA & AIR

At first, all you see is what looks like a little puff of smoke on the ocean surface. Out of the corner of your eye you spot it, and your attention becomes riveted to the spot like a magnet on steel. A closer look -- and there it is again -- but it quickly disappears.

You watch, waiting, but the sea is quiet. A row or cormorant glides past, a dozen murres are paddling around, and for a moment you forget why you're out here on the briny blue. Then your daydreams are popped by a giant tail, the size of a lifeboat, breaking the sea surface.

A moment later, the head and back of a gray whale surges into view.

After you have seen a whale -- a real, live friendly sea monster -- you will never again look at the ocean in quite the same way. Anybody who saw Humphrey in the Bay or Delta will attest to this. By seeing a whale you often regain the feeling that this world of ours is still a place where great things are possible. Because a whale is one of those things.

And there are 18,000 of them swimming along the California coast through the first of the year, cruising 50 to 100 miles per day within the range of charter boats, small airplanes and many shoreline lookouts. Seeing one not only makes you feel special, but can instill the kind of excitement that will stay with you for many years. Every time you look at the ocean, you will remember it.

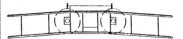

These giant air-breathing creatures average more than 40 feet long and 30 tons. They do not act threatened and will often pace alongside a boat, spouting, occasionally emerging to show their backs. As they gain confidence they may fin you -- give you a tail salute -- and if you're particularly lucky, do a half breech in your full view. In one spectacular 20-minute sequence off the Half Moon Bay coast, I saw 10 or 15 huge humpback whales leaping completely out of the water in full 180-degree pirouettes. They landed in gigantic splashes on their backs beside the boat, perhaps trying to clean off the barnacles. Now and then, a pair would even crisscross like Wilkinson Sword Blades in front of our path. This occurred while on a fishing trip, and it was just luck that we ran into the rare humpbacks.

However, there is little luck involved in spotting gray whales.

The gray whale migration is a 5,000-mile trip from Arctic waters to Baja, a migratory route that brings them along the Bay Area coast from January through April. You don't need a boat or airplane to see them, but it can help.

Northern Airventures offers whale watching from a seaplane, a fantastic adventure. The price is $60 per person for an hour. This plane will cruise across the open ocean in search of the tell-tale spouts that indicate a whale's position. After one is spotted, the plane will zero in on it.

Since the whales cruise along the surface, from a seat in a plane you can often see the entire top of the whale from snout to tail, or at least a silhouette of its body. That's quite a different experience from a boat, where you must wait for the whale to poke through the sea surface.

Another advantage is since you are not on the water, the whale senses no vibrations or motor noise, such as produced from a boat. This allows you to approach completely undetected.

If you don't like the $65 price tag or the idea of flying in a small plane, a whale-watching boat is the next best world. Some whales seem attracted by the big boats and will play tag with you on the southern route, disappearing and reappearing several times over the course of an hour.

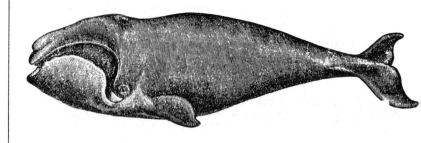

Skippers have learned that most gray whales will follow a migratory course from Point Reyes on southward past the Farallon Islands near the continental shelf. Most skippers will start the day by heading to Point Reyes and then heading south, hoping to pick up some whales and cruise parallel to them for many miles.

worn behind the ear by commercial fishermen and Naval officers.

The final option is to skip the boat or plane and drive to a lookout along the coast. However, don't expect to see much of the whales. You will see whales from considerable distances blowing their steam. Still, even from afar, it's an exciting affair. From the San Mateo County coast at Pigeon Point, I have seen as

Whale-watching trips by boat cost an average of about $25 out of Fisherman's Wharf, Sausalito or Bodega Bay. Trips of shorter range out of Half Moon and Monterey Bay cost $15 and $10, respectively.

Before boarding a large vessel for an ocean cruise, you'd be well advised to take a seasick preventative. The best on the market is called Sea-Tone, which has in it the same drug used in prescription patches

many as 200 whale spouts before we stopped counting.

The best vista points are from the bluffs at Davenport in Santa Cruz County; Pigeon Point, San Gregorio or Pillar Point in San Mateo County; or the tip of Point Reyes in Marin County.

Binoculars and a clear day can do wonders.

And if you see Humphrey, try to keep him on course.

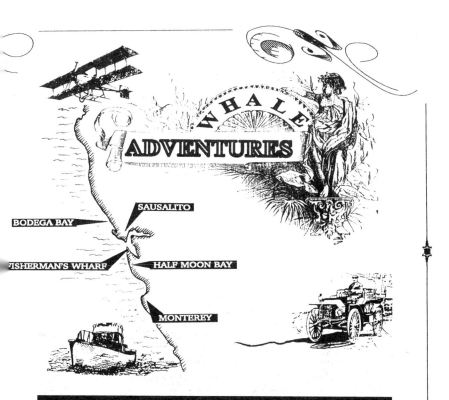

WHALE ADVENTURES

BODEGA BAY

SAUSALITO

FISHERMAN'S WHARF

HALF MOON BAY

MONTEREY

☞ **INFORMATION**

General information: Call the Oakland Whale Center in Oakland at (415) 654-6621.

Monterey: Call Sam's Charters in Monterey at (408) 372-0577; $10 for adults, $5 for children under 12.

Half Moon Bay: Call Huck Finn at (415) 726-7133 or Capt. John's at (415) 726-2913; $15 for adults, $10 for children under 12.

Fisherman's Wharf: Call Wacky Jacky at (415) 586-9800, Butchie B at (415) 457-8388, or Easy Rider at (415) 285-2000. Trips cost in the $20 range.

Sausalito: Call Salty Lady at (415) 348-2107 or New Ray Ann at (415) 584-1498; trips cost in the $20 range.

Bodega Bay: Call the Challenger at (707) 875-3344; trips cost $17.50 for adults.

Aerial flights: Plane flights out of Pillar Point Harbor can be arranged by calling the Oakland Whale Center at (415) 726-2903.

COASTAL FUN

HALF MOON BAY

A 10-MILE ANACHRONISM

Depending on which eye you look out of, the San Mateo County coast can provide something you might be searching for.

Out of one eye, you might see the Half Moon Bay coast as something of an anachronism; small towns, dirt streets, cowboys on horseback, and sprawling fields of Brussels sprouts give rise to thoughts of an earlier time. In a 10-mile area quality fishing, horseback riding, hiking and camping are available.

But out of the other eye, you might see quite a different picture: Expensive seaside restaurants, crowded roads, and on sunny days, beaches packed with folks for whom life's desires seem to end with a suntan and a drink.

Because Half Moon Bay can satisfy people with opposite interests, it has become one of the most popular places for a weekend visit.

Close? By Highway 92, its only 12 miles from San Mateo, 27 miles from Hayward. Via Highway 1,

Half Moon Bay sits 13 miles from Daly City, and from San Francisco starting from Highway 280, it's about 20 miles away. But there's a catch, of course. Because the highways are two-laners with no passing, one slow vehicle of any design will jam up traffic for miles and it will look like a parade of frustrated gerbils.

The centerpiece of the area is Pillar Point Harbor at Princeton. Salmon and deep sea fishing trips on sportfishing vessels are offered here for $30, a boat ramp ($6 launch fee) is available, and several fine restaurants ring the harbor. Many folks like the walk down Princeton Pier to look at the boats, and in the afternoon, watch fishermen return from with the day's catch.

But if it's walking that you like, then head instead to the Fitzgerald Marine Reserve in Moss Beach -- or at the northern end of Montara at McNee State Park. The Marine Reserve offers an extensive

tidepool system. When the ocean rolls back on low tides, unveiled are miles of tidepools -- and suddenly visible is the unique seal life within. Access and parking is free. At McNee State Park, from sea level you can hike to the top of Montara Mountain and its spectacular vistas, a gut-buster of a climb of 2,000 feet in 3.8 miles. Access is also free.

If you want someone else's feet to take you, horse rentals are available just north of Half Moon Bay, on the west side of Highway 1. Riding a horse along the beach here can be a classic trip, though the horses seem to be on automatic pilot when your time's up and it comes to returning to the barn. On weekends you may have to wait an hour before getting your mount.

The most overlooked element of the area is camping at Half Moon Bay State Beach, which seems to be taken advantage of primarily by out-of-towners touring Highway 1. The cost is $10 per night, and it's one of the closest campgrounds to the San Francisco Peninsula.

The beaches along the coast here can really be packed on warm sunny days, so if you're heading to the beach, wear some kind of footwear to protect yourself from broken glass hidden in the sand.

In most cases, however, the problems are few, and the adventures and scenic backdrop outstanding. In many ways, Half Moon Bay can seem the perfect place to be.

☛ HALF MOON BAY TRIP FACTS

Fishing: Deep sea and salmon fishing trips are offered at Pillar Point Harbor by Huck Finn Sportfishing, (415) 726-5677, and Capt. John's Sportfishing, (415) 728-3377. Most trips cost in the $30 range.

Marine reserve: The Fitzgerald Marine Reserve is located in Moss Beach, with a well-signed turnoff on Highway 1. Access is free. For information, call (415) 728-3584.

Horseback riding: Horse rentals are available at Sea Horse Ranch (408) 726-2362 and Friendly Acres (415) 726-9871. Trip cost ranges from $10 per hour for horses, or $2.50 for 15 minutes for kids on ponies.

Camping: Campsites are available at Half Moon Bay State Beach for $10 per vehicle. For information, call (415) 726-6238.

Hiking: To hike Montara Mountain, park at the northern most end of Montara, just south of Devil's Slide, and enter McNee State Park -- which is marked only by a gravel road with a pipe gate across it, and a small yellow state park sign. Access is free. For information, call (415) 726-6238.

COASTAL FUN

COASTSIDE HORSEBACK
RIDING

SITTING TALL IN THE SADDLE

If you have dreams of the days of open rangeland and watching sunsets from a saddle, there's still a path for you -- and a horse waiting as well in the coastside town of Half Moon Bay. For $10, you can put a cowboy boot in a stirrup, saddle up and literally ride off into the sunset.

You don't have to be John Wayne, and even if you have never ridden before, the cowboys at Friendly Acres Ranch will find a horse to match your ability. For small children, Friendly Acres provides a special pony corral, where $2.50 will get junior 15 minutes with Old Paint. Should junior start to get visions of the Grand National, another buck will get him 15 more minutes.

Horseback riding is remarkably popular in Half Moon Bay, an area that is something of an anachronism, where dirt streets, hometown post offices, and vast farms give the coast its special brand of country -- all just on the edge of the Bay Area. And one way to share in this is to hop in the saddle and go trotting on down to the beach. With 80 horses and eight ponies to pick from, finding a relatively fresh and well-mannered horse to match your size and experience is not a problem.

One Sunday afternoon I climbed aboard Moon, a big, strong horse which gives the rider a sense of cowboy outlaw spirit that Waylon Jennings captures in song. Ol' Moon and me trotted on out to the beach and watched the sun sink clean into the Pacific Ocean, the light refracting for miles across the water. Behind us, a special hue of orange was cast across Montara Mountain, and any moment I ex-

pected Waylon to come by and singing, "Don't let your babies grow up to be cowboys."

Well, I've always felt you shouldn't let your cowboys grow up to be babies. I almost started singing "Luckenbach Texas," but Moon suddenly decided that with the sun down, it was time to head for the barn.

Over yonder, a buddy of mine, Dave Zimmer, was experiencing a similar phenomenon, his horse heading hell-bent for leather for the barn. "Slow doooown," he yelled at his horse. Dave hanging onto the big saddle horn with both hands, the reins flapping loosely. "I'm outta control," he shouted, disappearing around a bend.

Up until this point, the relationship between Moon and me had been something like the Lone Ranger and Silver. I mean, whenever Moon would pull his ears back and snort, I would pat him on the neck and say, "Good horsey," and he would behave.

But after that sun went down and my buddy disappeared, no matter how many "good horsies," it did no good. With a snort, Moon had decided the hour was up and he was heading for the barn as well. He knew there was some hay waiting for him, and that it was time for me to get a little shuteye.

☞ COASTSIDE HORSEBACK RIDING TRIP FACTS

How to get there: From the north, take Highway 1 past Princeton Harbor. From the east, take Highway 92 to Half Moon Bay, then head north on Highway 1 for three miles. Friendly Acres Ranch is on the west side of Highway 1, between the city of Half Moon Bay and the town of Miramar, and is signed.

Trip Cost: Horse rentals cost $10 for an hour. Pony rentals in a corral for children cost $2.50 for 15 minutes, $3.50 for a half-hour.

Trip Tip: Get a horse that matches your riding ability -- and never abuse the animals.

Who to contact: For information, call Friendly Acres Ranch at (415) 726-9871.

COASTAL FUN

MONTEREY BAY

COMBINING THE BEST OF NORTH & SOUTH

CANNERY ROW

BY

JOHN STEINBECK

A unique niche called Monterey has been carved on the California coast.

The area seems to stand apart from the rest of California, both north and south. Monterey takes the best of both worlds, Southern California's weather and Northern California's rural beauty, and offers it as the ideal short vacation spot for Bay Area residents.

The area became famous in the early 1940s because of Steinbeck's Cannery Row. But after the sardine industry was wiped out by overkill

in 1948, Monterey became better known as a hangout for the rich and seclusive. For many, it has taken the opening of the Monterey Aquarium to draw them back to the area.

And people like what they see. There is as much variety for outdoor recreation as any place in the state. Spring is the best time to visit, when the salmon are still swimming along inshore areas, the hills are green, and fields of wildflowers are in full bloom.

The Monterey Aquarium can be the focus of a multiday trip to the area. The giant tanks are like glass houses, where people are allowed an inside view to all the levels of marine life in Monterey Bay. Recreations of a kelp forest, deep reefs, and a sea otter playpen are the big attractions. But the sideshows are just as fascinating.

For example, you can dip your hands in the water and touch a stingray or look through a microscope at tiny sea creatures.

A three-hour aquarium tour can provide the inspiration for several miniadventures. You can take what you've seen on a small scale at the aquarium and expand it to the wild outdoors. A sampling includes fishing, hiking, whale watching, scuba diving, ocean kayaking, or camping on a beach or in a forest. Take your pick.

Monterey Bay is cut by a deep underwater canyon that extends west from Moss Landing. For years fishermen have had great success here, and exhibits at the aquarium explain why. The 5,000-foot deep canyon generates nutrient-rich water that sets off one of the West Coast's most diverse marine systems.

Right in Monterey Bay, good runs of salmon arrive every spring from the north, and by mid-summer, schools of albacore come from the south. It's the best of both worlds. On a typical trip, fishermen aboard the Point Sir Clipper can score limits of salmon. It trolls just offshore from Moss Landing.

Because the Monterey Peninsula juts out into the Pacific Ocean, it is a prime area for whale watching, by boat or by shore. Point Pinos, Cypress Point, Point Lobos or the Asilomar State Beach in Pacific Grove all provide lookouts for whales. Sightings should remain good through April.

Monterey is known for its first-class and expensive lodging and restaurants, but during the warm days of spring and summer, a camp-out is a good alternative.

You have your pick of parks set on ocean frontage or in pine trees. Coastal state parks on Monterey Bay's shoreline include Sunset, Seacliff and New Brighton State Beach. If you want trees, Big Sur State Park is located south of Monterey on Highway 1. If you want more solitude, you can take it to the outback in Los Padres National Forest.

Monterey Bay is a remarkable area, and you can sense it just by watching the waves roll in. The water seems a deeper blue than anywhere along the California coast. It has a tranquilizing effect.

You can search the Pacific Coast and find few places that come close to matching it.

☛ MONTEREY TRIP TIPS

Monterey Aquarium: Located at the north end of Cannery Row, the aquarium is open from 10 a.m. to 6 p.m. daily. Admission is $7 for adults, and $3 for kids 12 and under. For more information, call (408) 375-3333 or (408) 649-1770.

Fishing: Salmon and rockfishing trips are available on the Point Sir Clipper. For information, call Sam's Sportfishing at (408) 372-0577.

Whale Watching: Sightings should remain frequent through the first of the year. Chris' Charters, (408) 375-5951 makes whale-watching trips. By shoreline, Point Pinos and Asilomar State Beach are prime lookouts.

Scuba Diving: Reefs and the underwater trench are rich marine regions that are top areas to explore. For information, call Bamboo Reef at (408) 372-1685, or Aquarius Diver at (408) 375-1933.

Ocean Kayaking: You might have a sea otter as your partner. Instructions and rentals are available from Sea Trek. For information, call (408) 372-2772.

Big Sur State Park: One of California's top state parks, it's located off Highway 1 just south of Monterey. For information, call (408) 667- 2316.

Beach Camping: Camping by the bay is available at Marine Dunes, Sunset, Seacliff, and New Brighton State Beaches. For information, call California Department of Parks at (408) 649-2836.

Hiking/Backpacking: Hundreds of miles of trails cut through Los Padres National Forest, which is located just inland from Big Sur State Park. For information, call (408) 385-5434.

Lodging/Restaurants: For a list of Monterey's accommodations, call the Monterey Chamber of Commerce at (408) 649-1770.

EIGHT MENDOCINCO COAST
ADVENTURES

QUIET ON THE SEASHORE

The Mendocino coast is so quiet you can practically hear the flowers bloom.

Without driving very far in terms of miles, it's about as far as you can get from the Bay Area in terms of style. Three hours up Highway 101 and over to the coast on Highway 128 and you enter a new world. Instead of concrete, condos and traffic jams, you get redwoods, wildflowers and miles of untouched Pacific Coast.

But more than anything else, you get quiet. It doesn't matter what you

choose to do -- walk the beaches, watch for whale spouts, hike the redwood forests or explore little towns like Elk or Mendocino -- you get quiet. You can camp in a forest, rent a hotel room for a night or book at an expensive coastal inn. It doesn't matter. You get quiet.

It's just what many Bay Area residents need and that makes the Mendocino coast an ideal retreat. Spring is a perfect time to visit because the whale migration is in full swing, all kinds of wildflowers are blooming in the nearby hills and the air is sparkling clean.

The coast has a different look to it here than along points to the south. In many areas, giant blocks of rock tower in the ocean shallows, rocks that look like they have been sculptured by an angry giant with a hammer and chisel, complete with tunnels and cutaways. They give the area a rugged, primitive feel.

Ocean and redwoods, you get it all on the Mendocino coast:

■ Van Damme State Park:

One of the coast's best hikes is here. It's the Fern Canyon Trail, a gently sloping 5-miler that cuts along the bottom of a lush creek. Because the park is located in a perfect setting for car campers heading up Highway 1, many people discover this hike by accident in the summer. You can beat the traffic though by going in the spring.

Who to contact: Call Mendocino Parks at (707) 937-5804.

■ Whale watching:

See what looks like a puff of smoke on the ocean surface? Look closer. It's more likely a whale spout, and watching the annual whale migration is one of the area's more popular events. In April, Fort Bragg hosts the Mendocino Whale Festival, which includes an arts and craft show and a two-mile run. Big ocean-going boats run whale watching trips through April out of Fort Bragg.

Who to contact: For more information, call the Fort Bragg Chamber of Commerce at (707) 964-3153, or Sportsman's Dock at (707) 964-4550.

■ Fishing:

Some of Northern California's best deep-sea fishing is out of Noyo Harbor in Fort Bragg. Fishermen catch many species of rockfish, along with lingcod and cabezone. By summer, salmon becomes king. At times the area gets some of the best salmon fishing on the Pacific Coast. Because salmon from the Klamath River migrate as far south as Fort Bragg and salmon from the Sacramento River migrate as far north as Fort Bragg, it's like fishing two runs of fish at the same time.

Who to contact: For more information, call Sportsman's Dock at (707) 964-4550.

■ Hiking:

Some 40 of the Mendocino coast's best walks are detailed in the book, "The Hiker's Guide to the Mendocino Coast." Most of the walks suggested are two or three miles and set in Mendocino County's most beautiful coastal areas.

Who to contact: The book is available for $10 from Bored Feet, P.O. Box 1832, Mendocino, CA 95460.

■ Coastal Inns:

On the more than 100 miles of coast, from Westport to Gualala, there are about 70 lodgings, varying from little countryside inns to more standard hotels in town, to vacation cottage rentals.

Who to contact: For more information, write Coast Chamber, P.O. Box 1141, Fort Bragg, CA 95437, or phone (707) 964-3153.

■ Camping:

There are 25 public and private campgrounds along the Mendocino coast. The settings include redwood forests, such as at Russian Gulch State Park, (707) 937-5804, near Point Cabrillo Lighthouse, or beach frontage, such as at Wages Creek, (707) 964-2964, at Westport.

Who to contact: For a listing, write Coast Chamber, P.O. Box 1141, Fort Bragg, CA 95437. Or check out the book California Camping which describes 1500 campgrounds throughout the state (Foghorn Press, San Francisco).

■ Ocean kayaking:

Sound crazy to you? It's not. It's fun, exhilarating and anybody can do it.

Who to contact: Rentals are available at Big River Lodge. Call (707) 937-5615.

■ Horseback riding:

Trails lead either into the redwood forest or to the beach at Ricochet Ridge Ranch which is located near Cleone. In addition, special horse-pack trips can be booked into the Mendocino mountain wildlands.

Who to contact: For more information, call Ricochet Ranch at (707) 964-PONY.

There are other activities, like visiting the wine country, photographing the coast, cruising the craft shops, but you get the idea.

After a few days here, your biggest problem in visiting Mendocino is you may never want to leave. After all, quiet is an easy thing to get used to.

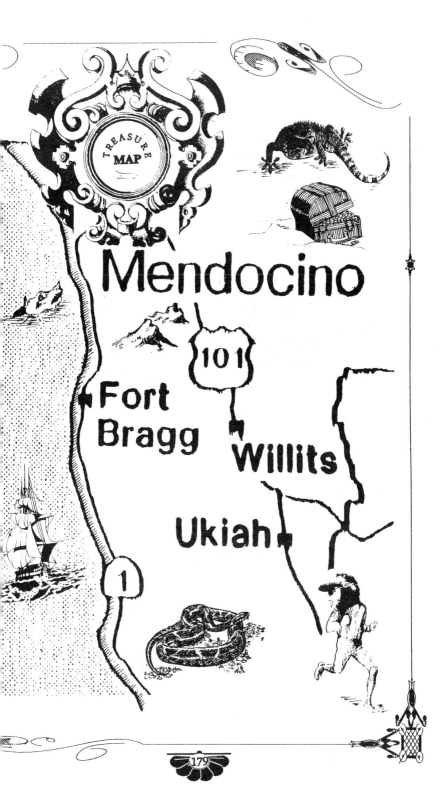

TREASURE MAP

Mendocino

101

Fort Bragg

Willits

Ukiah

1

COASTAL FUN

PATRICK'S POINT
STATE PARK

TUNNELS THROUGH VEGETATION

Patrick's Point State Park is a remarkable stretch of turf carved out of California's north coast. You get the best of both worlds. It's loaded with a classic fern undergrowth, yet bordered by the rockstrewn Pacific, where you can go tide pool hopping, rock fishing, and whale watching.

But what makes Patrick's Point unique is its virtual wall-to-wall plant growth within the park's 625 acres. Often the trails are nothing more than tunnels through vegetation. Hikers can become completely sheltered and isolated by the mammoth walls of ferns. The first time I stopped here was back in 1978, and like most folks, it was more by accident than intent. We just wanted a campsite for the night while on a fishing trip to the Klamath River (40 miles north), but got much more.

The park sits adjacent to Highway 101, and from the road, you have little idea of the beauty sheltered here. It's always a stunner for first-timers. It's like a rain forest jungle, where the dense undergrowth can only be experienced by foot. The Rim Trail, an easy two-miler, follows the edge of the bluff around three sides of the park, and short yet steep cutoffs can take walkers to the best vistas in the park -- Wedding Rock, Palmer's Point, Patrick's Point, and Agate Beach. From these lookout, it is common to spot migrating gray whales. It's nearly a year-long adventure here. Spring and fall are best for whale watching, however, because the air can be crystal clear.

During the summer, dense fog can cover Patrick's Point, as well as the tourists within. Water droplets trickle from the ferns and tourist's noses, and many folks believe it to be raining. It isn't; just fogging. This drip-drip, low visibility stuff

only rarely envelops Patrick's Point in spring and fall.

The muggy days of Indian summer set off the warmest days of the year here.

Four campgrounds offer 123 campsites, and like most state parks, they come with a sturdy table, barbecue stove, and cupboard. Water faucets and restrooms with hot showers are provided a short walking distance away from each campground. Play it safe and get a reservation.

A good idea is to plan your trip for when a low tide will roll back the Pacific and unveil the tide pools. Tiny marine organisms will conduct their little wars at your feet, as you hop from one pool to another. In addition, fishermen will discover good prospects for lingcod, cabezone, and sea trout during low tides, because one can walk to the outer reaches of the tidal basin. On high tides, on the other hand, anglers will be casting into a shallow, rocky sea floor where a snag per cast is the likely result.

It isn't often that you have a chance to come to Patrick's Point. For this reason, a side trip to Agate Beach is a necessity. Here you will find a shoreline, loaded with semi-precious stones polished by centuries of sand and water.

Pick one up and put it in your pocket. Someday when you're going undergoing a day of frustration, the little rock in your pocket will provide a connection to a day of happiness and near contentment.

☞ **PATRICK'S POINT STATE PARK TRIP FACTS**

How to get there: Simply take Highway 101 straight up the coast. Patrick's Point is located about 40 minutes north of Eureka, about 10 miles beyond Trinidad.
Driving time: From San Francisco, if you leave at 6 a.m., figure to be there by at least 1 p.m., including a stop for breakfast -- about 6-1/2 hours.
Trip Cost: The charge for campsites is $10 per night.
Reservations: Camping reservations are made through Mistix at (800) 444-7275.
Who to contact: The park can be reached by phoning (707) 677- 3570, or by writing Patrick's Point State Park, Trinidad, CA 95570. North Coast headquarters for state parks can be reached at (707) 443-4588.

CHAPTER 4

BAY AREA LAKES

WITH

12 ADVENTURES

CONTENTS:—

PUBLISHED BY FOGHORN PRESS

SAN FRANCISCO

QUALITY OUTDOOR BOOKS

BAY AREA
LAKE–BY–LAKE ROUNDUP

A FISHERMAN'S RESOURCE

H ere are 26 Bay Area Lakes with fishing potential.

■ Alpine Lake (Marin County):

This foothill lake has a small population of large resident trout. It offers good bass fishing from March through May. No boats are allowed. No fish stocks.

Who to contact: For more information, call (415) 456-5454.

■ Lake Anderson (Morgan Hill):

This once-giant lake, purposely drained by the local water district, is expected to fill during the winter.

Who to contact: For more information, call (408) 463-0711

■ Bon Tempe Lake (Marin County):

This lake is stocked with eight to 11-inch trout by Fish and Game in winter.

Who to contact: For more information, call either (415) 459-0888 or (415) 456-5454.

■ Campbell Perc Pond (Campbell):

It's stocked with catchable rainbow trout by Fish and Game.

Who to contact: For more information, call (415) 688-6340.

■ Calero Reservoir (Coyote):

A health warning on eating fish (mercury) has made this a catch-and-release recreational fishery for small bass and catfish. No stocks in years.
Who to contact: For more information, call (408) 463-0711.

CAUTION

■ Lake Chabot (Castro Valley):

Shorefishing for rainbow trout at Coot Landing, Indian Cove. There's big bass.
Who to contact: For more information, call (415) 582-2198.

■ Chesbro Dam (Coyote):

There's some crappie along corners of the dam and in the coves.
Who to contact: For more information, call (408) 463-0711.

■ Contra Loma Reservoir (Antioch):

A few fishermen take occasional striped bass to 22 inches by casting deep-running shad lures along the east shore.
Who to contact: For more information, call (415) 757-0404.

■ Cottonwood Lake (San Jose):

It's stocked with eight to 11-inch trout.
Who to contact: For more information, call the ranger at (408) 225-0225.

■ Coyote Reservoir (Coyote):

It has some trout stocks in winter and some bass.
Who to contact: For more information, call (408) 463-0711.

■ Cull Canyon Reservoir (Castro Valley):

This is a longshot for small catfish. No trout stocks.
Who to call: For more information, call (415) 531-9300, Ext. 2208.

■ Del Valle Reservoir (Livermore):

There's good trout fishing from the narrows on up toward the dam.
Who to contact: For more information, call (415) 449-5201.

■ Don Castro Reservoir (Hayward):

It's stocked with eight to 11-inch trout.
Who to contact: For more information, call (415) 531-9300, Ext. 2208.

■ Lake Isabel (Pleasanton):

This lake has the highest catch rate in state with a four trout-per-rod average. There is an access fee.
Who to contact: For more information, call (415) 462-1281.

Lafayette Reservoir (Lafayette):

Stocked by Department of Fish and Game with trout, this lake offers good prospects.
Who to contact: For more information, call (415) 284-9669.

Lagunitas Lake (Marin County):

This lake has been converted to support a self-sustaining trout fishery. Designed by Cal Trout, it has strict catch regulations.
Who to contact: For more information, call (415) 392-8887, or the ranger station at (415) 459-5267.

Lake Merced (San Francisco):

Heavily stocked, this lake boasts trophy-size trout.
Who to contact: For more information, call (415) 753-1101.

Parkway Lake (Coyote):

Parkway produces more trout weighing five pounds or better than any other lake. There is an access fee.
Who to contact: For more information, call (415) 463-0383.

Phoenix Lake (Marin):

Stocked by Department of Fish and Game with eight to 11-inch trout.
Who to contact: For more information, call (415) 456-5454.

Pinto Lake (Watsonville):

This can be an excellent lake for crappie and trout.
Who to contact: For more information, call (408) 722-8129.

San Pablo Reservoir (El Sobrante):

The reservoir is stocked heavily with rainbow trout from eight inches to five pounds. Bass fishing is an option.
Who to contact: For more information, call (415) 223-1661.

Sandy Wool Reservoir (San Jose):

This ranch pond has been converted to a park and trout lake. It's stocked with catchable-size trout by Fish and Game.
Who to contact: For more information, call the Fish and Game at (415) 688-6340.

Shadow Cliffs Reservoir (Pleasanton):

Once a water hole for a rock quarry, this lake has been converted to a park and now provides good fishing at the end of the panhandle. Stocked by the Department of Fish and Game, with bonus trophy fish by park district.
Who to contact: For more information, call (415) 846-3000.

■ Stafford Lake (Marin County):

The bass habitat improvement project should pay dividends. No trout stocks.

Who to contact: For information, call (415) 456-5454.

■ Lake Temescal (Oakland):

This little lake can provide limit fishing after a stock.

Who to contact: For information, call (415) 531-9300, Ext. 2208.

■ Uvas Reservoir (Coyote):

This is the best bass lake in Bay Area, and offers some giant catfish, too. In winter, it's stocked with trout.

Who to contact: For more information, call (408) 463-0711.

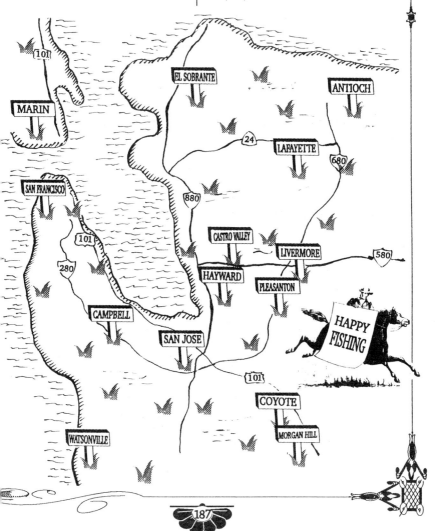

EIGHT MARIN
LAKES

FISH, PICNIC & HIKE

Marin County has eight hidden lakes, but most people don't even know of one. They are ideal for fishing, picnics and hikes. They vary widely, from little Phoenix Lake and its superb spring trout fishing to hidden Soulejule Reservoir, where each evening crappie fishing can provide the spark for anglers of all ages.

The lakes are ideal for a family adventure, or going solo. Several of the lakes are perfect for an evening picnic: Lagunitas, Bon Tempe and Stafford lakes. Just bring your fried chicken.

A number of the lakes also provide ideal jump-off points for hikes. One of the best is Bon Tempe, with trails that connect to a network of routes that lead to several other lakes. One of my favorite areas is the far side of beautiful Alpine Lake which has an extensive trail system. The hikes here are steep, remote and provide overlooks of Alpine Lake.

For more information on any of the lakes, call Western Boat in San Rafael at (415) 454-4177 or the Marin Water District at (415) 924-4600 or the North Marin Water District at (415) 897-4133.

Here's a capsule look at each of the lakes.

■ **Alpine Lake:**
Alpine is the most well-known of the Marin lakes. It's a big reservoir set in a tree-bordered canyon along Fairfax-Bolinas road. It is larger and prettier than any first-timer would expect. Trailheads for several excellent hikes can be found here, and all can lead you

back into pristine woodlands. This lake has a few very large rainbow trout and largemouth bass. It's not stocked, and the resident fish are very smart and elusive. The best bet is walking around the back side of the lake, casting plugs such as deep-running Wee Warts, Rebels or Rapalas patterned after a shad minnow.

How to get there: From Highway 101, take the Sir Francis Boulevard off-ramp and head west to Fairfax. In Fairfax, turn left on Pacheco, go less than a block, then turn right on Broadway. Drive past the Fairfax Theatre and turn left on Bolinas. Continue for five miles; the road borders the lake.

■ Bon Tempe:

This is headquarters for hikers, picnickers and shore fishermen. A network of outstanding hiking trails start at Bon Tempe, a pretty lake that is probably the most popular of all the Marin lakes. Why? It seems to get more sun than the others. It is stocked with rainbow trout by the state Fish and Game Department twice per month through the spring, and recent shore fishing has been excellent. Many five-fish limits of eight to 11-inch trout have been the rule rather than the exception. There's no secret to it: Bait fishing with salmon eggs and marshmallows along the shoreline. It's a good way to spend a pleasant evening.

How to get there: Same directions as for Alpine, but from Bolinas Road, drive 1.5 miles then turn left at Sky Oaks Toad and continue to the lake.

■ Lagunitas:

This little lake gained national attention because California Trout Inc. tried to have it support a natural trout fishery with no future stocks. To do that requires a special slot limit, with all fish 10 to 16 inches being released, along with a new law mandating the use of artificials with single barbless hooks.

The anglers having the most fun are using dry flies and a Cast-A-Bubble and catching and releasing during the evening rise. This lake also has an idyllic picnic area along the west side of the lake, just below the dam.

How to get there: Same directions as for Bon Tempe Lake. Lagunitas sits directly above Bon Tempe Lake.

■ Phoenix:

This has been the Number One fishing spot in Marin County during May. Fishermen arriving for the morning or evening bite take limits of rainbow trout. They're bait fishing from the shore on the southern side of the lake. A fly fisherman can have some fun here fishing the mouth of the feeder stream.

This lake is less accessible than Alpine, Bon Tempe, or Lagunitas, and requires a half-mile hike. That's just far enough to keep a lot of people away -- and ensure good fishing for those willing to hoof it. The shore is undeveloped for picnickers, but for hikers it's one of Marin's jewels. A network of trails connect Phoenix Lake to Bon Tempe, Lagunitas and Alpine lakes.

How to get there: From Highway 101, take Sir Francis Drake Boulevard heading west. Turn left on Lagunitas Road and continue for a few miles into Natalie

Coffin Green Park. You can't see the lake from your car. After parking, hike a quarter of a mile on the signed trail.

■ Kent:

The only way to get here is to hike, and when you first see the lake, its immense size will astonish you. Space for parking is poor along Sir Francis Drake Boulevard, and after you've found a spot, it's another half-hour walk before you reach the lake. The area is undeveloped for recreation. It's primitive with just one trail that loops the lake. And the fishing is not easy (no stocks are made). The resident trout and bass have taken plenty of smart lessons. Best bet is to bring a minnow trap to the lake, catch your own minnows (taking foreign minnows to the lake is illegal), then use the live bait with a sliding sinker rigging. Best prospects are to the left of the dam, along the back side.

How to get there: From Highway 101, take Sir Francis Drake Boulevard and head west for about 10 miles. Go through the town of Lagunitas and park on Sir Francis Drake Boulevard just before reaching Samuel P. Taylor Park. A small sign is on the gate on the left side of the road -- a ranch road that is the trail to the lake, about a mile hike.

■ Nicasio:

This lake has been the surprise of spring, providing good bass and crappie fishing during the evening. Shoreliners casting surface plugs such as the Jitterbug are enticing strikes from largemouth bass in the eight to 12-inch class. You can drive right to this lake because three-quarters of it is accessible by road. There are no picnic tables, so you have to improvise, and that is just how some people like it. It is only fair for hiking, since the area isn't wooded.

How to get there: From Highway 101, take Sir Francis Drake Boulevard and head west for about seven miles. Turn right on Nicasio Valley Road. Follow that for another five miles and it will take you directly to the lake.

STAFFORD LAKE

■ Stafford Lake:

This little lake was a local project to improve the bass and red-ear sunfish fishing. It was drained to repair the dam, then volunteers completed a habitat-improvement project. It is now full of water and bass, and bluegill have been stocked and are becoming re-established. The lake is open for hiking (which is only fair since the hillsides here are sparsely wooded) and just recently reopened for fishing. There is a picnic area on the west side of the lake.

How to get there: From Highway 101, take the San Marin exit and head west until you reach Novato Boulevard. Turn right and continue directly to the lake.

■ Soulejule:

This is a little-known, hike-in lake in northern Marin. You can drive to the base of the dam; a short hike will get you to lake's edge. It is a small, hidden spot where crappie and small largemouth bass are abundant. It provides the county's best crappie fishing, with shoreliners using chartreuse and yellow crappie jigs.

How to get there: From Highway 101, take the San Marin exit and head west until you reach Novato Boulevard. Turn right and continue nine miles to Petaluma/Point Reyes Road. Turn right, continue for a quarter of a mile, then turn left on Wilson Hill Road. Continue for three miles and turn left on Marshall/Petaluma Road. Continue for five miles to the lake entrance signed on the left side of the road. You can drive to the base of the dam.

MARIN LAKES

BAY AREA LAKES

SEVEN SANTA CLARA LAKES

SURPRISES FOR PENINSULA ANGLERS

Long-term Bay Area residents are often surprised when they learn of the Santa Clara County lakes that are tucked away south of San Jose.

Here are some close-to-home spots where you can match a weekend adventure to fit your style, be it power boating, fishing, paddling a raft or just enjoying an evening picnic. Rules prohibiting motors on some lakes, yet allowing water skiing on others, has a way of keeping everybody happy.

A little homework, however, can go a long way in choosing the right lake for the trip you've planned. The first step in preparation should be to talk to Earl Bradford at (408) 463-0711, who owns Coyote Discount Bait and Tackle and doubles as one of my fieldscouts. Bradford fishes extensively and as a result, can provide on-the-spot details for all of the Santa Clara County lakes. He also offers a free map to the lakes to anybody willing to pick it up. Always check first for water levels.

■ Uvas Lake:

No motors are allow on this lake, making it ideal for canoeists, rafters, or fishermen using float tubes. The latter can often discover what could be the best lake in the Bay Area for largemouth bass fishing. It is best in spring and early summer when the lake is full to the brim with water. Fishermen do best with a purple plastic worm, jigged slowly along the bottom in shade-covered coves.

■ Parkway Lake:

Parkway put recreational trout fishing on the map, where more 10-pound trout are caught than anyplace else in Northern California. Fishermen are charged an $9.50 fee, and have a honest chance to catch trophy rainbow trout in the six to eight-pound class, as well as a good number of 13 to 14-inchers. No private boats or motors are allowed on the lake.

■ Lake Anderson:

This lake, the county's largest, is a skiing capital, with all types of power boating allowed. However, a five mile per hour speed limit on the southern half of the lake provides quiet water for anglers. Anderson is the only lake in the county with a full-scale marina. Fishing for bluegill (on worms) and crappie (minnows or small jigs) can be quite good during the evening, but since spots tend to get picked over quite a bit, bass are spooky and wary. Some huge catfish are sometimes caught here.

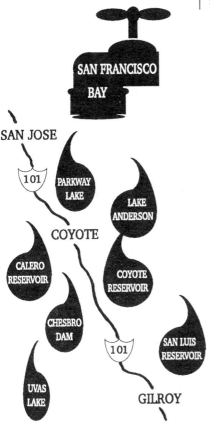

SAN FRANCISCO BAY

SAN JOSE

101

PARKWAY LAKE

LAKE ANDERSON

COYOTE

CALERO RESERVOIR

COYOTE RESERVOIR

CHESBRO DAM

101

SAN LUIS RESERVOIR

UVAS LAKE

GILROY

■ San Luis Reservoir:

Striped bass to 45 pounds have been landed here, providing an indication to the kind of fishing that is celebrated here in the fall. It is similar to ocean fishing; you follow schools of baitfish (threadfin shad) which are indicated by bird activity, then cast lures such as the Krocadile, Kastmaster or Hair Raiser from boat or shoreline. Wind can be a problem in spring and summer, but rarely in the fall. Most stripers tend to be small.

■ Coyote Reservoir:

Coyote was drained completely, in fall of 1985, but was filled during the winter and stocked with trout. It provides a fair winter and spring trout fishery, starting in mid-December. Power boats are allowed on the lake, with a 35 mph speed limit.

■ Chesbro Dam:

This can be a frustrating lake for bass fishermen. The bass tend to be very, very small, or giant, so you end up catching midgets or getting your tackle busted. A sprinkling of crappie are a sidelight. Gas engines are prohibited, but electric motors are allowed.

■ Calero Reservoir:

After high mercury levels were discovered in the fish here, most folks have ignored this lake. Good catfishing can still be had on fall and summer evenings, though a health warning is out on eating the fish. Good catch-and-release fishing.

HENRY W. COE
STATE PARK

BAY AREA'S SUBURBAN WILDERNESS

$100 ONE HUNDRED DOLLARS

Great solitary fishing spots are like $100 bills -- the supply never seems to equal the demand. But just a short drive from the San Francisco Bay Area is such a place, a hidden wildland that you can use as your personal fishing reserve.

Imagine catching and releasing dozens of black bass in a weekend, landing native rainbow trout that range to 26 inches, chasing scads of bluegills, and locating fat crappies and sunfish.

That's what you'll find at Henry W. Coe State Park, which sits on the edge of the Bay Area metroplex southeast of San Jose in the Gavilan Mountains. Coe Park contains more than 100 square miles of wildlands, some 68,000 acres, with 74 lakes and ponds, more than half of which

support viable fisheries. The prime fishing areas can be searched out on the 150 miles of trails and long-abandoned ranch roads. It is a place for the person who wants solitude and quality fishing in the same package and isn't averse to rugged hiking to find it. If there's a catch, that's it -- the lakes and ponds can be reached only by trail, not car.

For starters, you should obtain a map of the park. (See trip facts.) With map in hand, you can plan your route whether you are spending a weekend or a week here. Without a map, you can wander around to many of the lakes and possibly miss much of the quality fishing.

One of the park's prettiest settings is at Mississippi Lake, an 11-mile hike from headquarters and a haven for the few that know it. The lake is a home for wild trout with a remarkable growth rate -- reaching 16 inches in as little as two years. The first time I fished this lake, I was astounded to catch and release several 16 to 20-inch rainbow trout.

"I've seen 26-inchers and have heard of 28-inchers," said Barry Brecking, unit ranger at Coe Park. "I wouldn't doubt any story I hear about those trout at Mississippi."

In order to protect the quality trout angling at Mississippi Lake, a one-fish, 18-inch minimum size limit is in effect.

Another surprising trout prospect in the park is the Middle Fork of Coyote Creek, four miles from headquarters. The upper stretches of the creek provide the best hopes, with many eight-inch trout and a sprinkling of 12 to 15-inchers.

However, some fishermen ignore trout fishing to pursue bass action at several lakes. The best bets for bass are Coit Lake, Hoover Lake, Kelly Lake, and the ponds in the Orestimba and Red Creek drainages.

"In the spring, there are times when you can catch and release 200 bass in a weekend at Coit Lake," said ranger Breckling. "I told this one guy that he could catch a bass per cast here. He came back from his trip a few days later and said he did even better than that -- he caught two bass at once on the same lure."

Most of the largemouth bass at Coit Lake are in the 10 to 13-inch range, with an occasional larger fish providing a surprise. Hoover, Kelly and Paradise Lakes have bass ranging to larger sizes, and Kelly has the bonus of some big crappies as well, including some in the 14-inch class.

The lakes are virtually untouched, and in some cases, the fish are even stunted from lack of fishing pressure and overpopulation. How is it that almost no one is aware of the fishing here? The answer lies in the history of the park. Much of the land was once owned by rancher Marvin Coit, who built most of the ponds and reservoirs 30 to 50 years ago. then stocked them with fish for his personal use. This property was added to Coe Park just a few years ago; thus, some of the lakes have

> *After hiking several miles at Coe State Park, you can be thirsty enough to think you can drink a lake, but you won't find any fountains out here. You will be relying on creeks and small lakes for your drinking water. A key is to protect yourself from microscopic organisms in the water that can cause diarrhea and abdominal cramps -- a painful souvenir of your trek to the Coe wildlands. The simplest and safest way to protect yourself is to buy and use one of the lightweight water filtration systems available at backpacking stores. They are fast and effective. A free yet slower option is to boil water for two to three minutes. This can be frustrating, however, since few thirsty hikers desire to drink hot water rather than cold. Water purification tablets, such as iodine or chlorine, do well in killing bacteria, but can be unreliable against some organisms, such as Giardia.*

almost never been fished in a 50-year span.

The park is about an hour's drive from San Jose. If you're planning on taking advantage of the fishing ahead, I suggest calling or stopping at Coyote Discount Bait located 11 miles south of San Jose off State Highway 101. Owner Earl Bradford is a good source for up-to-date information and fishing tips for the area. Another good idea is to call Coe Park for angling and camping conditions. (See trip facts.)

Once you reach the park, you should contact the rangers to acquire a wilderness permit for overnight backpackers. For drive-in campers, there are only 20 campsites at headquarters, each with a picnic table and barbecue. It's on a first come, first served basis, with no reservations allowed. a more appealing plan is to obtain a backpack permit from park headquarters, then hike into one of the 22 wilderness camps. They are spaced apart so that you can hike for five days without having to camp twice in the same area, and in the process, sample the wide variety of fishing the park provides.

Since open fires are not permitted in the park, a lightweight backpacking stove should be taken along. A water purification system is also worth the expense; dehydration can be a problem for some hikers on California's warm spring days.

Since thoughts of outstanding fishing can set off ambitious plans, your feet should snugly fit into a quality pair of hiking boots.

Most hikers travel fairly light, and that includes fishing equipment. Five or six-piece backpack rods, micro spinning or lightweight fly reels, and tiny boxes that will fit into your shirt pocket are the most practical equipment. I use a six-piece, graphite pack rod -- which can be used for spin or fly fishing -- along with a spinning reel filled with four-pound-test line, and a Plano "micromagnum" tackle box. The latter will fit into a shirt pocket, yet it holds $70 worth of lures and flies.

What to use? The thinking angler would do well to listen to scientist Jerry Smith of San Jose State, who has studied the feeding patterns of trout at Mississippi Lake. The major source of food for trout there it the water flea, according to Smith.

Water fleas are tiny swimming crustaceans. Fly fishermen casting small dart patterns, particularly nymphs, can do quite well in the spring months. Small midge, mosquito, and gnat patterns should be included in your box. At times, it can be necessary to use fly patterns as small as a No. 16 in order to match the size of insects the trout are feeding on. Pinch down the barb on your hooks to make it easier to release your catch without injury.

Usually by June, Mississippi Lake will stratify, and one of the layers will be a narrow oxygen band. This is where the trout will always be found, according to Dr. Smith. In

COE PARK'S TOP 10 FISHING SPOTS

With 74 lakes and several streams at Coe State Park, you could spend more time searching and less time finding when it comes to fishing here. Some 35 to 45 of the lakes and ponds in the park provide fisheries, according to biologist Tom Taylor. Here's a snapshot guide to the 10 top prospects, in order of hiking distance.

1. Frog Lake: *Since it is just a 1.5 mile hike from park headquarters, this pond gets more fishing pressure than many of the others. It has bass that top out at 18 inches, though most are smaller, along with bluegills, and some catfish.*

2. Bass Pond: *Golden shiners provide an excellent forage fish for the bass and bluegill in this lake. Two miles out, it's a good resting stop on your way to the outback.*

3. Mahoney Pond: *This tiny pond (you can cast across it) was originally stocked with just six bass and two bluegill. It now provides an abundant fishery, though most of the fish are stunted. Figure about a six-mile hike.*

4. Middle Fork of Coyote Creek: *The upper stretches of the stream are quite good for rainbow trout. Eight-inchers are common, with a few 12 to 14-inchers. The largest trout are in the 16-inch range.*

5. Hoover Lake: *Eager bass fishermen often stop to hit Hoover en route to Coit Lake. Eight miles out, you can't blame them, with largemouth bass in the 12 to 14-inch class.*

6. Coit Lake: *A long hike, 11 miles with an elevation climb of 1,600 feet, will bring you to a lake where a bass-per-cast is possible on spring evenings. Most of the fish are in the 10 to 12-inch range, with some larger. A bonus at this lake are large green sunfish that will hit bass plugs.*

7. Mississippi Lake: *This is the promised land for many. Rainbow trout grow fast here, like to 16 inches in just two years, and fish ranging to 26 inches have been caught. A one-fish, 18-inch minimum size limit will be in effect. Expect a rugged hike, almost 12 miles from headquarters with a 2,000-foot elevation gain.*

8. Kelly Lake: *A good dose of large crappies in this lake makes it a winner, though at a distance of 13 miles from headquarters, it is rarely fished. Bass and green sunfish are also present.*

9. Paradise Lake: *Like most lakes in the Orestimba drainage of Coe Park, it provides larger bass than elsewhere in the park. It is best in the spring, and usually avoided after mid-May, when it takes a long, hot hike to get here.*

10. Hartman Reservoir: *Close to Paradise Lake and quite similar in the fishery it provides. You'll find larger bass than at Coit Lake, the benchmark for bass fishing in the park.*

the warmer months, a fisherman who is persistent enough to test different depths until he finds that oxygen band, and then stay there, can experience some remarkable fishing.

It is not necessary to be a fly fisherman to catch trout in Coe Park, either at Mississippi Lake or the Middle Fork of Coyote Creek. Small flashy lures, particularly in silver, not gold, can also be effective. My favorites include the Super Duper, blue/silver Kastmaster, and the Met-L Fly.

The bass are less picky about what they strike. Some of the lakes have golden shiners as a forage fish, and anglers should take a tip from that: In the spring, shad-type plugs in the one to three-inch range are the most effective. I use the floating Rapala in blue/silver, Countdown Rapala in black/silver, and the black/silver Shad Rebel Shorty. For fly fisherman, small bass poppers gently laid out along lines of tules with floating fly lines can inspire strikes from bass and bluegills alike. Crappies hit best on small white jigs.

In addition to the fishing, springtime at Coe Park is highlighted by explosions of wildflowers. In some areas, entire hillsides will change color when the Shooting Star blooms. Your hike can take you to summits of 3,000 feet and along hillsides studded with oak, madrone, buckeye, and pine. The valleys are bright green from the crackling fresh grasslands.

Blacktail deer and ground squirrels are common sightings; you will likely see far more of them than you will other people. If you spend enough time exploring, you may see a wild pig, coyote (or at least hear one), or a golden eagle. Mountain lions and bobcats are widespread, but their cautious nature makes sightings rare. Footprints from many of these species can often be found in the mud at the edge of some lakes.

San Jose — Henry Coe State Park

Anderson Reservoir

Dunne Avenue

Morgan Hill

"This is one of the best parks in California, yet few know of it," said Harry Battlin, District Superintendent of the Gavilan Mountain District. "It offers solitude, yet is close to an urban area. People who spend all week cooped up in an office can set out for Coe Park when they get off work Friday, camp at headquarters, then head for the hills Saturday morning."

The best time to visit Coe State Park is from February through May, prior to the arrival of the blast-furnace heat of summer. In the spring, the lakes are full to the brim, and the fish are awakening from their annual winter slowdown. They are hungry and will do their best to prove it to you -- and it won't take much proving before you'll draw the conclusion this place is your own private fishing wonderland.

☞ Trip facts about Henry W. Coe State Park

How to get there: To reach the park from the Bay Area, figure about an hour's drive from San Jose. Anglers should drive south from the Bay Area on State Highway 101 to Morgan Hill, turn east on the East Dunne Avenue, then continue past Lake Anderson on the winding two-lane road for about 30 minutes to park headquarters.

Maps: A map of the park is available by sending $2 to Henry Coe State Park, P.O. Box 846, Morgan Hill, CA 95037. Hikers may be interested in a newer, more detailed map, which shows elevation gains and losses, and is for sale for $4 at park headquarters.

Fishing: All anglers should remember to possess a valid California fishing license. They are available at most tackle shops for $19. Before you get to the park, I suggest calling or stopping at Coyote Discount Bait, (408) 463-0711, located 11 miles south of San Jose off State Highway 101. Owner Earl Bradford is a good source for up-to-date information and fishing tips for the area. Another good idea is to call Coe Park at (408) 779-2728 for angling and camping conditions.

Camping: For drive-in campers, there are only 20 campsites at headquarters, each with a picnic table and barbecue. It's on a first come, first served basis, with no reservations allowed. With a backpack permit, you can hike into one of the 22 wilderness camps. They are spaced apart so that you can hike for five days without having to camp twice in the same area.

Camping fees at Coe Park are $6 per night at the drive-in campground near headquarters, and $2 per night at the hike-in wilderness campsites.

Wilderness permits: As soon as you reach the park, you should contact ranger Breckling or John Neef to acquire a wilderness permit for overnight backpackers.

Day trips: If you're just staying the day, a $2 charge per vehicle is assessed.

Who to contact: Call Coe Park at (408) 779-2728.

ADVENTURE
5

BAY AREA LAKES

LAKE MERCED

THE CITY'S BACKYARD FISHING HOLE

A new trout program at San Francisco's Lake Merced may be one of the nation's top urban fishing programs. In late winter, Merced is stocked by private hatcheries with 100 rainbow trout weighing five to 12 pounds and thousands more trout averaging 12 to 14 inches. Fish and Game continue to stock 1,200 pounds of trout per month, with each fish weighing an average of 1-1/2 pounds. Add it up and San Francisco Bay Area fishermen have a chance at quality close-to-home fishing.

Anglers at Lake Merced pay a $2.50 per-day fee, with 70 percent of the monies turned back to purchase more and larger rainbow trout -- more than at any time in the lake's 100-year-plus history.

Dave Lyons of San Francisco, 72, a veteran Merced fisherman, can tell you firsthand about the lake's revival. He caught his legal limit (five fish per day) on forty-six of fifty trips, often catching and releasing ten to fifteen trout per visit.

"My best went about 22 inches," Lyons said. "I only fish a few hours during the evening, yet they tell me the fishing here is going to get even better."

The lake has some other unique advantages, particularly during the winter/spring transition. Because the lake is spring-fed, it is often clear in late winter, even when most other lakes in California are turbid from heavy storm runoff. In addition, it provides a good option to fishing in the bay and ocean, which have the roughest water conditions of the year from February through May.

The region's coastal breezes and summer fog keep the waters cool enough to sustain a top trout fishery.

Although Merced sits within a few miles of San Francisco's 700,000 residents, it seems to have carved out its own niche far removed from the city's concrete and skyscrapers. The lake is located just a half mile from the Pacific Ocean, adjacent to the Harding Golf Course and San Francisco Zoo. It's a pretty place with the water surrounded by tules and set amid rolling green hills. It's also the only lake in between San Francisco to San Jose, that allows public access.

Lake Merced is actually two lakes separated by a sliver of land, along with a third body of water, a pond named the Impoundment. The lakes cover 386 surface acres, and are surprisingly rich in marine life. In 1956, aquatic biologist Bill Johnson of the California Fish and Game Commission called Merced "the richest trout lake in the state." More than 30 years later, it is much the same. The lakes are filled with freshwater shrimp, a natural for the trout, along with perch, bullheads, catfish, and largemouth bass.

As a result, survival rates of stocked fish are high, and they often seem stronger than trout stocked at more barren reservoirs. In a recent trip, I hooked a 14-inch rainbow trout that spun off about 30 feet of line before making a turn. Imagine what a 10 pounder would do. But with the coming stocks, it isn't imagination that you need, but some time-out fishing on the lake. In the past year, the trends at Merced have become clear: Fishermen using boats outcatch shore fishermen by as much as three-to-one; the North Lake produces larger rainbow trout than in the South Lake, but results are sporadic; and the South Lake has a steady catch rate for trout, usually averaging two to three per rod, but the fish are smaller -- rarely longer than 20 inches. The South Lake also

---

RIGGING FOR BIG TROUT

The simplest way to rig your outfit for big trout is to slide a small barrel sinker over your line, then tie on a snap swivel. From there, tie on three feet of leader and a No. 8 or 10 hook.

But you can take it a step further. Midway up your leader, tie a small dropper loop, then add a second hook. This gives you the ability to double your chances; after a hungry trout has stolen the bait off one hook, you still have a shot at catching it on the other.

For an advance lesson, use no weight at all. A nightcrawler for bait will provide enough casting weight. Hungry trout are easily spooked by the sensation of any unnatural weight attached to a baited hook. Dave Lyons, Merced's fishing master, is happy to show people how to rig their lines. He's available at the Merced Bait Shop, Harding Road, San Francisco, CA 94132 or call (415) 753-1101.

has some big largemouth bass hiding along the tules, but they are difficult to catch.

If you want the closest thing to a guarantee at Merced, or want to get a kid turned on to fishing, then rent a boat and fish the South Lake. If you want a chance at catching a trophy-sized rainbow trout, like one of those 10-pounders being stocked this month, then the North Lake is your best bet.

Either way, all anglers over age sixteen are required to have a California sportfishing license in possession.

Boat ramps are available for both lakes, but no gas engines or boats with gas motors affixed are permitted. Canoes, prams, and small boats set up for rowing or rigged with electric motors are ideal. There is a launch fee. (See trip facts.)

Some anglers prefer to fish from shore. The favorite spots are the beach on the North Lake, and the bridge and fishing pier on the South Lake. The public can use the fishing pier except when special children's programs are being conducted by the San Francisco Police Athletic League.

Best results, however, come to boat fishermen who are willing to explore Merced's tule-lined shore. Dave Lyons, the master of Merced, suggests tying up your boat along the tules, then casting 10 to 30 feet from the tules.

Since the trout here have so much natural forage at their disposal, they often are reluctant to strike spoons, spinners, or plugs. Instead, bring a variety of baits, including nightcrawlers, salmon eggs, cheese, marshmallows, and if you can get them, mealy worms. Over the course of a few hours, Lyons will use them all, often in combination.

A light-duty spinning rod is the best outfit for Merced fishing. The simplest and most effective set-up is a two-hook rigging. On the bottom hook, thread half of a nightcrawler partially on the hook so it will lay straight and have a natural appearance in the water. On the top hook, mold a small piece of cheese on the shank of the hook, then pop a salmon egg on the point of the hook.

Another strategy is to inflate the worm like a little balloon by using a worm inflater (a small, plastic bottle with a hollow needle.) With an inflated worm, the bait will float off the bottom of the lake, just where the big trout swim. The same effect can be achieved by topping off the nightcrawler with a small marshmallow.

After you cast out and let the bait sink to the bottom, you must be alert for even the most subtle signs of a nibble. On a windless day, simply watch where the line enters the water -- if it twitches even an inch, you're getting a pickup. A technique Lyons suggests is to just lay down your rod, leave the bail of your spinning reel open, and place the line under a light plastic lid of a worm tub.

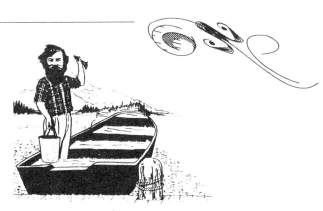

"There's virtually no resistance, so it doesn't spook the fish," Lyon said. "But when the line gets pulled out from under that lid, I know darn well what's going on down there."

What's going on most likely is a rainbow trout on the prowl -- a premium stocking program has made sure of it. Merced receives approximately 210,000 trout per year, a tremendous number when compared to most other lakes. Bon Tempe Lake in Marin County, for instance, receives about 10,000 trout per year, and most of them are rainbow fingerlings. The difference is that in addition to stocks from Fish and Game, special plants are made from the funds accrued from the Lake Merced fishing permits. So as more fishermen try their luck, the trout stocks improve at the same rate.

In a typical year, 80,000 fishermen will average 1.5 fish per rod at Merced according to lake manager Chris Senti. The largest fish documented in the 1980s has been a 10-pound rainbow trout landed in the North Lake by Ed Hamack of Pacifica in 1985, and an 8-pound 10-ounce largemouth bass caught in the South Lake by Mike Rainey of San Francisco in 1987.

Since Merced was converted to a reservoir in 1877, a number of fishing programs have been attempted. Many have failed. In 1891, carp were stocked, but they roiled up the lake so much that nineteen sea lions were trapped and put in the lake to clean them out. Two years later, 90,000 muskies were stocked and never heard from again. Officials next tried largemouth bass, but few anglers could figure out how to catch them. It wasn't until 1944 that trout were planted, but because of the lake's infestations of carp, hitch, and squawfish, sport fishing didn't have much of a chance to get established. Finally in 1949, the lake was poisoned with rotenone to clear out the trash fish, then restocked with rainbow trout and opened to fishing in 1950.

But it hasn't been until the late 1980s that anything like the present trout-fishing program has been attempted. So before you head to some faroff place in search of quality rainbow trout fishing, first try San Francisco's backyard fishing hole -- Lake Merced.

☞ TRIP FACTS

How to get there: From Interstate 280, take John Daly Boulevard west, turn right at Skyline Boulevard and continue to the lake.

Lake Merced Fishing Permit: Required for anglers ages 16 and over, $2.50 for North Lake, $1 for the South Lake. An annual fee for the South Lake is available for $8, with a $4 discount for fishermen 62 or over. Kids under age 16 do not need a California sport-fishing license or a South Lake permit. If parents want to take their kids to the North Lake without purchasing the $2.50 permit for each of them, kids under twelve may share a permit with another angler. Permits are available at the Merced Bait Shop.

California State Fishing License: Fishermen ages 16 and over must have a state fishing license in possession, which costs $19 for residents. One-day permits are also available to both residents and nonresidents for $5.50 per day. For additional information, contact the California Fish and Game Commission, 1416 Ninth Street, P.O. Box 944209, Sacramento, CA 94244-2090, or call (916) 445-5708.

Boat rentals: Row boats and canoes are available for $5 per hour, $14 for three to five hours, $19 for a full day. Boats with an electric motor cost $7 per hour, $20 for three to five hours, $29 for a full day. A $20 deposit is required, $30 with an electric motor.

Launch fee: The launch fee is $2.50 a day or $20 a year.

Fishing rod rentals: Rod and reel rentals are $4 per day, with a $20 deposit.

Limits: A five-fish limit is in effect for trout or bass, 10 for catfish.

Whopper Club: Any trout or bass over three pounds wins a free whopper button from the Merced Bait Shop. The largest trout caught each month wins a quality spinning rod-and-reel combination.

Who to contact: Contact the Merced Bait Shop, 1 Harding Road, San Francisco, CA 94132. The phone number is (415) 753-1101.

BAY AREA LAKES

LAGUNITAS LAKE

MARIN'S NATURAL TROUT FISHERY

What started as an experiment in Marin County may end up a national discovery for fishermen.

Lagunitas Lake near Fairfax is being converted to support a one-of-a-kind natural sustaining trout fishery. If it works, it will be the only program like it in an urban area in the country.

Other programs, like at some 20 other lakes in the Bay Area, rely on repeated stocks of rainbow trout to maintain fish populations. That can be changed, according to California Trout, the organization that is directing the effort at Lagunitas.

"What we're trying to do is emulate the natural system," said Dick May of Cal Trout.

To do that, a special "slot limit" took hold at Lagunitas. A two-fish limit is in effect, but all trout between 10 and 16 inches must be released. Anglers are permitted to use only artificials (lures and flies) with single barbless hooks so that survival rates of released fish will be high. Bait and hooks with barbs are not permitted.

Lagunitas was selected for the program primarily because it has feeder creeks that rise high enough in the winter and spring to allow trout upstream to spawn. If the fish spawn naturally, and angler take is sufficiently restricted by the slot limit, Lagunitas could provide a first-class trout fishery that could run indefinitely on automatic pilot.

It is a pretty lake, set in the wooded Marin foothills, and seems a perfect spot for such an experiment.

It started when the lake was drained -- then rid of all fish, and volunteers worked to improve habitat. Heavy rains in that year through December and January brought lake levels back up, and the next phase of the project was ready to be implemented.

A trout that spawns in winter had to be located and stocked, a fish that would only spawn when the feeder creeks are running high. Fish and Game chose the Shasta Rainbow, and sent a tanker truck down from a Northern California hatchery with 9,000 of them to make what may be the first and last stock.

The last piece of the puzzle was found when a huge aerator was set in place, pumping oxygen near the lake bottom. This will allow the trout to live during hot weather, when small lakes such as Lagunitas can become depleted of oxygen.

The big problem so far has not been fishermen -- who have been happy to release what they catch -- but raiding birds.

"We were sitting there watching the trout rise and the birds were having a field day," said May of Cal Trout.

"The laws of nature will take hold. The strong and smart will survive. The weak will end up in the stomachs of mergansers, ospreys and comrorants."

No more trout stocks are scheduled for Lagunitas. Instead, the lake will settle into a "natural fishery," possible only if the trout spawn in the winter and fishermen release what they catch. The former is up to the trout. The latter has been accepted by area anglers.

One reason for that is because trout plants scheduled for Lagunitas are instead being sent to nearby Bon Tempe and Phoenix lakes, where a five-fish limit is in effect. So the sum effect is that three lakes have improved fisheries.

At most lakes around the Bay Area, the quality of fishing is tied directly to the quality of trout stocks. To get more and larger trout, anglers in some cases are willing to pay special entry fees. The highest is $9.50 at Parkway Lake, located south of San Jose, where the trout average 13 to 16 inches. In the long run, anglers may get similar quality at Lagunitas -- with no more trout stocks.

☛ TRIP FACTS ABOUT LAGUNITAS LAKE

How to get there: Exit off of Highway 101 at Francis Drake Road. Drive west to the town of Fairfax. In Fairfax, turn onto Broadway westbound. At Bolinas Road go left and drive until you reach the Sky Oaks Road crossroad (at 700 Bolinas) and turn left.

Fishing license: Yes, it's required.

Trip cost: There is $3 day use fee.

Trip tip: The lake serves as a watershed primarily and has few recreational facilities.

Who to contact: Call the Sky Oaks Ranger Station at (415) 459-5267.

PARKWAY LAKE

WHERE GIANT TROUT COME TO YOU

A key part of the puzzle has been found for fishermen who want a chance at giant trout. Instead of you searching for the fish, at Parkway Lake the fish come to you.

In one three-month span here, more than 50 rainbow trout weighing 10 pounds and up were landed, including three going 13 pounds or better. In addition, the overall fish-per-rod average is usually quite steady, ranging from 3.1 to 3.3.

"You know, I know and the people know that the fish are here," said Earl Bradford, who helps manage Parkway. "With access a problem at many lakes, compounded by management problems, we offer a good option. Your search ends here. We bring the fish to you."

Parkway Lake is located about 10 miles south of San Jose, just off Highway 101. It originally opened in April of 1981 -- the first time anything like it was offered in Northern California -- and more

than 60,000 anglers flocked here in a 14-month span. Torrents of rain in February of 1983 raised Coyote Creek, broke the levee and ripped out the lake. It re-opened in late 1984, and again, has experienced remarkable success.

It's no accident. The $9.50 access fee charged anglers is returned almost entirely for the purchase of trout from a private hatchery. So unlike other Bay Area lakes, there is no reliance on the Fish and Game.

A good comparison is Bon Tempe Lake in Marin County, which receives about 10,000 eight-inch trout for the entire year from Fish and Game. A typical allotment for Parkway is about 15,000 trout per month -- many larger than eight pounds. In fact, one stock of 6,000 pounds of trout consisted of fish all five pounds and up -- half of which were bigger than eight pounds.

Why can't Fish and Game do the same? "That's because of the

government bureaucratic bull," said Bradford. "They should turn the fish raising over to private enterprise, where it gets done right."

Parkway attracts beginner and expert alike. Experienced anglers use Parkway like a hunter practicing with his shotgun at a skeet range. A fishermen can come here and practice his technique. At times, it can be difficult not to catch trout here. You see all kinds. One gent was shorefishing with a 6/0 reel and a stout five-foot rod more suitable for 300-pound tuna. Fish and learn.

However, most folks prefer light tackle, and fishing from the shoreline. The popular rigging is to use bait such as salmon eggs and small garlic marshmallows -- and use an "Adjustabubble," which should be partially filled with water. This allows your bait to slowly sink to the bottom; almost all big fish have been hooked when the bait is on the move. Lures such as the Roostertail, Panther Martin, Mepps Lightnin' and a woolly worm fly have been the ticket to the largest fish.

You don't need heavy tackle. Richard Brown of San Jose, using just four-pound test line from the shore, nailed a giant rainbow trout going 13 pounds, 2 ounces. It required a 20-minute fight.

Though some anglers disagree with the hatchery concept for raising fish, it does provide good fishing in urban settings -- fishing that otherwise would not be possible.

Parkway Lake is a small lake, with just 40 surface acres, but at 40 feet deep, has the water volume to be a home to big fish. The lake is quite clear; rarely, if ever, suffering from roily water problems. If you're tired of searching for the fish -- or want to get a kid hooked on angling -- then Parkway is made to order for you. Here the giant trout are practically beckoning for you to try and catch them.

☛ PARKWAY LAKE TRIP FACTS

How to get there: From Highway 101 south, go past San Jose, take the Bernal Exit to Monterey Road, then turn left on Monterey. Then turn left on Metcalf, go over the bridge and make a left at the entrance gate at Parkway Lake.

Trip cost: Admission is $9.50 for adults, $4.50 for kids 12 and under. Kids five and under can fish for free with an adult.

Boat rentals: Boats go for $15 per day, or a half day for $12.

Fishing license: Because it is a private compound, no fishing license is necessary.

Who to call: For information, call Coyote Discount Bait & Tackle at (408) 463-0711, or (408) 463-0383.

BAY AREA LAKES

ANDERSON LAKE

PRIME FOR A PICNIC

Lake Anderson has everything going for it, but that in itself can be quite a problem for someone searching for solitude.

As a recreational lake, it is ideal for all kinds of boating, along with fishing, picnics, or suntans. And since it is just four miles from Morgan Hill, anyone from the Bay Area can tool down Highway 101 and get there in a flash.

And that's the problem. A great place that is easy to reach equals people, lots of them on weekends. Although courtesy seems the rule here rather than the exception -- including water skiers. One warm Sunday, we plopped a canoe and a raft in the lake and didn't get buzzed even once. At Berryessa, we would have been swamped.

Anderson is the largest body of freshwater in Santa Clara County, and the barnburner heat of the south valley turns the lake into something akin to a big bathtub by August every year. This makes it ideal for water skiing, swimming and rafting.

After launching at Holiday Marina, water skiers head to the north end of the lake, leaving the southern end to fishermen. This is an ideal arrangement and prevents conflicts between the two user groups. Anglers like quiet water, and you'll find it -- along with bass, bluegill, crappie and catfish -- at the southern end of the lake, just beyond the Dunne Avenue Bridge. Submerged trees provide ideal haunts for fish, but again, so many people work over these spots that the big bass are quite wary. In an hour-long stretch, while we were tied up to a tree and catching

bluegill, I saw 10 different bass boats hit the same spot, then leave. You get the picture.

Casting small jigs, or letting a live minnow roam wild under a bobber, is the best bet for bluegill and crappie. Bassing can be downright tough, but experts with plastic worms have a chance at a sprinkling of giants that do live here. Catfishing is best for folks who hunker down at a spot during the evening and wait it out with a nightcrawler for bait.

Though the lake is quite popular, you can still pick out your own personal picnic site by simply landing your boat/raft/canoe/kayak anywhere along the shoreline, or hoofing it to a spot. Mosquitoes are not a problem, though yellow jackets in pursuit of your fried chicken dinner can be an occasional nuisance in some on-shore areas.

Holiday Marina, located on the southwestern side of the lake, has a small store, tackle shop, and gas pump. Rental boats are also available at the dock. Although the prices for all of these services are out of sight, lakeside convenience makes it handy.

Add it all up and Lake Anderson is a good bet, and so easy to reach that the number of people sharing good times on weekends is a minor inconvenience.

☛ LAKE ANDERSON TRIP FACTS

How to get there: Head south on Highway 101 to Morgan Hill, then take the East Dunne Avenue turnoff northeast. After 3.3 miles, take the Holiday Drive turnoff, which will lead you to the boat ramp.

Trip time: From the Highway 101/Highway 680/280 turnoff in San Jose, figure about 20 minutes driving.

Trip cost: Access to the lake is free. The Marina charges $5 for boat launching, $3 for canoes, with a $2 parking fee. Boat rentals: A 12-foot aluminum fishing boat with motor and gas is $32 per day. Sailboards cost $8 per hour, jet skis cost $30 per hour, and water ski boats that hold six people cost $150 per day.

Who to contact: Coyote Discount Bait & Tackle at (408) 463-0711 is a good contact for fishing tips, and provides a free road map to south county lakes. Holiday Marina can be reached at (408) 779-4895.

BAY AREA LAKES

ARASTRADERO
LAKE

HIDDEN IN THE PENINSULA FOOTHILLS

A truly hidden lake on the Peninsula offers a new opportunity for hiking, fishing, birdwatching and picnics.

It is called Arastradero Lake. It has been open since 1987, and is the only lake that allows public access south of San Francisco to San Jose. It is set in the foothill country above Palo Alto as part of a new 600-acre nature preserve.

There are some 30 lakes around the Bay Area, but Peninsula residents have long been frustrated by no-trespassing signs set up by "public" agencies that are supposed to serve them. The Peninsula has several magnificent lakes -- Crystal Springs, Pilarcitos, Felt, Searsville,

Boronda -- but they are all off limits to the public at large.

Belmont has a tiny, squarish reservoir that is public-accessible, but it provides little recreational opportunity and can't be called a lake by any definition.

Park rangers are stretching it a bit too, calling Arastradero a lake, but the recreational opportunity here makes a visit worthwhile anyway. The best time would be a warm summer evening, when the birds are feeding and the fish are jumping.

The lake looks more like a farm pond, circled by tules and set gently in the foothill country. It was created by a small earth dam built across the canyon, then filled with water from the winter run-off from a small creek.

It takes a 10-minute walk from the parking area to the lake, and even though you know the lake is there, it is still a surprise when you top the rise and see it for the first time. It is prettier than you might anticipate.

The bird life is abundant, and on a quiet evening, it makes for an idyllic setting.

The area is a good one for a short walk, say just to the lake and back. If you have kids, it's short enough to keep their attention and long enough to get rid of their ya-yas.

But the area is worth exploring on a longer trip. The Perimeter Trail connects to both the Acorn Trail and Corte Madera Trail, and from that you can visit most of the preserve. At the most, there is a 300-foot rise, so it is comfortable for hikers of all ages.

My favorite piece of trail is the Corte Madera Trail above the lake, where it borders the Arastradero Creek watershed. A map that details all trails is available for free in a box at the parking lot.

The birds and wildflowers provide a good sideshow. In the foothill country, there are a lot of hawks circling around, looking for prey. As you near the lake, there is more diversity, both songbirds and waterfowl. In less than an hour, we spotted more than a dozen species of birds.

The area is exceptionally pretty as spring gives way to summer. The hills are still green, though fading, and there are blooms of lupine, blue-eyed grass and California poppies to give the hillsides some close-up color.

If there is a frustrating element to the trip, it is that the fishing should be great at Arastradero Lake. But it isn't because of overregulation and poor management by the Palo Alto Department of Recreation.

The lake is set in an area where climate, food production and cover make for abundant populations of largemouth bass and bluegill. The lake is creek fed, so it is full, another plus. The fish are in there, some big ones -- I know, because I have seen them.

But fishing for them is virtually impossible and a shame, especially for the kids in the area who have no place else to try.

The fishing problems are shoreline access, weed growth and a rule that makes fishing from a raft or float tube illegal. There are just a few breaks in the tules along the shoreline where a kid could try to

fish. But even if you are lucky enough to get a spot which isn't taken, the heavy weed growth in the shallows makes every retrieve a frustrating experience.

The solution would be to fish from a raft or float tube, as is so much fun at farm ponds in the Central Valley. But, alas, the city of Palo Alto has deemed that illegal. As a result, they have screwed up the one public-accessible fishing spot between San Francisco and San Jose. What's left is a chance to catch a small bluegill or two, that is if you can get them through the weeds.

Regardless, the Arastradero Preserve provides a good surprise adventure for visitors. It is hidden, known by a few local residents and few else, and is pretty, warm and peaceful.

And you won't find any signs that proclaim "no trespassing." That's the best news of all.

☞ TRIPS FACTS ARASTRADERO LAKE

How to get there: The park is located in the foothills above Palo Alto. From Highway 280, take the Page Mill Road entrance and head west. Turn right on Arastradero Road. A signed parking lot is available on the right side of the road.

Trip cost: Admission and parking are free. A trail map is available for free in a box at the parking lot.

Pets: Dogs are permitted Monday through Friday and must be leashed at all times.

No, no, no: No boats, flotation devices, or swimming at Arastradero Lake, no camping, and no bicycles on the Perimeter Trail.

Who to contact: Call headquarters at Foothills Park at (415) 329-2423.

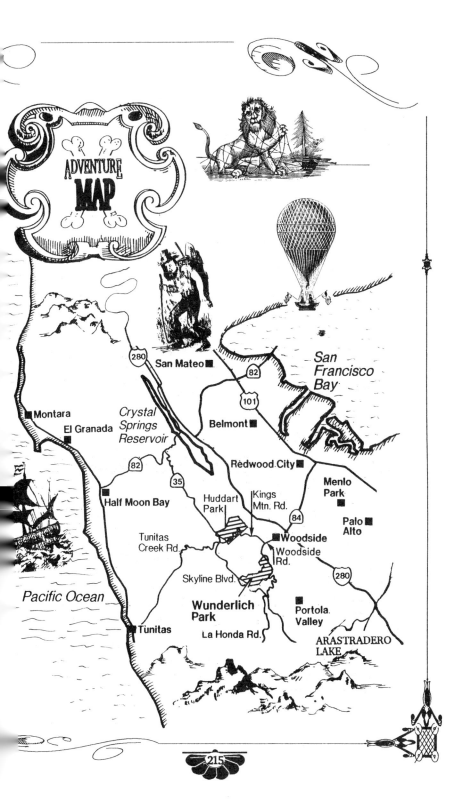

ADVENTURE MAP

San Mateo

280

82

101

San Francisco Bay

Montara

El Granada

Crystal Springs Reservoir

Belmont

82

35

Rèdwood City

Menlo Park

Half Moon Bay

Huddart Park

Kings Mtn. Rd.

84

Palo Alto

Tunitas Creek Rd.

Woodside

Woodside Rd.

280

Skyline Blvd.

Wunderlich Park

Portola Valley

Pacific Ocean

Tunitas

La Honda Rd.

ARASTRADERO LAKE

ADVENTURE 10

BAY AREA LAKES

SAN PABLO
RESERVOIR

CLOSE TO HOME TROUT FISHING

Many husbands wait until the pleas from their kids turn into threats from their wife before they will arrange a family fishing trip. They don't like the long drive and they don't like opening their wallet for megabucks with a chance of getting zilched.

But San Pablo Reservoir in the East Bay provides a solution for that. This lake is tucked away in a canyon between Richmond and Orinda, and despite being centered in the Bay Area metroplex, is one of the best fishing lakes in California. It's a good hideaway as well for hikers, joggers, or people with boats that can be hand-carried to the lake. For the fisherman, San Pablo is a pick-and-choose lake with rainbow trout, largemouth bass and catfish all on the prowl.

The good fishing at San Pablo is a testimonial to proper habitat conditions. A few years ago it was discovered that the San Pablo Dam was not earthquake proof and that

an improved dam had to be constructed. And that meant draining the lake. Then nature took over. While the lake was drained for dam repairs, low-lying chaparral bushes and even some trees sprouted on the lake bed. And when the dam was repaired, the lake filled, the abundance of underwater structure provided an ideal fish habitat.

Man did the rest. To park your car at San Pablo, you pay a $2 fee, money which is funneled directly into an extensive trout stocking program. With the extra dough, trophy-size trout are bought and stocked in the lake. In addition, the Department of Fish and Game also plants trout and catfish -- and are electro-shocking bass from other lakes and transplanting them into San Pablo. The result is that Bay Area anglers can arrive without a long drive, fresh and eager for the bite of a big fish. A launch ramp is available, though car-top boats, canoes or rafts will do just fine. If you're

216

without such a craft, a boat and motor can be rented. If you prefer keeping your feet on solid ground, many folks set up shop for a quiet evening of fishing along the bank, complete with a picnic dinner.

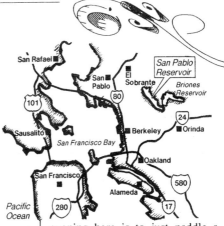

While no trail system around the lake has been built, Old San Pablo Dam Road is closed to vehicles and extends 4.5 miles, the length of the reservoir. It is used now by hikers and joggers, providing scenic glimpses of the lake from above. However, since the road is in a state of disrepair, it is not recommended for bicyclists.

Sometimes the simple and elemental can please one most. One of my favorite ways to spend an evening here is to just paddle a canoe with a friend across the lake and into Scow Canyon, with a few fishing lines dangling over the side. The little whirlpools from paddle strokes in quiet water can be almost hypnotic, but the tug of a big trout on your fishing line has a way of waking you up in a hurry.

☞SAN PABLO TRIP FACTS

How to get there: The simplest route is to take Highway 80 to San Pablo, then head south on San Pablo Dam Road to the reservoir. Another route is from Highway 24: At Orinda, head north on Camino Pablo Road, which connects directly to the lake.

Trip cost: A $2 parking fee is charged, and on weekdays, be sure to bring two $1 bills for the machine at the gate. A $1 fishing fee is charged, and tackle can be purchased at the San Pablo Boathouse.

Boat rentals: Row boats can be rented for $4 per hour, $12 for five hours, $15 for the full day, with a $20 deposit. Motor boats can be rented for $8 per hour, $20 for five hours, and $27 for a full day, with a $30 deposit and a driver's license. Senior citizens are offered discounts on weekdays.

Who to contact: Rangers can be reached at (415) 223-1661 for all information, including fishing tips.

BAY AREA LAKES

DEL VALLE
RESERVOIR

LIKE THE SIERRA NEVADA

Many fishermen equate trout fishing to a Sierra Nevada adventure along a babbling stream on a hot summer day, a mosquito nipping at your neck.

At Del Valle Reservoir, it is a year-around event, the trout can be quite a bit easier to catch than their Sierra Nevada counterparts -- and there are no mosquitoes drilling holes in you. And since Del Valle is just a short drive out of Livermore, you arrive fresh and eager.

It is a good fishing trip for the weekend angler, especially for kids. A new fish stocking program by the East Bay Regional Park District has resulted in some of the better trout fishing available among Bay Area lakes.

If you want to make an over-nighter out of it, there are 100 campsites available Hiking, bicycling and boating are popular, with fishing boats and canoes available for rental. It is one of the top combination fishing/camping/hiking

adventurelands in the Bay Area.

The lake spans 750 acres with 16 miles of shoreline, and is snuggled in oak-covered rolling hills just 20 miles from Hayward. As part of the East Bay Regional Park District, four miles of scenic trails for hikers or horseback riders have been cut.

Del Valle is a good fishery for the expert and beginner alike. In addition to trout, Del Valle is stocked with bluegill, black bass and catfish, and also holds a sprinkling of striped bass to 30 pounds that have been pumped in via the California Aqueduct. The rejuvenation trout program makes Del Valle's quite an attraction, providing action from both boat and shoreline.

As with all lakes stocked with hatchery-raised fish, bait is the ticket to the top catches, with the favored entreaty being a combination plate of a marshmallow and salmon egg.

In the summer months, kids can catch bucketfuls of bluegill with just a worm for bait and a bobber for a float. When that bobber starts to dance, then disappears under the surface, then you know a hungry bluegill has claimed his dinner.

Black bass and striped bass can be quite an elusive challenge at Del Valle, and that attracts the experts to this lake. Black bass tend to roam fairly deep off rocky underwater

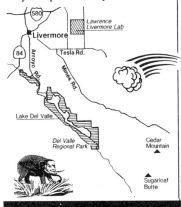

shelves, and are vulnerable to a dark-colored plastic worm retrieved very slowly and bumped on the bottom. Occasionally someone lands a five or six pounder.

Stripers also tend to go deep, especially in the dam area. From the adjacent shoreline here, fishermen will cast deep-diving lures like the Big Mac. Every now and then, bass in the 30-pound class are hooked.

Though summer afternoons can be windy, winter days between storm fronts bring the quietest of water, making it ideal for a canoeist exploring the hidden coves on the lower end of the lake. And on any cast with your fishing rod, you might be able to tell of the kind of fishing you thought you had to go to the Sierra Nevada on a summer day to get.

☛ DEL VALLE RESERVOIR TRIP FACTS

How to get there: From Highway 580, take the North Livermore Avenue exit and drive south toward Livermore. Follow the road through town until it turns into Tesla Road -- then take a right on Mines Road, then veer right on Del Valle Road and continue to the park.

Trip cost: A $2.50 parking fee is charged, and anglers ages 16 and older pay a $1.50 fishing access fee.

Boating: Canoes rent for $3.50 per hour, or $12 per day; row boats $4 per hour, or $15 per day; motor boats for $8 per hour, or $27.50 per day. Launch ramp use is $2.

Trip tip: The boating concession is closed Mondays and Tuesdays.

Who to contact: For fishing and boating information call Del Valle at (415) 449-5201; for maps and brochures, call the East Bay Regional Park District at (415) 531-9300, Ext. 2208.

LAKE ISABEL

WHEN YOU WANT ACTION, NOT SOLITUDE

It can seem like wall-to-wall trout at Lake Isabel, the Bay Area's answer for parents who want to take their kid fishing -- and have them get action. Kids don't want the tranquillity of a mountain stream, they want fish on the hook, and Isabel is doing much to satisfy that wish.

At Isabel, you cast out your bait and watch the fishing line settle on the lake surface, tailing out in little curls. Just as you start to absorb the rays from the warm spring morning, your line straightens, your rod tip dances. Got one!

It's not always that easy to catch trout at Lake Isabel, but just the same, not too many folks spend their time howlin' at the moon waiting for a bite.

Lake Isabel is a new Bay Area phenomenon for fishermen who cannot or will not take the time and the money for long-distance trout trips. For eight bucks, you get access to this private lake that is stocked weekly with rainbow trout measuring nine to 13 inches, plus occasional plants of trout in the five-pound class. Most Bay Area lakes receive bi-weekly stocks of microscopic trout measuring just six to eight inches from the Department of Fish and Game. Not Isabel. All trout come from a private hatchery, which is owned by the lake managers.

In a unique management plan, every trout that is caught by fishermen is logged -- so lake officials know almost exactly how many trout are in the lake, as well as a precise fish-per-rod average. It adds a special degree of credibility to their fish reports. Fish-per-rod averages ranging from 2.5 to 4.1 are typical in the spring, when water temperatures here are still cool.

Suppose, however, that you get flat-out zilched. No problem. When

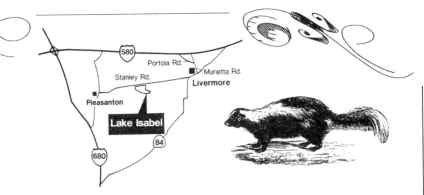

you pass through the check station, you will receive a Skunk Card, which discounts your next visit.

Many fishing methods are popular, and if you need help rigging, the lakeside tackle shop will provide assistance. Most anglers agree that the two favored techniques here are casting a nightcrawler dangling below a bobber -- or using a marshmallow/nightcrawler combination with a sliding sinker, so the bait will float just off the bottom.

The kicker at Isabel is that some giant fish are finning about in the lake, eluding the pursuits of anglers. The lake record trout weighed eight pounds, 12 ounces, and the top bass checked in at nine pounds, 7 ounces. Other fish in those size classes have been hooked and lost. Maybe this weekend it will be your turn to try and land one of those monsters -- or just to take a kid along and show him that trout fishing in a lake is more than sitting on the bank.

It can involve catching a few fish as well.

☛ LAKE ISABEL TRIP FACTS

How to get there: From Highway 580, take the Portola Road exit. Continue on Portola to the first stop sign, which is Murietta Road, and turn right. Head 1.5 miles to Stanley Road and turn right, and then drive three quarters of a mile to the well-signed Lake Isabel turnoff.

Trip cost: Adults are charged $8 (five-trout limit), and kids aged 11 and under are charged $4 (three trout limit).

Best time: In the spring, from 3 p.m. to sunset is usually the best time. In the summer, early morning is best.

Trip tip: The best bet for the big trout is to use a nightcrawler for bait, and fill it with air with a Worm Inflater (cost $1.49).

Who to contact: For information, or an up-to-date fish report, call the Isabel boathouse at (415) 462-1281.

CHAPTER 5

NORTHERN
CALIFORNIA LAKES

WITH
18 ADVENTURES

CONTENTS:—

PUBLISHED BY FOGHORN PRESS
SAN FRANCISCO
QUALITY OUTDOOR BOOKS

NO. CALIFORNIA LAKES

50 LAKE VACATION
DESTINATIONS

WHERE TO FISH, CAMP & BOAT

FISHING HOLE

Where are you going for vacation this year? You don't know yet? The following list may have the answers you need -- Here are 50 of my favorite lakes that provide good camping and fishing.

But picking which one for your adventure can be a real mystery. The following list gives you the lowdown, providing the detective work necessary in planning your summer adventure.

Detailed in this lake-by-lake report is whether campgrounds are primitive or developed. A primitive camp has few facilities and may not have piped water available, but is free or very low cost. A developed camp has piped water, some facilities, and reservations are often necessary.

Bay Area

■ 1. Lake Chabot (Alameda County):

No private boats are permitted, but rentals are available year around. It has a developed campground.
Who to contact: For more information, call (415) 582-2198.

■ 2. Del Valle Reservoir (Alameda County):

The lake level drops from mid-July through August, but the boat ramp is operable all summer. It has a developed campground.
Who to contact: For more information, call (415) 449-5201.

■ 3. Pinto Lake (Santa Cruz County):

A boat ramp is available all summer. There's good trout fishing. It has a developed campground.
Who to contact: For more information, call (408) 722-8129.

■ **4. Spring Lake**
   (Sonoma County):
No motorboats are permitted. There are two trout plants per month. The campground is developed.
Who to contact: For more information, call (707) 539-8082.

■ **5. Uvas Reservoir**
   (Santa Clara County):
Allows carry-in boats only. The campground is developed.
Who to contact: For more information, call (408) 274-6121 or (408) 463-0711.

Foothill Country

■ **6. Lake Amador**
   (Jackson County):
The boat ramp is operable through summer. There's no water skiing, but has good trout fishing. It's a developed campground.
Who to contact: For more information, call (209) 274-4739.

■ **7. Lake Berryessa**
   (Napa County):
Boat ramps are operable most of summer. There's good trout trolling. Camping is allowed in private resort areas.
Who to contact: For more information, call (707) 966-2111 or (707) 966-2134.

■ **8. Camanche Lake**
   (Calaveras County):
Good bass fishing is to be had. There are both developed and primitive campgrounds.
Who to contact: For more information, call (209) 763-5178.

■ **9. Clear Lake**
   (Lake County):
This lake offers nine boat ramps and complete recreation facilities. It has excellent bass fishing and is very popular.
Who to contact: For more information, call (707) 279-4293.

■ **10. Collins Lake**
   (Yuba County):
There's one boat ramp available. The campground is developed.
Who to contact: For more information, call (916) 526-6900.

■ **11. Lake Don Pedro**
   (Tuolumne County):
The boat ramp is operable through late summer. Developed and boat-in camping are available.
Who to contact: For more information, call (209) 852-2369.

■ **12. Folsom Lake**
   (Sacramento County):
Reservations are required for camping. There's good bass fishing.
Who to contact: For more information, call (916) 363-6885.

13. Indian Valley Reservoir (Lake County):

Boat ramps are operable to mid summer. Bass fishing is good. The campground is primitive.

Who to contact: For more information, call (916) 662-0607.

14. New Melones Reservoir (Calaveras County):

One ramp is expected to be operable to late summer. There's good bass fishing. The campground is developed.

Who to contact: For more information, call (209) 984-5248.

15. Lake Nacimiento (San Luis Obispo County):

There's one boat ramp and it's operable all summer. There's good bass fishing and the campground is developed.

Who to contact: For more information, call (805) 238-3256.

16. Lake Natoma (Sacramento County):

Boat ramp is operable most of summer. There is a speed limit on the lake. The campground is developed.

Who to contact: For more information, call (916) 988-0205.

17. New Hogan Lake (Calaveras County):

One boat ramp is operable to mid summer. There's a developed campground.

Who to contact: For more information, call (209) 772-1462.

18. Lake Oroville (Butte County):

There is at least one boat ramp open all summer and full marina services and boat-in camping. The campground is developed.

Who to contact: For more information, call (916) 534-0605.

19. Pardee Lake (Amador County):

One boat ramp is operable through summer. There's good trout fishing and a developed campground.

Who to contact: For more information, call (209) 772-1472.

20. Pillsbury Lake (Lake County):

Three boat ramps are available all summer. There are cabin rentals, a marina and a developed campground.

Who to contact: For more information, call (707) 743-1573.

21. San Luis Reservoir (Merced County):

A boat ramp is available all summer. It gets very windy in the afternoon. There's a developed campground.

Who to contact: For more information, call (209) 826-1196.

22. Lake Sonoma (Sonoma County):

The boat ramp is available through summer. There's good bass fishing and excellent boat-in camping.

Who to contact: For more information, call (707) 433-2200.

23. Turlock Lake (Stanislaus County):

There's a boat ramp available. The campground is developed.

Who to contact: For more information, call (209) 874-2008.

Sierra Nevada

24. Boca Lake (Nevada County):

Only carry-in boats are permitted in the late summer. Both primitive and developed campgrounds are available.

Who to contact: For more information, call (916) 587-3558.

25. Davis Lake (Plumas County):

One boat ramp is available through mid-summer. The trout fishing is outstanding. The campground is developed.

Who to contact: For more information, call (916) 283-6773.

26. French Meadows Reservoir (Placer County):

Two boat ramps are operable to mid-summer. Both developed and primitive campgrounds are available.

Who to contact: For more information, call (916) 367-2224.

27. Frenchman Lake (Plumas County):

This offers a primitive campground. The short drive to Reno is a bonus.

Who to contact: For more information, call (916) 253-2223.

28. Ice House Lake (El Dorado County):

Carry-in boats are only permitted in late summer. The campground is developed.

Who to contact: For more information, call (916) 644-2349.

29. Jackson Meadows Reservoir (Nevada County):

One boat ramp is operable most of summer. There are primitive and developed campgrounds.

Who to contact: For more information, call (916) 265-4531.

30. Little Grass Valley Reservoir (Plumas County):

Three boat ramps are available through mid-summer. It has a primitive campground.

Who to contact: For more information, call (916) 675-2462.

31. Loon Lake (El Dorado County):

Low and dropping, carry-in boats are only permitted after July 1. The campground is primitive.

Who to contact: For more information, call (916) 644-2349.

32. Hell Hole Reservoir (Placer County):

One boat ramp is available. Developed campground and good primitive boat-in campsites are both available.

Who to contact: For more information, call (916) 644-6048.

33. New Bullards Bar Reservoir (Yuba County):

Carry in boats are allowed only after July 1. The campground is developed.

Who to contact: For more information, call (916) 288-3231.

34. Pinecrest Lake (Tuolumne County):

The boat ramp is available all summer. There's a full marina, good trout fishing, a developed campground and plenty of company.

Who to contact: For more information, call (916) 288-3231.

35. Prosser Lake (Nevada County):

Boat ramps are available to early summer. There's a primitive campground.

Who to contact: For more information, call (916) 587-3558.

36. Sly Park Lake (El Dorado County):

There's primitive camping.

Who to contact: For more information, call (916) 644-2792.

37. Stampede Reservoir (Sierra County):

The boat ramp is operable and the campground is developed.

Who to contact: For more information, call (916) 587-3558.

38. Lake Tahoe (Placer County):

Cave Rock launch will be usable all year. You'll find complete marina facilities, developed campgrounds and crowds.

Who to contact: For more information, call (916) 541-5255.

39. Union Valley Reservoir (El Dorado County):

Carry-in boats are allowed only in late summer. Developed and primitive campgrounds are available.

Who to contact: For more information, call (916) 644-2349.

Northern California.

40. Lake Almanor (Plumas County):

The boat ramp is operable through most of summer. There's good salmon fishing and both primitive and developed campgrounds.

Who to contact: For more information, call (916) 258-2141.

■ 41. Lake Britton (Shasta County):

Two boat ramps and marina services are available. It's state park camping.
Who to contact: For more information, call (916) 335-2777.

■ 42. Bucks Lake (Plumas County):

Boat ramps are available. There's good trout fishing. Both primitive and developed campgrounds are available.
Who to contact: For more information, call (916) 534-6500.

■ 43. Eagle Lake (Lassen County):

Four boat ramps are open all year. There's good trout fishing. Both primitive and developed campgrounds are available.
Who to contact: For more information, call (916) 825-2191.

■ 44. Keswick Lake (Shasta County):

This lake is full with boat ramps operable all summer.
Who to contact: For more information, call (916) 243-2643.

■ 45. Lewiston Lake (Trinity County):

Boat ramps are operable all summer. It's an idyllic setting with primitive and developed campgrounds.
Who to contact: For more information, call (916) 243-2643.

■ 46. Ruth Lake (Trinity County):

There is one boat ramp open. It has a developed campground and boat-in camping.
Who to contact: For more information, call (707) 574-6418.

■ 47. Shasta Lake (Shasta County):

Campgrounds include both developed and primitive.
Who to contact: For more information, call (916) 243-2643.

■ 48. Lake Siskiyou (Siskiyou County):

The lake is full, with a boat ramp available year around. It's a beautiful spot set at foot of Mount Shasta. The campground is developed.
Who to contact: For more information, call (916) 926-2618.

■ 49. Trinity Lake (Trinity County):

Complete recreation facilities are available.
Who to contact: For more information, call (916) 243-2643.

■ 50. Whiskeytown Lake (Shasta County):

Boat ramps are available through summer. The campground is developed. There's good kokanee salmon fishing.
Who to contact: For more information, call (916) 243-2643.

LAKE BERRYESSA

THE BAY AREA'S BACKYARD FISHING HOLE

SUMMER

Lake Berryessa is one of the most popular areas in America during the summer months -- but it is in autumn when Berryessa becomes most enticing.

Instead of a cyclone of wild vacationers swirling about the lake, Lake Berryessa becomes a hideaway for quiet waters and fishermen, cool breezes and houseboaters, and trees aflame with color and folks just out to simply kick back and savor it all. It is located just 20 minutes east of Napa -- less than an two-hour drive from San Francisco and just 60 miles from Sacramento. A round trip can require less than a tank of gas.

From Memorial Day to Labor Day, Lake Berryessa is the water skiing capital of the western hemisphere. Ninety-degree temperatures turn the lake into a big bathtub, and skiers celebrate at high speed, roaming free along the 160 miles of shoreline. But come autumn and the skiers start moving out and houseboaters, campers, and fishermen start moving in.

Most people have never even boarded a houseboat, much less considered navigating one. But they provide a singular perspective while exploring the lake, come complete with all the amenities, and are as easy to drive as a bike with training wheels. They can be rented from Markley Cove Resort from $115 per day, a price which is usually split among a half-dozen friends that share the trip.

With 750 campsites at seven resort areas, Berryessa can look like "Tent City" during three-day weekends. But during autumn, reserving a quiet spot by the lake to camp is a simple matter of arriving with a tent -- or $30 to rent a cabin at Putah Creek or Steele Park resorts.

And don't forget your fishing rod. Berryessa is home for trout, bass, crappie, bluegill, catfish, and even king salmon. But it is the fall trout fishing that is the strongest magnet, drawing anglers on fly-in trips from as far away as Texas. Every October, rainbow trout that average 14 to 16 inches -- with some brutes 24 inches and beyond -- come to the surface and rip into schools of threadfin shad. Fishermen who simply dangle a live minnow along the shoreline can experience the top trout fishing you can get within 150 miles of the Bay Area.

If you don't like using bait, the ticket can be offering flies or small flashy lures near the surface in coves or at the mouths of creeks. The swirl of a 20-inch trout inhaling your fly is quite a sight. You don't believe it? Then just consider the brute of a trout taken in Markley Cove, a 14-pound rainbow trout, measuring 38 inches, that gobbled a minnow near Monticello Dam. It's a lake record.

The average size trout planted at Berryessa will be raised by an average of three inches also under a new experimental plan by the Department of Fish and Game to give the lake a trophy-trout fishery.

However, to accomplish it, 100,000 trout will be stocked per year instead of the previous allotment of 150,000. A DFG biologist says it will add up to a plus, providing for higher survival and growth rates.

"We're hoping to provide a trophy-trout fishery and at the same time have more fish available to anglers," said Frank Gray, biologist for the DFG.

Lake Berryessa is visited by several hundred thousand fishermen and water skiers each year. The trout fishing is the centerpiece, both during the summer for trollers and in the fall, when the trout come to the surface and provide the best fishing of the year.

In the past, trout 10 to 11 inches long have been stocked at Lake Berryessa. They are usually planted in the spring, and if not caught by fall, average 13 to 14 inches.

Under the new plan, trout 12 to 13 inches will be stocked, and by fall they will be 15 to 16 inches long and double in weight, according to Gray.

He says both growth and survival rates will be much higher by stocking fewer trout because the lake's reduced numbers of threadfin shad, which the trout feed on, won't be spread so thin.

So this new program will be conducted on an experimental basis for two years.

"We will evaluate the growth and survival rates to determine the effectiveness of the program," Gray said.

Lake Berryessa has long been the Bay Area's "Backyard fishing hole." Although the Bay Area has 30 lakes, Berryessa attracts the most boaters and fishermen because of its size, fishing and distance insulation from the Bay Area.

The lake is 25 miles long and has 165 miles of shoreline. It is just 20 miles east of Napa, yet is separated by mountains, giving Bay Area

vacationers the illusion that they are far away from their homes.

The fishing is best for bass in the spring, for trout in the fall. In the summer, when water skiing is popular, warm surface temperatures drive the fish deeper to a cool, oxygenated layer of water called the thermocline.

Anglers who troll lures in this layer of water, set 30 to 45 feet deep, are the ones who catch the trout. But many summer visitors fish too shallow and get the impression that "there aren't any fish here."

☛ LAKE BERRYESSA TRIP FACTS

How to get there: Several routes are available, but the fastest is to take Interstate 80 east, then turn north on the Suisun Valley road overpass. Turn right on Highway 121, and at Moskowite Corners, take Highway 128 and continue on to the lake.

Cabins: Lakeside accommodations are offered at Putah Creek Resort by calling (707) 966-2116 and Steele Park Marina by calling (707) 966-2330.

Camping: Tent and RV camping are available at Rancho Monticello, (707) 966-2116; Berryessa Marina, (707) 966-2161; Spanish Flat, (707) 966-2338; South Shore, (707) 966-2172; Putah Creek and Steele Park.

Fishing guide: Claude Davis often guarantees limits of trout for his customers. Call him at (916) 787-3925.

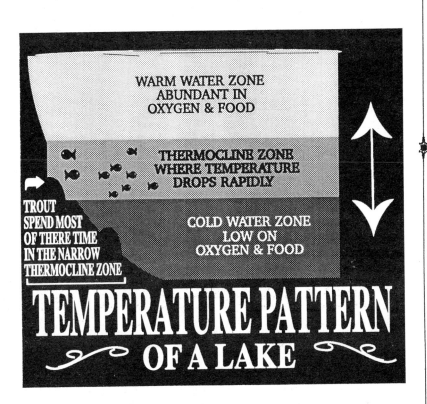

WARM WATER ZONE
ABUNDANT IN
OXYGEN & FOOD

THERMOCLINE ZONE
WHERE TEMPERATURE
DROPS RAPIDLY

TROUT
SPEND MOST
OF THERE TIME
IN THE NARROW
THERMOCLINE ZONE

COLD WATER ZONE
LOW ON
OXYGEN & FOOD

TEMPERATURE PATTERN
OF A LAKE

That impression can change in a hurry in late October, when cold nights cause the lake to "turn over" and the temperature zones flip-flop. The warm layer on top sinks to the bottom and is replaced on the surface by the cold, oxygenated layer -- and with it come the trout.

Examiner fieldscout Claude Davis, a former guide, has even offered a guarantee that his clients will catch a limit of trout on every trip with him.

Gray said anglers may complain at first at the thought of 50,000 fewer trout being stocked a Berryessa. But he added that those sentiments will change in a hurry when the complainers catch 16-inchers instead of the little "Slim Jims" that now are more common.

NO. CALIFORNIA LAKES

LAKE SONOMA

A VERY WELL KEPT SECRET

Lake Sonoma is California's mystery spot -- but soon the only mystery is going to be why people haven't visited it yet.

Sonoma is California's newest lake, created with the construction of Warm Springs Dam, located north of Santa Rosa.

The creation of this lake provided the government with a chance to do something right, and alas for their track record, they have succeeded. It is a perfect lake for camping, fishing, water skiing (in designated areas), canoeing, and sailing -- but has some other key elements that make it particularly special: Boat-in camping, 40 miles of hiking and horseback riding trails, and an 8,000 acre wildlife area.

It takes less that a two-hour drive to reach the lake from San Francisco, and the first stop should be the Sonoma Overlook at the south end of the lake. From here, you get an ideal picture of the adventure ahead of you. The big lake is set in rich foothill country with thousands of hidden coves to be explored by boat or trail.

From the dam, the lake extends nine miles north on the Dry Creek arm, four miles to the east on Warm Springs Creek. Each of the lake arms has several fingers and miles of quiet and secluded shore. The public boat launch is located near the junction of the the lake arms.

If you don't own a boat, rentals are available from the marina. If you don't want to rent one, but still desire a secluded lakeside campsite, there are eight that can be reached by trail.

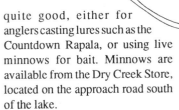

At some lakes, such as Berryessa and Shasta, for instance, water skiers and fishermen are in constant conflict. At Sonoma, that has been solved by providing a large area for water skiing and jet skis -- and out-lawing skiing elsewhere. Two miles of the Warm Springs Creek arm is off limits to skiing, along with al-most five miles on the Dry Creek arm.

As a result, water skiers can "hit the coves" without worrying about running over fishermen, and fisher-men can sneak up on quiet shoreline spots and not get plowed under by skiers. Each has large areas to do their own thing.

As the word gets out, the fishing here is going to attract some excite-ment. Right now, the bass fishing is

quite good, either for anglers casting lures such as the Countdown Rapala, or using live minnows for bait. Minnows are available from the Dry Creek Store, located on the approach road south of the lake.

The key for fishing is habitat. When Lake Sonoma was created, trees were left on the upper stretches of both lake arms. In turn, there is now ideal underwater habitat provided for bass and red-ear sunfish.

If you are interested in a visit, you should obtain the Lake Sonoma brochure, which details campgrounds, trails and posted areas for boating. (See trip facts.)

The centerpiece for campers is the Liberty Glen Campground, with 113 developed sites. Each campsite has a tent pad, barbecue grill, picnic table, and developed restrooms, which include hot running water and showers. Water spigots are spaced about every for or five sites. No electrical hookups for motor homes are provided.

There are no reservations. Campsites are available on a first-come, first-served basis, with a maximum 14-day stay.

Two large group camps are also available.

If you want a more secluded, lakeside option, 15 primitive shoreline camps are available. Seven can be reached only by boat, eight are accessible by boat or trail. All are spotted on the Lake Sonoma Map.

For hikers, there are 40 miles of trails, located on the Warm Springs Arm of the lake, In addition, there is an 8,000-acre reserve set aside as a wildlife management area. Limited hunting is permitted for wild boar here.

When visitors first see Lake Sonoma, the first comparison will likely be to Lake Berryessa, which is in a similar setting. But when it comes to solving the water skier/fishermen conflict, and opportunities for secluded camping, boating and hiking, Sonoma kicks booty on Berryessa's.

☛ LAKE SONOMA

How to get there: From Highway 101 at Geyserville, take Canyon Road five miles west to the lake. Fishermen should take the Dry Creek exit at Healdsburg, which will route them past the Dry Creek Store, which has live minnows for sale.

Marina: Boats with motors, canoes, and paddleboats are available for rental. For information, phone (707) 433-2200, or (707) 526-7273.

Trip tip: A special access point for car-top boats is provided at the quiet, north end of the lake from Hot Springs Road.

Camping: Camping is on a first-come, first-served basis. with a maximum stay of 14 days. The Liberty Glen Camp has 113 developed campsites and opens April 13. There are 15 boat-in sites, eight which can also be reached by trail. Two large group camps are available, each which can hold 50 to 75 people. Reservations are required through the park office by phoning (707) 433-9483.

Maps: Maps and brochures detailing posted lake areas, campgrounds and trails are available for free. Write Corps of Engineers, Lake Sonoma, 3333 Skaggs Springs Road, Geyserville, CA 95441-9644, or phone at (707) 433-9483

NO. CALIFORNIA LAKES

CLEAR LAKE

WHERE EVERYTHING FALLS INTO PLACE

Dear Tom: I dream of a place where I can set up a tent along the shoreline of a beautiful lake. I'm talking about a place where my boy and I can walk a few feet from our campsite and catch fish in the evening, yet launch a boat without any problem in the morning. Is there such a place? Or am I dreaming?
-- Mark Speir, Kentfield.

Dream on. Clear Lake State Park offers such an oasis -- lakeside campsites, good fishing for largemouth bass, catfish and crappie, and a camping fee of only $10 per night. It's a bargain.

Clear Lake is located north of the Bay Area, about a three-hour drive from San Francisco. It is just far enough away to make each trip here

a special event; a place where you can make memories, rather than talk about them. Because it is a lake made by nature rather than man, Clear Lake has a natural beauty and everything seems to fall in its rightful place. And ancient Mount Konocti, the big mountain to the west, gives the area a definite sense of historical permanence.

"When you live here you get the idea that this lake has been here a long, long time before any of us were around," said the late George Powers. "You also get the feeling it's going to be here a long while after we're all gone. Knowing that makes you think different, act different."

This kind of sentiment, along with the adventures available here, make Clear Lake an ideal place.

Although there are resorts of every kind that ring the lake, Clear Lake State Park offers about 50 classic lakeside campsites at its Kelsey Creek Campground.

Another 100 campsites are available in the park, all in nice settings that provide drinking water spigots, table, food lockers, and barbecue stove. Reservations are strongly advised, and are a must from Memorial Day through Labor Day. You can obtain them through Ticketron outlets, and you should allow at least two weeks to obtain even a weekday reservation, according to rangers.

You will learn why after you've fished here a few days. Right in Old Kelsey Creek, a slough that turns into the park, you can get in on some good catfishing at night (clams for bait), and decent bass and bluegill fishing during the day (live minnow or red worm for bait, respectively). If you have your own boat, some of the best bass fishing territory in the entire lake is along the tule-lined shoreline within a mile or two of the park. In the spring, largemouth bass move into the shallows, often in as little as six inches to a foot of water along the shoreline.

What I like to do is camp at Kelsey Creek Campground, then launch my canoe and paddle slowly along the shoreline, the only sound being that of quiet strokes dipping in calm water. We'll cast a bass plug such as a Rapala Fat Rap, Rapala Minnow, or a Rebel Shad, and plunk it as close to the tules as we dare without snagging. There have been times where if you could cast within two or three inches of the tules -- then surprise! -- a bass would rip into the plug almost as soon as it hit the water, yet casts of less precision would go unrewarded. Because these are often bass preparing to spawn, we return almost all that we catch.

Clear Lake can be a paradise for kids, especially in the summertime. Lake surface temperatures of 75 degrees make it ideal for swimming

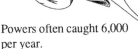

during the day, and bluegill or crappie fishing in the evening. You can often catch either by the bucket full here.

For bluegill, a redworm on a small hook dunked below a bobber is the ticket. When that bobber start to dance and then disappears, you're in business. For crappie, you're better off using live minnows. For the best bet, fish at night under a bright light, which acts as a bug and fish attractor, and cast white crappie jigs. And catfish? Old-timers joke Clear Lake has "wall-to-wall catfish." In fact, George "Mr. Catfish"

Powers often caught 6,000 per year.

Add it up and you see why you're not dreaming when you envision a Northern Californian hideaway such as this. Clear Lake is real.

☞ CLEAR LAKE TRIP FACTS

How to get there: From the Bay Area, there are several choices. The most popular is to take Highway 80 to Highway 29, then follow 29 through the Napa Valley to the lake. Another route is to take Highway 101 north to Hopland, then turn right on Highway 175 east to the lake (no trailers allowed on this route) and follow the twisty route east to Lakeport. Drivers of RVs often reach Clear Lake via Highway 20, which intersects with Highway 101 and Highway 5.

Driving time: It's 100 miles from San Francisco, about a 2.5 to 3-hour drive from San Francisco.

Trip cost: Costs vary dramatically according to your tastes, from as little as $10 per night for a campsite at the state park to an average of $35 per night at a resort. An aluminum boat and motor can usually be rented for $25 per day.

Who to contact: Clear Lake State Park can be reached by calling (707) 279-4293. Campsite reservations are made through Ticketron. A complete list of private resorts as well as state park information can be obtained from the Clear Lake Chamber of Commerce, P.O. Box 629, Clearlake, CA 95422, or call (707) 994-3600. It's free.

NO. CALIFORNIA LAKES

MOTHER LODE
LAKES

A TAKE-YOUR-PICK DEAL

S nuggled away in the Mother Lode country of the Sierra Nevada foothills is a four-lake circuit that offers genuine diversity that seems made-to-order for any boater or fisherman. At Amador, Pardee, Camanche or New Hogan lakes, all about a two-hour drive from San Francisco, you can self-style a weekend or a week to fit your exact needs. Although remarkably close to each other, each lake has its own personality, as well as adventures to offer.

■ **Lake Amador:**
Amador is famous for producing giant black bass -- like the record two-man limit of 10 fish that weighed 80 pounds, or the Northern California record bass going 15 pounds, 13 ounces. A bonus for anglers is that no water skiing or jet skiing is allowed.

The lake opens either the last Friday in January or the first Friday in February. It is not unusual for a 10-pound bass to be caught the first weekend of operation. However, do not believe these giant fish are easy to come by. They're not, and it usually takes long hours and persistence, as well as patience.

The best technique is using a live crawdad for bait, then letting it roam wild on the bottom in one of the brush-lined coves, your reel on free spool. In most cases, you have to let the big bass take the bait, then play with it before setting the hook. It takes a degree of touch.

The lake is fairly small, and good for small boats. When the big bass get a case of lockjaw, trout fishing can be a

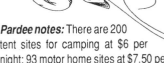

good alternative up the Jackson Creek arm.

Amador notes: There are 150 drive-in campsites available at $8.75 per night. Reservations are suggested. Boat-use fee is $3.25 per day. All important facilities are available. Amador has 13 miles of shoreline.

Who to contact: For more information, call (209) 274-4739.

■ Pardee Lake:

Pardee is a little jewel of a lake that provides some of the best trout fishing in the central Valley, and like Amador, no water skiing is permitted. This means that you can plop your raft, canoe, or small boat in the lake and never fear getting blown off the lake by a power boater. The lake opens every year in mid-February.

Both shore anglers and trollers do quite well at Pardee, with some trophy-sized rainbow trout and kokanee salmon in the deal. One of the easiest ways to catch trout in California is to just troll a Needlefish lure here from five to 15 feet deep. My preference is to connect with the trout at Pardee in the morning, then head over to nearby Amador for the evening bass bite. It can be a spicy combo.

The lawmen at Pardee have a reputation as being no-nonsense types, and tend to deal quite quickly with groups that even hint of getting out of line. Depending on your point of view, that fact is worth remembering.

Pardee notes: There are 200 tent sites for camping at $6 per night; 93 motor home sites at $7.50 per night, or $45 per week. No water skiing, swimming or wading is permitted. All facilities are available. Pardee has 43 miles of shoreline.

Who to contact: For more information, call (209) 772-1472.

■ Camanche Lake:

Come the first warm days of spring and some of the best lake fishing in Northern California can be had at Camanche Lake. The bonus is variety, with Florida bass, largemouth bass, crappie, bluegill, and catfish all sustaining in good populations. In just a few hours of fishing, it is possible to tangle with all of these species. Some of the best fishing is for crappie during the early summer, particularly at night under a bright light. The campgrounds are giant, and come three-day weekends, look like tent cities. Almost never is anybody turned away at any time for space reasons. Camanche is the largest of the four Mother Lode lakes, and since the surface temperature can reach the high 70s in the summer, it's a favorite for all water sports, including water skiing, jet skiing, and swimming. It is open throughout the year.

Camanche Lakes notes: Some 1,100 campsites are available for tents and motor homes. There's a full service marina and all facilities are available. Horseback rentals are a bonus. Camanche has 53 miles of shoreline.

Who to contact: For more information, call North Shore at (209) 763-5121 and South Shore at (209) 763-5178.

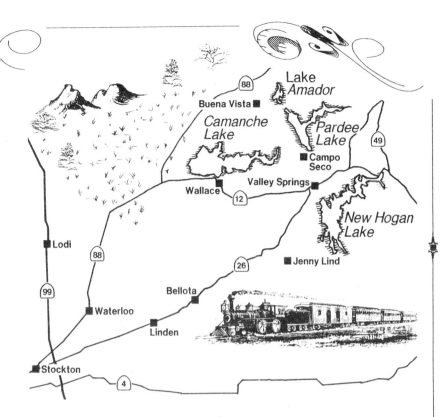

■ New Hogan Reservoir:

New Hogan sits less than 10 miles from Camanche Lake, and is always a good option if the fishing at the latter goes sour. March and April are the most beautiful times here, with lavish wildflower displays exploding into color. This is the only lake of the four that has been stocked with striped bass. The jury is still out on that decision. Although stripers get big, many fishermen believe what was once a promising black bass fishery is getting annihilated by the hungry stripers.

Even on crowded weekends, it is possible to find seclusion at New Hogan -- at the Deer Flat Campground on the east side of the lake, accessible only by boat.

The officials at New Hogan haven't yet figured out what to do about fishermen/water skier confrontations. Water skiing is permitted, but many coves are restricted against water skiers -- except that the skiers here traditionally ignore that law.

New Hogan notes: There are 193 campsites for tents at $6 per night; some 160 spaces for motor homes, also $6 per night. Some 70 undeveloped sites are free. Full facilities are three miles distant at Valley Springs. New Hogan has 50 miles of shoreline.

Who to contact: For more information, call (209) 772-1462.

NO. CALIFORNIA LAKES

LAKE AMADOR

NORTHERN CALIFORNIA'S BIG BASS FACTORY

nia. Amador is located east of Lodi, so it's not a head-spinner drive from the Bay Area, and its population of a strain of bass from Florida make it like a factory for big fish. It's a winning combo: A nearby lake with some whopper big bass.

Even though bass can't read a calendar, when spring arrives, their inbred alarm clocks go off just the same. Mr. Bass will awaken from his winter slumber, stretch and fin the sleep out of his eyes, then realize how hungry he is after months of the doldrums. He'll go on morning and evening prowls, and every crawdad and minnow in the area will be endangered.

And that's where you come in. With bass on their annual spring feed, March and April will bring some of the best bass fishing of the year. It's the time to schedule a trip to Lake Amador, the best lake for hog-size bass in Northern Califor-

One of the largest bass caught in Northern California history, 15 pounds, 13 ounces, was landed here in fall of 1984. A 15-2 was checked in during the spring of 1985, just after Amador opened for the year. In the six weeks that followed 15 bass going five pounds or better were caught. Just a start, just a start.

The arrival of spring is marked by the sun crossing the equator in its annual move northward. Astronomers call it the vernal equinox, and it will bring spring's warmer temperatures, fewer storms -- and ultimately get black bass on their best bite of the year. And though there are many good bass lakes in Northern California, Amador is an ideal choice to fish for several reasons. Neither waterskiing nor speedboating are allowed here, so you get a guarantee of quiet water -- and the lake is stocked with rainbow trout, which provides an option for anglers, as well as more feed for the giant bass. A bonus is the lakeside camping, with about 150 campsites, which makes Amador a nice retreat from the Bay Area.

However, just because this is the home for giant bass does not mean you will get to tangle with one. But it does mean you will have a better chance than just about anywhere else, and with a little luck and know-how, sooner or later, you can score. One note, however: a boat is a necessity for big fish here. It doesn't have to be fancy, but without a boat, you're in trouble;

rentals are available at the Amador Lodge. With a boat under you, you have the mobility to probe the Jackson Creek arm, Carson Creek arm, Rock Creek, and the Mountain Spring areas. This is where the big bass lurk. Avoid open water, and stick to the coves, then work the lake bottom, just where it drops off. We're talking hawgs!

Many fishermen are content casting lures along the shoreline, occasionally nailing bass in the 10 to 14-inch class. Plugs such as the Rebel Shad Minnow can be quite effective. With a lot of fish taken on the surface, it can make for exciting fishing.

But if you're after a five to 15-pounder, a trophy wall mount, then you have to think differently. And

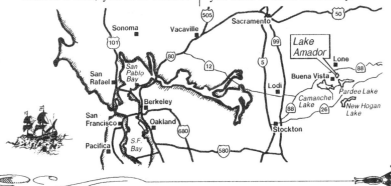

that means fishing the bottom. With what? Take your pick:

a. A live crawdad. Leave your sinkers at home, and instead tie a No. 8 hook directly to your fishing line. Hook the crawdad right between the eyes in order that it will swim about most naturally, then let it descend to the lake bottom. More 10 pound bass are caught with crawdads than anything else.

b. A leadhead jig with porkrind trailer. With your boat just inside a cove, cast the jig toward the shoreline, let it hit the bottom -- then "walk it" down the drop-offs, retrieving slowly. I caught a six-pounder with this trick.

c. A dark plastic worm. Position yourself similar to the way you should while using a leadhead jig, and cast the plastic worm right along the shoreline. Retrieve it so it "swims" along the bottom, appearing as natural as possible. This is how bass pros, who use artificial lures only, win their tournaments.

d. Luck. It's a much easier method to use to catch fish. But like a poker game, you have to practice to learn luck. Lake Amador is a good place to deal your hand.

☛ LAKE AMADOR TRIP FACTS

How to get there: From Stockton at Highway 99, take Highway 88 east for about 25 minutes, then turn right on Jackson Valley Road and continue for five miles. Amador Lake turnoff is well signed.

Camping: Campers are charged $8.75 per vehicle, which includes a day-use fee.

Boat/motor rentals: Aluminum skiffs with seven-horse-power engines can be rented for $35 per day, or $25 for six hours.

Fishing tip: Crawdads are not available for bait at Lake Amador, though they can often be purchased at a number of bait shops on Highway 88 en route to the lake.

Trip cost: Amador charges a $3.25 day-use fee, $1.50 trout stock fee, and $3.25 boat launch fee, which are collected at the Amador Lodge.

Who to contact: For a free brochure, write Lake Amador, 7500 Lake Amador Drive, Ione, CA 95640. For information or fishing tips, call (209) 274-4739.

NEW MELONES
RESERVOIR

CALIFORNIA'S NEWEST LAKE

If you were to gaze into a crystal ball and ask what lake will produce the top fishing in California over the next five years, appearing would likely be New Melones Reservoir. "I can tell you that, and I don't even have a crystal ball," said fishing guide Bob Leslie.

New Melones is California's newest lake, created when two consecutive winters of heavy rains filled it to the brim. Some 100 miles of shoreline are studded with submerged trees and brush -- an outstanding fish habitat that provides food, cover and ideal spawning conditions.

Landing rainbow trout to 24 inches is not a rare occurrence for skilled trollers, taking small black bass on 10 straight casts is possible during the evening rise -- and bucket fulls of bluegill and crappie are common for baitdunkers with a yearning for a fish fry. King salmon have also been stocked, some already reaching eight pounds.

To give you an idea of the newness of the lake, consider that the lake's first recreation area was opened in fall of 1983, providing a series of first-class boat ramps, parking and portable restrooms. Two different campgrounds provide 250 picnic sites and 220 overnight campsites.

The upper end of New Melones Reservoir was once a prime rafting area on the Stanislaus River, with one rafter even chaining himself to a rock to prevent the lake from being filled. Well, that rock is now about 150 feet under water and gone is the rafting. In its place is a haven for fishing and boating. The sheer-faced canyon walls that rafters tried to protect still tower above the lake on the upper end, and will always provide a spectacular setting for boaters. And fishing.

But deciding where and what to fish for is no simple matter. New Melones has 12,500 surface acres, and a map of the lake is a necessity for navigation. If you explore the lake arms, you will discover a tree-lined shoreline where bass plugging on the surface can be mercurial. Most of the top water fish are small, but if you probe deeper, like 15 to 20 feet down, you can find the bigger fellows with a plastic worm, or a jig hooked with a pork-rind trailer. The main lake area is prime for trolling for trout and salmon, especially at Black Bart Cove, Bostick Point, and at the mount of Angels Creek. Still fishing with worms for trout is best whenever you can find feeder creeks pouring forth water (and food), particularly on the lake arms.

Though New Melones is a new lake, some giant fish already live there.

NEW MELONES TRIP FACTS

How to get there: The simplest route from San Francisco is to take Highway 580 through Manteca, and continue on Highway 120, turning left at Rawhide Road at Jamestown. The turnoff is well marked.

Trip cost: If you own your own boat, launching is free. Guide Leslie charges $95 for two people for a day during the week, $120 on weekends.

Who to contact: A detailed map of the lake and adjacent areas is available for $5.70 including postage from Lake Map, 418 Calaveras Way, Sonora CA 95370. Expert fishing advice is available from guide Bob Leslie at (209) 532-4453.

NO. CALIFORNIA LAKES

SIX PRIME SIERRA NEVADA
DESTINATIONS

THE TASTE OF A MOUNTAIN MORNING

Most people long for what they do not have, and in the case of Bay Area campers, that yearning is often for the magic of the Sierra.

The air has the scent of pines up here, and on a pure mountain morning, the taste of crackling freshness. You awake and find yourself in a range studded with miles of forest, cut by classic trout streams, and sprinkled with lakes the color of blue sapphire gems. It remains one of the west's natural wonders, and can provide many classic spots for camping, lake and stream fishing, and backpacking. You can spend a weekend, a week, or a month.

For most it's been awhile. Yet Highway 80 can help zip you up to one of six prime camping, fishing and hiking areas near Truckee in about four hours driving time. You don't need a four-wheeler, just four wheels and an engine, and you can discover the Truckee River, Donner Lake, Martis Lake, and Boca, Stampede and Prosser reservoirs.

■ **Truckee River:**
Streamside campgrounds, easy access from Highway 89 (it borders most of the stream), and quality trouting make the Truckee one of California's best trout waters. The best stretch of water runs from Truckee upstream to Tahoe City. A prime trout area is from Squaw to Donner Creek, which is located near the entrance to Alpine Meadows. Although most of the fish are stocked rainbow trout, especially near the campgrounds, a few big brown trout hunker down in the deep holes. Rafting is also quite popular on the Truckee. An ideal day could be to sandwich morning and evening fishing trips around a midday rafting venture.

■ Donner Lake:

This can be a good choice for family camping. Since the lake sits directly adjacent to Highway 80, all facilities are provided, and the area is well developed with cabins and road. However, it is for those same reasons that many serious anglers skip Donner. Donner State Memorial Park at the east end of the lake is for weekend campers, and reservations are necessary through Ticketron. A public boat ramp is available at Donner Village Resort, where trout fishing is good in the summer with small Kastmaster lures. But if you hope to tangle with something big here -- like a 15-pound mackinaw or brown trout -- then be on the water at daybreak in a boat, and troll a Countdown Rapala or J-Plug adjacent to the northern shoreline.

■ Martis Lake:

This is a tiny jewel that has been set aside by the Department of Fish and Game as special fishing refuge. There's wild trout, but all fish are released, and the use of only artificial lures or flies with a single barbless hook is allowed. It's definitely not for a family camper. But for proficient fly fishermen, there is no better place to tangle with 18 to 24-inch wild trout, brown or Lahontan cutthroat. Boat motors are not permitted on the lake, so fishing from a float tube or small raft is ideal. The Sierra View Campground has hookups for motor homes, and provides fair sites for tent camping. To reach Martis Lake, turn south on Highway 267 at Truckee, then after six miles, turn east on the first turnoff to the lake.

■ Boca Reservoir:

A few giant -- yet elusive -- brown trout and a good sampling of stocked rainbow trout make Boca a good lake for trollers. During a warm summer evening, trollers often limit with a nightcrawler for bait trailed behind Ford Fender flashers. Boca Camp, on the far side of the lake, is the best spot to camp, and has boat ramp nearby. Motor home hookups are available as well near Boca Camp. Boca can be reached ìby turning north on Stampede Meadow Road, six miles past Truckee.

■ Prosser Reservoir:

Prosser is tucked away just five miles from Truckee, so supplies can be obtained with a very short drive. A 10-mph speed limit on the lake keeps skiers off, and with steady trout fishing, makes the lake a favorite for local anglers. Prosser Campground is perched on a wooded lake overlook and is a great spot. However, many campers do not learn of its existence when they first arrive, since they usually stop at the first campground they see here, Lakeside Camp. The lake is located five miles north of Truckee. From Highway 80, turn north on Highway, then turn right on Forest Road 18n74.

■ Stampede Reservoir:

If you want the classic Sierra experience, this is a good choice. It offers some 250 postcard-type campsites and consistent trout fishing year around. A bonus is an honest chance at big brown trout; troll a large Rapala directly across from the boat launch along the northern shoreline, and be on the water at dawn. Stampede is tucked away at 6,000 feet, 14 miles from Truckee, and eight miles off Highway 80 from the Stampede Road turnoff.

SIERRA ADVENTURE TRIP FACTS

Maps: The U.S. Forest Service has published a map that details all fishing waters, campsites, Forest Service roads, and backpack trails. Ask for the map of Tahoe National Forest and send $1 to the Office of Information, U.S. Forest Service, 630 Sansome Street, San Francisco, CA 94111.

Fishing tips: Call either Tahoe Truckee Sports at (916) 587-7436, Mountain Hardware at (916) 587-4844, or Tourist Liquor & Sporting Goods at (916) 587-3081.

Camping/lodging: Phone the Truckee Chamber of Commerce at (916) 587-2757, or write P.O. Box 2757, Truckee, CA 95734.

Who to contact: For more information, call (415) 556-0122.

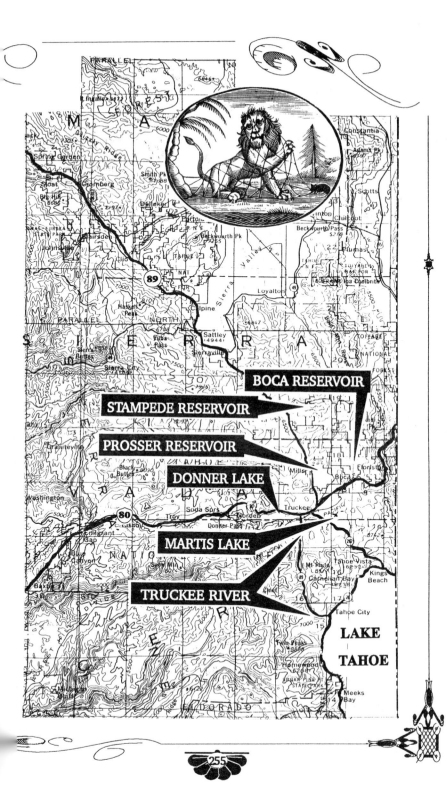

BOCA RESERVOIR

STAMPEDE RESERVOIR

PROSSER RESERVOIR

DONNER LAKE

MARTIS LAKE

TRUCKEE RIVER

LAKE TAHOE

BEARDSLEY RESERVOIR

❧ ❧ ❧

WHEN YOU CAN'T WAIT FOR OPENING DAY

The "twitch-twitch" at the rod tip never lies. Trout? You bet, maybe a big one. Brown trout to 15 pounds have been caught from Beardsley Reservoir.

Twitch-twitch. Bang! The rod was jerked, but then the line went limp. Nothing.

"I don't get it," said Ed Dunckel, a man of the Sierra Nevada who is one of my fieldscouts.

"Another bite, but no fish. Those trout are wily buggers. When we have out lines aboard, our hooks catch everything in sight, pants, shirts, the boat! In the water? Can't hook anything."

Some people can't wait for the opening day of the trout season, the last Saturday of each April. And yes, myself and fieldscout "Ed The Dunk" are two of the seriously afflicted.

Beardsley Reservoir is a good remedy. Hidden in the Sierra Nevada near Dodge Ridge at about 6,500 feet elevation and set amid mountains filled with cedars and pines, this Sierra lake is home for good populations of brown trout and a decent supply of rainbows. The road is paved all the way to the lake, and there is a large concrete launch ramp, as well as parking area. Although there are no developed campsites at the lake, the Forest Service provides a campground in nearby Pinecrest.

In the spring, snow is rarely a problem. The Sierra Nevada igloo is defrosting, with only patches of snow below 7,000 feet, and those few being in the shadows of north-facing slopes. Warmer weather, usually arriving by late March or early April, can get people thinking trout. And that's when it is time to think Beardsley.

Twitch-twitch went my rod. I set the hook hard, but the line again went limp. Just can't seem to hook these elusive critters.

Just about any concoction and strategy -- bait, spinners, flies, trolling or shoreline baitdunking -- can inspire strikes from the trout at Beardsley at one time or another. The trick is hooking them. In the spring from a boat, Ed The Dunk advises using small flashers, three feet of leader, and a half of nightcrawler on a No. 6 or 8 hook. We allowed the wind out of the west to push the boat along the southern shoreline.

Upon inspection of the bait, however, we kept finding the nightcrawler bit cleanly off at the edge of the hook. Lots of bites, no fish.

"Darndest thing I've ever seen," said The Dunk. "Well, we'll try something to fool 'em."

He tied a new hook, and from the excess line at the end of the knot, tied on yet another hook.

"A trailer hook," he said with a grin. The hooks were inserted at each end of the nightcrawler.

"Whichever end they grab, now we've got 'em!" shouted the Dunk, and let out a crusty laugh that echoed down the canyons. I rigged the same.

Bang! Almost immediately, I got a jolt of a bite. But then the line went limp again. I checked the bait and found that this time, the nightcrawler was bit in the middle, with two tiny pieces of each of two hooks.

In the next 15 minutes, the episode was repeated several times. Dunckel looked as confused as a mother chicken hatching a duck egg. Then his eyes suddenly brightened.

"I know what we'll do to get the sneaky little buggers," he said, retrieving his line. He shortened his bait to about a half-inch long, just a small piece of the nightcrawler, and had hooks sticking out of both ends.

"Let's see them try to get that!" shouted The Dunk. Almost immediately we had a trout on, a nice, little brown going about 11 inches. Then bang, The Dunk had one as well.

"Now we got 'em," said The Dunk with a grin. "Many are called but few are chosen."

He was right. In the next two hours, we both knocked quick limits of five fish apiece. And get this: Included were brown trout that measured 20 inches, 15 inches and 13 inches. A great limit and provided a classic Sierra fish fry that evening.

As we returned to his mountain home, Ed The Dunk laughed. "Hey, I hear the bass are starting to bite at New Melones. What do you say we..."

☛ BEARDSLEY RESERVOIR TRIP FACTS

How to get there: From the Bay Area, take Highway 580 to connecting route 205, then turn west on Highway 120/108 at Manteca. Continue on the highway through Sonora and up through Strawberry. The turnoff is well marked and is located about four miles from Strawberry.
Camping: No Forest Service campsites are provided at the lake, though camping is permitted. The One Loop Campground at Pinecrest, which is about five miles from the Beardsley turnoff, provides the nearest developed campsites.
Trip Cost: Access and boat launching at Beardsley Reservoir are free.
Who to contact: For fishing information, call Pinecrest Store at (209) 965-3597. For camping info, call the Forest Service at (209) 532-3671.

NO. CALIFORNIA LAKES

LAKE TAHOE

WHERE YOU COULD USE A LITTLE LUCK

The natural laws of gravity don't seem to apply at the casinos at Lake Tahoe. Although the gaming tables are perfectly level, your money seems always to slip a few feet away and into the grasp of a blackjack dealer. Those wary of this phenomenon know that the best bet you can make at Tahoe is to minimize your time at the casinos and instead take your chances with the fishing, boating and hiking.

Tahoe's excitement, adventures and remarkable natural beauty make it the Number One weekend vacation area for Californians. Just make sure you come home with your shirt; a lot of people don't.

Tahoe is "The Lake in the Sky," as Mark Twain called it, a natural wonder set amid miles of national forest. It is colored the deepest blue of any lake in California, a true gem situated at 6,000 feet. A definite tinge of mystery surrounds it. Just how deep is Lake Tahoe? Some scientists claim Tahoe is 1,648 feet deep, yet some old-timers say it is bottomless. The fact that boats and airplanes have disappeared in the lake, never to be seen again, seems to support the latter.

When it comes to the fishing, there are a lot more clues. Big mackinaw, rainbow, and brown trout, along with kokanee salmon, attracts anglers from throughout the Pacific Northwest. However, newcomers to Tahoe are usually quite surprised at the techniques used to catch these monsters.

The big fish, the mackinaw trout, are deep at Tahoe, and sportfishing boat skippers use downriggers to troll 180 to 260 feet deep. Your

fishing line is clipped to a separate reel of wire line and a 10-pound weight, and both lines are descended to the trolling depth. When you get a strike, your line pops free of the release clip and you fight the fish free of any lead weight. Skippers will troll just off the edge of the underwater shelf, using lures such as J plugs. If there are a few keys, it's to be on the water at first light, for the bite is often kaput by 10 a.m. -- and to fish when the moon is in its dark cycles.

Some locals in small boats score with rainbow and brown trout by trolling near the surface in coves. They use Rapala minnows or a flasher/nightcrawler combination. But for the big trout, you have to go deep, way deep. One fishing guide at Tahoe is so certain he can produce that he advertises a "no-fish, no-pay" deal. His name is Dean Lockwood and he operates out of Tahoe Sportfishing Center near South Lake Tahoe.

Timber Cove Marina, which is closer to the Stateline area, offers boat tours and scuba diving, in addition to fishing trips.

A tremendous number of campgrounds, motels, and resorts ring the lake, but reservations are still a must in the summer. After all, Tahoe is not exactly undiscovered.

If you want to break free from the crowds here, a good alternative is in the Tahoe National Forest, which borders the north shore of the lake. It provides good backpacking trails, as well as access to the famous Desolation Wilderness. And out here you don't have to worry about unfriendly dealers either.

Trout fishermen have two good rivers in the area. To the north is the Truckee River, a fine trout stream with excellent access, and to the south is the Carson River.

If your idea of breaking free is not camping, well, some of the finest motels in the Pacific Northwest can be found in the Tahoe Basin. If you want to stick to your car instead of hoofin' it on a trail, it takes about three hours to complete the loop drive around the entire lake, about 70 miles on a two-laner.

Just don't spend too much time at the casinos. Never forget that the blackjack tables claim their own special laws of gravity.

☞ **LAKE TAHOE TRIP FACTS**

Campgrounds: Five campgrounds are operated by the California State Park System, two by the U.S. Forest Service. Campsite reservations are available through Ticketron. For information on privately-operated campgrounds, contact the Tahoe Chamber of Commerce or refer to California Camping: The Ultimate Guide.

Tahoe National Forest: For information or permits (for Desolation Wilderness), call the U.S. Forest Service at (916) 544-6420.

Fishing: Dean Lockwood, Tahoe Sportfishing, South Lake Tahoe, (916) 541-5448; Lake Tahoe Excursions, (916) 541-7177.

Boat tours: A wide variety of cruises are available. For the M.S. Dixie, call (702) 588-3508; for the Tahoe Queen, call (916) 541-3364. Rentals of small boats are available at many marinas around the lake.

Lodging: Call the Tahoe Visitor's Bureau toll-free line at 1-800-822-5922.

Who to contact: Contact the Tahoe Chamber of Commerce at (916) 541-5255, or by writing P.O. Box 15090, South Lake Tahoe, CA 95702.

NO. CALIFORNIA LAKES

SHASTA LAKE

NORTHERN CALIFORNIA'S FAVORITE PLAYLAND

The lure twitched on the lake surface, sending little ripples across quiet water -- and almost instantly, the plug disappeared in a swirl of a big bass on the attack.

"Got one!" shouted Darrell Burroughs, my fishing compadre, his rod suddenly alive.

Excitement is the name of the game when fishing with Burroughs, a guide at Shasta Lake, and a unique fellow who has come as close to anybody to mastering bass angling. Burroughs was born with legs that end at the shin, yet has a remarkable zest for life that has made him one of the best fishing instructors in the West Coast. Burroughs lives in a home that practically sits on the lake, and it is here at Shasta where he has developed his art.

Shasta Lake is one of the true outdoor recreation capitals of the west, a massive reservoir with 365 miles of shoreline, 1,200 campsites, 21 boat launches, 12 marinas to rent houseboats, and 35 resorts. Want

more? Got more: A remarkable 22 species of fish live in the lake. It's easy to reach. It's a straight 250-mile shot up Highway 5; close enough to reach in a morning of driving, yet far enough away to merit a sense of remoteness.

Popular? Every year, a million people try fishing at Shasta. In the case of largemouth and smallmouth bass, that has smartened up the fish considerably. That's where the wiles of a man like Darrell Burroughs come on strong.

"Look at the leeward side of that island," said Burroughs, pointing just ahead of his boat. "See the muddy water along the shoreline? That's where the bass will be. In the rest of the lake, the water is so clear that the threadfin shad (a minnow) have no protection. They'll try to hide in the muddy water. The bass go right in after them inside the mudline."

From my seat on the boat, I casted a surface plug that landed on the shoreline, then with a twitch of the rod, plunked the lure in the turbid water. Almost instantly, a bass smashed into the plug.

Although bassers have thousands of lures they can buy at tackle shops, Burroughs uses few on a regular basis: (1) A white spinner bait; (2) A small jig called a Get's It; (3) A surface plug called a Zara Spook; (4) Surface buzz baits styled for a fast retrieve.

He prefers working the Pit Arm of Shasta Lake, particularly the lower reaches of it. After reaching the fishing grounds, Burroughs directs his boat with an electric trolling motor, probing coves, rock outcroppings, and tips of islands. You cast lures along the shoreline as you go.

Strikingly, in several coves on our trip, we saw gigantic schools of tiny, black fish -- less than 1/16 of an inch long -- crowding in hordes along the shoreline. They were baby bass, newly hatched; a good spawn that bodes well for future years. Despite a come-and-go wind, we did quite well on our trip, with a six-pound largemouth tops for the day. All fish were released.

If the thought of bass fishing doesn't stoke your fires, you have a choice of many different species, as well as other activities. Trolling for trout, baitfishing for catfish, or minnow dipping for crappie provides plenty of variety.

Shasta is also one of America's top lakes to houseboat on. Figure a week's vacation if you want to see the entire lake.

This is also one of the few places in California that can handle the overflow crowds of the holiday weekends -- Memorial Day, 4th of July, and Labor Day -- there's plenty of room here for all.

☛ SHASTA LAKE TRIP FACTS

How to get there: Drive straight up Highway 5 past Redding, a distance of about 250 miles.

Fishing: For fishing information, call Shasta Marina at (916) 238-2284, Bridge Bay Resort at (916) 275-3021, or Jones Valley Resort at (916) 275-1204.

Houseboat rentals: Houseboats rent from $900 to $1800 per week and sleep six to 14 people. For information, call Shasta Cascade at (916) 243-2643.

Camping: For a map locating campgrounds around Shasta Lake, write either Shasta Ranger District, 6543 Holiday Drive, Redding, CA 96003, or write Shasta Cascade, 1250 Parkview, Redding, CA 96001.

Shasta caverns: Tours are offered daily for $7 per person ($3 for kids under 12). For a brochure, write P.O. Box 801, O'Brien, CA 96070.

ADVENTURE 12

NO. CALIFORNIA LAKES

LEWISTON LAKE

RUB YOUR EYES

When you roll out of your sleeping bag at your campsite alongside Lewiston Lake, you might rub your eyes a few extra times to make sure you're still on earth, not in heaven.

This jewel of a lake laps quietly at the bank, and a few trout rise to the surface, just a few feet from your campsite. You rub your eyes some more. Thickly wooded mountains rise around you, and in the distance, the snow-covered alps provide a backdrop. Is this Montana? Canada? Switzerland? Hardly. This is another adventure in our own California; Lewiston Lake, tucked

away 30 miles west of Redding in Northern California, snuggled below the Trinity Alps.

It's a unique place that provides quality camping, fishing, boating, and hiking, yet is just far enough away from the Bay Area -- a five-hour drive -- to keep it from becoming a summer zoo of vacationers.

Four campground facilities provide 100 campsites, and if tents are not for you, there are several private resorts along the northwest end of the lake that offer cabins or hookups for motor homes. But a tent is all that is needed at the Mary Smith Campground, a truly idyllic spot at lake's edge. It has 18 sites for tent camping and is the first campground you reach in your drive along the lake.

Lewiston Lake is just big enough, with 15 miles of shoreline, so that it remains uncrowded both for camping and boating. A 10-mph speed limit on the lake makes it ideal for canoes and small aluminum boats, and keeps high-powered boats out. You don't have to contend with skiers, only the fish. And there can be plenty of the latter.

Like at any lake, the fishing runs in cycles, but kokanee salmon, rainbow trout, and a few giant but elusive brown trout can be in the deal. A key here is that Lewiston is actually the forebay for Trinity Lake -- and that means that water in this lake is cold year around, since it comes from the bottom of Trinity Dam.

Some of the best fishing in the summer is just before sunset at the upper end of the lake, particularly above Pine Cove Marina, just where you can start to see current on the lake surface. This is the haunt for rainbow trout, most averaging 13 to 14 inches. By boat, you should anchor in this area, and let a nightcrawler flutter in the current, testing different depths.

If you're without a boat, then bring chest waders and from above the Lakeview Terrace area, wade outside the tules and either cast a threaded nightcrawler, with split-shot for weight, or flycast. Spin fishermen might also try using a bubble and a fly in combination. Evening bites can be quite good.

Typical daytime fishing is not as good, but trollers using flashers and

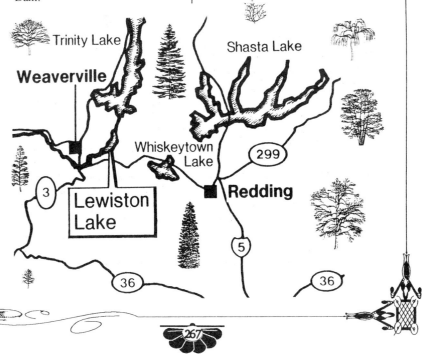

a needlefish lure or a nightcrawler can take good scores of kokanee salmon and rainbow trout in the 10 to 12-inch class.

Boat and motor rentals are available at Pine Cove Marina, Lakeview Terrace (for guests only). Rentals costs run $12 to $15 for a half day, and $22 to $25 for a full day.

A good option, especially for families, is to rent a boat for a half-day trip and fish the evening bite -- and spend the morning and mid-day exploring a trail on neighboring Trinity Lake. A good suggestion is the trail that runs from Clark Springs Campground and runs three miles to Cedar Stock Resort.

If you're roughing it, and need supplies while you're here, there are small grocery stores at Lewiston (southern end of lake) and Pine Cove Trailer Park.

That leaves little to worry about here. You just show up, kick back, and try to remember that you're not in some far corner of the world, but still in California. But then again maybe you don't even need to remember that.

☞ LEWISTON LAKE TRIP FACTS

How to get there: Just head up Highway 5 to Redding, take the Central offramp and head west on Highway 299. Continue on 299 for 23 miles, and turn north on the Lewiston Road -- which takes you to the lake. Figure a five-hour drive from San Francisco.

Camping: Campsites are free at Cooper Gulch, Ackerman, and Tunnel Rock, but cost $4 per night at Mary Smith Campground. All are operated on a first-come, first-served basis by the U.S. Forest Service. For information, call (916) 243-2643.

Motor home hookups: Available for $10 per night at Pine Cove Trailer Park by calling (916) 778-3838 and Lakeview Terrace Resort by calling (916) 778- 3803.

Boat rentals: Boat and motor rentals are available from Pine Cove Marina at (916) 778-3770.

Cabins: Lakeview Terrace offers cabins for $30 to $65 per night, depending on the number of rooms. For information: (916) 778- 3803.

Who to contact: For free maps, brochures, directions, and fishing tips, call Shasta Cascade Wonderland Association at (916) 243- 2643, or write at 1250 Parkview, Redding, CA 96001.

PHOTO
OPPORTUNITY

NO. CALIFORNIA LAKES

LAKE SISKIYOU

IN THE SHADOW OF SHASTA

Lake Siskiyou provides the classic camp setting. It's a small jewel of a lake with campsites along its shore, good fishing for both trout and bass, and located in the shadow of nearby Mount Shasta, a dominate sight with its 14,000 foot peak.

It is one of the best camping/fishing lakes in the North Country and is bordered by wild, primitive country, yet is accessible to anyone with four wheels and an engine. At 3,400 feet elevation, Siskiyou sits above the blowtorch heat of Redding, yet below the icebox cold of Mount Shasta.

A bonus is that the Siskiyou Campground is an ideal base camp for exploring a network of backcountry roads leading into relative wilderness. Nearby Gumboot Lake, for instance, is one of 35 alpine lakes in the Trinity and Shasta forests, and can provide excellent trout fishing, especially for anglers equipped with float tubes.

Lake Siskiyou itself is one of the few reservoirs in the western United States created with the sole intent as a recreation center. Because it is used for neither hydro-electric power or flood storage, the level remains consistent year around, and conditions are often optimum for fishing. A key is that a large stretch of the lake bottom is studded with tree stumps which makes for an ideal habitat for big fish, both brown trout and black bass. It was here that I hooked the largest trout I've ever tangled with, a 15 pounder. Since crawdads are so abundant in the lake, plugging with diving crawdad lures is often the ticket for the bass.

Summer vacationers are often content to rent an aluminum boat and troll 40 to 50 feet deep for the stocked rainbow trout. Many fish are caught in this manner during the morning and evening bites.

Siskiyou Campground is an ideal base camp for your adventure.

There are 290 campsites, each with a fire pit, picnic table, and food locker. You just drive right up. Most of the spots have RV hookups. It is so close to Highway 5, that the easy access causes the area's one foible -- people. Especially on hot weekends, there are too many people, and it distracts from the outdoor experience.

For others, however, it is just what they want. There is a good swimming and a beach area, along with volleyball and frisbee games. Take it or leave it. Regardless, the area remains very clean, the air has that mountain taste to it, and of course, there is that awesome mountain, always looming above. Indian legend has it that Mount Shasta was formed when the great spirit poked a hole in the sky and shaped a tepee with the fallen pieces.

Some of the fish in Lake Siskiyou seem big enough to have been create in a similar manner.

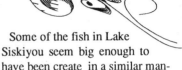

☞ LAKE SISKIYOU TRIP FACTS

How to get there: Take Highway 5 north past Redding, then take the exit ramp at the town of Mount Shasta and head west for a half mile. Turn left on Old State Road and continue to Siskiyou Lake.

Supplies: A small country store and marina tackle shop are available for supplies, the latter providing the latest tips.

Trip Cost: Campsites cost $7 per night for two people, with an additional $1.50 charge for each additional person. Boat and motors can be rented for the half-day for $20, and $32 for a full day. To launch private boats, a $1 fee is charged. It's free if you are camping.

Who to contact: Write or call Shasta Cascade at 1250 Parkview Avenue, Redding, CA 96001, (916) 243-2643, or Siskiyou Campground, P.O. Box 276, Mount Shasta City, CA 96067, (916) 926- 2618.

NO. CALIFORNIA LAKES

SAN LUIS
RESERVOIR

WHERE THE FISH ARE IMPORTED

It is not without a certain degree of irony that a fisherman celebrates his catch at San Luis Reservoir. If you have ever wondered where the Delta striped bass go that are swallowed by the giant California Aqueduct pumps near Tracy, San Luis Reservoir provides much of the answer. The lake is full of bass, catfish, and bluegills pumped down the California Aqueduct. But outdoorsmen who live nearby from San Jose to Los Banos have few complaints, and that is a key reason why after 20 years of pumping fish and water from the Delta to San Luis, the state has yet to solve the dilemma.

The striper fishing is clearly what makes the San Luis State Recreation Area most inviting, although boating, water skiing, camping, and hunting (in season) are also popular. It is a good wild card bet for an adventure, and is relatively nearby, located between Gilroy and Los Banos, just south of Highway 152. Instead of a limit of two striped bass, as is law in the Bay and Delta, San Luis Reservoir has so many striper that there is a five-fish limit. And instead of an 18-inch minimum size limit, at San Luis, anglers are urged to keep all fish.

When I fished here, I caught a few little stripers, about eight inches long, and tossed them back, wishing I was throwing them back in the Delta instead of in this reservoir. But that is how the locals look at it. I approached one fellow who had three little stripers on a stringer, all about eight to 10 inchers.

He was excited and happy. "Man, they're really hitting today," he

said. "I had a big one on, but it got away." Well, it turned out the "big one" was about a 14 incher.

Small fish here are generally the rule rather than the exception, although a sprinkling of stripers in the 15 to 20-pound class are caught by trollers, right at daybreak, using deep running lures. Occasionally, 30 and 40 pounders send shockwaves around the area. The best fishing here is almost always during the fall on days when the wind is down and the lake quiet.

In the fall, the stripers will often chase down and corral schools of threadfin shad. From the shoreline, you can see the fish going wild. By either boat or bank, it can be an exciting affair to chase down these roaming hordes of hungry fish then cast white Hair Raiser jigs into the swirl. From the shoreline, your car becomes as important as your fishing rod -- you literally race your way around the lake, trying to follow the ranging school of feeding stripers.

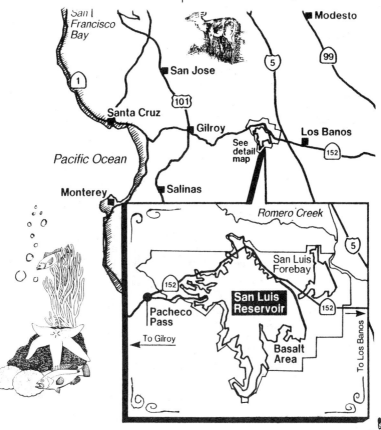

At the Basalt Area next to the lake, there are 79 campsites available, each with a table, cupboard, and barbecue grill. Most are set next to a mix of eucalyptus and pine. At the Medeiros Area at O'Neill Forebay, there is a primitive area that can hold up to 500 campers, an alternative if the Basalt Area is full.

During the booming heat of summer, water skiing is quite popular here, but boaters should beware of afternoon winds. A special warning light sits at Romero Overlook to warn of gales exceeding 30 mph.

The Pacheco Pass area can be like a wind tunnel, especially in the spring, so call first before hitting the road. With calm weather, it can be worth spending a weekend here, except when the blistering sun of July scalds everything it touches.

At the west end of the reservoir is a specially designed wildlife area where the ideal habitat attracts hawks, owls, falcons, and occasionally, even golden eagles. Waterfowl hunting is permitted here during the winter, in season.

☛ SAN LUIS RESERVOIR TRIP FACTS

How to get there: Take Highway 101 south to Gilroy, then take the Pacheco Pass cutoff (Highway 152) to the lake. It is about an hour's drive from San Jose to the campgrounds.

Reservations: Campsite reservations are advised through Ticketron. The state park requires reservations be made here at least 10 days ahead of your trip.

Fires: Fires are allowed only on campground grills.

Dogs: Dogs are allowed, but must be kept on a leash, and proof of rabies vaccination is required.

Trip Cost: The day-use fee is $2, campsites cost $6 per car per night and the boat launch fee is $2.

Who to contact: The San Luis State Recreation Area can be reached by calling (209) 826-1196, or writing 31426 West Highway 152, Santa Nella, CA 93635. For fishing information, call the Santa Nella Trading Company at (209) 826-6020.

LAKE NACIMIENTO

WHERE ANGLERS HAVE NO LIMIT

Dear Tom: I want to get my son excited about fishing, but I have no interest in the stocked trout at the Bay Area lakes. Can you tell me a good lake where we can catch a lot of bass? -- Bill Wolter, San Bruno

There may be no better lake than Lake Nacimiento to get anyone -- newcomers or old-timers alike -- excited about fishing. In fact, there are times here that the sport should be called "catching," rather than fishing.

Nacimiento is situated west of Paso Robles, and because it's a good four-hour drive, many Bay Area anglers overlook it. But from March through May, the bite here can often measure up to any lake in the western United States. For starters, consider the white bass; there are so many that there is not even a limit on how many you can take. Plus, the smallmouth bass action here can be some of the best you can find in California. A sprin-

kling of largemouth bass provides the kicker.

However, do not go to Lake Nacimiento with visions of landing some giant fish for a trophy wall mount. As the locals say, "There just ain't no such critters." We're talking quantity, not quality, and when it comes to action -- just the ticket to getting a kid hooked on fishing -- this is the place to come. Most of the white bass are like big crappie; the lake record is only four pounds, two ounces. But if you use light spinning tackle, you can still have a real kick. I use a five-foot, graphite rod and an ultra-light spinning reel filled with 2-pound test line.

All you have to do at Lake Nacimiento is tie on a lure such as a Roostertail, Mepps, or Kastmaster, and start casting in one of several key spots. When you connect, you're apt to start taking fish literally one after another. But where? That's the one variable that can foil first-timers here. With a minimum of homework, you can solve that bugaboo.

White bass go on wild feeds just after they move into one of several tributaries to spawn. Buy a lake map, then locate spots such as the narrows of the Nacimiento River, as well as in Las Tablas and Town Creeks.

If you want the closest thing to a guarantee, then the timing of your trip is a key. The white bass go wild the first time the water temperature hits 58 degrees. Hordes of a small baitfish called threadfin shad are the key to the fishery here. If you ever see the shad literally bubbling right on the surface, then stop and cast. More than likely, a pack of angry white bass will be lurking below.

If your arms get tired of reeling in the white bass, then you can switch your tactics for smallmouth bass, which range primarily from one to two pounds. White spinner baits, small plastic jigs are the favored lures. Where? OK, my favorite spot: At the western end of the lake in the "narrows," casting along the rocks.

If you own your own boat, Lake Nacimiento has three launch ramps. For overnighters, you can either stay at Nacimiento Resort, or camp at Devil's Gorge or Pine Knoll Campgrounds.

Nacimiento is primarily a spot for the camper fishermen, but if members of your expedition don't have a yearning for a tug on the rod, then there are other adventures available as well. Hiking trails, swimming areas, and rental of pontoon boats are popular. A full service marina, grocery store and resort are also available.

If you were to arrive here on a Friday evening, you'd be set for almost two days of action. Not a bad weekend. And if you want to get a buddy hooked on fishing for keeps, there are few better places to go.

☞ LAKE NACIMIENTO TRIP FACTS

How to get there: Take Highway 101 south past King City and continue to the town of Bradley -- where County Road G-19 will take you to the lake.

Trip length: It's about 100 miles from Monterey, so figure about two to three hours driving time to reach Nacimiento.

Facilities: A snack bar, restaurant, grocery store, bait and tackle shop, boat rentals, hot showers, and resort are available.

Trip Cost: Campsites are $7 per day, full RV hookups are available for $14 per day, and a boat launch ramp fee is $2.

Who to call: Woody's, a reliable source for fishing information, can be reached at (805) 238-3256.

FOUR TOP
CRAPPIE LAKES

WHEN YOUR YOUNG ANGLER WANTS ACTION

The best way parents can get their kids excited about fishing is to remember one key lesson: They want action.

Not solitude. Not watching the flowers bloom. Not watching the water roll by. They want sizzle. Taking them to a place where they can catch one fish after another can provide it.

Some say no such place exists. But if you are fishing for crappie, an abundant, good-eating panfish, you can find that place.

At Clear Lake, people can catch 25 to 30 crappie apiece in an area called Clearlake Oaks, also known as the Keys. Lake Berryessa has also been a good spot, with stringerfuls of crappie being caught around submerged brush piles and tree stumps. In the Bay Area, the window of opportunity has opened at Uvas Reservoir, south of San Jose and Lake Chabot near Castro Valley.

My first successful fishing trip as a kid came when crappie fishing at Clear Lake. My family arrived late one Friday evening, and I could scarcely wait for the station wagon to stop before jumping out with my fishing rod. I ran down to a boat dock, where bright lights were attracting a lot of bugs, mainly gnats.

Right from the dock, you could see schools of minnows near the surface, attracted by the gnats. I flipped out a short cast using a small crappie jig, and instantly had my first crappie on. In the next two

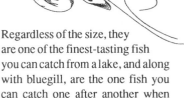

hours, I caught 30 or 40 of them, and for a kid, it was the most exciting two hours of my life. It was the first thing that could beat hitting a baseball.

That was a lucky night, to be sure, but anybody can approach the same kind of fun with just a little bit of homework. This is one time when "fishing" might be renamed "catching."

One key is understanding the food chain at a lake. Crappie eat minnows. So fishing at areas where minnows are likely to be in abundance is the first step, and that means around submerged brush piles, tree stumps (also called "stick-ups" from fishermen), or submerged piles of rocks, such as are common along the edges of earth dams. At night, bright lights attract bugs, which in turn attract minnows, so fishing under bright lights is another time and place to fish for crappie.

Crappie average about seven or eight inches. It is a white fish speckled with black spots (though before they spawn, they turn quite dark). Sometimes you might catch one just three or four inches long. Sometimes you get a big one, like 14 inches, better than a pound.

Regardless of the size, they are one of the finest-tasting fish you can catch from a lake, and along with bluegill, are the one fish you can catch one after another when you find a school.

It helps to have a boat, but it's not the critical factor. Mobility is. If you aren't getting the bites at one spot, then pick up and move on to another likely looking spot. Search the lakeshore for the right kind of habitat, the trees, brush, or rock piles.

Use either a live minnow or a small crappie jig, whatever you prefer.

Most people like using a live minnow, because you get to "see" the bites. You start by tying a No. 8 hook on your line, then attach a small bobber three feet above that. The minnow is then hooked through the back or through the lower jaw. You just toss it out and keep a close watch on that little bobber. If you get into the crappie, it will start dancing, maybe get tugged right under and disappear. Set the hook, hoss, 'cause you've got a fish on.

Others prefer using small jigs, an artificial lure that imitates a minnow. They can be preferable since you don't have to buy or fuss with live minnows. However, the crappie can get mighty picky when it comes to jigs, and it is advisable to use several different types in the

search for just the right one for that day's fishing. Some people use a pencil bobber with a jig, the bobber serving as a strike indicator in order to retain the visual excitement factor.

An added bonus is that when using a minnow or a lure that imitates a minnow, you might catch other fish besides crappie. At Uvas recently, I snuck up on a cove that I thought was filled with crappie, and tossed in a mini jig. Wham! I caught bass on back-to-back casts. They weren't monsters, just 10, 11-inchers, but what the heck, it's action.

And that's what a kid wants. If you want to get your kid fascinated with the sport, you have to provide it.

That's what crappie can do. But let me issue one warning: Remember what happened to me when I was a kid on that first, historic trip to Clear Lake. I had so much fun I became an outdoors writer.

TOP CRAPPIE LAKES

Clear Lake:

Once considered the crappie capital of the western United States, Clear Lake now has fewer, but larger, crappie. Located northeast of San Francisco, about a three-hour drive from the Bay Area, it's the largest natural lake inside California.

Who to contact: *Call either the Clear Lake Chamber of Commerce at (707) 994-3600 or Clear Lake State Park at (707) 279-4293.*

Lake Berryessa:

The Bay Area's backyard fishing hole is located northeast of Napa, about a two-hour drive from San Francisco. The best crappie spots are in coves in the arms of the southern end of the lake, and around submerged trees in coves in the Putah Creek arm, at the north end of the lake.

Who to contact: *Call any of the following: Putah Creek Resort at (707) 966-2116; Steele Park at (707) 966-2330; Spanish Flat Resort at (707) 966-2338; Markley Cove Resort at (707) 966-2116.*

Lake Chabot:

This lake is the centerpiece of the East Bay Regional Park District. Crappie tend to be a bit smaller than at other lakes, and the use of live minnows is not permitted. Regardless, results can be good in protected coves using mini jigs.

Who to contact: *Call either the East Bay Regional Park District at (415) 531-9300 or Lake Chabot Marina at (415) 582-2198.*

Uvas Reservoir:

Uvas is the best of the lakes in the Santa Clara Valley south of San Jose. It's located near Coyote. Live minnows drifted near the dam or around submerged trees have been the ticket to good crappie catches.

Who to contact: *Call Coyote Discount Bait at (408) 463-0711.*

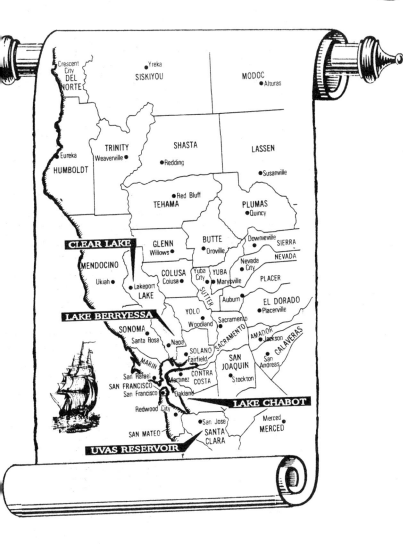

CRESCENT City
DEL NORTE

Yreka
SISKIYOU

MODOC
Alturas

TRINITY
Weaverville

SHASTA
Redding

LASSEN
Susanville

Eureka
HUMBOLDT

Red Bluff
TEHAMA

PLUMAS
Quincy

CLEAR LAKE

GLENN
Willows

BUTTE
Oroville

Downieville
SIERRA

NEVADA

MENDOCINO

Ukiah

Lakeport
LAKE

COLUSA
Colusa

Yuba
City

YUBA
Marysville

Nevada
City

PLACER

Auburn

EL DORADO
Placerville

SUTTER

LAKE BERRYESSA

SONOMA

Santa Rosa

YOLO
Woodland

Napa

SACRAMENTO

Sacramento

AMADOR
Jackson

CALAVERAS

SOLANO
Fairfield

San
Andreas

MARIN

San Rafael

CONTRA
COSTA

SAN
JOAQUIN

Stockton

Martinez

SAN FRANCISCO
San Francisco

Oakland

LAKE CHABOT

Redwood City

SAN MATEO

San Jose

SANTA
CLARA

Merced
MERCED

UVAS RESERVOIR

NO. CALIFORNIA LAKES

TRINITY LAKE

SOLITUDE & SMALLMOUTH BASS

Come every February, when most bass in California lakes are deep in winter slumber, the alarm clock seems to go off in Trinity Lake and awaken a huge population of smallmouth bass.

Almost nobody seems to know of it during the cold weather of February, March and April. The lake is practically abandoned, with the exception of a few smart bass fishermen who try to keep their lips sealed about the secrets they've learned. This lake is a beauty in the early season as it is situated below the snow-capped Trinity Alps. It's cold out here, and that does much to keep many people away, but the skies are often clear, the water flat calm, and in the lake's coves, the smallmouth bass are just starting to go on the bite.

Trinity Lake has much to offer. Lakeside cabins secluded in pine trees, mountain campsites, week-long houseboat rentals, and good trout fishing -- shoreline anglers can nail 14-inch trout at Stuart's Fork, just tossing out a nightcrawler with a marshmallow topper.

But it seems that Trinity is a for-gotten refuge until Memorial Day Weekend. Ironically, by then, the best fishing is often long gone. The smallmouth bass bite best from February to early April. Unlike their big brother, the largemouth, smallmouth get active in cooler water.

From any type of boat -- canoe, raft, aluminum skiff -- you should approach Trinity's coves in silence, then cast a spinner bait, jig, or plastic worm actually on the shoreline. With a flip of your rod, you dart the artificial bait into the water, letting it sink 10 to 15 feet -- bang! That's when the smallmouth hits. The best fishing is from sunrise to 10 a.m., when you need to wear several layers of clothing to keep warm. By mid-morning, when the sun is on the water, you should switch to tiny jigs, not more than inch long, for the best angling bet.

With 175 miles of shoreline, there are plenty of coves to sneak up on to try these techniques. The best fishing, however, is usually on the north end of the lake on the east fork of the Trinity, at an area the locals call the "Dredger Tailings."

If you are searching for a classic cabin hideaway, there are several options available. At Trinity Center, the cabins are tucked away in a canyon alongside Swift Creek. How isolated is this? Well, put it this way:

They finally got phones with dials on them in 1984. Cabins along the lake are available at Cedar Stock Resort and also at Wintoon.

If camping is for you, waiting for warmer weather is advised. By late May, 23 campgrounds with 723 sites are opened up by the U.S. Forest Service. Only a few are open prior to mid-April. Motor home hookups are available year around at Wintoon Park.

If you own a trailered boat, there are four public ramps (free access) and five private. The best launch ramp is at Tannery Gulch, which is adjacent to Stuart's Fork on the western side of the lake. Two other good ramps are located at Fairview Marina, which is adjacent to the

massive Trinity Dam, and also at the northern end of the lake at Recreation Plus.

One of the little-known features at Trinity Lake is that above Swift Creek is the trailhead for several wilderness-styled backpack trips. Several trails cut their way to a series of primitive lakes, and others can take you high into the Trinity Alps. Such hikes should not be attempted until mid-June, when snowmelt opens the trails. If your interest is primed, the Forest Service has a new map available detailing the Trinity Alps Wilderness.

But until warm weather arrives in mid-May, you're best off sticking to the lake, casting along the shoreline for smallmouth bass. Most of these fish are not giants, but have the spunk to give you a good tussle.

While you're at it, at some point be sure to stop, and just gaze at the scenery around you. The Trinity Alps are on one side, laden with snow and glistening in the sun, the Trinity Mountains on the other. But be careful. You might not want to ever go home again.

☞ TRINITY LAKE TRIP FACTS

How to get there: Head north on Highway 5, take the Central Redding offramp, then continue on Highway 299 to Weaverville -- then turn right on State Route 3 and continue to the lake.

Maps: For a free map and a list of accommodations, either call Shasta Cascade at (916) 243-2643, or write them at 1250 Parkview Avenue, Redding, CA 96001.

Cabins: Cabins cost from $25 to $45 per day, or about $250 per week. They include a full kitchen and can accommodate up to four people per cabin. Call Cedar Stock Resort at (916) 286-2225, Wintoon Park at (916) 266-3337, or Ripple Creek at (916) 266-3505.

Motor homes: Hookups are available year around at Wintoon Park. The price is right at $8.50 per day, $49 per week, or $135 a month.

Camping: A few U.S. Forest Service campgrounds are open year around, but most are not accessible until late May. For information, call the Weaverville Ranger District at (916) 623- 3121.

Fishing: For information, call Brady's Sportshop in Weaverville at (916) 623-3121.

TRINITY ALPS'
TROUT

AN OFF-THE-TRAIL CHALLENGE

The rocky chute rose almost straight up, and from my perch on a narrow ledge, it seemed like trying to climb the backbone of a huge monster.

Below was 1,500 feet of rock, above was the Sawtooth Ridge of the Trinity Alps. Climbing, as we were, off-trail, in search of wonders, unknown lakes and big trout, means accepting mystery and danger.

Rivers, lakes and ocean will attack you. Mountains are different. They wait for you to make a mistake.

I reached up and grabbed hold of a rock, and it gave way and went crashing down the talus slope like a bowling ball -- and my heart shook at the thought it could be our bodies doing the same. Then I remembered my old wilderness adage:

Don't fight the mountain. Accept it, think it through, and move forward. Deep inside of you, right in your chest, is a window, and when that window opens, the power of the universe will flow through you. Don't let the window shut and lock. Settle down and let it open, and you will move forward and achieve the greatness for which you are meant.

With that thought, now more settled, I grabbed another rock. It held. I pulled myself up, a booted foot lodged in a crevice for support. A light breeze coming up the canyon made the sweat tingle on the back of my neck. The next foot came easier. Made it through a top spot, just like that.

We scrambled to the mountain rim and peered from a ridge notch as if we were standing on the edge of the earth. Below us was the Trinity Alps Wilderness, located northwest of Redding, immense wildlands with 585,000 acres, 82 lakes, 50 mountain peaks and 550 miles of trails.

Bigger-than-life rainbow trout.

The biggest mountain-bred rainbow trout of the West live here in remote, little known lakes. But to reach them, you must leave the trail. One such lake, Little South Fork Lake, is said to have trout that average 15 to 18 inches and that practically say, "Catch me." But in a guidebook for the area, author Wayne Moss called reaching this lake a task for "deranged souls."

Three likely candidates for such a title are Jeff Patty, Michael Furniss of Eureka, and myself. Over the years, we have gone off-trail in search of Bigfoot, hiked the entire John Muir Trail, and climbed Shasta, Whitney and Half Dome, among many other adventures. Patty, a wilderness explorer/photographer, and Furniss, a scientist, don't have any squeaky parts, but are a bit crazy.

And the idea of giant rainbow trout in remote wildlands was enough to inspire another trip.

The Trinities may be the prettiest land in the Western United States. The granite chutes on the mountain rims make it look like the Swiss Alps. The lakes are actually rock bowls carved by glacial action, then filled by snowmelt. Every deep canyon looks like a sea of conifers.

From the trailhead at Coffee Creek, we hiked in 12 miles to the Caribou Lakes Basin, spent the night, then stared hard at the map, studying the terrain and slope.

"There's no easy way in to Little South Fork Lake," Patty said. "No easy way out."

"Perfect for three 'deranged' souls," answered Furniss.

There would be an altitude drop of 2,500 feet, then a climb of 3,500 feet without the benefit of a trail. In our way were two mountains, and we decided to lateral around them, taking bear paths and deer trails to get there. It wasn't long until we ran into a massive brush field, and one after the other, the three deranged souls disappeared into it.

We'd grapple with the limbs, scramble for a toehold, fall down, and cuss the brush. After several hours, our forearms were scratched up like we'd been in a fight with a pack of bobcats and lost.

"Getting caught in that brush makes you feel like a bug in a spider web," Furniss said.

But there is no fighting it. You lose every time. Remember the window in your chest. Let it open and you can move on.

Fighting off a swarm of bees.

Later, after dropping elevation and heading through a forest, Patty spotted what looked like a bear trail, and we were able to take one good step after another for the first time in hours. The air smelled of pines, and you could faintly hear the sound of a small stream. I took a deep breath and felt like I was in a time machine, back in the 1830s when the first trailblazers came west.

Suddenly, right then, there was a terrible stinging sensation on my right hand. Then bang! Again, in my arm. And again, right in the butt. I looked down at my stinging arm and hand and saw bees swarming around me.

I let out a howl, and in a flash, I unhitched my pack and went running through the forest, then stopped to see if I had outrun them. No such luck. Some 20 bees were clamped onto my pants, trying to sting my legs. Others were circling.

"They've marked you, they've marked you," shouted Furniss. "Run, run!"

In a panic-stricken rush, I swept them off my legs, and went running through brush, around trees. I would have given a million dollars for a lake to jump in. But there was no lake. A minute later, after being chased by a swarm, it was over.

Patty, certified for emergency medical treatment, immediately grabbed me.

"Do you have an allergic reaction to bee stings?"

"No," I answered, and he then slid the stingers out, using care not to break the poison sack.

"You must have stepped on a bee hive," Furniss said. "You're lucky you didn't get stung a hundred times. One time they got me in the head, but they only got me three times."

"A lot of people get hurt when they're running from a swarm of bees," Patty added. "In panic, they don't watch where they're going and break an ankle or leg. Then, while laying there, the bees get them anyway."

Later, we dropped down the canyon stream, hoping to rockhop straight up the river, eventually reaching the lake. The plan was working well until we ran head-on into a surprise, a 100 foot waterfall. We named it Crystal Falls, because the falling water droplets with sunlight refracting through them looked like crystals.

But as pretty as it was, that waterfall blocked our route. To get around it required backtracking, then scrambling up a 120-degree talus slope to gain altitude on the canyon wall, lateraling across thick brush, and then rock-climbing our way to a rock basin. It had required 10 hours for us to travel under two miles -- but we could finally see it, Little South Fork Lake.

It was just before sunset. It is a particularly beautiful lake, small, but deep blue and surrounded by steep, glaciated granite. Even from a distance, you could see the insects hatching and the trout rising.

Feeling like we were on top of the world.

We could hardly wait to fish, and after a night of recovery, gave it a try. At times it was hard to believe. In one stretch of seven casts, I has five strikes and landed rainbow trout measuring 12, 13, and 16 inches. The biggest of the trip was 17-1/2 inches. I had another on that ripped off 20 feet of line in two seconds before spitting the hook.

Yes, the fish were as big as the rumors. And there is logic to explain why.

Even though the Trinity Alps look like the top of the world, the elevations are 5,000 to 6,000 feet, much lower than the Sierra Nevada or Rocky Mountains.

"That's why there is more terrestrial productivity here than in the high Sierra," said Furniss, whose speciality is soil and water science.

"There is more soil, more trees, more algae in the bottom of the lakes and more insect hatches."

In other words, more life in general, including fish. Big ones. There was no "evening rise," like at most lakes. The fish were feeding continuously. A gold Z-Ray and small Panther Martin spinner were the lures that enticed the most bites.

At night there was a remarkable calm at this remote lake. Deer, sometimes 15 at a time, could be seen browsing in the bright moonlight within 100 yards of the camp.

Patty pointed to the granite rim above the lake. "When it's time to get out of here, let's climb that," he said. "No way do we want to fight the brush, the bees and that waterfall again."

Patty smiled and started suggesting possible routes. Nearby, a big trout jumped and landed with a splash. Fifty yards away, a deer stared at the surprise visitors, the three deranged souls.

Furniss sized up the ridge bright in the moonlight, and smiled.

"It looks just about impossible to climb," he said with a laugh.

A minute later, he spoke again.

"Mother Nature saves her best for those willing to struggle to find her."

CHAPTER 6

NORTHERN

CALIFORNIA RIVERS

WITH

11 ADVENTURES

CONTENTS:—

PUBLISHED BY FOGHORN PRESS

SAN FRANCISCO

QUALITY OUTDOOR BOOKS

NO. CALIFORNIA RIVERS

M^cCLOUD RIVER
PRESERVE

WHERE THE CHAIN IS NEVER BROKEN

Comes a time when a person wishes he could live in an earlier time, a time when deer roamed without fear, old trees were left standing, and wild rainbow trout were kings of the stream. At the McCloud River Preserve, Californians have the chance to live in such a time. You can experience the wild native wonder of California that trailblazers found in their first steps out West.

Hidden east of snowcapped Mount Shasta, the McCloud River remains close to its native state. A person can choose to walk among the woods, or fish hip deep for wild trout, and get the feeling that this is much as it was 200 years ago, before the white man had ever thought of dams and chainsaws. And it will always remain this way. The Nature Conservancy, a non-political organization dedicated solely to purchasing and preserving unique wildlands, now manages more than six miles of the McCloud watershed. While fishing access is permitted for free, it is restricted to no more than 10 rods on the river, all trout hooked must be released, and anglers must use single barbless hooks on flies or lures.

No hunting, tree cutting, or wood gathering is allowed. When it comes to fishing, the ethic of the Nature Conservancy is clear: A wild trout is too valuable to be caught only once.

It was a warming spring morning on the McCloud, my waders marked to the hip by river water, and I watched insects hatching on the river surface. "Caddis," I thought to myself.

My wrist twitched with my fly rod; I already had a fly patterned after a caddis tied on my fishing line. My old friend, Joe Kimsey, 60, a guide and fly fishermen extraordinaire who was born in the nearby town of McCloud, had tipped me off the previous day. Casting not more than 25 feet, I laid the fly in a riffle, and watched the current take it downstream, the fly tumbling as if no line was attached. Then, suddenly -- got one! A remarkable red flash in the water was at the end of my line, and after a few minutes, was brought to my side: A wild rainbow trout, about a 12-incher, not a giant by any means, but colored with nature's most vivid red. Unhooked, it swam away to freedom.

"Did you see the red cheeks and stripe on that fish," asked Kimsey. "It's like that nowhere else in the world. Last fall I got a 29-incher here, and that trout was so bright red that it would make you blind."

Trout here are a special breed; they are the Shasta Rainbow. According to the Nature Conservancy, it is from the McCloud strain that most hatchery trout in many parts of the world have descended. In 1872, an egg-taking station was situated at the mouth of the river, resulting in the introduction of the fish to places such as New Zealand, where it now provides a world-class fishery. Though the 10-pounders of New Zealand draw anglers from thousands of miles, there are enough 15 to 30-inchers in the McCloud to entice Bay Area residents to make the eight-hour drive a few times each spring and summer.

However, do not get the false impression that just because the fish "know" they will be released, that they will commit Hari Kari on your hook. Many first timers are skunked. According to a logbook kept by the Nature Conservancy, the average catch during the morning or evening bite is four to five rainbow trout per angler. Experienced anglers do better, especially for larger trout.

To learn, you have to get out on the stream, and start casting. No amount of words or pictures can make you know this special river in the sense that you should.

However, a few keys can aid you in your attempt. For one, bring chest waders and a wading staff (an old ski pole is well suited). The rocks here are coated with a light film of algae, and are slippery, particularly the large flat ones. One fellow outdoor writer slipped and took the plunge three times in a single morning. A good lesson for all. Take your steps with care, avoiding large rocks, and search instead for gravel pockets between large rocks.

Another key here is detecting the delicate bite of the trout. Rarely is there a distinct jerk, as with hatchery fish, but instead, the only signal is often a misdirection of your fly line as it drifts downstream with the current. "You see anything phony looking about your line as it drifts downstream, and darn it, you set the hook," advises Kimsey. Anglers learning this craft usually have to pay their dues. Those are the rules of the wild.

The McCloud River is unique. Its source for thousands of years has been a huge 44-degree volcanic spring from the underground waterways of nearby Mount Shasta. The surrounding area has never lost its wild character either. Squirrels with giant tails play in the leaves; mountain lions hide in the woods. The picture comes into focus. One morning, we even saw a wild turkey running straight up the side of a mountain.

☛ MCCLOUD RIVER PRESERVE TRIP FACTS

How to get there: Take Highway 5 straight up the California Valley, past Redding to Mount Shasta City, and turn east on Highway 89. Continue to the town of McCloud, turn right at the Shell gas station, and follow the signs past McCloud Reservoir to the Preserve.

Reservations: Only 10 rods are allowed on McCloud Preserve. Reservations can be made by phoning the Nature Conservancy at (415) 777-0487.

Guide: Fishing guide Joe Kimsey, is available at a rate of $125 per day for two people, and can be reached at (916) 235-2969.

Camping: The camping fee at the primitive campsite Ah-Di-Na Campground is $6.

Hotel: The nearest lodging to McCloud is Park Motor Hotel, which rents rooms for $19 per day, fully-equipped apartments for $35 per day. They can be contacted at (916) 964-2300.

Who to contact: For general information on fishing, hotels, directions, and maps, call the Shasta Cascade Organization at (916) 243-2643, or write at 1250 Parkview Avenue, Redding, CA 96001. The Nature Conservancy can be contacted at 156 Second Street, San Francisco, CA 94105.

"I've been fishing this here Mc-Cloud practically since the day I was born," said Joe Kimsey. "Last year we came around a bend and saw what looked like two little kittens playing in the dust. I couldn't believe it. They were baby bobcat, like nothing you ever seen."

A few bald eagles, mink, wild turkey and river otter may be seen on the McCloud Preserve. A hundred years from now, their descendants will remain. The chain of wildlife here will never be broken.

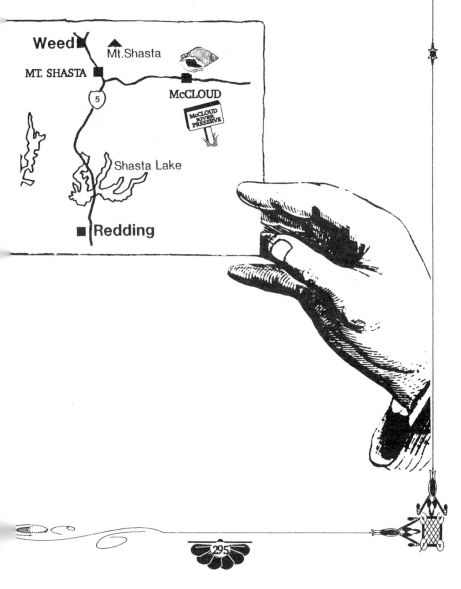

BURNEY: CALIFORNIA TROUT
PARADISE

WHERE DREAMS ARE MADE

I n the northeastern corner of California is a valley where nature has carved and sowed two of the finest trout streams in the Western United States. Hat Creek and Fall River are not created by the many trickles of melting snow like most streams along the slopes of California's Sierra Nevada, or Oregon and Washington's Cascade ranges, but are spring-fed, each bubbling fresh out of the ground from the underground waterways of nearby Mount Lassen, a volcano that blew its top in 1914.

The area is tucked away near Burney, about 50 miles east of Redding via Highway 299, about a five-hour drive from the metroplex of the San Francisco Bay Area. It is a paradise for fly fishermen, but offers angling and camping opportunities as well

for anybody who wants to set up a tent and plunk a bait in a nearby stream or lake. In addition to Hat Creek and Fall River, which have designated "Wild Trout Sections" with special angling restrictions, the area has several prime trout streams and reservoirs that can provide action for all fishermen. Upper Hat Creek, Pit River, Burney Creek, Baum Lake and Lake Britton provide a network of trout fishing opportunities just minutes apart.

But the focal points here are the two spring-fed streams, Hat Creek and Fall River, where fly fishermen find contentment rolling out casts and watching the line settle quietly in the gentle flows. As anglers know well here, the wash-tub sized swirl of big rainbow trout taking a dry fly is not a sight quickly forgotten. And big the trout do get, as a result of the streams' unique habitat.

Rather than strewn with pebbles, the river bottoms of Fall River and Hat Creek are moss covered, ideal

homes for insect larvae. When the temperature reaches 60 degrees and warmer, the larvae will emerge from the moss and hatch on the surface. At Fall River, the hatch can be so thick that it can look like San Francisco fog. Locals call it "Hatch Madness." The trout will gorge themselves on the insects with almost every summer day evolving into an all-you-can eat smorgasbord. A native 14-inch rainbow trout can be considered an average specimen in this haven where fish are often measured with scales, not rulers.

For either Hat Creek or Fall River, a good fly line is a No. 5. Figure on using about nine feet of leader when using nymphs, and in excess of 12 feet when using dry flies.

Who to contact: For maps and a list of campgrounds, motels and fishing guides of the entire area, call the Shasta Cascade Wonderland Association at (916) 243-2643 or write at 1250 Parkview Avenue, Redding, CA 96001.

■ Hat Creek:

This is the most popular stream in the area because it offers both a pristine setting and good access. It is a classic chalk stream, and the lower 3.5 miles of river have been designated by California's Department of Fish and Game as a Wild Trout Stream -- no hatchery fish have been planted in 15 years. The wild trout here average 10 to 16 inches, with an occasional rainbow trout in the 22-inch range. Some particularly elusive monster brown trout also roam free; in 1980, a 17-pound female was caught.

Highway 299, the two-laner that feeds into the Burney area from Redding, actually crosses Hat Creek, providing excellent access. Anglers can arrive, from the drive, take a hard look at the river, then choose whether to hike upstream or downstream. The farther you walk -- to reach rarely fished areas -- the better the angling can be. Typically, however, fishing is best on Hat Creek in the evening hours of summer.

From Powerhouse No. 2 to Lake Britton, Lower Hat Creek is a designated Wild Trout Stream, where only flies and lures with a single barbless hook are allowed -- and a two-fish 18-inch minimum size limit applies. It is primarily a flyfishing stream, where anglers use small patterns and two and four-pound test tippets, so the wild trout will not detect their presence. Though the fly patterns vary in size according to season and hatches, in

the hot weather from mid-summer on, fishermen use very small flies, even as small as No. 20. According to guides, some of the best patterns are: Adams, Blue Dun, Dark Blue Upright, Quill Gordon, Jerry, Yellow Stone, Pale Evening Dun and Yellow Stone. Spincasters with lures should stick primarily to lures such as the Kastmaster, Rooster Tail, Krocadile, Mepps Spinner and Panther Martin. Small sizes are usually best.

This area is home to some of the wisest fishermen in California (for example they selected this beautiful area to live). Just a few of the smartest anglers are willing to provide up-to-the-minute information on Lower Hat Creek. One of them is Steve Vaughn, (916) 335-2381, at Vaughn's Sporting Goods, 1713 Main Street, Box AV, Burney, CA 96013. If you drop Steve a stamped, self-addressed envelope, he will be happy to send you, free of charge, his "Fishing Guide Map" for the Burney Basin. Hat Creek Anglers, also in Burney, are willing to provide guide service and fishing tips. They can be reached at (916) 335-3165, or by writing 3193 Main Street, Johnson Park 96013.

Four motels are available in Burney, with about a dozen sitting in the inter-mountain area. Reservations are strongly advised. A complete list, along with additional fishing information, can be received from the Burney Chamber of Commerce by phoning Caldwell's Corner at (916)335-4994 or by writing them at 1819 Main Street, Burney, CA 96013.

Campgrounds are abundant along Highway 89, which intersects Highway 299 about 10 miles east of Burney. The U.S. Forest Service operates eight campgrounds, with some specially tailored for recreation vehicles. For brochures, write U.S. Forest Service, Hat Creek District, Fall River Mills, CA 96028. The Pacific, Gas & Electric Company also provides campgrounds, with information available by writing Area Manager, PG&E, Route 1, Box 50, Burney, CA 96013. The McArthur-Burney Falls State Park is exceptionally popular and reservations are necessary through Ticketron.

■ Upper Hat Creek:

A favorite campground here is the Big Pine Camp, operated by the U.S. Forest Service, which is nestled at streamside along Upper Hat Creek. It is an ideal alternative for fishermen who want to have a trout barbecue once the trip is completed, instead of releasing almost everything you hook, as is practiced at Lower Hat Creek and Fall River. The stream is well stocked with hatchery fish, and bait-fishing is not only allowed, but has evolved into the favored tactic to catch a trout dinner. The preferred entreaties are crickets, worms and salmon eggs. Most of the trout here are of the pansize variety in the eight to 11-inch class.

Additional Angling Opportunities

Cassel Forebay, Baum Lake, Lake Britton, Burney Creek and Pit River provide additional angling opportunities in a relatively small area near Burney. For more information, call Vaughn's Sporting Goods at (916) 335-2881, Shasta Cascade at (916) 243-2643, or Burney Chamber of Commerce at (916) 335-4994. A capsule summary:

Cassel Forebay:
Located east of Burney, Cassel provides a well-stocked stretch of water with a 10-fish limit. Most anglers use traditional baits like red eggs or crickets, but fly-fishing can be effective. A PG&E Campground is available at Cassel Park.

Baum Lake:
This is big fish country, where german and rainbow trout grow to surprising sizes. A 24-pounder was taken back In 1985, and most trout average one to two pounds. Baum can be fished by boat or bank, but no motors are allowed on the lake. Most fishermen dunk worms or nightcrawlers; a few others cast flies under a bubble.

Lake Britton:
This is a popular lake for vacationers, with campgrounds available on the north shore and also at McArthur-Burney Falls State Park. It's a take-your-pick fishery, with bass, crappie, bluegill and trout stocked in the lake.

Burney Creek:
Burney Creek is a pretty setting, the river gurgling over rocks polished by centuries of rolling river water. Access is excellent and it is a well-stocked creek, although most fish are small.

Pit River:
One of the west's most unheralded trout streams despite providing a quality fishing experience. The stretch of river below Pit River No. 3 powerhouse can be particularly good. A problem here is a brushy shoreline, providing access problems to first-timers. A phone call to one of the sources previously listed should be considered mandatory before heading out.

■ Fall River:

Snow-covered Mount Lassen sits above this trout paradise, watching as it has done since its last violent eruption 70 years ago. If you lose a few big trout on Fall River, you might blow your stack too.

When the trout explode in a surface feed, there can be so many pools from rising fish that it can look as if it is raining. And these trout are big, with many measuring 16 to 20 inches with a genuine sprinkling of five to eight-pounders. The water can be so clear during summer months that fly fishermen will use leaders as long as 20 feet; otherwise the fish will detect the fly line. On some days you can spot a dime at the bottom of 30 feet of water and reach in the stream with your hand thinking you can pick it up; Fall River is that clear.

This is a stream that flows so gently that it can be fished in a float tube. On the upper river near Glenburn, gasoline engines are prohibited and any form of fishing other than with flies is considered sacrilege. The only sound is that of your small craft, either aluminum boat or canoe, pushing water aside. Electric motors are popular.

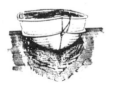

The favored fly patterns are the paraduns -- olive, tan or yellow -- with a No. 16 as a good starting size. Nymphs such as the Zug Bug, Black AP, Black Leech, and Hare's Ear can also get the desired result. With the wild and varied hatches, it can be an entomologist's dream.

But here is where the problems start. The river is bordered by private land, primarily owned by ranchers, most who get their shotguns out at the slightest trace of "another Bay Area trespasser." As a result, access is severely restricted. While this keeps fishing pressure low so the river retains its wild identity, it also can be a source of irritation for anglers. But regardless, that factor can be overcome.

Two lodges and the lone public access point operated by the organization Cal Trout are all an angler has to choose from here. Rick's Lodge at Glenburn is my favorite, providing the best access on the prime upper stretch of river. Anglers can gain fishing access by renting a room for $40 per night, $60 for double occupancy. Boats and electric motors ($30 per day, or $20 per half day) are also available,

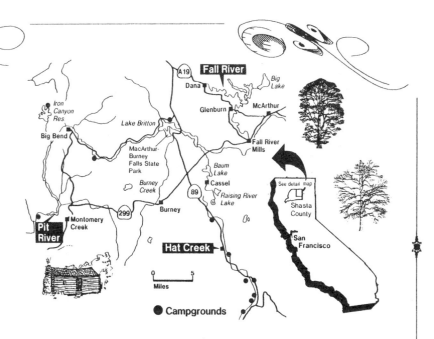

Fall River

Hat Creek

● Campgrounds

0 ─────── 5
Miles

as is advice and custom-tied flies. Fishing classes and week-long package deals are available. A free pickup service at the airport at nearby Fall River Mills is a bonus here, along with a full bar and restaurant. Rick's Lodge can be reached by phoning (916) 336-5300, or by writing Star Route Glenburn, Fall River Mills, CA 96028.

Lava Creek Lodge also sits on Fall River, and offers a similar deal. Rooms can be rented for $45 for double occupancy, $35 for a single. Boats and electric motors can be rented for $35 per day, with guides available for hire. A pickup service at the nearby airport brings a $15 charge. A complete restaurant and bar is open during the trout season. For information, call (916) 336-6288, or write Lava Creek Lodge, P.O.Box 615, Fall River Mills, CA 96028.

The only public access point to the prime stretches of Fall River is at the Island Bridge, where a tiny parking lot has been constructed by California Trout, a conservation organization. The lot will only hold about four or five vehicles, and no nearby areas are available for parking -- and on some summer days, a single recreation vehicle can take up all the available space. For information, phone Cal Trout at (415) 392-8887, or write at P.O. Box 2046, San Francisco, CA 94126.

NO. CALIFORNIA RIVERS

SACRAMENTO RIVER
SALMON

TALKING REALLY BIG

My friend Pete said, "Let me tell you how good the salmon fishing is on the Sacramento River." And then continued, "It's so good, people are canceling trips to Alaska to head up the Central Valley and fish the river north of Red Bluff."

I looked at him like he had antlers growing out of his head. Then he went on, "First we were getting 20 and 30-pounders, now there are some 50s. Everybody's limiting. The river releases from Shasta Dam into the river are at 8,000 cubic fee per second, and you know that's perfect for salmon fishing. From mid-August to mid-November we'll get the biggest fish of the year."

Now having a passion for the pursuit of truth, I naturally headed to the Sacramento River for proof of Pete's story. I mean, nobody cancels a trip to Alaska, not even if they get hit by a train and have to go in two pieces.

So at 7 a.m., we were on the river to set the record straight. The boats were whistling down the Sacramento River, the crisp morning air sending a few shivers down our backs. We had hired guides out of Balls Ferry Resort, located just east of Anderson in the north valley, where a fine piece of water attracts the largest salmon caught in California. The state record 88-pounder was caught on this river. And after hearing Pete talk, it sounded like a 100-pounder might be caught any day.

Pete and I were in separate boats. My guide was Gene Satterfield, and with us was field scout Ed "The Dunk" Dunckel, a man of unquestioned veracity to act as witness.

The boat stopped just downriver from a popular spot called the "Barge Hole." On weekends there have been boats lined up practically nose-to-nose for 300 yards drifting through the area. Guide Satterfield said he was considering canceling trips on Sundays because of the boat traffic. "Darn near impossible just to fish," he said. "Catching a fish is even tougher."

Even when you get the two-fish limit up here, the fishing is almost never fast-paced. You tend to grind out the fish, working the river for hours, hoping to get a bite every hour or so. If you have persistence with spirit -- and don't miss the sets when you get a hit -- you have a chance at a limit in a guide's eight-hour day. But if your attention wanders, if you start watching mermaids float by on the driftwood, you don't have a chance.

It was early and only four boats were at the spot. I let my line out, felt the lure twitch against the river current, then two seconds later, sensed a subtle pull-down on the line. Wham! I set the hook. It was a nice one, and I tangled with it for 15 minutes before finally bringing it to the side of the boat. About a 12-pounder.

"We're here all of five seconds and you catch one," said Ed the Dunk. "Maybe I should cancel my trip to Alaska, except I don't have one planned."

In the next five hours, we worked seven different spots, all deep river holes that the big salmon use to rest on their migratory journey. The guide will position the boat at the head of a hole, keeping it pointed upriver and the engine running, giving it just enough gas so the boat is nearly motionless in the current. Behind the boat, we let our lures or bait dangle in the hole. With a lure, the river current imparts the motion. With bait, you raise and lower your rod, "walking" the bait along the river bottom.

I was using a large, silver Kwik-fish lure, with a three-inch fillet of sardine tied on its undersize with plastic thread. A four-ounce sinker, which is connected to a three-way swivel three feet above the lure, helps keep the lure near the river bottom. Ed the Dunk was using sal-

mon roe for bait, placing it on a treble hook then tying it in place with the plastic thread.

By 1 p.m., Ed the Dunk had landed one, a shade larger than mine. We'd also taken a four-pound steelhead. Clear skies and an 80-degree sun seemed to make the day perfect as we worked, probed and waited for baits. It wasn't the kind of adventure that could make you cancel a trip to Alaska, I would remind Pete, but it's a good day fishing, said The Dunk.

Just then, his pole twitched, and the hook was set. You could sense immediately that this was no guppy. The rod was bowed in a U-shape, and when you put some muscle to it, the fish would rip 15, 20 yards of line off as if you'd stuck him with a cattle prod.

"A good fish," said guide Satterfield, "A good fish."

A half hour later, he was still saying, "A good fish." And the good fish was still on the line, still ripping

line when pressured. We had passed the rod around a few times, enjoying the fight. You could sense the immense weight of the fish, and feel it thrash the line as it jerked its head from side to side. I had the rod when the fish came near the surface to be seen for the first time. It looked better than four feet long with a mouth the size of a salad bowl.

In the next 10 minutes, the salmon was worked near the boat five times. But each time it would whip its tail and shoot off, disappearing into the murky, green river. Finally, though, it seemed I had turned the big salmon. It was on the surface, about 15 feet from the boat. I leaned back with the rod -- and pop! -- the hook pulled out and flew past my head like it was shot out of a cannon. The big salmon swam away free.

Back at the dock that afternoon, we met Pete. He had caught a 23-pounder, and his partner had a 37-pounder.

"Well, I wouldn't cancel a trip to Alaska for it," I told him, admonishing him for even thinking about exaggerating a fish report. I mean, the truth only is supposed to have one version.

"Now let me tell you about this salmon we had on that got away," I continued. "The first time it came up to the boat it almost swamped us in river water. "When it jumped, the river level went down two feet. One time it attacked the boat and we had to hit it with our oars to protect ourselves. Then it jumped near a boat, and the hole it left in the water was so big that the boat fell into it and disappeared.

"But cancel a trip to Alaska, Pete? C'mon. You should never exaggerate when talking about fish."

Who to contact: For a list of guides, write Shasta Cascade, 1250 Parkview, Redding, CA 96001, or phone (916) 243-2643.

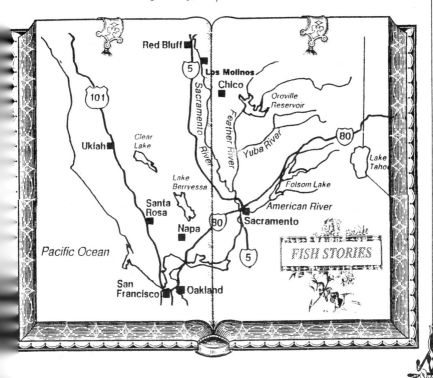

NO. CALIFORNIA RIVERS

THE EEL
RIVER

GOD'S COUNTRY SALMON

Northern California is often called "God's Country" and anybody who fishes for salmon on the Eel River during fall is likely to find out why.

Adventures here can feel like they are straight from the marrow of life. The Eel runs through some of the West's most beautiful country, rumbling northward past redwoods, firs and mixed conifers. And some years, the scenery is matched by the quality of fishing.

By boat or bank, the Eel was the salmon capital of the West during the fall of 1987. There are days when anglers caught and released a dozen salmon apiece, and kept a big one for the smoker. Newcomers and old-time river wolves alike were in celebration. Guides with drift boats reported two-fish limits for their customers virtually every day. Many shoreliners matched it.

"1987 was the best salmon run on the Eel in 25 years," said Dan Gracia. "We had weekends where three of us would catch and release 30 salmon, shorefishing. Absolutely fantastic."

"It gets to the point where you expect limits," said driftboat guide Dale Lackey. "There are a lot of rivers to choose from, but when the salmon run started, I spent every day on the Eel. It has become one of the West's great rivers."

The fall salmon run on the Eel has been so good that guide Jack Ellis has had trips booked a year in advance.

The surge is part of a big upswing for salmon on Northern California's streams. The best example is on the nearby

Klamath/Trinity system, where salmon counts are well documented by the California Department of Fish and Game. A big increase was counted from 43,000 salmon in 1984 to 199,000 in 1987.

199,000

The upswing may have been even greater percentage-wise on the Eel. To estimate fish populations on the Eel, the Department of Fish and Game does not have the money or the manpower to use advanced methods. Instead, they count the number of salmon carcasses on tributary spawning areas in the same spots, year after year.

On Sproul Creek, for instance, a small feeder to the South Fork Eel, there is an average of 300 spawners counted per year -- but last year there were 2,100 counted. That is seven times the historical average. On little Redwood Creek (not to be confused with the Redwood Creek that runs through Orick), 215 salmon were counted in the fall of 1987 -- four times the average.

"It is the relative numbers that are important," said Paul Wertz of Fish and Game. "Just based on those two spot checks, it confirms what fishermen are saying about the big runs on the Eel."

In a parallel, the good news continued on the Trinity River, which attracted a record spring run. It is all part of a bigger picture.

Several reasons account for the big increase, but the key one is that the take of commercial trollers has been severely limited in order to allow stocks to rebuild.

In 1984, a month and a half of the commercial season was closed, and in 1985 it was closed altogether. Then catch quotas were initiated in 1986 (50,000 fish) and 1987 (120,000) fish. Since the commercial take had previously averaged 180,000 per year, the cutbacks allowed thousands of salmon to survive and return to spawn.

The benefits of the closures are now being seen. Fishing one of the West's salmon rivers can be a real grind of a day, but on the Eel, there is a sense of electricity. It comes with the expectation of greatness.

That's how it was for me when I made my first cast on a warm October day, standing on a sandbar on the main Eel. The water was low and green, but the hole that accepted my cast was deep, a likely place for salmon to keg up on their migratory journey.

I was using fresh salmon roe for bait, just a split shot for weight, and it drifted gently downstream into the hole, the line with a steady bow in it. Then suddenly, the bow in the line straightened a bit. Something deep inside me told me to strike. I hesitated for a moment, maybe out of nervousness, then reared back, hard!

Instantly, I could feel the weight of a big salmon, and the fight was on. After five minutes, I leaned on him hard, and he came out of the water and landed with a big splash, leaving a ring the size of a big washtub. Well, it wasn't the biggest salmon in the world, a 16-pounder, but hooking him on the first cast of the season felt as if a magic light had been cast upon me. It turns out a lot of anglers on the Eel have had the same sensation. Good fishing can do that to you.

The key for fall fishing on the Eel is rainfall, of course. It is ideal for it to rain enough to attract fish in the river, but not enough to muddy the water. That's a real paradox on the Eel and fishermen here are always prisoners of hope as fall arrives.

Heavy rainfall can muddy up the Eel quickly, ending the prospects, but the big storms usually start in December. That is well after the brunt of the salmon run, which arrives from early October into December.

If you are a first-timer and do not wish to hire a guide, call ahead to get stream conditions, as well as the general area where fish have been located.

Good sources of information for the main Eel include Bucksport Sporting Goods in Eureka at (707) 442-1832, Fernbridge Market;

The numbers

The rise in Northern California salmon runs has been closely documented by California's Department of Fish and Game. This chart refers to the number of adult salmon, not jacks, that have entered the mouth of the Klamath/Trinity river system during the fall run:

Year	Number
1979	50,100
1980	44,500
1981	77,300
1982	65,200
1983	57,900
1984	43,300
1985	59,300
1986	186,300
1987	199,000

phone (707) 725-3852. For the South Fork Eel, Brown's Sporting Goods at (707) 923-2533.

Highway 101 follows much of the river and there are many access roads. The best spots are the holes with slow-moving river current. These are perfect for salmon to rest while fighting their way upriver. In some rare cases, you can even see the salmon milling about near the stream bottom, providing you have a high enough vantage point.

If a big hole is a productive one, you can expect company from fellow fishermen. In some cases, the shoreline will have many anglers, and a driftboat might be working it as well. Cooperation and courtesy can go a long way. There seems to be plenty of salmon to go around.

One crazy element in the year's past was the baits that proved effective. Believe it or not, the preferred entreaty has been a cocktail shrimp topped off with a small white marshmallow. Crazy? Yes, but salmon make rules of their own.

Fresh roe is the more traditional offering. But some anglers also swear to the use of tuna balls for bait, wrapping them in moulin cloth to keep it on the hook.

"I catch 95 percent of my fish on fresh roe," said fieldscout Darrin Brown. "If you fish it right, it's the best bait."

Regardless of your bait, the consensus is that you should fish it on the drift -- and keep close watch on your line. At times the only indicator will be the steady downstream bow in your line will straighten a bit. Then strike! It may indicate a salmon has stopped the drift of your bait. Very rarely will a salmon hit a bait hard and scream off with it.

Brown prefers fishing the South Fork for salmon before the rains of early winter arrive. The rigging he advises is very simple: No swivel, just a splitshot or two for weight on the line, and a No. 2 Kamakatsu hook.

"The less stuff you put on the line the better," Brown said. "And I use just 10-pound line. Salmon don't seem to be able to see as clearly as steelhead, but you don't want to give yourself away."

"When the water greens up, I might add a Wobble Glo as an attractor about 2-1/2 inches above the bait."

If you use a driftboat, the favorite put-in points on the South Fork Eel include a spot about a mile above Mendocino County Line, and behind Garberville. Good boat access is also available at Dean Creek or the Miranda Bridge.

Most guides use driftboats and almost all use the same style: They will position the boat at the head a hole, then oar against the current to maintain position. Meanwhile, the fishermen aboard will either bounce roe off the river bottom or let a plug flutter in the river current. The most popular lures include the Wee Wart, Hot Shot and Hot 'N Tot.

If you are new to a river, hiring a guide is one of the best ways to learn the water and catch fish your first time out. A list of licensed river guides is available from the Department of Fish and Game.

To share in this fishery, you need to know a few rules. Of course, you must have a state fishing license in possession. The limit on the Eel River is three trout or salmon in combination, but no more than two salmon in possession.

FISHING LICENSE

N327569
SALMON
16 POUNDS
EXPIRES ON
BIRTHDAY

If you fish the Klamath or Trinity Rivers, you will need a salmon punchcard. The Klamath/Trinity has many special and complicated regulations and you should study the Fish and Game rulebook before heading out on the stream. If the laws are unclear to you -- and the joke up here is that you need a lawyer to interpret them -- you should call the Fish and Game office in Eureka for clarification.

One other factor are river flows. In years where there is little rainfall after late September, fishing can be temporarily closed down due to low stream flows. In very low water conditions, the salmon become vulnerable while waiting in river holes for higher water to continue their journey.

The minimum flow standards apply to portions of the Eel, Van Duzen, Mattole, Redwood Creek, and Smith River systems.

What typically occurs is that it will rain just enough in early October to sweeten up the river and attract salmon from the ocean. Thousands of adult kings will then stack up in the river holes -- and the fall salmon run is on.

That's when the fun starts. It won't take long for you to realize why they call this place "God's Country." Maybe even on your first cast.

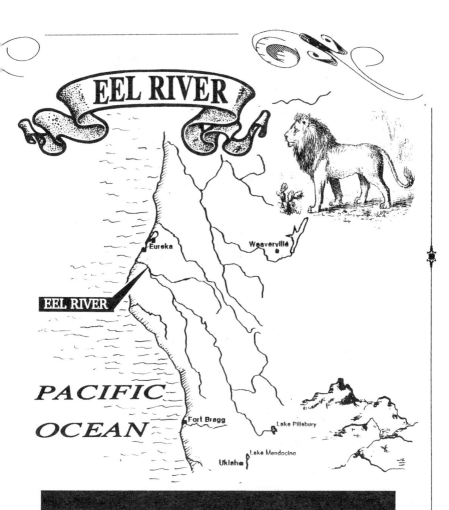

EEL RIVER

Eureka

Weaverville

EEL RIVER

PACIFIC
OCEAN

Fort Bragg

Lake Pillsbury

Lake Mendocino

Ukiah

☛ **EEL TRIP FACTS**

Rules and regulations: They are complicated. For interpretation or clarification, you should call the Fish and Game office in Eureka at (707) 445-6493.

River guides: A list of licensed river guides is available from the Department of Fish and Game by writing 1416 9th Street, Sacramento, CA 95814.

Who to contact: Good sources of information for the main Eel include Bucksport Sporting Goods in Eureka at (707) 442-1832, Fernbridge Market; phone (707) 725-3852. For the South Fork Eel, Brown's Sporting Goods at (707) 923-2533.

NO. CALIFORNIA RIVERS

CAMP YOUR WAY
TO STEELHEAD

TRADING IN BAD WEATHER FOR GOOD FISHING

How would you like the chance at a world-class fishing trip -- but instead of paying thousands of dollars, you pay just the price of gas and fishing tackle?

The trip would include battling one of the West's fightingest fish and your choice of staying at some of Northern California's most pristine areas.

Sound good? It is. And that is exactly what you can get when you go steelhead fishing and camp along the way. The time for exploring California's great rivers and camping at beautiful streamside settings is from winter to early spring. Instead of money, what you supply is the effort -- and a little know-how, of course.

There are some 40 campgrounds set along steelhead rivers in Northern California and they provide the opportunity for an inexpensive, but first-class fishing adventure. Most of the camps are very low cost, just a few dollars payable on the honor system, and are within walking distance of a steelhead stream.

To pull it off, a little homework is necessary. You need a variety of campgrounds to choose from, a good map to make it easy to reach them, a reliable vehicle, a system to keep your gear uncluttered -- and the means to stay dry and warm no matter what weather you confront.

As a steelheader, one thing you learn fast is that the most inportant piece of fishing equipment you can have is your vehicle. Make sure you can rely on it. Your car or truck provides mobility, the ability to drive from one river to another, and in the process gives you the best chance possible to catch fish. That kind of flexibility is critical during

winter, when come-and-go storms can change fishing conditions overnight.

Your fishing luck is often tied to water conditions, including river height, clarity, temperature and flow velocity. The chance for localized storms and the unique characteristics of each river mean that your favorite river can be running high and muddy, while another, just a morning's drive distant, can be in good fishing shape.

A good example of what you may face happened on one of my trips last year. I was camped at Richardson Grove State Park along Highway 101, fishing the South Fork of the Eel River. This is a great river, providing good bank fishing access and the best success rate for big steelhead of any river in California. But alas, the Eel also muddies up quickly after a good storm -- and that's exactly what hit.

The rain pounded on my tent like somebody was standing on top of it firing a machine gun. The next morning, the Eel was brown and high, and very unfishable. As the oldtimers' say, it was "too thick to drink, too thin to plow." I broke camp and headed north. While en route, I checked out several streams -- the Mattole, Van Duzen, Mad, Redwood Creek -- all were running chocolate brown. I just kept on driving, eventually reaching the Smith River in the northwest corner of the

state near the Oregon border.

Well, the Smith had been hammered by the storm too, but this is one river that can take it. It's the fastest clearing steelhead stream in California. I set up camp at Jedediah Smith State Park, and the next day by 10 a.m., I was fighting a 15-pound steelhead, having the time of my life.

With a few tricks, you can do the same. Be ready to react spontaneously to weather conditions and the up-amd-down quality of fishing. If it rains hard, be prepared to drive to another camp or another river where stream conditions are better. If the fish aren't biting, then don't keep hammering your head against the wall, instead pick up and move. The next spot may be the Promised Land.

Remember the camper's motto: Keep it simple. And that goes for fishing gear, too.

My favorite steelhead rod is an 8 1/4 foot long graphite rod. It is long enough to cast well, strong enough to handle big steelhead, sensitive enough so I can tell the difference between a rock and a light bite.

The rod should be matched with a small level-wind, revolving-spool reel. Revolving-spool reels are much better suited for steelhead fishing than spinning reels, because you have a much more direct connection to your bait. In turn, that allows you to have better "feel" which is required to set the hook on big steelhead.

STEELHEAD CAMPGROUNDS

The following is a selection of my favorite campgrounds on steelhead rivers available in Northern California.

Eel River:
1. Huckleberry
2. Madrone
3. Oak Flat
(All at Richardson Grove State Park, (707) 946-2311)
4. Hidden Springs
5. Burlington
(All at Humboldt Redwoods State Park, (707) 946-2311)

Klamath River:
7. Aikens
8. Bluff Creek
9. Pearch Creek
(All Forest Service Campgrounds, (707) 442-1721)
10. Dillon Creek
11. Oak Bottom
12. Fort Goff
13. O'Neil Creek
14. Sarah Totten
15. Beaver Creek
16. Trees of Heaven
(All Forest Service Campgrounds, (916) 842-6131)

Mad River:
17. Clam Beach County Park, (707) 445-7652

Mattole River:
18. A.W. Way County Park, (707) 445-7652

Salmon River:
19. Matthews Creek
20. East Fork
21. Shadow Creek
22. Trail Creek
(All Forest Service Campgrounds, (707) 842-6131)

Smith River:
23. Jedediah Smith Redwoods State Park, (707) 458-3310
24. Panther Flat
25. Grassy Flat
26. Patrick Creek
27. Cedar Rustic
28. Big Flat
(All Forest Service Campgrounds, (707) 442-1721)

Trinity River:
29. Tish Tang, Forest Service Camp, (707) 442-1721)
30. Denny
31. Gray's Falls
32. Burnt Ranch
33. Hayden Flat
34. Big Bar
35. Big Flat
36. Pigeon Point
(All Forest Service Campgrounds, (916) 246-5222)
37. Junction City, Bureau of Land Management, (916) 246-5325

Van Duzen River:
38. Van Duzen County Park, (707) 445-7652
39. Grizzly Creek Redwoods, (707) 777-3683

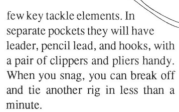

Fill the reel with fresh 10 to 12-pound test line. Shoreliners can count on a lot of casting, so you should feel 100 percent comfortable with your gear.

Your terminal rigging should be as simple as possible. The most effective method is "bumping roe," which means using roe for bait, casting it upriver, then bumping it downstream with the current. You retrieve as it drifts, keeping the rod tip at a 45-degree angle.

To rig, start by tying a three-way swivel to your line. From one swivel, tie on three feet of leader and your steelhead hook. From the other, tie on four or five inches of leader, with a dropper loop, which you clamp on a pencil sinker.

This way, if your sinker snags, you can just break it off. Instead of having to re-tie the entire rigging, you can just tie another dropper for your sinker, then clamp on some pencil lead.

Anglers who fish a lot will set up their fishing vest in advance with a few key tackle elements. In separate pockets they will have leader, pencil lead, and hooks, with a pair of clippers and pliers handy. When you snag, you can break off and tie another rig in less than a minute.

That happened to me on a trip to the Smith River. I had set up camp at a little-known, primitive spot called Big Flat, along the South Fork of the Smith. Nearby, I was fishing a long, deep slick that was fed by a tumbling, minature waterfall.

The problem was that in that slick was a submerged rock that I kept snagging. I was certain a big fish was lying behind the rock, out of the main current, and I kept casting to it. I snagged up five straight casts, re-tying quickly, before getting my bait to drift right alongside that rock.

Then, for an instant, it felt like my weight was gone, and I knew something strange was happening down there. What the heck, sets are free, and I set the hook hard! Instantly, a big steelhead jumped out of the water, my hook in its mouth.

When that fish hit the water, it tore off downstream. In a split second, it

hit a rapid and was gone.

Keep your camping gear as simple as possible. Bring essentials for cooking, sleeping, fishing, and the weather, and keep them in separate containers. If your gear gets jumbled up, your only reward will be a complete sense of futility.

Even if you have plenty of room in the camper of your pickup truck, you should still minimize the amount of gear. If you bring too much gear, it will inevitably crumble into a large, formless "pile of stuff," probably similar to how your garage looks. If you plan on sleeping in your camper, you'll have to throw the pile outside to make enough room -- and if it rains, it will become a wet, cold and disgusting pile.

If that wet pile contains some of your spare clothes, or worse, toilet paper, and you need either, life will be quickly reduced to a miserable, losing struggle.

A trick is to always keep a small tent stashed away. It can serve two purposes. One is when you bring more gear for a long trip, and plan on sleeping in your vehicle, you can make plenty of room by stowing your gear in the tent for the night. Another is if the weather is dry, and you find a good sandbar along a river, you can set up a camp within casting distance of a good fishing spot.

Regardless of your choice, you must be able to get dry and warm after you have finished the day's fishing. Steelheading and cold,

rainy weather often occur together. Expect it to rain, and if it doesn't, chalk it up to luck. That means you must have quality rain gear, waterproof boots, and rain-proof hat -- and then expect to get wet anyway. Always keep an emergency stash of clothes in a plastic bag in your vehicle.

It is also advisable to wear boots that have Vibram soles, not cheap rubber boots. Cheap boots with rubber soles provide little traction on rain-slickened rocks and, in an instant, you can go sliding from your perch at streamside into the river. I know from experience: 10 years ago, while trying to land a trophy steelhead at the bottom of a gorge on the Smith, I slipped and went thundering into the river, getting completely dunked.

Usually the excitement of a steelhead/camping trip is confined to catching big fish. With camping options available, you can zip from river to river, fishing where conditions are best. The final result is more and bigger steelhead and, in turn, a great trip.

For the money, it can be the most exciting winter adventure in the West.

☞ STEELHEAD TRIP FACTS

Maps: Maps detailing Forest Servece land, camps and access roads are available for $2 apiece from Maps, U.S. Forest Service, 630 Sansome Street, San Francisco, CA 94111. For information, call (415) 556-0122.

Fishing Reports: For up-to-date fishing information and streamflow conditions, call the following -- Lower Eel: Fernbridge Market, (707) 725-3852; South Fork Eel: Brown's, Garberville, (707) 923-2533; Mad, Van Duzen, or Lower Eel: Bucksport Sporting Goods, Eureka, (707) 442-1832; Klamath, Salmon or Trinity: Shasta Cascade, Redding, (916) 243-2643; Trinity River: Brady's, Weaverville, (916) 623-3121; Mattole: Honeydew Store, (707) 629-3310.

Fishing Guides: Jack Ellis, (707) 526-9066; Dale Lackey, (916) 275-2878.

Trip cost: Anglers must have a valid California fishing license ($19) in possession. Most Forest Service campgrounds cost $4 to $6 per night, payable on the honor system.

NO. CALIFORNIA RIVERS

1⁹ STEELHEAD
STREAMS

MY FAVORITES

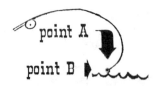

M y rod tip dipped, and I reared back, hoping to set the hook on a big steelhead, but the line went limp; barely missed the set, a fraction of a second late. Again.

Guide Tim Kutzkey looked up at the sky and closed his eyes. "Please God, put a fish on his hook."

Then he looked at me. "The rod tip is Point A," Kutzkey said. "The water is Point B. When Point A meets Point B, that means it is time to set the hook."

Just then, in the flash of an instant, I got another rip on my rod, but missed the set again, just as quick.

"When your arm is pulled into the water, it means that you are getting a bite," Kutzkey said with a laugh.

When you're the best guide on the best steelhead river in California, you can afford to joke.

This was on the Klamath River, way up near the Oregon border below Iron Gate Dam. We're talking cold country, like in the 20s daily in mid-December, where the prime steelhead fishing as well as a good jacket is what keeps you warm. This is the one river in the state where you can afford to miss the set.

In eight hours of fishing in two days, a compadre and I boated nine steelhead -- yet missed setting the hook on some 20 of the 30 bites. Steelhead are supposed to be hard to catch, but Tim Kutzkey has been changing that on the Klamath for some time.

The son of legendary guide Al Kutzkey -- who is credited with inventing drift fishing -- Tim oared his first boat at age 12. Now in his forties, Tim Kutzkey has drifted the upper Klamath from Iron Gate Dam

to the mouth of the Shasta River enough times to know each hole, crevice and rock as if he'd personally placed them there.

In December, fishermen aboard his boat commonly average four to eight steelhead per trip. Misses and all. The limit is three per fisherman. Bait? Nightcrawlers, roe, Wee Warts, Hot Shots -- all can do the job. But get them deep, just off the bottom, working the edges of holes, currents and eddies.

And that goes for several rivers. Here are my favorites:

■ 1. Carmel River:
The deep and lower stretches of river provide the top angling opportunities here. There has been heavy poaching activity on this stream, so if you see any snaggers, be quick to call the Fish and Game poaching hotline number (1-800-952-5400). The stream is open from the mouth on up to Robles Bridge at Robles Del Rio on Wednesdays and weekends.

■ 2. Pescadero Creek:
Located about 15 miles south of Half Moon Bay, and about five miles south of San Gregorio Creek, this stream supports a modest steelhead run that can be fished only on Wednesdays, Saturdays and Sundays. Most of the fish caught here are tricked at sunrise during December's and January's high tides, which raises the river level and allows the fish to enter the stream. Most anglers do so by offering bait from the Highway 1 bridge up some 200 yards.

■ 3. Lagunitas Creek:
This stream tumbles into Tomales Bay at its southernmost point. Most fish pool up in the lower stretches of the river, waiting for rain and the resultant higher water before moving upriver. The stream is open only from the mouth on up to the Highway 1 Bridge.

■ 4. Russian River:
Thousands of steelhead still enter the river every fall, and there are hopes the new fish hatchery here will boost angling prospects. The river level can fluctuate wildly, capable of going from creek level to flood stage in a weekend. Wait a week to 10 days after a heavy rain for the color to return to the river. The mouths of Dry Creek, Fife Creek, and Austin Creek are the best spots.

5. Gualala River:

This is a smallish and unpredictable stretch of water that can provide the full range of steelhead -- big fish stories to zilch. The best fishing is at the mouth of the river, which can be low and clear enough to fish with flies during winter dry spells. The steelhead usually school up in holes at those times. Almost all of the tributaries to the river are closed to fishing.

6. Garcia River:

The mouth of the river is at Point Arena (the point, not the town) with fishing allowed only from the mouth to the Eureka Hill Road Bridge. The major run hits usually in December and early January. If you can time it after a moderate rainfall coincides with a high tide from the ocean, you can be in business. That's when steelhead enter the Garcia in good numbers.

7. Navarro River:

Highway 128 follows this river all the way to the ocean, providing good access. Bait and spinners seemed to be used almost exclusively on the lower river, where it can get surprisingly big near the mouth. The Navarro is open to fishing from the mouth of Greenwood Road Bridge.

8. Noyo River:

This river starts just west of Willits and tumbles its way to Fort Bragg. Local anglers who are close enough to react quickly to changes in conditions catch 90 percent of the fish here. Fishing is allowed from the mouth to below the Silverado Area Boy Scout Camp.

9. Mattole River:

This is a personal favorite. A small two-lane road follows the Mattole (pronounced Muh-Toahl) to the stretch with the best fishing. Lots of rain hits the King Mountain Range, so come prepared. Fishing is permitted from the mouth of the river to the county road bridge at Petrolia.

10. Eel River:

Here is the southernmost of the major North Coast steelhead rivers. In November, river levels are usually high enough to bring steelhead in from the mouth, through Fortuna and on to Rio Dell. Bait and spinners are the top entreaties. After Thanksgiving, the fish are predictably scattered all the way to the South Fork past Garberville. From January through March, the South Fork is usually the best stretch of water. Try your luck as far upriver as is necessary to find green water. When heavy rains hit this area, the Eel can be unfishable for weeks due to roiled flows.

11. Van Duzen River:

Steelhead enter this river at the end of November, providing the area has received sufficient rainfall. The Van Duzen forks off from the Eel, and can be subject to closures because of low flows. The backlash is that when the river is high, it is difficult to fish. Not high on my list.

12. Mad River:

This is an unpredictable stretch of water that pours into the Pacific at Arcata. Fish move into the river in surges, often split by weeks of inactivity. It can also muddy up quickly after heavy rains. As a result, locals who are tipped off early get in on most of the action. The Mad is open for fishing from the Highway 101 bridge on up to the Country Road Bridge near Maple Creek.

13. Klamath River:

This is the primary steelhead stream in California. Steelhead can usually be caught from August through March, providing you work the right stretch of river. Before the heavy rains hit in the fall, the stretch from Weitchpec to Klamath is a good bet using nightcrawlers or roe. After moderate rains, the mouths of the Salmon and Scott Rivers as well as the mouth of Clear Creek can be good spots. After heavy rains, work from the Scott River on up to Iron Gate Dam. Star Route 96 follows the river and provides good access.

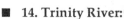

■ 14. Trinity River:

This is a rock-hopper's heaven, where you bounce along the shoreline, picking and choosing your spots. The best fishing is downriver from Douglas City, and between Salyer and Burnt Ranch. Use roe and nightcrawlers, and dress for cold weather.

■ 15. Salmon River:

This is a clean and often clear river where fly fishermen are best tested in December. From Cecilville to Somes Bar, there are many good-looking spots. A gravel road follows both forks of the river and provides access. The river is open to fishing from the mouth on up to Cecilville on the south Fork and to the county bridge at Sawyer's Bar on the North Fork. This river sits at the bottom of a steep canyon, so it is shaded for much of the day. The lesson? Dress for very cold weather.

■ 16. Smith River:

The Smith is one of the fastest clearing rivers in the world and it is a good thing, because it rains like crazy up here -- as much as 240 inches per year in parts of Del Norte County. Some huge salmon and steelhead lurk here, with the steelhead usually opening in December and continuing through mid-February at a good clip. Glo Bugs, Hot Shots, spinners, roe, nightcrawlers, and flies can induce bites at the right time, according to river height and clarity. The South Fork is closed from George Tyson Bridge upstream to its confluence with Craig Creek. Come prepared for rain.

■ 17. Sacramento River:

The steelhead run here always follows the fall run of chinook salmon. The steelhead like munching on salmon roe, especially below the Red Bluff Diversion Dam. The thickest concentrations of steelhead are always between Colusa and Red Bluff, particularly at the mouth of feeder streams such as Mill Creek, Deer Creek and Rock Creek. Cottonwood Creek can be quite good. The river is closed in several places in the Shasta and Tehama counties to protect spawning salmon, so consult your rulebook.

■ 18. American River:

This river runs right through Sacramento so it receives the heaviest angling pressure of any of the steelhead streams. After heavy rain, the gates at Numbus Basin are often opened and that's when the steelhead move upriver full blast. Although it can get crowded, Nimbus Basin at Fair Oaks on downstream is usually the obvious place to start fishing. Warning: Check Fish and Game regulations for special season river closures.

■ 19. San Lorenzo River:

Wild card. Located at the northern end of Monterey Bay, the fishing has improved tremendously in recent years. Bait fishing with nightcrawlers is the way to go, bank fishing at the mouth, or "lagoon," or hitting upriver spots near Santa Cruz. New runs of steelhead enter this stream during high tides. Good luck!

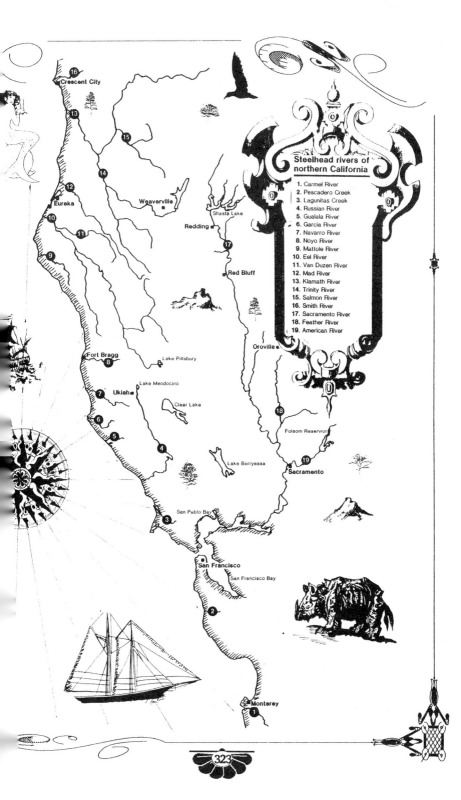

Steelhead rivers of northern California

1. Carmel River
2. Pescadero Creek
3. Lagunitas Creek
4. Russian River
5. Gualala River
6. Garcia River
7. Navarro River
8. Noyo River
9. Mattole River
10. Eel River
11. Van Duzen River
12. Mad River
13. Klamath River
14. Trinity River
15. Salmon River
16. Smith River
17. Sacramento River
18. Feather River
19. American River

Crescent City

Eureka

Weaverville

Shasta Lake

Redding

Red Bluff

Fort Bragg

Lake Pillsbury

Ukiah

Lake Mendocino

Clear Lake

Oroville

Folsom Reservoir

Lake Berryessa

Sacramento

San Pablo Bay

San Francisco

San Francisco Bay

Monterey

RUSSIAN RIVER

CLOSE-TO-HOME STEELHEAD

The Russian River is one of the great playlands just on the outskirts of the Bay Area and is an attraction all year long.

In the winter, the Russian is the closest large stream to the Bay Area that can provide good steelhead fishing. "Steelhead!" Just the sound of the word can quicken your pulse. The river is also ideal for kayaking and canoeing, from Healdsburg on downstream, through early summer when streamflows are moderate.

In the summer, several small temporary dams are put in place to keep the Russian from draining dry. Fishing for smallmouth bass, catfish (Guerneville area), and trout (north of Cloverdale) -- plus there's camping and hiking in the nearby Armstrong Redwoods.

But when most fishermen hear the word "steelhead," something funny clicks on in their mind, and off they go to the Russian. Steelies range to 15 pounds here. The best fishing is from Healdsburg on downriver at spots such as the mouths of Dry Creek, Austin Creek, and Fife Creek. However, the migrant fish can be intercepted any many spots; from Duncan Mills on up to Healdsburg. Additional prime spots are almost all where the river bends and sand bars have formed on the inside of the bend.

The best bet for most anglers is to tie loose roe on a No. 2 hook with thread, using a three-way rig with a small pencil sinker. (All inexpensive and available at area tackle shops.) Cast upstream, then retrieve as the roe tumbles its way downstream through the hole.

Because of the Russian River's proximity to the Bay Area -- just 15 miles north of Santa Rosa -- you can jump in your rig with a minimum of tackle, and be on the water fishing in practically a flash. One of the better sources for on-the-spot fishing information is at King's Tackle in Guerneville.

The Russian is also the best close-to-home river for canoeing or kayaking. A good first run is from Healdsburg to Guerneville, where the flows are easy and a bit of the streamside is junglelike. If you want to pick up swifter water, put your craft in at Cloverdale and paddle to Healdsburg, a distance of about 30 miles, a good weekend trip for beginner/intermediates.

If you don't own your own canoe, you can rent one from Burke Canoe Rental in Guerneville (opens early summer) or from Trowbridge Canoe Rentals in Healdsburg. Trowbridge offers 11 different trips, and if you own your own canoe or kayak, for $3 they will provide you with a ride back to your launch point.

If you prefer to keep your feet on solid ground, an ideal redwood hideout is located just north of Guerneville at Armstrong Redwoods. It consists of 5,000 acres of wildlands, much of it studded with giant redwood trees up to 1,000 years old. It was set aside in the 1870s, when most giant trees were being felled as quickly as loggers could sharpen their blades. Armstrong Redwoods provides 24 drive-in campsites, along with three primitive hike-in sites.

There are tremendous adventures available out this way, most of it in solitude, yet it sits just 90 minutes from San Francisco by car. The last time you cruised up Highway 101, your foot heavy on the pedal, you probably sailed past the Russian River turnoff at Healdsburg like a Concorde jet. Next time, slow down and turn west. You might be surprised.

☞ RUSSIAN RIVER TRIP FACTS

How to get there: Take Highway 101 to Healdsburg, then turn west on the Russian River Road. To get directly to Guerneville, take Highway 101 to Santa Rosa, then turn west on Highway 116.

Trip tip: Since streamflows are constantly changing due to weather patterns, always call to learn river conditions before heading out.

Steelhead: For fishing information, call King's Tackle in Guerneville at (707) 869-2156.

Canoe rentals: In Healdsburg, call Trowbridge Adventures at (707) 433-7247 for a free brochure. In Guerneville, call Burke's Canoe Rentals at (707) 887-2258.

Camping/hiking: For information call Armstrong Redwoods at (707) 865-2391.

Trip Cost: Canoe rentals cost about $30 per day. If you own your own canoe or kayak, Trowbridge Adventures will provide a ride back to your launch point for $3. The campsite fee at Armstrong Redwoods is $6 per night.

NO. CALIFORNIA RIVERS

THE AMERICAN
RIVER

A YEAR ROUND ANGLING RUN

The American River is the crown jewel of the Sacramento area; a gurgling, crackling-fresh stream that is home to good fishing within minutes of thousands of anglers who live in the vicinity of our state's capital.

It provides nearly a year-around fishery as well, getting runs of steelhead, striped bass, shad, and salmon. The American is also one of the most favored rivers in California for rafters, and is one of the few places I've ever fished where rafters and anglers co-exist on a peaceful level.

The past few winters, the American River has stunned anglers by attractions some of the largest steelhead taken in the state. A 10-pounder, which is a genuine trophy, became almost passe, with 15-pound and even 20-pounders arriving to win fish derbies.

Little rain and low streamflows slow steelheading on the American. However, it is nothing that a moderate rain can't cure. And anglers in this area are not ones to fret. Why? Because another run of fish always seems on the way.

Winter time is steelhead time, when anglers shake off cold, foggy mornings for a chance at the kind of fish that can send a chill down your spine. Some of the best steelheading, particularly for the big fish, usually continues through to third week of February.

Given good water conditions, steelhead can be caught through March, and rarely, in early April. But by that time, fishermen around these parts have something else on their minds -- shad!

Home to one of the state's big shad runs, the American attracts hordes of these fish in early May. By boat or bank -- fly or spinning gear -- shad provide great sport. Casting shad darts is most effective, but fly fishers with gaudy, silver shad flies do quite well on the early summer evenings.

By June, most of the shad action is upriver at Nimbus Basin, and by July, the shad fishing really tails off.

What? Me worry? No problem. Come July and August, arrives a surprising run of striped bass, feeding on crawdads, the prime bait here. Jumbo minnows can also do the job. Simultaneously, light run of summer run steelhead also can provide some jolts.

From September to December, the fall run of salmon kicks in. By boat or bank, you can take your pick. The favored method is to backtroll from a boat, using roe. However, many anglers fish from the bank, casting a large Mepps Spinner, or a 1/2-ounce to 5/8-ounce spoon, such as a Little Kleo or Krocadile.

By January, the cycle starts anew; steelhead time. Anglers are advised to check Fish and Game regulations for any special closures.

The best spots on the American are well-known by long-time fishermen around these parts. From downriver on up, they are named Grismill, Mather Rapids, Goethe Park, behind Ancil Hoffman Golf Course, Rossmoor, El Manto, Lower Sunrise, Upper Sunrise, Sailor Bar, and Nimbus Basin.

☛ AMERICAN RIVER TRIP FACTS

How to get there: From the Bay Area take Highway 80 to Sacramento, veer off the Highway 50 exit. The river generally parallels Highway 50 from Sacramento to Fair Oaks.

Maps/brochures: For free maps or brochures of the American River, write Juan Quinday, Department of Parks and Recreation, 4040 Bradshaw, Sacramento, CA 95827, or phone at (916) 366-2072.

Fishing: One of the more reliable tackle shops for information is Fran & Eddy's in Rancho Cordova at (916) 363-6885.

Rafts: Raft rentals are available from Rent-A-Raft, (916) 635-6400. Rates vary according to size of raft, from $16 per day for a two-person raft, to $55 for 14-person raft. The most popular rental is a raft designed to hold six people at $24 per day.

NO. CALIFORNIA RIVERS

SACRAMENTO RIVER
SHAD

MORE THAN JUST ONE FISH

Some people might think there is just one fish in the world, and it is passed around among fishermen for photographs. A weekend of shad fishing on the Sacramento River can change that assessment.

"The average person can catch 10 or 12 shad, even if they are just learning to fish," said John Reginato of the Shasta Cascade Wonderland Association.

What sets shad fishing apart is the number of fish -- the river is full of them. Your odds are just plain higher. Skilled anglers during a good evening bite might catch 25 or more, from boat or bank, and newcomers usually get at least 10.

This is an ideal trip to parlay fishing with camping and touring. The best area for fishing is on the Sacramento River between Corning and Red Bluff. Camping areas include Woodson Bridge State Park, Red Bluff Diversion Dam, and several private campgrounds and motor home parks. For information, write Shasta Cascade.

A number of good side trips can add enjoyment to the weekend. A few destinations to consider are Lassen Volcanic National Park to the east, Weaverville to the west and its historic Gold Rush past, and to the north, the massive Shasta Dam and its Vista Point overlook.

The idea is to fish for a few hours during the morning or evening, then use the rest of the day to explore the area. But it is the shad fishing that puts the sizzle into the trip.

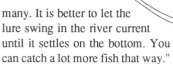

By boat or bank, this is one time you can just about guarantee you will catch some fish.

To be prepared, you should come equipped with a spinning rod and reel that would make a good match for trout fishing, the reel filled with four or six pound test line. The best lures are small jigs, such as the red-and-white Shad Dart with a fluorescent tail.

You just tie on the jig, wade out in the stream, then start casting. The water temperature is about 60 degrees, but a number of fisherman will wade up to their belt line without using waders. It is more important to have a pair of tennis shoes or wading shoes for traction.

"The lure must bounce on the bottom," Reginato said. "The best way is to cast upstream. After the lure hits the water, the flow of the river will sweep the lure downstream, just above the bottom.

"Right when the lure sweeps downstream and the line starts to straighten out is when the shad will take it.

"When the line starts to straighten out, a lot of people will bring their line in, and they won't catch as many. It is better to let the lure swing in the river current until it settles on the bottom. You can catch a lot more fish that way."

Shad don't strike hard. They actually just seem to stop the lure as it drives downstream. So a good tip is to watch the drift of your line -- and if it start to bend, then strike. "Once you understand this and see this, you can catch millions of shad," Reginato said.

These fish average 2.5 to 4 pounds, rarely bigger. They are bright silver and there is often a fluorescent sheen to them when first taken from the water. If you apply much pressure during the fight, they can jump several times.

"I was down to the river just the other night," Reginato said. "In two hours during the evening, we caught and released about 20 fish. The biggest was about 5 pounds."

If you have a boat, it can help. There are two good launching ramps, one at the Red Bluff Diversion Dam, another at Mill Creek Park at Los Molinos. A gravel ramp is available at Woodson Bridge State Park east of Corning.

If you plan to fish from shore, plan on wading, of course -- and don't drive up without knowing your access points.

The favorite fishing spot is the Tehama Riffle, located downstream of Tehama Bridge. To reach it, take the Tehama/Los Molinos exit off Highway 5, then drive east. At Tehama, run right on County Road A8 and drive a few blocks and cross the Sacramento River; turn left on a dirt road and park immediately under the Tehama Bridge.

This is a popular parking spot for fishermen. You'll see them in the river, just downstream of the bridge.

This sport is something of a celebration. Expect to share in it with others. It's common for 40 or 50 anglers to fish the Tehama Riffle at once.

☞ SACRAMENTO RIVER SHAD FISHING TRIP FACTS

How to get there: From the Bay Area take Highway 80 to Sacramento, veer off the Highway 50 exit. The river generally parallels Highway 50 from Sacramento to Fair Oaks. The best shad fishing is along the river from Corning to Red Bluff.

Trip tip: Shad fishing is best from late May through mid-July.

Special rules: There is a 25-fish limit, no minimum size. A 1988 sportfishing license must be in possession.

Shad as food: Most anglers release what they catch because shad have so many tiny bones. They are best prepared by soaking the fish in a brine solution, smoking them for six hours, then finishing the job in a pressure cooker.

Boat ramps: Located at the Red Bluff Diversion Dam, Mill Creek Park in Los Molinos. A gravel ramp is available at Woodson Bridge State Park east of Corning.

Campings: Camping is available at Woodson Bridge State Park, Red Bluff Diversion Dam and several private campgrounds.

Who to contact: For information on lodging, fishing, camping, guides and maps, write Shasta Cascade, 1250 Parkview, Redding, CA 96001, or phone (916) 243-2643.

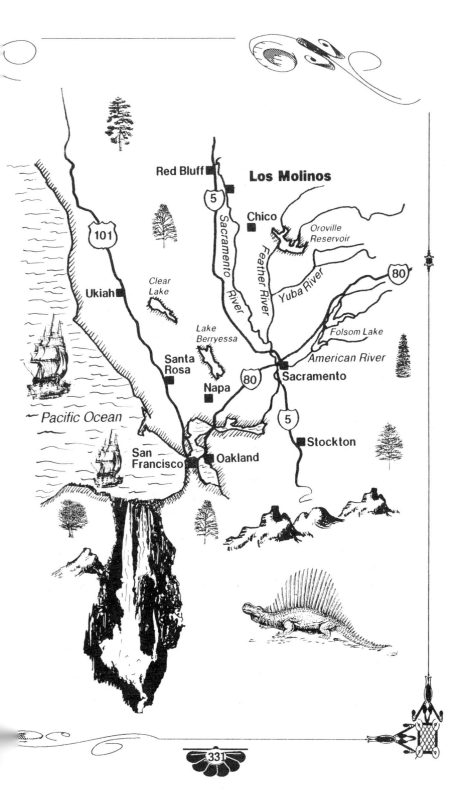

Red Bluff

Los Molinos

5

Chico

Oroville Reservoir

101

Ukiah

Clear Lake

Sacramento River

Feather River

Yuba River

80

Lake Berryessa

Folsom Lake

Santa Rosa

80

American River

Napa

Sacramento

Pacific Ocean

5

Stockton

San Francisco

Oakland

ADVENTURE
10

THE DELTA

ALL YOU NEED IS A BOAT

If you are losing your zest for life, some doctors prescribe "looking at everything as if you are seeing it for the first time."

The Delta provides another option -- because there is so much to explore, everything you see can literally be for the first time, every day, for the rest of your life. You don't need a psychologist. What you need is a boat.

"I've been exploring this son-of-a-gun Delta my whole life and I still haven't seen all of it," says Tony Addimando of Livermore. "I'm 57 and I'm going to keep at it the next 57 years just to see how much I can see. But you know, we'll never see it all. There's just too much out there."

The Delta is one of America's largest recreation areas of any kind, and for boaters, likely the best. The only waterway comparable is the Okefenokee Swamp that runs over the state line between Georgia and Florida, a tangled bayou web where the public is barred without a guide and a permit.

The public is welcomed to the Delta, on the other hand, and there is room to play for pleasure boaters, fishermen, skiers, and houseboaters alike. It seems to have no end, with 1,000 miles of navigable waters, 46 boat launches and 44 public and private campgrounds.

If you don't own a boat, there are many options. Houseboat rentals are available at 16 locations, skiff rentals can be made at five marinas, and one and two-day trips on tour boats are available out of Stockton, Brentwood, Isleton, Sacramento and Oakland.

Hey, you might even see a whale. Just kidding -- Humphrey the whale's aberrant swim from the ocean, through the Bay and into the Delta in 1985 is considered a once-in-a-lifetime event.

The Delta is located about 60 miles from San Francisco, but when you are on the water, it can feel like you're a million miles away from any city. Access routes by car include Highways 4, 12 and 160, which gives you an idea of its relative size. The Delta is fed by two of the West's largest rivers, the Sacramento and San Joaquin, along with many big feeder rivers...the Mokelumne, Stanislaus, Tuolumne, Merced, and Kings. All of them start as little trickles from melting snow high in the mountains, but eventually join at the Delta, then as one, rumble to San Francisco Bay.

When viewed from the air, a mosaic of smaller connecting rivers, sloughs, and islands make the Delta look like intricate masonry work, By boat, it can look like paradise.

The first thing you notice is that no matter where you go, you are shadowed by that big mountain, Mount Diablo. At 3,849 feet, it isn't so tall when compared to peaks in the Sierra Nevada, but since it is surrounded by the Bay Area and Delta at virtual sea level, it can be seen for hundreds of miles.

On the water, old Diablo gives you a reference point, a connection to something familiar, something strong and still amid stirring waters. It also provides a backdrop for spectacular sunsets in the fall, when orange sunlight refracts through Ansel Adam clouds and across the slopes of Diablo and the Delta's waterways.

"I love this old Delta," said Jay Sorensen, 52, of Stockton. "I've lived here since I was 10 months old, and in the past 30 years, I've been on the water five days a week. One time I was out 30 straight days, just on my own.

"I'm a fishing guide because I just plain love being on the water. We catch a lot of fish, but a few days you just don't get 'em. Lots of customers don't mind, because they're out here on the Delta. There's a special feeling to this place."

George Bruns of Lodi made it simple. "Sometimes I just like to watch the water go by," he said.

Musician David Crosby even recorded a song about the Delta on a Crosby, Stills & Nash album, which was awarded a gold record for sales.

The gold for boaters and anglers, however, is in the variety of fisheries the Delta supports.

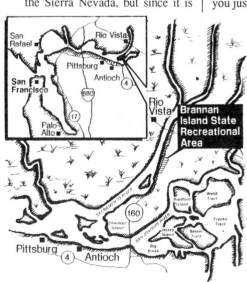

"It's not like the 'good old days,' but you can still have a heck of a good time," said Luther Harris, 67, of Bethel Island. "A lot of guys go big for the striped bass, but I kind of like the catfishing."

There are plenty of choices. It is one of the most well-rounded fisheries anywhere in the West, with both sizzle and steak.

The biggest attraction is the striped bass, which begin to arrive in their annual fall run. Also in the fall, salmon migrate through the Delta, headed upriver to spawning grounds on the upstream rivers. Resident fish that live here year around include catfish, black bass, bluegill, and, of course, the giant sturgeon.

How big do sturgeon get? Well, consider the tale of Bill Stratton, who was fishing for striped bass in the lower Delta on a November day in 1981. It was a warm day, but when "something huge" took his bait, a cold tingle went down his spine. Several hours later, when the fish was finally brought alongside the boat, it looked like some kind of whale.

That's because it was. It was over eight feet long and weighed 390 pounds, a world record for 30-pound test line.

"I wasn't even fishing for sturgeon," Stratton said with a grin when the fish was being weighed.

He had been fishing for stripers, like most of the others who are attracted to the Delta during the fall and winter. The striper has been severely impacted by state and federal water projects, but still number about 750,000 according to Fish and Game estimates. It's a viable fishery.

Sometimes it is better than "viable." In one recent winter season, guide Barry Canevaro and his customers caught 1,300 stripers, releasing many -- these are remarkable numbers by any standard. Some years are not as productive. Weather, water flows, and fishing skills are key determinants.

During November the first sprinkling of striped bass arrives to the Delta. The big school locates in San Pablo Bay, where it awaits rain and freshened-up waters before heading home.

Most fishing guides are predicting that time will come in early November, with several traditional spots attracting fish: Big Break, mouth of False River, San Andreas Shoals, and the mouth of the Mokelumne on the San Joaquin River; Sherman Lake, southern tip of Decker island, just upriver of the Rio Vista Bridge, and the shoal at the river bend between Rio Vista and Isleton, on the Sacramento River.

You don't have to fish to have a good time on the Delta. You can go houseboating for a week, take a two-day tour boat ride from Sacramento to San Francisco's Fisherman Wharf. Or show up on a hot Indian Summer weekend and water ski all your willies out.

Or maybe you could just pick out your own spot and watch the water go by. No extra pushing needed.

DELTA TRIP FACTS

How to get there: The San Joaquin Delta is crossed by Highways 4, 12, and 160, with a network of county roads also providing access. A detailed map of the Delta can be obtained from any area tackle shop for $2.25, or by mail for $2.75 to Delta Map, P.O. Box 9140, Stockton, CA 95208.

Boat rentals: Available at Paradise Park Marina at King Island at (209) 952-1000; Rainbow Resort at Brannan Island at (916) 777-6172; Kourth's Pirate Lair on the Mokelumne River (916) 777-6464; and Martin's Marina at Sherman Island at (415) 860-5105.

Boat Launches: Available at Collinsville, Rio Vista, Brannan Island, Antioch Bridge, west tip of Sherman Island, Bethel Island, Walnut Grove, Terminous, Del's near Clifton Court Forebay, West Stockton, and King Island, among others.

Camping: Brannan Island State Park is the most popular public area with 32 tent sites, 15 sites for motor homes, 102 sites for tents or motorhomes, and a boat launch. For information, phone (916) 777-6464. Private campgrounds are spotted on Delta maps, and are detailed in the book, California Camping (Foghorn Press).

Fishing: Phone Hap's Bait in Rio Vista at (707) 374-2372; Panfili's in Antioch at (415) 757-4970; Delta Sportsman at Bethel Island at (415) 684-2260; Tony's Tackle in Livermore at (415) 443-9191; and Bill's Bait in Tracy at (209)835-3203.

Fishing guides: Three excellent fishing guides are Barry Canevaro at (916) 777-6498; Jay Sorensen at (209) 478-6645; and Bob King at (707) 374-5554.

Houseboating: There are 16 Delta house boat agencies that can be reached through the chambers of commerce for Antioch (415) 757-1800 and Stockton (209) 466-7066.

Tour boats: One and two-day deluxe tours on large double-decker boats are available out of Stockton by calling (209) 464-2590, Brentwood by calling (415) 634-2890, Isleton by calling (916) 777-6411, Sacramento by calling (916) 372-3690, and Oakland by calling (415) 834-3052.

ALAMEDA CREEK
FOR LOCAL TROUT

LET'S GO FISH NILES CANYON

This is a story about a Bay Area trout stream.

A what? You heard right -- believe it or not, there is such a place -- a clean, free-flowing river that has plenty of rainbow trout. It is provides good fishing, and is proof that you don't need a tank of gas and a free weekend to reach a trout stream.

It's called Alameda Creek, but for those who fish there, it's known better as "Niles Canyon," as in, "Let's go fish Niles Canyon!"

Well, let's go, because the Department of Fish and Game stocks it in April, May and June.

Niles Canyon Road is the two-laner that connects Fremont with Highway 680 at Sunol in the East Bay. Right alongside the road is this nice, meandering stream -- that's Alameda Creek. And if you want stream fishing for trout in the Bay Area's backyard, this is the choice.

The only other stream in the Bay Area that has trout is Redwood Creek in the Oakland hills, but because the trout are a one-of-a-kind native strain, no fishing is permitted. A few years ago, during February of 1983, there was trout fishing in Coyote Creek south of San Jose. But this was an accident. Flood waters broke the levee at Parkway Lake, and the trout there swam downstream and temporarily glutted Coyote Creek.

On the Bay Area's coastal streams, such as Lagunitas Creek in Marin County, or Pescadero Creek in San Mateo County, the "little trout" some see are actually baby steelhead. You'll never see one bigger than a few inches. They spend the summer growing and, come the rains of winter, will head out to the ocean. No fishing is permitted during the summer and fall in order to protect the smolts.

That leaves Niles Canyon, and even though it's the only game in town, few people other than locals seem to know about it.

The four-mile stretch road west of Sunol provides access to the best stretch of river. A good place to start fishing is a mile above Fremont's Mission Boulevard. You'll see a small concrete coffer dam, over which the river flows. Try from there and further upstream a few miles.

The best technique is to simply tie a small hook, like a No. 8 on the end of your line. Two feet above that, make a dropper loop and add another hook. On the bottom hook, use half of a nightcrawler for bait. On the top hook, put a salmon egg or a chunk of Zeke's Floating Cheese.

If you have light enough spinning tackle, no weight is necessary. At the maximum, a small split-shot sinker will do. You should cast upstream in the current, then let the bait swing past as if no line is attached, retrieving as it drifts.

The trout will fin in the current, facing upstream, waiting for food to come drifting by. If they see your bait, they will dart over and take a look -- and if they sense no weight,

they will grab it.

Most strikes will come on the first 10 or 15 feet of drift, just as the bait starts to swing downriver. Almost never will you catch a fish while working downstream, because the bait will not have a natural, free-drifting appearance.

You can always use small lures such as the Panther Martin spinner, blue/silver Kastmaster, yellow Roostertail or Super Duper. Some anglers try fly fishing, but to keep it straight here, the best results are usually on bait.

For additional tips, you can stop in at one of the local sporting good stores in the area. The Fisherman, owned by Frank Wong, is the best for what we call "local knowledge."

There's a concession and picnic area on the stream if you want to make it a family outing.

On trout fishing trips in the mountains, sometimes it feels good just to watch the river roll by. Believe it or not, there is a place in the Bay Area where you can apply the same philosophy.

☞ NILES CANYON TRIP FACTS

How to get there: From San Francisco, take the Bay Bridge, then Highway 17 (880) south to Decoto Road in Fremont. Then head east, toward the hills, and turn right on Niles Boulevard, and continue for several miles to Niles Canyon Road. If approaching from Highway 680, take the Sunol exit and head west.

Who to contact: Call Frank Wong, owner of The Fisherman Bait and Tackle, at (415) 793-3474. For general information, call the East Bay Regional Parks District at (415) 531-9300, Ext.2208.

CHAPTER 7

SALT WATER FISHING

WITH
17 ADVENTURES

CONTENTS:—

PUBLISHED BY FOGHORN PRESS
SAN FRANCISCO
QUALITY OUTDOOR BOOKS

SALTWATER FISHING

THE GULF OF THE
FARALLONES

FISHING FOR SALMON OUT THE GATE

The richest marine region from Mexico to Alaska is along the San Francisco Bay coast, a unique area that provides the longest ocean season anywhere for salmon fishing. That's the steak -- the high catch rates add the sizzle. It is called the Gulf of the Farallones, an underwater shelf that extends 25 miles out to sea until dropping off to never-never land. The plankton-rich waters here attract shrimp, squid, anchovies, and herring, and in turn, are like a magnet for hordes of feeding salmon. It means that on any given day of the nine-month season, a fisherman has the chance to head out on the briny deep and tangle with the king of the coast.

The salmon range from four to eight pounds, but there are enough going at 15 to 25 pounds to keep fishermen on edge at all times. The limit is two, with a minimum-size limit of 20 inches, and there are several periods every season when every angler aboard every boat will limit out.

One key is finding the baitfish. Do that and you find the salmon. To accomplish that, the most popular method of fishing is trolling, which allows anglers to cover the maximum amount of water in the minimum amount of time. The 30 big sportfishing vessels from the Bay Area ports will fan out across the Gulf of the Farallones like spokes in a turning wheel in the search. When one finds the fish, the skipper will alert the rest of the fleet -- private boats will follow -- and everybody catches fish.

If the baitfish are shallow, tightly schooled and easy to locate, such as becomes common in mid-summer and early fall, a number of anglers will abandon trolling. Instead they drift mooch, using light tackle, anchovy-baited Shim jigs, and set the hook on each fish. This technique produces lower catch rates, but the average size of the salmon is much larger.

If you are new to the game, learning how is as easy as tumbling out of bed in time for the 6 a.m. boat departure. A list of the fulltime, sport-fishing vessels is included with this adventure to get you pointed in the right direction. Trips cost $35 to $40, and include bait, instruction, and a heck of a boat ride under the Golden Gate Bridge. Rod rentals are available for $3 to $5, along with leaders, sinker releases, and sinkers. You should bring a lunch, drinks, warm clothing, and, if vulnerable to Neptune, seasick pills.

Before heading out to sea, the skippers provide brief instructional lessons. They will explain that the strategy is to troll anchovies amid the school of baitfish, and with the bait appearing wounded, this method will attract strikes. A two or three-pound cannonball sinker is used to get the bait down, and is attached to a sinker release. The universal rigging is to tie the sinker release to your fishing line, then use three to six feet of leader from the sinker release to the bait. If you need help, the deck hand will tie your rig for you.

After the cruise to the fishing grounds, the fishermen aboard will drop the baits overboard and the trolling begins. Most often, the rods are put in holders, and the angler stations himself nearby. When a salmon strikes, the sinker is released and drops to the ocean floor -- and the tip of the pole starts bouncing.

This is where the excitement starts. You grab the rod and immediately sense the throbbing weight of Mr. Salmon. I've caught hundreds of salmon, and it still gets to me every time.

The first key is keeping your drag set light, particularly at the beginning of the fight. Many salmon escape in the first few seconds after taking the bait, when the excited angler clamps down too hard on the lie. Well, salmon are too strong for that. Slam the brakes to 'em, and the hook will pull out in a flash.

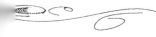

Instead, take your time and enjoy the fight. Keep a bend in the rod, given them no slack, but don't muscle them either. It takes an "in-between" touch to land big salmon, kind of like the "just right" feel when a good mechanic tightens a bolt. Not too tight.

When you eventually lead the salmon alongside the boat, the deck hand will provide the crowning touch with the net. If you own a private boat, this should be done with a single, knife-like down-and-up motion. Don't try to reach, scoop or chase the fish with the net -- if you hit the line, it will be "adios muchachos."

You can maximize trolling results with a number of additional inside tricks which are particularly effective on private boats. Experimenting with the use of downriggers, plastic planers, dodgers, flashers and mixing the use of Krocodile and Andy Reeker spoons, hoochies, anchovies clasped in Salmon Rotary Killers, and probing from the surface to the ocean bottom can result in bonanza catches. These advance lessons are detailed in my book, California Salmon Magic.

Another technique that is gaining in popularity is mooching. In Monterey Bay, where salmon fishing is best in the early season, the big sport boats mooch virtually every day. Off the Bay Area coast, the technique is relatively new to the industry, but the concept has fascinated anglers.

Instead of trolling, the skipper turns the engine off, and lets the boat drift in the current. Instead of putting the rods in holders, you keep it in your hands. Instead of a heavy sinker and an anchovy, you use a 1\2-ounce Shim jig and a small chunk of anchovy. My experience for the big salmon is that the best rigging is to fillet an anchovy from its dorsal fin on back to the tail, including the tail in the fillet -- then hooking it near the front of the fillet on the jug. You let the line out just 15 to 35 feet as the boat drifts.

With rod in hand, you feel every nibble, twitch and bite. Don't jig it, but keep it steady; the sway of the boat will do the work. You might catch rockfish, kingfish, jacksmelt, mackerel and even perch along the way, particularly if working inshore reef areas. With the engine off, the ocean is peaceful and quiet. That ends abruptly in the explosion of a salmon attack.

When a salmon grabs the bait, there is no doubt about it, but you must be ready for it. Underwater filming of attacking salmon by my pal Dick Pool shows that they arrive at full velocity from the underside of the bait. As a result, when you get a strike while mooching, you get

1\4-foot HMG, is a popular stick. Another one of my favorites is a shorter graphite with a stiffer tip, like the LCI 7 1\2-foot GBB764. Level-wind reels make good companions, with 10 to 16-pound lines.

Make certain you have your reels filled with fresh, premium line. Salmon, particularly the big ones, can both bulldog you and run in erratic spurts. All it takes is one nick on some old line and it's goodbye. If you rent a rod-and-reel combination on the boat and the line is low and old, demand something better. You deserve it.

Spring is a unique time in the Gulf of the Farallones, because it marks a switch in the feeding pattern of the salmon. In March, salmon feed primarily on shrimp. But with the arrival of April and May comes the migration of huge schools of anchovies from southern waters into the area. The salmon will chase down the baitfish like Jesse James running down a stagecoach.

During this time of year, the schools of bait will often move to inshore areas, along the Marin Coast and also San Mateo County coast near Daly City, Pacifica and Half Moon Bay. The salmon will follow them.

This is your chance. The fish are out there waiting for you. All it takes is a boat ride, a fishing rod, and your bait -- and by the end of the day, you likely will be telling the tale of tangling with salmon, king of Golden Gate fishing.

some immediate slack in the line. If you do not reel down to the fish immediately and remove that slack, that salmon will be one long-gone desperado before you can regain your composure.

Good tackle can help, both for trolling and mooching. For trolling, I like a seven-foot rod with a tip strong enough to withstand the weight of trolling the cannonball sinker. The rod should be matched with a medium-weight, revolving spool saltwater reel with 20-pound test line.

For drift mooching, you need lighter, more sensitive tips, since you are using just a quarter-ounce or half-ounce of weight. A good steelhead rod, like the Fenwick 8

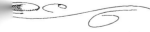

Where to Book a Boat for King Salmon Trips

The following list of sport vessels that run daily trips for salmon is provided by the Golden Gate Fisherman's Association.

All phone numbers, except where noted, are in the 415 area code.

San Francisco:
Butchie B, 457-8388
Chucky's Pride, 564-5515
Ketchikan, 981-6269
Lovely Martha, 621-1691
Miss Farallones, 352-5708
New Easy Rider, 285-2000
New Florie S, 878-4644
New Holiday IV, 924-5575
Quite A Lady, 821-3838
Viking, 469-0464
Wacky Jacky, 586-9800

Sausalito:
Flying Fish, 453-6610
Ginnie C II, 454-3191
Louellen, 668-9607
Mr. Bill, 892-9153
New Merrimac, 388-5351
New Ray Ann, 584-1498
Pacific Queen, 479-1322
Salty Lady, 348-2107
Sea Otter, 824-1068
Stardust, 924-1367

Berkeley:
El Dorado, 223-7878
Gertha L., 638-7497
Nerka, 937-7518
New Capt. Pete, 581-4000
New Donna D, 222-4158

Emeryville:
Mamasan, (408) 374-8295
(six customer limit)
New Fisherman III, 837-5113
Huck Finn
Salmon Queen
Rapid Transit, all at 654-6040

Half Moon Bay:
Capt. John, 726-2913
Huck Finn, 726-7133
Red Baron, 726-2525

Bodega Bay:
Jaws and New Sea Angler,
  (707) 875-3495
Bodega Bay Sportfishing,
  (707) 875-3344

Santa Cruz:
New Stagnaro, (408) 425-7003
Rain Song, (408) 462-3553
Sea Dancer, (408) 476-2648

Monterey:
Monterey Sportfishing,
  (408) 372-2203
Sam's Fleet, (408) 372-0577
Chris's, (408) 375-5951

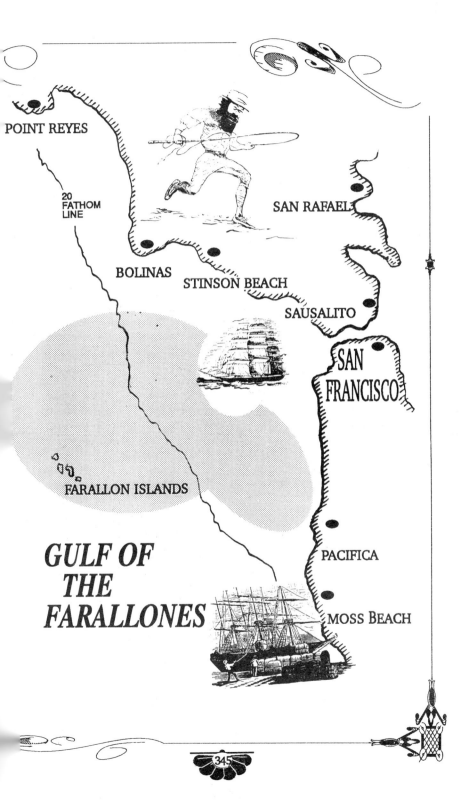

POINT REYES

20
FATHOM
LINE

SAN RAFAEL

BOLINAS

STINSON BEACH

SAUSALITO

SAN
FRANCISCO

FARALLON ISLANDS

*GULF OF
THE
FARALLONES*

PACIFICA

MOSS BEACH

SALTWATER FISHING

POTLUCK PRIZES
OF SAN FRANCISCO BAY

VARIETY WITH A VIEW

Fishing on San Francisco Bay can be like opening up a mystery box on your birthday -- you never quite know all the surprises that are in store.

It starts with a boat ride while surrounded by national treasures like Alcatraz, the Golden Gate Bridge and the San Francisco skyline. It often ends with big striped bass, halibut, lingcod, rockfish and sometimes even salmon. In between you can get some of the West Coast's top fishing excitement, dangling a live anchovy or shiner perch for bait on the bay bottom, where you never know for sure what might grab it next.

Skippers call it "potluck fishing," and the striped bass is the centerpiece. Every May, stripers begin arriving en masse at bay waters after a winter's stay in the California Delta. First come the "scout fish," the five to 10-pound bass. Shortly thereafter arrive the big fellows, the kind that make for magazine pictures and for great summer days on San Francisco Bay.

But there's more. Simultaneously, halibut will start moving into bay waters after a winter in the ocean. By June, 10 to 25-pound halibut will be thick in many spots. In fact, the largest halibut caught in the bay that I know of, a 46 pounder, was caught one June day aboard a potluck boat, the Huck Finn out of Berkeley.

Skippers will spot key parts of each day's tide to maximize their luck for the prizes, stripers and halibut. If the bite slows, they can fill the day by drifting over reefs for rockfish and in the process plump-

ing up anglers' bags. Thus it is possible to catch many species of fish on a single trip. In addition to stripers, halibut, lingcod and salmon, you might hook a cabezone, china rockfish, blue rockfish, bolinas cod, flounder or shark. There can be many surprises.

Other elements that are often unexpected, especially for first-timers, are the late departure, short boat ride, and fishing methods.

Trips aboard potluck vessels usually leave at 7 a.m., and rarely any earlier. This is one of the latest departures on the West Coast for major sport-fishing vessels. The reason is because it is the tidal patterns that key the bite of the stripers and halibut, not how early you get on the water. As a result, you can get a full night's sleep before your trip, and when you're rested instead of exhausted, it can really make a difference in your spirit, attentiveness and, ultimately, how many fish you catch.

Skippers charge an average of $35 per day, which includes a boat ride, live bait, the expertise of the deckhand, and the fish-finding ability of the skipper. You supply your own lunch, drinks and fishing license, which must include the $3.50 striper stamp. Rod-and-reel rentals are available on the boats for $3 to $5. For a complete rundown on the Bay Area potluck boats and boat ramps, see the accompanying box.

A shocker for many is how quickly you begin to fish after departure from the dock. There is no lengthy boat ride to points unknown. For instance, the best striper spots include the South Tower of the Golden Gate Bridge, Yellow Bluff (located on the north shore just east of the Golden Gate Bridge), a ledge located just east of Treasure Island, the "rockpile" west of Alcatraz Is-

Private Boat Information

Launch ramps: If you own your own boat, you can launch at one of several good ramps that ring bay waters: Berkeley Marina, (415) 849-2727; Caruso's, Sausalito, (415) 332-1015; Loch Lomond Marina, San Rafael, (415) 456-0321; Richmond Marina, (415) 236-1013; Oyster Point Marina, South San Francisco, (415) 871-4057.

Live bait: Live bait can be purchased at two locations. Meatball Bait, (415) 441-0111, located at Pier 45 at San Francisco's Fisherman's Wharf, sells live anchovies by the scoop. You can cruise right up the bait receiver here. The largest supplier of live shiner perch is Loch Lomond Live Bait in San Rafael, (415) 456-0321. Set on a dock, boaters can buy their bait and be fishing in minutes.

land, and just west of Angel Island in Raccoon Strait. All of those spots are within short reach of any boat in the bay. So even though the boats leave relatively late, the fishing begins quickly.

First-timers are common to bay potluck trips, and prior to departure the skipper will provide a short instructional period. The first thing they will describe is the terminal rigging.

They keep it simple, using the three-way swivel concept. From one of the swivels, you just tie on your fishing line. From another, you tie off your sinker with about eight inches of leader. And from the remaining swivel, you tie on a three-foot leader and a short-shanked live-bait hook. Skippers will have pre-tied rigs available on the boat for you.

When you reach the fishing grounds, anglers will gather around the live-bait tank and grope for a wiggling anchovy or shiner perch. Anchovies should be hooked through the nose, vertically, or in the gill collar. Shiners should be hooked through the nose horizontally.

The skipper will not anchor, troll, mooch, or turn his boat engine off. Instead, he will allow it to drift with the tide over the prime spots. In turn, fishermen dangling their baits near the bay bottom will have their baits swimming right through the prime territory, vulnerable to a big striper or halibut.

"The rocks down there are home for the striped bass," says skipper Cliff Anfinson of the *Bass-Tub*. "When you bounce a sinker on his house it's like knocking on his door, and they like to come out and see who's there."

The down side is that many of the prime spots are real tackle grabbers. It usually takes newcomers several tries to get the feel of how to drift a good ledge that is holding stripers. The key is staying in close touch with your sinker and bait, so you always have a feel of "what is going on down there," as skipper Chuck Louie of Chucky's Pride calls it. Never permit any slack in your line, and instead "walk the bait" up a ledge, reeling as the bottom gets shallower. The anglers who get the hang of this are the ones who catch the big bass.

Good tackle can help keep you in close touch with your bait, so you can catch fish instead of snags. Three of the best rods are the Fenwick 847, Sabre 500C, and Contender 70LJ. A revolving spool reel, such as the Penn Jigmaster No. 500, 2/0 Senator or their equivalent in Newell, Daiwa or Shimano are appropriate. They should be filled with fresh 20-pound line.

One idiosyncratic element of bay potluck fishing is that when the stripers aren't biting, the halibut often are. It's because of how tide patterns dictate feeding; stripers like strong-moving tides, and halibut prefer slow-moving tides. Since tide cycles in-and-out of phase, fast to slow, on a weekly pattern, skippers have quality stripers or halibut to shoot for virtually every day from mid-May through the summer. And with all the other species you might catch, it makes for a prime fishing trip on bay waters.

A mystery box? You bet, and now is time to open it up.

Bay Potluck Boats

The following open-party boats offer potluck fishing trips in San Francisco Bay. Information about prices, schedules, departure times, recommended tackle and current fishing conditions may be obtained by contacting the following sources by phone:

San Francisco: Bass-Tubb, skipper Cliff Anfinson, (415) 456-9055; Chucky's Pride, skipper Chuck Louie, (415) 564-5515; New Mary S, skipper Collin Wing, (415) 752-0670.

Berkeley: Happy Hooker, skipper Jim Smith, (415) 223-5388.

Emeryville: Huck Finn, skipper Art Roby, (415) 849-2727.

San Rafael: Loch Lomond Marina: Superfish, skipper Dick Steinhart, (707) 763-5380.

Richmond: New Keesa, skipper Mike O'Connell, (415) 787-1720.

SALTWATER FISHING

SUPER SYSTEM
FOR STURGEON

OFFERS NO MISS CATCHES

The sky looked like a scene out of the Ten Commandments with yellow and orange rays of sunlight refracting through clouds and across the water. We were fishing on San Francisco Bay for big sturgeon, a fish strong enough to make you say your prayers -- but an elusive devil.

The sun was just hitting Mount Tamalpais to the west when there was a sudden downward pump on the rod tip. Then, just as quickly, there was nothing. The rod straightened. The master, Keith Fraser, pounced on the rod and gently took hold and tilted it forward, using a unique rod board as an axis point.

"This looks like the start of a classic sturgeon bite," Fraser whispered, staring at the rod tip like he was the sphinx. All was quiet and still, then the rod tip pumped down again, and in an instant, Fraser reared back hard and set the hook home.

Fraser leaned back on the rod and watched the line disappear off the reel; a good run, 60 or 70 yards. He looked over at Tommy Mannion, a 12-year-old protege, and passed him the rod. "Go for it Tommy," Fraser said. "Have some fun."

Well, it wasn't the biggest sturgeon in the world, but at 80 pounds it gave little Tommy everything he could handle before the fish was brought to the boat and released. Fraser, the founding president of United Anglers of California, releases almost all the fish caught aboard his boat.

And he catches a lot of them, especially big sturgeon -- using a one-of-a-kind system he invented that parlays a fishing rod holder he calls a "sturgeon board" with specially-designed rods for sturgeon and a study of how tide patterns produce optimum three and four-hour periods. Any angler can employ these tricks to catch more sturgeon and put a lot more success into his

fishing and the excitement that goes with it.

It takes most anglers days and days on the water to hook up with a big sturgeon, particularly in the San Francisco Bay system. Not Fraser. In 41 trips over the winter season, Fraser hooked 86 sturgeon (keepers over 40 inches) and had only 10 missed sets. In one period, he hooked 26 straight. Virtually all of the fish were released, including two well over 200 pounds.

In the past few years, many anglers have become disciples of the Fraser system and are catching more sturgeon because of it. Every fall, Fraser conducts two public seminars in Corte Madera in Marin County, where he teaches his system. He has drawn crowds of up to 1200, with 500 turned away at the door -- including one lady who passed out from the excitement in the building. The big crowd prompted the Corte Madera fire chief to attempt closing down Fraser's seminar, but he gave up when he discovered that half of the town's firemen were at the seminar, refusing to budge.

One of Fraser's proteges is Ross Peterson of San Rafael, who fishes three and four times per week during the winter and spring bay season.

"I tried hard, but it just wasn't happening until I started listening to Mr. Fraser," Peterson said. "Listening is kind of against my nature, but I just wasn't catching much, no matter how hard I tried, no matter how many hours I spent on the water. So I listened real close and put it to use. Now I expect to get 'em every time out, and often do."

Peterson has caught and released numerous sturgeon over 100 pounds in the past two years.

It was a similar experience in my case: several years of futility before trying the Fraser system in 1981, then catching 100 and 150-pounders on back-to-back days. The big one measured 7-foot-1 and cleared the water twice in jumps. Thereafter, I didn't make a sturgeon trip without catching at least one.

One of the keys to the system is the unique rod holder Fraser has designed. It is called the "sturgeon board." It measures 58 inches long and 2 1\2 inches wide. At the top is a 3\4-inch piece with a slot in the center where the rod is placed. There are also two vertical pieces three inches high on each side of the board located 16 inches from the bottom. They keep the reel upright and in place.

The board, with the rod in place, is rested at a 45-degree angle against the boat rail. The rod is left untouched until a fish bite is registered.

Most people with average garage tools can make a sturgeon board -- and many have done exactly that.

"Obviously it keeps your rod from flopping around when the seas are bumpy," Fraser said, "but it does a lot more than that.

"The thing to remember is that even though sturgeon are huge, their bite is often very delicate,

more of a soft pump than anything else. Also the fish are very sensitive to anything unusual, they feel any movement or agitation with the bait, or vibration. If you jiggle the rod at all, they're gone.

"What happens with the uninformed angler is that when he gets a bite, he immediately picks his rod up, or stands with it, getting ready to set the hook, waiting for another pump. Sturgeon are so sensitive than just by moving the rod around like that, Joe Angler often spooks Mr. Sturgy. The fish never comes back and the angler gets skunked again. It happens over and over."

A rod board can solve that. When you get a bite, you should carefully lift the butt of the rod, which consequently tips the rod forward -- using the slotted forepiece of the board as an axis point. Now you are ready. When the rod tip is pulled down again by the sturgeon, you are in strike position.

If you bump or jerk the rod, the movement will often be telegraphed to the fish at the other end of your line. "Anything that causes any agitation can spook the fish," said Fraser.

To provide an additional edge, Fraser prescribes rods with light tips (but not whippy), and enough backbone to whip a 100-pounder. His favorite is the 7-foot Sabre 870. Another good one is the Fenwick 1870C. If you prefer graphite rods, the LCI GBT704 is my favorite.

Several kinds of reels are well suited. Fraser prefers the Newell G344F. The key here is to tighten the drag 100 percent for the set.

"You have to set the hook hard on sturgeon," Fraser said. "Their mouths are tough. To get hook penetration, you don't want any line slippage at all. We use 30-pound line and really sock it to them on the set, then immediately back off on the drag for the fight. That's what works.

"Another key is being attentive. You must keep constant vigilance on that rod tip."

To catch 86 sturgeon in 41 trips, like Fraser has done, you might think he practically lives in his boat, fishing all the time. On the contrary, Fraser rarely fishes more than three or four hours at a time.

USING A STURGEON BOARD

The sturgeon board keeps the angler from unnecessarily moving his rod when a sturgeon is biting. Sturgeon are wary, sensitive fish and can spook at the slightest unusual movement of the bait. The rod rests in the board prior to the first sign of a bite. After a strike, the angler carefully picks up the rod by its butt which, in turn, lowers the rod tip and offers the sturgeon a few feet of line, while keeping the rod blank in contact with the slotted forepiece of the board. When the bites get stronger and the rod tip is pulled down, the angler grabs the rod from the holder and lifts sharply to set the hook.

What he does is identify key tidal periods when optimum sturgeon fishing can be projected. In general, the best sturgeon fishing in the San Francisco Bay system is during outgoing tides just before and during a cycle of minus low tides. All tide books identify these periods. They phase in and out in two-week cycles throughout the winter and spring.

Fraser has had his greatest success during the latter part of outgoing tides during the winter. Since minus tides occur late in the day during winter, the sturgeon fishing is often best from 3 p.m. to sunset (5 p.m. to 5:30 p.m.). To fine-tune it a step further, the best fishing is often during the two days just prior to when the minus low tides begin.

"When the fish are on a good bite, all you need are moving tides," Fraser said. "In the summer, the incoming tide seems the best. In the winter, we like the outgoing."

There have been many days when we will see frustrated anglers leaving at 3 p.m. after a full day of no action. Meanwhile, we will just be heading out, excited at fishing during a prime two-hour period -- and then catch and release two or three big sturgies, sometimes even getting doubleheaders.

One skunked angler looked at me and said, "Next time, I'll say my prayers."

It is not a prayer you need answered. It is a winning system. Keith Fraser has exactly that.

☞ STURGEON FISHING TRIP FACTS

Sturgeon seminars: Keith Fraser's seminars are scheduled for the first weekend of November. For information, call (415) 456-0321.

Sturgeon boats: Bass-Tub, San Rafael, (415) 456-9055; Superfish, San Rafael, (415) 456-0321; New Keesa, Point San Pablo, (415) 787-1720; Happy Hooker, Berkeley, (415) 223-5388; Fury, Point San Pablo, (415) 357-4390.

Tackle shops: The Trap, Rio Vista, (707) 374-5554; Panfili's, Antioch, (415) 757-5343; Harris Harbor, Pittsburgh, (415) 458-4904; Martinez Bait, (415) 229-3150; Rodeo Lucky Bait, (415) 799-9070; Loch Lomond Bait, San Rafael, (415) 456-0321; Berkeley Marina, (415) 849-2727; Hi's Tackle Box, San Francisco, (415) 221-3825; Modern Bait, San Francisco, (415) 824-5450; Sun Valley Bait, San Mateo (415) 343-4690; Alviso Boat Dock, (408) 262-3885.

SHARK FISHING
IN THE BAY

HOW TO CATCH YOUR OWN SET OF JAWS

The problem with sharks is that every once in a while they decide to eat somebody. Men of the sea have this common haunt, hidden somewhere in the back of their minds: They are tossed overboard by a sudden wave, and while they are kicking to stay afloat, they see a giant fin cutting the surface, speeding toward them. What could be more terrifying than a snapping mouth of razor blades?

Well, the truth is that more people are killed by lightning bolts than munched by sharks. But it still can be astonishing to learn the size of some of the sharks right in San Francisco Bay. As you read this, sharks ranging from 200 to 400 pounds are likely to be roaming the Bay, hungry for a meal; the angling record for the Bay is a 545-pounder. The biggest I have tangled with was a 170-pounder -- hooked just west of Alcatraz -- eight-feet long with a mouth as big as a large salad bowl. It's enough to keep you from dangling your legs in the water again, even though these are bottom feeders, not mid-water munch machines like their cousin, the Great White.

Shark fishing in the Bay remains a unique sport, the kind of adventure that most anglers would like to try at least once. One of the best times is in the fall at the annual Bay Shark Derby, which is sponsored by United Anglers of California and the California Striped Bass Association.

If you're new to shark busting, you'll find it a unique adventure.

For some sport and good eating, the leopard shark and dogfish can be easy to come by. Your ticket?

Just use a standard two-hook surf leader, with hunks of squid for bait on 6/0 hooks, and dangle it on the bottom in the Bay's channels or deep holes. Leopard sharks, named for the leopard-like black spots dotting their body, are the most prolific in the Bay and range from three to six feet. Be sure to cut the tail and bleed the fish immediately in order to preserve the quality of meat for the dinner table. If you do not plan on eating the fish, cut your leader and return the shark to the Bay; the hook will erode in three days. At no time should the life of one of the Bay's fish be wasted, including sharks.

You want to set yourself up for a spree with Jaws Jr.? Then plan on playing by an additional and special set of rules.

Heed one word of warning: Although the sharks common to San Francisco Bay are not man-eaters, they still have an instinct to bite at just about anything they can get their teeth into. That includes you, if you're within range. Any shark larger than five feet should not be brought aboard any sportfishing boat, but rather should be tied off and kept in the water. That lesson should not be difficult to remember the first time you look down into the water and see an eight-footer coming up, mouth open, teeth exposed, and jaws snapping.

This is an unusual sport and the methods reflect that. The key aspects include bait, tackle, rigging, and knowing the right spots. The latter is well known by sharkbusters; the deeper the better. The best spots are located outside the entrance to Sausalito, where the bottom is 250 feet deep (adjacent to a small green building on the shore), in a hole west of Angel Island, and in the channel off of Hunter's Point.

Other good spots, especially for leopard sharks, include off of Richmond, and also in the South Bay, in the main channel near the Dumbarton Bridge on southward.

For bait, remember that sharks are cannibals and often like nothing better than munching a wounded brother. Some of the biggest sharks ever caught in the Bay have been hooked by fishermen using a whole stickleback shark, or at least massive hunks of one, for bait. In fact, Reno Montanelli of Oakland used a three-foot stickleback shark for bait and enticed the bite of a 337-pound seven-gill shark that measured 10 feet long. That occurred aboard the Fury, the shark boat out of Point San Pablo.

To deal with a fish like that, you must have the right rigging, otherwise the attempt is hopeless. The rigging for big sharks has been perfected by Jim Siegle of Siegle's Hunting and Fishing in Oakland and skipper Ernie Tritto: Use a one-pound sinker, from which five feet of 25-pound plastic-coated wire leader extends to a size 14/0 hook. This insures the bait will be right on the bottom, where the giant sharks feed.

Do not expect the fight to be a short one. They have bulldog strength and a mean spirit, and 300-pounders have been known to strip the line off a reel without even breathing hard.

According to marine biologists, the six-gill shark can reach 15 feet long and 1,600 pounds. Perhaps in the near future, you will tangle with one.

☞ SHARK FISHING TRIP FACTS

Charters: The Bay's only sportfishing vessels that specialize in shark fishing are the Fury, (415) 357-4390, out of Point San Pablo, and the Fishing Fool, (916) 777-6498, out of Emeryville.

Fishing tips: The men at Siegle's Hunting and Fishing in Oakland have the know-how when it comes to chasing big sharks. Talk to Jim Siegle, (415) 655-8789.

SALTWATER FISHING

DEEP SEA
FISHING

A DIFFERENT KIND OF MOUNTAIN GOLD

There's a nearby mountain range that is constructed something like the Sierra Nevada, but you won't find it on any road map. It's buried beneath miles of sea water.

Tucked below the ocean surface along the Bay Area coast is rock ridgeline, complete with craggy peaks and canyons that drop thousands of feet. And similar to how the Sierra is a home for wildlife, this underwater range is perfect for fish.

A wild variety of big rockfish, along with cabezone, and lingcod to 50 pounds hold court here. September and October is a special time,

when the big lings will emerge from the depths of the canyon bottoms to spawn along many of the mountain tops.

The highest peak is 22 miles west of San Francisco, where the Farallon Islands break the surface. The ridgeline extends for about 100 miles, to just north of Bodega Bay. Reefs (south to north) such as the Farallones, Soap Bank, Fanny Shoals, and Cordell Bank attract vast schools of rockfish year around, and big lingcod every fall.

Fishing for them is a sport for newcomers and experienced hands alike. In any case, you are likely to fill up your freezer with some of the finest food fare in the sea. Autumn is the prime time, when it is common for anglers to bring home burlap bags plugged with limits on trips to these spots. The best lingcod spots are at Cordell Bank, southwest of Bodega Bay, and at the Soap Bank, which us just south of Cordell.

The Sea Angler from Tides Wharf in Bodega Bay ventures to Cordell Bank daily when seas allow it. On a typical trip in the fall, boat loads of 25 to 35 fishermen will catch 30 to 60 lingcod, in addition to limits of 15 rockfish per rod. "This is the time of year when nothing surprises me," said skipper Ricky Powers.

The Soap Bank, a rarely fished spot due to its distance from sportfishing ports, can offer even better action. Lingcod to 50 pounds are caught every fall. The only sportfishing vessel fast enough to reach the Soap Bank is the Cobra out of Richmond Marina, a 196-footer that hits this spot daily. In many cases, the boat ride takes longer than it does for fishermen to limit out.

The rigging is quite simple. Most people buy a shrimpfly rig, that is, a pre-tied leader with three red/yellow shrimpflies. Small strips of squid are baited on the hooks, then it is dropped to the ocean bottom-usually 200 to 450 feet deep.

The boat does not anchor, but drifts over the reefs, and the speed of the drift is controlled by the intensity of the wind. In turn, this is the variable that decides how much sinker weight is required. It can vary from eight ounces to two pounds, though one-pound weights usually do the job. But instead of lead sinkers, you can add some excitement to your trip with an option -- try a 16-ounce, chrome-plated Diamond Jig or Yo Ho Ho jig for a sinker. A chrome jig dangled near the sea bottom is the ticket for big

ling cod, which will often smash into it in order to protect the territory they have staked out.

The problem is that these jigs, complete with large treble hooks, can snag up so fast on the bottom that it can seem the rocks are biting better than the fish. On calm autumn days, when the boat drift is a slow one and fishermen have plenty of time to dangle baits over the reef, it is common for everybody aboard to catch two or three fish at a time.

A few years ago, on one trip to the Farallon Islands, a gent shouted for the gaff -- which usually means a big fish is on the line. But when skipper Ricky Powers looked over the side, he instead saw what looked like a stringer of 15 fish.

"What the heck are you doing using a stringer," Powers said. "This is the ocean. We put them in a burlap bag out here. You put them on a stringer and all you're going to do is attract a bunch of sharks."

The fishermen just grinned. "Look closer," he said.

We all did. It turned out that the man had a custom-tied leader with 15 baits on at once -- and had caught a 15-fish limit on one drop.

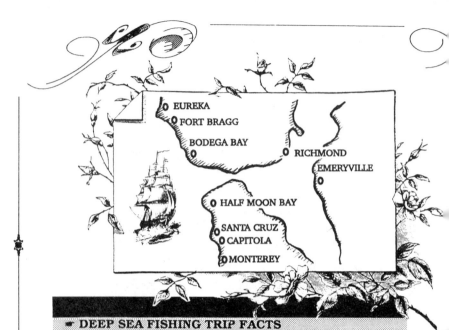

☛ DEEP SEA FISHING TRIP FACTS

Cordell Bank: The Sea Angler makes trips daily out of Tides Wharf in Bodega Bay. Call (707) 875-3495.

Soap Bank: The Cobra, the fastest sportfishing vessel in the Bay Area, hits Soap Bank regularly out of Richmond Marina. Call (415) 283-6773.

Fanny Shoals: Hank Schramm occasionally sends deep sea trips here during fall and winter. Based at Emery Cove Marina. Call (415) 654-6040.

Farallon Islands: This is the favorite spot for the Capt. John from Princeton in Half Moon Bay. Call (415) 726-2913.

New Year Island: Stagnaro's Fishing Charters sends boats here from Santa Cruz. Call (408) 425-7003.

Capitola: Fishing the edge of inshore kelp beds in shallow water can be productive. Skiff rentals are available at Capitola Wharf. Call (408) 462-2208.

Monterey: The Holiday works the Monterey underwater canyon. Call (408) 372-0577.

Fort Bragg: The Trek II out of Noyo Harbor runs Friday through Sundays to local reefs. Call (707) 964-4550.

Eureka: The Moku makes two half-day trips out of Easy Landing to Table Rock, or in Humboldt Bay. Call (707) 442-3474.

ALBACORE OFF THE
COAST

A TORPEDO WITH FINS

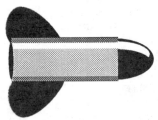

Most fishermen have never experienced the phenomenon of looking down at their fishing reels after hooking a fish -- and seeing the line disappear so fast it looks like it is melting.

That's because they have never hooked a big tuna.

But fishermen now have that rare chance. The annual late-August/early-September arrival of warm ocean currents along the Monterey and Bay Area coasts brings schools of tuna within boating range.

A tuna is like a torpedo with fins, and that goes for the albacore or its more rare and larger cousins, the yellowfin or bigeye. Everything about them, their shape, muscle and range, is designed for speed and power.

Schools of albacore begin arriving in late August, 20 to 30 miles west of Point Sur off Monterey. Then they show up at a spot called Guide Seamount, which is located about 40 miles west of Half Moon Bay.

On a typical trip, the boat Nautilus II out of Emeryville will find water 62 to 64 degrees at the Guide and return to port with 65 albacore -- with all the fish ranging 15 to 30 pounds.

That is the kind of news that will make anybody who has fished for albacore start taking a blood pressure check.

But it is new territory for most Bay Area fishermen. There just is no other trip like it. You usually leave late at night, like 1 a.m., sleep while the boat cruises far out to sea, then wake up and start fishing at sunrise. On the Nautilus II, the trips include bunking, meals, and unlimited drinks.

362

And it doesn't come cheap at $125 for a one-day trip, $250 for two days.

The techniques for albacore are unique. After cruising far out to sea in the night, the fishing starts at daybreak when four rods will be rigged with feather jigs and trolled at eight to nine knots. Albacore commonly cruise at 200 to 500 feet deep, but will flash to the surface to hit the jigs.

At that point, the boat will be stopped and deck hands will chum live anchovies overboard, hoping to induce the entire school of albacore into a surface bite. Fishermen will rush to the railing and toss out a live anchovy for bait.

One of the most exciting moments in all of fishing is when you find yourself in the midst of a genuine tuna feeding frenzy -- everybody aboard hooks up simultaneously, fishing lines go every which way imaginable. It's a combination of total confusion, excitement and insanity, all at once. And there's nothing else like it.

But what is more common is a heck of a long boat ride, and then finally a hookup on one of the jigs. The boat is stopped, and a few more tuna are picked up on bait.

Just about everything about the trip is different than other ocean-going adventures. Even the water looks different, a deeper blue than you've ever seen. The ocean is deep out here, 5,000 feet deep, and there's no land in sight.

Traditionally, September is the peak season, with late August and early October providing the start and finish.

A variable is always water temperatures. In the winter, inshore ocean waters often measure 48 to 54 degrees off the local coast, far too cold for albacore.

Tuna fishing can be like the old shell game, but fishermen can win at it.

☞ ALBACORE TRIP FACTS

Bay Area: In the Bay Area, special long-range albacore trips will be offered by Emeryville Sportfishing Center, (415) 654-6040; on the Cobra, (415) 283-6773, out of Richmond Marina, and on the Red Baron by Huck Finn Sportfishing, (415) 726-7133, and Outlaw by Capt. John's, (415) 726-2913, out of Half Moon Bay. Out of Santa Cruz, Stagnaro's Fishing Charters (408-425-7003) also chase albacore.

Monterey: Trips are also offered out of Monterey. Monterey boats are generally closer to the action which makes for shorter boat rides. Call (408) 372-0577.

SALTWATER FISHING

SUISUN BAY
STRIPERS

WHERE YOU LEARN HOW TO COUNT

T he rod tip dipped, then straightened. Fish on? Fish off? With the reel on free spool, I thumbed the line, waiting like a safecracker for any detectable sign. Suddenly, again I felt pressure, and under my thumb, I felt the line start to leave my fishing reel.

"One, two, three," I counted out loud, while some 15 feet of line was stripped -- then rammed the hook home. Bass on!

Fishing the fall run of striped bass in Suisun Bay can not only be the ticket to some big fish -- fish gorged from a summer of feasting on anchovies in San Francisco Bay and Pacific Ocean -- but a style of fishing that can cause the kind of tingles that anglers search for.

Because mudsuckers and bullheads are the preferred entreaties, you cannot simply strike at the first indication of a bite. Instead you must allow the fish to mouth the bait, run with it, and begin to eat it. If you wait too long, the bass will feel the steel and drop the bait. If you are too anxious, the hook will never be in the fish's mouth. So a certain touch must be developed. Those who have it often tell of some of the best action of the year in Suisun Bay.

Want more? Got more: While you're anchored and waiting for a bass to come by, a giant sturgeon may happen to gobble your bait by accident. Some of the biggest sturgies in the past 10 years have been caught this way -- by accident.

Access to the prime areas is quite easy. On the southern shoreline, private boaters will find ramps at Martinez, West Pittsburg, Pittsburg, and Antioch. On the northern shoreline, launch ramps are

available at Pierce's Harbor at Montezuma Slough, plus there is a free ramp in Benicia.

Party boats that specialize in this style of fishing leave daily from Martinez and Crockett. Trip cost? A day of fishing on the Nobilis out of Martinez, for instance, goes for $30 to $35, including bait. Rod and reel rentals cost $5.

If you want to keep your feet on solid ground, the Benicia shoreline has several good areas to cast from. But boaters have tremendous advantage, being able to sample many areas on any day. The best spots are often the southern part of Honker Bay, Suisun Cut, Garnet Point, and just south of Roe Island.

Back-to-back storms in the fall will pump enough fresh rain water into the Delta/Bay waterways to set the striper migration in full gear. In San Francisco Bay, the bass will take off, heading through San Pablo and Suisun bays, then onward for the Delta.

High and outgoing tides seem to set off the best fishing for stripers in Suisun (pronounced Soo-soon). A prerequisite to every trip should be a phone call for wind conditions. At times during early winter, Suisun Bay can be like a wind tunnel. However, it is often quite calm between storms.

As winter approaches, some one million stripers will head up to the Delta. Most will rest in Suisun Bay in order to acclimate themselves to the freshwater of the Delta. The best fishing lasts from mid-October through early December.

And if you don't believe it, just try counting to three after a big bass has picked up your bait.

☛ **SUISUN BAY TRIP FACTS**

How to get there: From San Francisco, take Highway 80 to Highway 4, which borders the southern edge of Suisun Bay.

Fishing boats: The Great Escape (707) 864-2222 berths at Martinez, while the Skip-A-Loo, Capt. K. Marauder, and the Morning Star berth at Crockett (415) 787-1047.

Fishing tips: For up-to-date fishing information, call Harris Harbor in Pittsburg at (415) 458-4904, Martinez Bait at (415) 229-3150, or the Tackle Shop in Benicia at (707) 745-4921.

Trip cost: Boarding a sportfishing boat for a day costs about $35, which includes bait. Rod and reel rentals are available on all boats, usually for about $5 per day.

SALTWATER FISHING

STRIPERS IN THE
SURF

THE SEA WOLVES OF THE BEACH

Battling big striped bass in the surf with nothing more than a fishing rod has a unique appeal for people who want to strip themselves of extras and instead meet the sea on a one-to-one basis.

The first time you dig your shoes into the sand, unleash a long cast into the Pacific surf, then feel the surge of sea water at your legs, you immediately realize what you may have missed before. There is a certain reliance on the self that is missing from the lives of many, and surf fishing supplies exactly that.

In July and August along the San Mateo County coastline, surf fishing provides a chance to catch big striped bass, most ranging from eight to 25 pounds. You write your own ticket, and big bass jump on for the ride.

The first big striper run of the year usually arrives in late June, when a school of stripers will corral a mass of anchovies, pinning them against the back of the surf line. Surf casters will toss metal lures such as the Miki Jig and the Krocadile as far as possible, barely reaching the bait activity -- and hook and battle big stripers for short sprees. The action comes and goes, and fishermen search and don't always find. It magnifies the magic when you find yourself in the midst of a hot run.

Access to the prime areas is a simple matter of driving your vehicle to the coast. The fish roam wild in the sea, but the best spots are San Francisco's Thornton Beach, Pacifica's Mussel Rock, Sharp Park, Rockaway Beach and Linda Mar, and Half Moon Bay's Venice Beach. Never set out on a surf trip blind. Always call one of the contacts listed on the checklist for a tip.

Birds never lie. A diving pelican indicates that baitfish are on the surface -- driven there by feeding stripers below. However, many fish can be caught without a wild bird scene that indicates an undersea feast is going on.

One rule is that if you cast from beach areas, you should use metal lures. When you venture to rocky coves such as Pacifica's Rockaway Beach or Pedro Point, the big plugs such as the Pencil Popper are most effective. Another key is tides. The best catches often occur just at the top of the high tide because it often sets off intense baitfish activity, primarily anchovies.

Just like the adventure itself, surf fishing calls for a stark outlay of equipment. All you really need is a 12-foot long surf rod and a matching reel filled with a 20 to 25-pound test line, and a small box of lures. Spinning reels can handle the widest weight range of lures without problem, but revolving spool reels attain the longest casts (with metal lures), and there are many times when the stripers seem just beyond your casting range.

Chest waders are popular for anglers who are out regularly. Rather than open up Fort Knox for the expensive models, however, many Sea Wolves are now opting for the inexpensive "stocking waders," and wearing tennis shoes over them.

This adventure, admittedly, is not for everybody. A special bond links those of us who share in this type of excitement.

☞ STRIPERS IN THE SURF TRIP FACTS

How to get there: From San Francisco, take Highway 280 to Highway 1 and continue on into Pacifica. From the Peninsula or East Bay, take Highway 92 to Half Moon Bay, then head north on Highway 1 into Pacifica.

Trip tip: Surf fishermen share a common bond. If you're driving in Pacifica or Half Moon Bay and see a vehicle with a surf rod sticking out, hail down the driver. He may have a hot tip on the latest bite.

Trip Cost: Access is free. A California fishing license with a striped bass stamp is required by state law.

Who to contact: In Pacifica, call Coastside No. 2 at (415) 355-9901, or Pacifica Pier at (415) 355-0690. In Half Moon Bay, call Hilltop at (415) 726-4950.

SALTWATER FISHING

PERCH IN THE
BAY

EARLY-SEASON SCRAPPERS

A good many spinning rods sit in garages during winter, cobwebs forming in the guides, a fine coat of dust covering the reel. With trout season still more than two months away, most anglers figure there is little to do but sit back in an easy chair with the most recent issue of Field & Stream and dream about spring fishing.

But for many licensed anglers in Northern California, perch can provide some fine early-season angling action. On calm days, you can find good perch fishing in coves and bays from Monterey on northward. Tomales Bay, north of San Francisco, is a perch spawning ground that offers exceptionally good fishing from midwinter through March. Humboldt Bay, near Eureka, is also

a very good area to fish. San Francisco Bay, however, is one of the best perch fishing spots on the California coast.

Some thirteen species of perch are caught in the state's waters, but the most common perch caught in San Francisco Bay is the pile perch, often called the splittail perch. This fish can reach 18 inches and is a real battler.

Terminal tackle for perch is simple to rig. Tie a No. 6 hook on the end of your line, then clamp on a small split shot 18 inches above that. Hook your bait, and you're set. Many trout rods are fine for perch fishing. Most anglers use light spinning gear. My personal choice is an ultralight graphite spinning rod with a small reel filled with four-pound-test monofilament.

For bait, use a single live grass shrimp, rigged so the shank of the hook follows the back of the shrimp and only the point of the hook protrudes. A half-pound of grass shrimp costs $3.50 and is usually plenty for two anglers. An alternative is to use a piece of pileworm, which can be the top bet when fishing in deeper areas. When the perch are really biting, they will even hit shiny metal lures. One of the most productive is the 1/16 or 1/8 ounce silver/blue Kastmaster.

As with almost all saltwater fish that live in San Francisco Bay,

---

Puzzling Perch:

Some fishermen practically need an Ouija Board to correctly identify all the species of perch in California. With some 13 in abundance, cases of mistaken identity are common.

A few years ago, four anglers in the same boat called what biologists term a Calico Surfperch a (1) pogie, (2) silver, (3) rubberlip, and (4) walleye. All are acceptable names for different kinds of saltwater perch.

Instead of a seer, the book How To Fish The Pacific Coast, by Ray Cannon, is the first and still the best guide to identifying different saltwater species of fish, including perch. The late Cannon was a renowned expert on Pacific fishing, and in this book he included a special section on fish identification that separates fact from fancy. The book, originally published by Sunset Books in Menlo Park, is no longer in print. However, you may be able to find copies in some bookstores, or in your local library.

---

perch are tide-oriented, and the times they feed are dictated by tidal currents. Tide books are available at most bait and tackle shops and ship's stores. They are usually inexpensive, and may be available for free. It is essential to learn how to read a tide book in order to properly assess the strength of each day's currents. To figure the amount of current, simply subtract the difference between the low and high tides. For example, a low tide of 1.2 feet followed by a high tide of 6.2 feet would set off a current of five feet of moving water -- a fairly strong incoming tide by San Francisco Bay standards. According to my logbook, tidal sequences with less than 3 feet of water movement tend to provide slow perch fishing. In addition, low outgoing tides, or minus low tides, also put the fish off the bite, or take them to deeper water. If you don't fish from a boat, this can be a problem.

If you're limited to shore fishing, your best bet will be to restrict your perch fishing to high tides where you get four to five feet of moving water. After several years of keeping track of trip results, I have found that the two hours before and after a tide peaks are often the most productive.

Perch in San Francisco Bay are almost never found in open water or along long, straight stretches of shoreline. The fish are usually found in large numbers around pilings, boat docks, submerged concrete blocks, and rocky areas. San Francisco Bay has many easy-access fishing spots with these features.

My favorite perch fishing areas are in South San Francisco Bay, and are accessible by boat. There are launching ramps at Oyster Point in Brisbane, Coyote Point in San Mateo, Redwood City Marina, Palo Alto Yacht Harbor, and Alviso Boat Dock.

Perch are often found in the South Bay along the pillars of the San Mateo Bridge or Dumbarton Bridge. The pilings in the South San Francisco industrial area and behind the San Francisco airport are also good bets, along with the rocky areas at the breakwaters at Coyote Point and Oyster Point marinas.

☛ PERCH TRIP FACTS:

Licenses and limits: The daily limit of perch is 20, with not more than 10 fish of any one species.

Who to contact: It's a good idea to check on the action before you go out. In South San Francisco Bay call Sun Valley Bait & Tackle, 620 S. Norfolk, San Mateo, CA 94401 at (415) 343-6837, or call the "fish line," at (415) 343-4690 for a recorded fishing report, updated daily.

Several good sources of information are available for San Francisco Bay perch fishing. In the East Bay, contact Berkeley Marina, 225 University Avenue, Berkeley, CA 94710, (415) 849-2727; or Siegle's Sportshop, 508 W. MacArthur Boulevard, Oakland CA 94609, (415) 655-8789. Both sell bait and tackle and can provide reliable and up-to-date tips. In San Francisco, contact Hi's Tackle Box, 4644 Geary Boulevard, San Francisco, CA 94118, (415) 221-3825; and Modern Bait and Tackle, 2975 Mission, San Francisco, CA 94110, (415) 824-5450.

In San Rafael, contact Loch Lomond Marina, Dock A, San Rafael, CA 94901, (415) 456-0321. Keith Fraser is a good source at Loch Lomond.

These shops also sell bait and tackle and offer up-to-date fishing information.

The latter two can be fished from shore, as can Redwood City Marina, and Showboat Slough in Burlingame.

In the main bay, there are several ideal perch fishing spots. The pilings along Berkeley Pier and Fisherman's Wharf can provide exceptional fishing from a boat or from the docks themselves. If you fish from a boat, some prime places to explore are the rocky areas on the Raccoon Strait side of Angel Island, and the Navy docks on the eastern side of Treasure Island. Boat ramps at Berkeley Marina, Sausalito, and Mission Rock in San Francisco, just south of the Bay Bridge, provide access to these areas.

Only rarely do perch frequent adjacent San Pablo Bay in late winter, since storm runoff can dramatically lower San Pablo's salinity. Since perch are a saltwater fish, an infusion of freshwater will flush them down to the saltier confines of San Francisco Bay. In the fall and early winter, however, perch are caught along the levee and docks at Loch Lomond Marina in San Rafael.

If you do not get a strike within 20 minutes, you should move to another likely spot. Since perch are a school fish, if you're not getting any strikes you are most likely casting in an area where there are no perch.

Keep these tips in mind, then wipe the dust off your spinning rod, and get ready for some of the best late-winter fishing San Francisco Bay has to offer.

FISHING ON
MONTEREY BAY

TURNING BACK THE CLOCK

Time has a way of altering every day, but when it comes to fishing at Monterey Bay, 25 years seem to have flashed by in a day or two. Little appears to have changed here.

It was back in 1962 when my Dad first took my brother and I to Capitola. While fishing, we'd listen to the Giants game; Willie Mays was hitting the left field wall, Billy Pierce was hitting the corners. And we were having the time of our lives, catching rockfish like crazy on the quiet waters of Monterey Bay.

More than 25 years later, Willie Mays is long gone, and the Giants struggle along. But at Capitola, the good times remain for the few people who know of the angling attractions waiting here.

The Capitola Wharf is one of the few places on the entire West Coast where you can rent a small boat for a day of fishing. Hence, awaiting is an adventure for any angler with the yearning for it. It is the perfect place for a father/son fishing trip. Just ask my dad.

At 7 a.m. or so, we'd arrive at Capitola, which is a relatively short drive (an hour to 90 minutes) from the San Francisco Peninsula. After hopping aboard a rental skiff, it would be just a five-minute ride to the prime fishing grounds, situated

at the edge of the nearby kelp beds. Like I said, little has changed. Spots such as Adams Reef, Surfers Reef, South Rock all produce outstanding fishing.

With rod in hand, you allow your bait to descend to the shallow sea bottom. Squid-baited shrimpflies, strips of mackerel, or cut anchovy chunks still entice a surprising variety of rockfish. A bonus is that very little weight is required to reach the bottom here, often just a few ounces. And in the fall, Monterey Bay gets its quietest water of the year, as well as its best rockfishing.

Most folks use light saltwater rods, with line rated at 12 to 20-pound test. Rod rentals are available at Capitola Pier for $3.

If you'd like to tussle with some heavyweights, autumn also brings with it a good number of blue sharks. For folks with even bigger plans, long-range trips are made this time of year in search of albacore and tuna. If you just want to stick to the pier, crabbing and fishing for mackerel can be productive.

Finding a common ground for a father and son can be difficult, but a fishing trip from Capitola can provide that rare space, and in the process, some special memories.

Maybe time doesn't alter every day after all.

☛ CAPITOLA TRIP FACTS

How to get there: Take either Highway 17 or Highway 1 to Santa Cruz, then head south on Highway 1. Take the 41st Avenue exit, then make a left on Capitola Road -- which will take you within a half block of the foot of Capitola Wharf.

Trip Cost: Skiff rentals cost $25 during the week, $30 for weekends. Rental includes a 7.5 horsepower engine and gasoline. Rod and reel rentals are available for $3 per day for boat use, $3.50 per day for pier use.

Don't forget: Anglers over the age of 16 must have a valid fishing license in possession.

Who to contact: For tips on fishing, weather, and sea conditions, call the Capitola Wharf at (408) 462-2208.

SALTWATER FISHING

BODEGA BAY

IT'S BETTER THAN THE MOVIE

The drive alone to Bodega Bay is enough reason to make the trip. A country-styled, two-laner from Petaluma meanders its way through a series of rolling hills and dairy farms, like something out of the midwest. But you'll know you are not in Iowa, and that you are just 100 miles northwest of San Francisco, when suddenly before you opens the vast expanse of the Pacific. It is a refreshing greeting.

Bodega Bay is best known as the place were Alfred Hitchcock filmed his famous horror flick, "The Birds." That honor often attracts first-timers this way out of curiosity. However, like myself, many find that they keep coming back for many other reasons.

Despite its short distance to the Bay Area, the area has managed to retain a special identity. Towns such as Freestone, Fallon, and Bloomfield have a definitive age, depth, and appeal. Like many of the towns along the coast north of the

Bay Area, what often draws people here is the sea, and the fishing that goes with it -- deep sea, salmon and shark fishing, and right in Bodega Bay, good clamming and perch fishing. There is also a tremendous variety of seabirds that frequent the area, so bring your binoculars.

Charter trips run year around out of Tides Wharf for deep sea fishing at Cordell Bank, one of the better spots on California's coast. The boats Sea Angler, Sea Dog, and Merry Jane often nail full limits for all customers aboard in a matter of hours. In the early 1970s, Cordell Bank was almost cleaned out by Soviet netters -- but since they were kicked out in 1978, the fish populations have rebounded in a big way. Anglers using shrimpflies baited with strips of squid often hook up with several fish at once.

This can be a favorite area to troll for salmon, with the best salmon fishing here usually from mid-June to August. An excellent two-lane

launch ramp at the western end of Bodega Bay provides access; get here early, the lines can get quite long on summer weekends. The prime salmon area is just outside the harbor at a red buoy called "The Whistler," about a 10-minute ride after launching. I have had trips here where we were releasing 10-pound salmon in hopes of better -- and came up with limits of 15 to 30-pounders.

If you have a yearning for the bizarre -- and want to tangle with a Great White shark -- drive your boat southward to the mouth of Tomales Bay, which is a known breeding area. Giant sharks have been hooked here, though few landed.

If the thought of a boat makes you kind of green in the gills, there are plenty of adventures on land. In the winter, minus low tides which come in cycles about every two weeks, uncover miles of tidal flats in Bodega Bay itself, particularly on the western side. This is a prime clamming area, though pretty gooey to walk in. Keep an eye on your tide book to determine when the next good set of minus low tides will arrive.

Many folks just show up with a picnic lunch and sit along the western shoreline of Bodega Bay during a high and incoming tide. They toss out a fishing line, munch on goodies and wait for a bite. Perch and flounder, and once in a while (in May through July) halibut, will come along to get in on the picnic.

One time at Bodega Bay, I saw a deer swimming out to sea; heading straight out of the harbor to the ocean. The Coast Guard rescued it.

That's as bizarre as it gets here. Despite what you may have seen in the movies, there are no bird attacks. Just good times.

☞ BODEGA BAY TRIP FACTS

How to get there: Take Highway 101 to Petaluma, where you turn west on Highway 116, and follow the signs to Bodega Bay.

Trip Cost: Deep sea trips to Cordell Bank out of Tides Wharf cost $30 per person, with rod rentals available for $3 to $5.

Area oddity: Bodega Bay often gets its sunniest and warmest weather in October and January.

Don't forget: For a bonus, bring your binoculars to scope out the tremendous variety of birds, including even flamingos at times. All species are of the non-attacking variety.

Who to contact: For information, call Tides Wharf at (707) 875-3595; New Sea Angler at (707) 875-3495; Bodega Sport Fishing at (707) 875-3344.

SALTWATER FISHING

TOMALES BAY

A BAY AREA RETREAT

Tomales Bay State Park is an ideal example of a quiet, secluded area within close range of millions of Bay Area residents -- that is rarely visited. While thousands of weekenders might descend on Point Reyes, Muir Woods or Stinson Beach, nearby Tomales Bay sits relatively undisturbed by anything except small waves lapping at the shoreline. The gentle surf-free beaches are a prime attraction for family picnics, and during minus tides, clamming is often outstanding. Hiking, surf fishing for perch, and cross-country running are also popular. Car-top boats can easily be launched in the quiet surf.

This state park sits on the Point Reyes Peninsula on the west side of Tomales Bay, with more than a thousand acres within park boundaries. It seems as if the retreat is much larger, however, since it is bordered by the Point Reyes National Seashore.

A unique element here is that Inverness Ridge acts as a blockade to much of the wind and fog that hammers away at the Pacific coast. When Point Reyes is buried in a rolling, 10-mph fog, Tomales Bay can be warm and sunny. It is a good secret to know.

The best hike here is on the Jepson Trail, a 6.5-mile trek, which crosses through one of the largest remaining virgin stands of Bishop pines. About 70 percent of the park is filled with pines, oaks and madrone. In this habitat, one can see fox, raccoon, badger, weasel and mule deer. However, my wildlife viewings here have largely been limited to chipmunks and the like.

If you want to get your hands dirty, then bring a clam shovel and pick a good minus tide. When the tide goes out, you will see acres of prime clam beds loaded with cockles. Two of the best spots are south of Heart's Desire Beach and north of Indian Beach. Be certain to have a fishing license, a measuring device, and to adhere to the limit of 50 cockles. Wardens commonly cite clammers here for not having licenses, which usually turns out to be a $50 to $300 fine; the exact amount depends on the Marin County judge.

On high and incoming tides, perch fishing can spice up an otherwise lazy day at the beach. Because of the relatively calm surf in the bay, giant surf rods are not necessary, although long, medium-weight rods can certainly help in attaining long casts.

If you instead choose to launch a car-top boat from the beach, it is not advisable to head out the mouth of Tomales Bay. Just south of the black buoy here, the water is very shallow -- which can turn into a dangerous chop with just a 15-knot wind.

Most folks, however, are content to explore the wooded areas or soak up the sun in relative isolation. That's how it is when you discover a place that seems to be one of the Bay Area's best kept secrets.

TOMALES BAY TRIP FACTS

How to get there: From the Point Reyes Peninsula, head north on Sir Francis Drake Boulevard through Inverness and then on three miles to Pierce Point Road where you turn right.

Trip tip: If you want to fish or clam, check tides carefully, with high and incoming tides best for perch; minus tides best for clamming. Dogs are not allowed on beaches or trails.

Mass transit: No buses get any closer than the town of Inverness.

Trip Cost: Day-use fee is $2 per vehicle. No camping is allowed.

Who to contact: For a free leaflet or information, call (415) 669-1140, (415) 456-1286, or (707) 576-2185 or write Tomales Bay State Park, Star Route, Inverness, CA 94937.

SALTWATER FISHING

FISHING FROM THE SHORE
OF THE BAY

STURGEON, JACKSMELT, PERCH

No boat? No fish? Thousands of Bay Area fishermen can empathize with that familiar quotient.

Because of the way fish are tidal-oriented in San Francisco Bay, a boat, any boat, can provide the mobility to move from spot to spot, hitting each at the optimum tidal period.

But in the winter, the have-nots can match the catch of the haves. No boat is necessary. Big fish? Try sturgeon to 60 pounds. Lots of fish? Try buckets of jacksmelt. Prime eats? Try a stringer of perch.

Where? How? The answers show how fishing can be easy and fun, rather than a duel of Men Against The Sea. For starters, you need to know how to go about it.

■ **Sturgeon:**

To catch a big sturgeon is the pinnacle of bay shore fishing, rarely accomplished and greatly celebrated. I've seen 25 landed by fishermen without boats in one day -- at Point Pinole Pier.

The pier is part of the East Bay Regional Park System, located on the edge of San Pablo Bay on the southeastern shoreline.

Sturgeon tend to congregate heavily in the Bay-Delta's freshwater/saltwater mixing zone, and a heavy storm runoff will push that zone right down to the Point Pinole area. In addition, when the Bay's herring spawn has finished, sturgeon are moving back upstream.

You should arrive at the pier at the beginning of the outgoing tide, when the water is deep, and has full power as it starts to move. In addition to your fishing rod, you will need a rope with a lasso (to land a big sturgeon), mud shrimp for bait, and extra tackle.

The rigging is simple enough. Slip a "slider" on your line, and then tie on a snap-swivel. From there, clamp on a pre-tied sturgeon leader which is available at tackle shops. From the slider, there is a clasp to attach your sinker. Use anywhere from four to eight ounces, depending on the tidal push.

Make sure you have plenty of line. Big sturgeon have been known to head for the Golden Gate Bridge, and they don't look back.

How to get there: To reach Point Pinole Pier, take Highway 80 to Hilltop Drive, which is in the Richmond area. From there, drive west to San Pablo Avenue, turn north, and continue to Atlas Road, then turn west. Proceed a few miles and turn south on Giant Highway and look for the park entrance on the right side. A shuttle bus will take you to the pier. No bait is available in the park.

Who to contact: For more information, call (415) 531-9300.

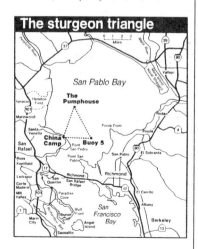

The sturgeon triangle

■ Jacksmelt:

Big schools of jacksmelt move into San Francisco Bay every March and April providing bucketfuls of fish for folks who know about it.

The best spot has been in South San Francisco Bay along the Burlingame shoreline -- less than a mile from Highway 101. Anyone can park a car along Old Bayshore Road, toss out a line, and start catching big jacksmelt. One of the better spots is just behind the drive-in theaters here.

All you need to do is tie on a No. 8 hook, and three or four feet above that, clamp on a large bobber. For bait, use a chunk of pileworm, enough to cover the hook. Arrive during a high tide; the best bite is just before and after the tide hits its peak.

Many shore anglers like fishing the outgoing tide because the tidal currents will carry their bobbers to deeper water.

You toss out your bait, and when the fish move in, your bobber starts to dance on the surface, then disappears momentarily. Got one! It's easy, fun and for residents of the San Francisco Peninsula, practically in your front yard.

How to get there: Off of Highway 101 on the San Francisco Peninsula, take the Old Bayshore exit in Burlingame. The road runs adjacent to the Bay's edge, with the best fishing near the drive-in theaters. A good bait shop is nearby in San Mateo.

Who to contact: Call Sun Valley Bait at (415) 343-6837.

■ Perch:

Perch hold along shoreline areas, schooling along piling and wharf areas. The pilings at Berkeley Pier are the top spot -- with luck you might catch 25 pounds in one sitting. The City's waterfront area can also be quite good.

Timing is critical, however. A key is to fish when the tides have moderate strength, eight incoming or outgoing. Slack water is bad news, and so are heavy currents. Since perch are a school fish, you can catch a zillion or none, dependent on when you hit the tide for each day.

Rigging is very simple. Just tie on a No. 6 hook, and about 18 inches above that, clamp on a splitshot or two for weight. The best bait is live grass shrimp, but sometimes that's difficult to attain. A chunk of pileworm is a good substitute.

You should toss it out in the moving current, letting it drift just past the piling where there are many species of perch.

So, you say you don't have a boat? No problem. March and April is one of the few times when you don't need one to score big in San Francisco Bay.

How to get there: To reach Berkeley Pier, take the University Avenue exit off of Highway 80, and follow the signs to Berkeley Marina.

Who to contact: A good bait and tackle shop is at the foot of the pier. For more information, call (415) 849-2727. The San Francisco waterfront is easily accessible, with a number of good bait shops nearby. Call Hi's Tackle, (415) 221-3825 or Modern Bait, (415) 824-5450.

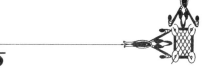

SALTWATER FISHING

PACIFICA PIER

SALMON WITHOUT BOARDING A BOAT

The idea of going salmon fishing usually brings thoughts of a pre-dawn wake-up, a long boat ride and a $50 tab for the boat fee, gas, parking and deck hand tip -- and the chance to catch the King of the Coast.

But at Pacifica Pier, the fishermen have a whole different way of thinking.

You just show up with your rod, buy your bait at the shop at the foot of the pier, and hope that luck is with you. Often enough, it is.

Pacifica Pier is the only place in the Bay Area, and on the California coast, where you stand a decent chance of catching salmon without boarding a boat. The price is right, the chances are fair, and this is one place where you definitely aren't going to get seasick.

The pier is located in the Sharp Park area of Pacifica, about 15 miles south of San Francisco. It juts out past the last ocean breaker line, right where salmon and striped bass will occasionally corral and trap schools of anchovies from July through August.

On premium days, when the bait-fish move in, as many as 200 salmon can be caught. About 30 to 50 is more common. On bad days, just a handful, and like they say, "that's fishing for you." Because it is a municipal pier, anglers are allowed two fishing rods (and not required to have a license). As a result, while waiting for a salmon to hit, you might throw out another line for perch, flounder or kingfish, or try a crab trap.

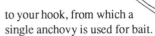

Another bonus is that the pier is lit, so when the fish are running you can stay into the night.

People will crowd all along the railing, and with so many fishing rods sticking out over the pier, it looks like a porcupine.

If you're new to the game, the folks at the bait shop at the foot of the pier, or the people at the nearby tackle shop, Coastside No. 2, will provide all the help you need.

The key, they will explain, is the arrival of baitfish, the schools of anchovies. That attracts salmon along inshore areas within range of the anglers on the pier.

In turn, that's why anchovy is such a perfect bait. To make it appear as natural as possible, the shops sell a special pier rigging for salmon fishing. The setup includes a float, a small mooching sinker, and then six feet of leader that is tied to your hook, from which a single anchovy is used for bait.

By using the float, you can see your bites instead of just feeling them through the rod, which adds to the excitement.

The whole affair is quite unique. You show up at the pier, excited at the prospect of catching a salmon without getting on a boat. When you see all the anglers out there, a sense of tension builds further, because you figure the big numbers mean a chance for big salmon.

When you actually get the bait in the water, though, a lull can set in, a sense of relaxation. You might notice the migration of brown pelicans is just starting. Murres and shearwaters are more abundant than in past months. The ocean seems to stretch out forever. For awhile, you might even forget you are fishing for big salmon.

But right then, that float might start to twitch, or better yet, get tugged under the surface. You set the hook and the battle is on.

Most salmon are in the 6 to 10-pound class, but there is always the remote possibility that a 20 or 30-pounder may grab your bait.

And that sets up another paradox: how do you land a fish that's measured in pounds, not inches? Try to handline it up to the pier and that fish will likely wiggle off and disappear faster than a gambler's pipe dream.

That's another reason crab nets are popular. A crab net can be lowered to the water, dipped under the fish, then raised to bring the fish to the pier deck.

A lot of people will work together to land a big salmon here, and if the fish is eventually brought to the pier deck, it can seem like a victory for all. You will find people of many nationalities at the pier, speaking different languages, but fishing is the common bond that transcends any differences.

Just watch what happens when a 20-pound salmon is hooked. Or better yet, watch when it happens to you.

☛ PACIFIC PIER TRIP FACTS

How to get there: From San Francisco, take Highway 280 to Highway 1 and continue on into Pacifica, where you take the Sharp Park exit. From the Peninsula or East Bay, take Highway 92 to Half Moon Bay, then head north on Highway 1 for 15 miles into Pacifica.

Trip cost: Access is free. No fishing license is required at Pacifica Pier. Two rods are allowed, but all other California State fishing regulations apply.

Who to contact: Phone Pacifica Pier at (415) 355-0690, or Coastside No. 2 Bait Shop at (415) 355-9901.

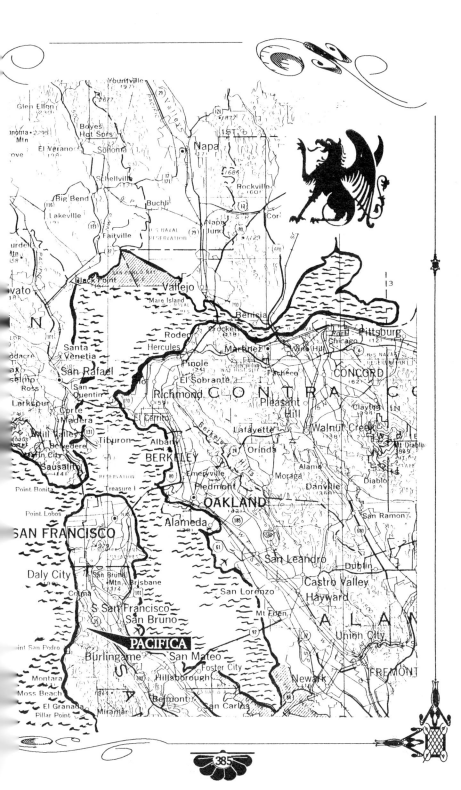

SALTWATER FISHING

BERKELEY PIER

MEDICINE FOR ALL

Some Bay Area folks complain of feeling like a hamster on a treadmill after a few years of a daily commute and the grind at work. The surroundings seem to merge. All looks the same, including the stop lights, and the cars blocking your way. One way to snap you out of that affliction is to take a slow stroll down Berkeley Pier, with or without a fishing rod.

At Berkeley Pier, you discover that waiting, the very thing people hate most about city life, is the very heart of pier fishing, a medicine that should be taken in regular dosages. Tension has a way of eating at you, but out here, you find yourself unworried, and that tight spring within begins to slowly uncoil. This ancient structure extends 3,000 feet

into San Francisco Bay, in the midst of some awesome landmarks that people travel around the world to see. You haven't looked lately? You're not alone.

Straight out to the west is the Golden Gate Bridge, a classic panoramic view. In a few hours, you see giant tankers come and go through the Gate. If you watch a sunset here, you will discover how the Gate got its name. It looks different out here than when you're burning up the road. Especially if you bring along a loaf of french bread and some cheese, plus something to wash it down, and maybe a fishing rod as well.

This has become one of the favorite ways to spend a day in the Bay Area since 1937, when Berkeley Pier was converted to a fishing pier. Since then, the pier has provided a place to spend a day on the Bay for old pros who just want some peace and quiet to young fishermen out for excitement.

Perch, jacksmelt, flounder, shark, sting rays, and bat rays are the most common catch here. Even the grand prizes of bay fishing: striped bass, halibut and even salmon, are occasionally caught here during their respective migrations, in spring, early summer, and fall. For decking the larger fish, it is essential to bring along a crab net, which can be dropped by a rope and then scooped under the fish. Anglers attempting to land a fish by hoisting it up by fishing line have lost some beauties in the past few years.

Several species of perch, including the big pile perch, are the most common from January through March. They tend to school around the pier's pilings; a live grass shrimp is just the ticket for good catches, particularly during moderate tides. Jacksmelt move into the area in April, May and early June, and can be caught on chunks of pileworm dangled under a float.

One of the Bay Area's finest fishing shops for bait, tackle, and most importantly, advice, sits at the foot of Berkeley Pier. Even if you don't need any tackle, you should always check in first here for the latest info.

However, don't get the idea that this is a complicated adventure. Most folks just hook on their bait, either grass shrimp, pileworm, or a chunk of anchovy, flip it out, take a seat and watch their line trailing out into the Bay in little curls, and enjoy the sights. Sometimes they get a bite, sometimes they don't. Somehow, it doesn't always seem to matter.

☛ BERKELEY PIER TRIP FACTS

How to get there: Berkeley Pier is in the heart of Berkeley Marina, which is located at the foot of University Avenue off of Highway 17. Take the University Avenue exit, then follow the signs to the marina.

Trip tip: A unique Fish and Game regulation allows anglers to fish with two lines here -- either two fishing rods, or a fishing rod and a crab trap simultaneously.

Time: Berkeley Pier is 3,000 feet long, so walking to the end takes an average of about 20 minutes. Many of the best perch fishing spots require just a short walk, however.

Trip Cost: Free. Since Berkeley Pier is a municipal pier, no fishing license is necessary.

Who to contact: Call Berkeley Marina at (415) 849-2727.

SALTWATER FISHING

POKE POLING THE
PACIFIC COAST

HOW NOT TO GET SNAGGED

The book "How Not To Get Snagged" might be a best seller for fishermen, except that it has not been written.

There may be no more frustrating element in sports than when you settle down for a quiet day of fishing, and then proceed to snag up on every cast and lose your gear. And that has been exactly the case for many when they head to the Pacific Coast to toss out a fishing line. After your 17th snag in a row, you might want to throw your fishing rod into the ocean. It turns out there's another solution, although a remarkably unusual one.

It is called "poke poling." What's that? Listen close: It's a simple, effective and inexpensive way to catch fish in greater numbers from the ocean shoreline than you might have ever thought possible. The bonus kicker is that you can eliminate snags almost 100 percent.

For equipment all you need is a long calcutta bamboo pole or its

equivalent, a pack of size 2/0 hooks, and bait, preferably squid, and a burlap bag for your fish. Sound confusing? It's not; it is the epitome of simplicity. From the end of the calcutta pole, you should tie a three-inch piece of wire leader to your hook. After baiting up, you hop your way along on the rocky spots along Pacific coast during low tides -- probably the same spots where folks have lost so much gear that they have quit fishing altogether.

From these rocks, with the burlap bag tied to your waist, you should poke the bait in crevices, under ledges, and in any deep holes you can find. For first-timers, it can be stunning to suddenly feel the pole stiffen and jerk; fish on!

Sea trout, cabezone, lingcod and eels lurk in these shallow holes among the rocks during the winter. The eel is an ugly fellow, but like the cabezone, is one of the finest tasting critters of the sea, regardless of preparation. I've been offered

$20 for a single cabezone; turned it down, of course.

You can maximize your success by fishing low tides, particularly minus tides. When the Pacific rolls back on low tides, it will unveil prime reef areas. It is the only time when you can walk out on reefs and poke pole in areas rarely fished by anybody -- and never by anglers attempting to cast from shore. Anybody trying to cast from shore to these spots just snags up on the rocks, and quick. I saw a gent hang up on seven straight casts before he finally just sat down with a beer and watched a poke poler in action!

The best areas for poke poling are anywhere along the Northern California coast where rocky areas and shallow reefs are abundant. In the Bay Area's backyard, such prime spots await along the San Mateo County Coast at Pedro Point in Pacifica, Fitzgerald Marine Reserve in Moss Beach, and from Pescadero to Pigeon Point.

Obtaining a Calcutta bamboo pole is as simple as plunking down a $6.80 at Hilltop Grocery in Half Moon Bay, one of the few shops anywhere to offer them. They sell a ready-to-fish poke pole, completely rigged with wire and hook, for $19.50. However, there are alternatives. Some fishermen use worn out CB antennas for a fishing rod, and they can do the job just fine.

Regardless, if you abandon the traditional surf casting techniques and instead take up poke poling, then you might just be ready to write that book, "How Not To Get Snagged" -- and catch a bag of fish right along with it.

☞ **POKE POLING TRIP FACTS**

How to get there: Highway 1 along the San Mateo County coastline provides easy access to all of the best spots along the Bay Area coast.

Pedro Point: Located in southern Pacifica across from Linda Mar Boulevard on Highway 1, gentle seas and low tides are prerequisites to success here. Call Coastside No. 2 at (415) 355-9901.

Moss Beach: Many species are protected in the Fitzgerald Marine Reserve, but poke poling is allowed for the most common species, such as seat trout, cabezone and eels. Call (415) 728-3584.

Pescadero: Several miles of good rocky spots are stationed from Pescadero to Pigeon Point Lighthouse. Call Hilltop Market in Half Moon Bay at (415) 726-4950.

Trip cost: Poke polers must have a valid state fishing license. A calcutta bamboo rod can be purchased for $6.80 in Half Moon Bay. Phone (415) 726-4950.

SALTWATER FISHING

CLAM DIGGING

BUSTING LOOSE FOR ALL AGES

A kid does not only want to do, he wants to do well. This is what makes clamming an ideal family adventure, because everyone's on even terms.

One need not be an expert to take a limit of clams. Techniques vary widely; on a single beach, one might see such tools as garden hoes, shovels and cultivators, or the long, narrow clammer's shovel or clam gun. I've even seen kids use a piece of abalone shell to dig for cockles, and after finding one, look at their dad like they were king of the world. It is a sight not easily forgotten.

But if you don't know when to go, you won't find clams, only lots of sand. During minus outgoing tides,

the Pacific Ocean will roll back and uncover the prime clamming grounds up and down the coast. With a little preparation, you can be ready.

Available for the taking will be Horseneck and Washington clams, in addition to cockles, depending on where you go. Don't expect to find clams on long, exposed stretches of beach. They need protection. Such ideal habitat is available at Bodega Bay, Tomales Bay, Half Moon Bay, south of Ano Nuevo, and in Elkhorn Slough at Moss Landing.

Cockles are my favorite, and are especially popular in Tomales Bay, Half Moon Bay, and Ano Nuevo. These little fellows will bury themselves in a rock and sand mix, usually just three or four inches below the surface. A three-pronged garden cultivator, used as if one were weeding a patch of lettuce, can produce a limit of 50 on a good day. Children prefer using a small hand shovel with the hands-and-knees technique. The minimum size cockle legally taken is 1-1/2 inches in diameter, and sportsmen must have a measuring device and state fishing license in possession when digging.

Where to Go Clamming

Bodega Bay: *During a minus tide, the harbor will completely drain except for the channel, leaving acres of prime spots, particularly on the western side. Horseneck clams are most abundant. Call Tides Wharf at (707) 875-3595.*

Tomales Bay: *This long, thin waterway offers more than 10 miles of prime clamming just 45 miles from San Francisco. Best bet is on the western shoreline in the Tomales Bay State Park. Call Tomales Park at (707) 576-2185.*

Half Moon Bay: *Just inside both the south and north ends of the harbor, or rock jetty, is a popular spot for locals and tourists alike. Call Hilltop at (415) 726-4950.*

Ano Nuevo: *The rock and sand mix cockles need is abundant in this area, but be careful not to actually dig on the Ano Nuevo State Reserve, where it is prohibited. Call Ano Nuevo Reserve at (415) 879-0595.*

Elkhorn Slough: *Located just 20 miles south of Santa Cruz at Moss Landing, this area has a legendary reputation for its Horseneck and Washington clams. Call Fish and Game at (408) 649-2870.*

Cockles are choice morsels when steamed and dipped in garlic butter sauce, the simplest of preparations. Horseneck and Washington clams, on the other hand, require a fairly extensive beating to soften them up. But their size makes up for the work. They get big, though state law requires any Horseneck or Washington clam dug must be retained until the bag limit is reached, regardless of size or broken condition.

For Horsenecks, you should be out during the minus tide, scanning the tidal flats, searching for the telltale sign of a small siphon hole in the sand. The hole is actually the neck hole for the clams, through which they feed. Should you spot the bubbling hole, dig, and dig fast. The clam will withdraw its long neck, leaving no sign of its whereabouts. But stand assured, somewhere below where that small hole appeared will be a clam.

The favored tool for these larger specimens is the clammers shovel, a long slender device engineered to dig a narrow yet deep hole in the least amount of time possible.

When you add it up, clamming is a simple adventure. And though adults may savor the tranquillity of a day on the coast, a kid wants action -- and clamming is one way to make sure he gets its.

CHAPTER 8

BONUS TRIPS

WITH

12 ADVENTURES

CONTENTS:—

PUBLISHED BY FOGHORN PRESS
SAN FRANCISCO
QUALITY OUTDOOR BOOKS

BONUS TRIPS

MOUNT SHASTA

THE CHALLENGE IN THE CLIMB TO THE TOP

S hasta is a mountain of fire and ice, a place where you can find a challenge and an answer, mysteries and truths. The challenge is the climb and the answer is that you can do it. The mysteries are of Lemurians, Yaktayvians and Phylos, creatures who are reputed to inhabit the inner mountain. The truth is only for you to find. At 14,162 feet, Mount Shasta rises like a giant diamond in a field of coal. It is the jewel of Northern California, located 60 miles north of Redding, where it occasionally can be seen for more than a hundred miles in all directions. We planned to reach the top of it in a single day.

Climbing Shasta is a one-in-a-million trip, one of the West's great adventures and one that most people have an honest chance of achieving. Climbing Half Dome in Yosemite and hiking the Grand Canyon might be comparable. But Shasta stands apart because of its sheer size -- a volume of 80 cubic miles, the highest of Northern California peaks, the largest of the Cascade volcanoes. Much of it is gouged with glacial canyons.

To put it bluntly, though, a one-day climb to Shasta's peak can be a punishing hike, an ascent of 7,000 feet over ice, snow and rock while trying to suck what little oxygen you can out of the thin air.

The big stopper is weather. The old mountain creates its own, and a sudden whiteout can turn your trip into a blackout. Mountain sickness, a combination of dizziness, nausea and wheezing, also claims a share of victims. If you're trying to make the summit in one day, the clock can allow too few ticks -- there is a maximum of 14 hours of daylight in summer, less at other times of the year.

According to the Forest Service, about half who try don't make it. That's why we chose early August, when Shasta gets its mildest weather of the year.

John Muir made it to the top. So did Josiah Whitney, the country's leading geologist in the late 1880s. Thousands of others have since tried. Whether you make it or not, many say, can seem dependent on a force well beyond your own. "Man is not always a welcome visitor in a kingdom he cannot control," said mountaineer Fred Beckey describing Shasta.

The Examiner Shasta Challenge Team included staff photographer John Storey, my brother Bob Stienstra Jr., and Michael Furniss, a scientist with the U.S. Forest Service. A couple year ago, my brother, Furniss, photographer Jeff Patty and I hiked the John Muir Trail in the Sierra Nevada, America's highest trail and one of its most rugged at 211 miles. With each step it seemed we were in the shadow of John Muir, and so it is at Shasta.

Other Examiner expeditions included rafting th 200-mile Klamath River in six days during spring's high waters, canoeing the Sacramento River 400 river miles from Redding to Fisherman's Wharf in five days, and a four-week search for Bigfoot in the remote areas of Northern California and southern Oregon.

Climbing Shasta stands apart. At Mount Shasta, you are a visitor at one of the world's true cathedrals. Like any sacred place, you become aware that not all are permitted to enter.

We made our base camp at 7,400 feet and, at daybreak, looked up at the old mountain through branches of red fir. Red Bank, a jagged rock outcrop of 12,900 feet, looked almost straight up, preceded by a 4,000-foot icefield.

There are many routes, but most start the trip at Horse Camp, a two-mile hike in from road's end at 6,800 feet on the southwestern side of the mountain. At Horse Camp you can get water, set up a base camp for the trip and prepare for the ascent.

From here, most figure eight, nine hours of scrambling to reach the peak and three or four hours to get back. Leaving at 5:30 a.m., you can be back by sunset -- if all goes well, that is.

At Horse Camp, we hid our large backpacks in the forest. We strapped on small daypacks that carried food, emergency weather gear and snow equipment.

The first few steps seemed so easy, a gentle climb over brown rocks, similar to much of the pumice that covers Shasta from its last eruption 300 years ago. The small porous rocks are from lava balls that blew right out of the top like puffed wheat.

"You can't get lost going up Shasta," said my brother, Bob. "Any direction going up is the right direction."

Timberline is at 8,500 feet, and as we entered the alpine zone, just a few little tiny flowers were sprinkled among rocks, wherever they could find a toehold. The first snow was at 8,600 feet. Just a little patch sits at the bottom of a gully, little fingers of it tracing up the mountain canyon. It was a warning.

Already the world below seemed to be opening up at our feet. Looking south, the entire Sacramento River canyon was in view, topped by Castle Crags, a series of granite spires near Dunsmuir. The sun wasn't up yet, but its glow lightened the tops of the Marble Mountains 40 miles to the west. Just a start, just a start.

Below in the valley, at 2,800 feet, you could make out cars and trucks traveling on Interstate 5, tiny images in the dis-

tance. I remembered how many times I had driven the highway, then looked up at Shasta, wondering of a day to climb it. That day had come.

At 9,100 feet, we reached the start of a long, narrow cut packed with ice and snow called Climber's Gulley, and stopped to strap crampons to our boots. Crampons are a metal framework with spikes, which dig into the ice to hold your position.

I jammed my ice axe in fully, sensed its hold, then pulled myself up a step, booted crampons holding the gain. Your short steps make a crunch-crunch sound as you begin

climbing the ice slope. The going is slow. A few steps, a few breaths, and you continue on.

Perfect quiet was in the air. It was so quiet, it was as if you could hear your heart beat. The icefield seemed to stretch on forever, and my ice axe was holding each step. But I had this strange, eerie feeling, as if I was being watched. Other people up here have had the same sensation.

"Look at that!" shouted Furniss, the scientist. No, it wasn't Bigfoot. Thousands and thousands of dark moths had hatched and were fluttering along the slope. So many that you could hear their wingbeats.

Stranger things have been reported on Shasta. A species of mysterious beings known as Lemurians are reputed to inhabit the inner world of the mountain. According to legend, they live in underground caves that are lined with gold. Some people say the Lemurians are tiny, while others identify them as seven, eight-feet tall.

Phylos is the most famous Lemurian. He is supposed to be able to materialize at will, wearing a flowing, white robe. A climbing party once claimed it was invited into his golden temple to listen to soft music. At 10,000 feet, we still hadn't seen any sign of Phylos.

Then there are the Yaktayvians of the Secret Commonwealth. They are said to have built the greatest bells in the universe, tuned so precisely that their ring will cause giant landslides. Some people claim to have hear the bells while driving on Highway 5. I am still listening.

Maybe it was the Yaktayvians who caused the rockslide at Helen Lake, which is actually a flat depression at 10,440 feet. It's one of the few spots where climbers can set up a camp, though it can be cold -- 20 degrees during our climb, when it was 105 in Redding. High winds are also common here. When we arrived, we were told of a rock the size of a Volkswagen that came tumbling down through the area, but missed all.

After a lunch of jerky, nuts, dried fruit and water, we moved on. At 12,000 feet, the slope reaches 35 degrees, and each step is a labor of passion. The climber will jam his ice axe in the snow, pull himself up a step, then rest for a moment to prepare to repeat the process.

It is below Red Bank, a huge red volcanic outcrop, where Shasta chews up most of its climbers. Some people start to wonder why

Answers to the 10 most frequently asked questions about climbing Mount Shasta:

1. Is it necessary to have any mountaineering experience to climb Mount Shasta? *No, in fact, only about 20 percent of those who try have mountain climbing experience. What is necessary is to be in good physical condition.*

2. What special equipment is necessary? *Be certain to bring a hat, sunglasses, sunscreen, ice ax, crampons for boots, and a day pack containing food, map, and foul weather gear.*

3. How long is the climb? *From Horse Camp to the summit is only about five miles, but with an elevation gain of 7,000 feet. People who successfully reach the peak do so in about eight hours.*

4. How long does it take to return from the peak to Horse Camp? *Usually about four hours, a bit more quickly if you ski or slide (which rangers do not advise).*

5. To shorten the climb, can you camp higher on the mountain? *Yes, you can camp at 10,440 feet at Helen Lake, which is actually a flat area, but this involves carrying all your camping gear up a long steep snowfield called Climber's Gully.*

6. What are the most dangerous problems of the climb? *Getting marooned at a high elevation during a sudden snow storm can cause hypothermia. The most serious injuries are caused when rolling boulders strike climbers. Climbers without crampons and ice axes can slip and fall at the chute at Red Bank.*

7. How many days should I plan for the trip? *Most people who set up a base camp will spend two nights on the mountain, with one day for the ascent and return.*

8. How many people will I see? *On weekends, an average of 15 to 20 people will attempt the climb.*

9. How much water should I carry? *A minimum of two quarts, with plans to refuel at 13,000 feet in the chute at Red Bank. Water is the lifeblood of the trip, and members of The Examiner team drank three to four quarts apiece.*

10. Who do I contact to rent equipment, or for maps and more information? *The Fifth Season in the town of Mount Shasta rents ice axes and crampons, and also sells an excellent guide map for $4 (including postage). They can be reached by phoning (916) 926-3606, or by writing The Fifth Season, 426 North Mount Shasta Boulevard, Mount Shasta, CA 96067. A 24-hour climbing report is available by phoning (916) 926-5555. For area maps, guide services, lodging and info, call Shasta Cascade at (916) 243-2643, or write at 1250 Parkview, Redding, CA 96001.*

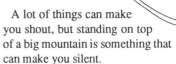

they're even here. Fun? Who said this was fun? It seems too steep. A slip and you might turn into a human snowball.

A few more steps, a few more breaths. It was near here during Whitney's geologic expedition in 1862 that three members of the team got mountain sickness and were scarcely able to continue. On this trip, our scientist, Furniss, was having the same problem. His face was so bleached that it looked like he'd seen a Lemurian.

"Dizzy, very dizzy," Furniss said. He slowed his pace, but continued. After scrambling through a steep rock/ice chute at Red Bank -- where a dangerous fall is near certain without crampons -- we were perched at 13,000 feet. Close, very close.

We crossed a glacier and ahead was what is known as Misery Hill, because to newcomers it give the false impression of being the summit. When you rise atop the hill, however, the true Shasta peak suddenly rises before you, a massive pinnacle of lava which seems to jut straight up into the air.

The air seems thin, and your lungs suck all you can get, but it is never enough. At the top, there is no snow. Wind has carried it away. Your steps are slow, but now you can see the goal. With a final push, your hands grabbing rock to pull you up, you take the last few steps, and you are standing on top.

A lot of things can make you shout, but standing on top of a big mountain is something that can make you silent.

Just over there is Shastina, Shasta's smaller volcano, a glaciated pond forming a bowl in its mouth. To the north is miles of Oregon, the Sisters peaks barely visible through binoculars. On rare clear days up here, you can see Mount Hood, Mount Lassen, the Siskiyous backbone, and 200 miles beyond.

Not today, with clouds obscuring the view. Some light hailstones fell, and they were like little puffs of cotton. At 14,000 feet, the sky is a deeper blue than you've ever seen, and on this day, scarcely a hint of wind is blowing.

To the side of the peak, a flume of sulfurous smoke still rises, a connection to the inside of the old volcano.

In 1875, John Muir almost froze to death when he was caught in a blizzard at Shasta's peak. He stayed alive by spending a night huddled near the mountain's hot sulfur gas vents.

As we were perched on top, I thought of Muir standing at the same point. And of Whitney's trip. And the thousands of other hikers who have since claimed Northern California's greatest peak.

You will feel their shadow, and some times, maybe even their ghosts helping you on your way as you step your way up the old mountain.

BONUS TRIPS

CUTTING FIREWOOD

FROM FOREST TO FIREPLACE

Y ou bring the great outdoors indoors every time you light a match to firewood you have cut and split yourself.

Part of it is the sweet smell. As your fire burns, the mountain scent of acres of pines, firs, cedars and madrones is recaptured in your living room. Then you notice a different kind of heat than you get from a thermostat, a penetrating warmth that gives your home that feel of a cozy, log cabin.

You toss another log on the fire and you get the satisfaction of a project started and finished with

results you can see and feel, from that nice stack of wood out back to a quiet night in front of the fireplace.

From forest to fireplace, cutting your own firewood can be easy, fun, and save hundreds of dollars in the process. It can add a special dimension to a weekend camping/fishing trip, even if you just spend a few hours at it, like in the middle of the day when the fishing goes flat. You end up bringing home a nice stack of firewood as well as memories of your good times.

And the price and time is right.

It costs only $10 to buy a firewood permit from the U.S. Forest Service, which allows you to cut two cords of wood from trees that are dead and down. Fall is an ideal time to cut, because timber companies are putting the wraps on summer logging operations, meaning there are plenty of slash piles -- unusable trees where you can cut a quick load of firewood.

It all makes for time well spent in the miles of mountain country that comprise our national forests.

In California, there are 95 ranger districts in the national forests -- mountain land that is owned and used by the public.

They are far different than national parks, such as Yosemite. A national park is considered something of a nature preserve, while a national forest is there to be used -- to be fished, hunted, hiked and to some extent logged.

The national forests closest to the Bay Area are Mendocino (east of Ukiah), Tahoe (east of Marysville), El Dorado (east of Placerville) and Stanislaus (east of Sonora). They are close enough so you can parlay a weekend camping trip with firewood cutting and come up a winner.

If you plan on visiting more distant national forests, such as Shasta/Trinity or Klamath, it is wise to finagle an extra day or two for your trip. Otherwise, you'll spend too much time driving and not enough time in the forest -- and instead of fun, it will seem like work.

It doesn't take long to cut a load of firewood, especially if you find a good slash pile, but trying to rush a trip in the mountains is like trying to rush a good bottle of wine.

You should take your time, decide which national forest you want to visit, then buy a map for it. For maps, simply send $1 apiece to the U.S. Forest Service, Office of Information, 630 Sansome Street, San Francisco, CA 94111. These maps detail all backcountry roads, as well hiking trails, streams and lakes that you previously may not have known even existed.

The next step is to call the district office and ask about firewood availability. In some areas, particularly where a timber sale has been completed, dead-and-downed logs are literally just lying around, waiting to be picked up. In others, it can be slim pickings.

You must show up at the district office in person to purchase your $10 firewood permit. While you're at it, the information officer will usually tell you precisely where to go. On two firewood trips I've taken, one to Shasta/Trinity and the other to Six Rivers Forest, the Forest Service even provided a free locator map to pinpoint the best spots.

On one trip, it took little over an hour to fill my pickup truck, which left plenty of time to hike, fish and explore the area.

If you don't have a pickup truck, you'll have to team up with some-

body who does, rent one or sharply limit the size of your load. Occasionally, some Bay Area neighbors share in the cost of renting a large flatbed truck, head to the mountains as a team and pool their permits, then cut, split and stack enough wood for all parties.

Wood is measured by the "cord," which describes a well-stacked pile that measures 4-by-4-by-8 feet. You can fit a cord of wood in a standard-size pickup truck bed, but only if it is carefully stacked. Most people will settle for about half a cord, since a cord brings with it a lot of weight.

With a wood-burning stove or fireplace insert, two to three cords is usually enough to get you through a winter in the Bay Area. People living in mountain areas use about six cords per year.

The savings? Your $10 permit will get you two cords of firewood -- which would cost you anywhere from $250 to $450, depending on how much you are gouged. In mountain areas, the price is cut in half. The cost of hardwoods, such as oak or madrone, is usually 25 percent higher than softwoods, like pine or cedar, because hardwoods burn hotter and longer.

Mixing hardwoods and softwoods can make for the ideal fire -- the pine will keep your flame, but the oak will throw off more head, and burn all night long.

You don't need much equipment, but you'll be lost without a few essentials.

A good chainsaw, of course, is a prerequisite, and most cost in the low $200 range. Some rental companies have them available.

My preference is for a chainsaw with a 20 to 24-inch bar. Smaller ones, the chainsaws with 12 or 14-inch bars, are designed for limbing, not logging. The big 36-inch saws are heavy and powerful, designed

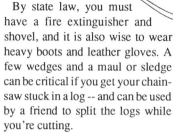

for professional tree fallers, and can be dangerous for newcomers.

Homelite, McCulloch, Stihl, Echo and Husquavarna are the most popular brands. I own two different kinds, and family members own two other brands. All have performed well. Consumer Reports has completed an excellent safety study on them, describing how manufacturers have changed design to virtually eliminate kickback.

By state law, you must have a fire extinguisher and shovel, and it is also wise to wear heavy boots and leather gloves. A few wedges and a maul or sledge can be critical if you get your chainsaw stuck in a log -- and can be used by a friend to split the logs while you're cutting.

The most important safety factor is always to make the trip with a friend, and to alternate cutting and loading. Otherwise, fatigue gradually sets in, and without even being aware of it, the cutter can become vulnerable to a serious accident.

The most common error, which increases as fatigue sets in, is to look directly down at your cut. If the saw were to jam on a knot and kick back, your face would be directly in

☞ WOOD-CUTTING FACTS

How to get started: Get the Forest Service brochure on firewood cutting by writing the U.S. Forest Service, Office of Information, 630 Sansome Street, San Francisco, CA 94111, or phone (415) 556-0122.

How to get a map: Send $1 for a detailed map of the respective national forest at Office of Information, 630 Sansome Street, San Francisco, CA 94111.

How to know where to cut: Stop in at the district office, purchase a cutting permit for $10, then receive directions pinpointing areas to cut your firewood.

What to bring: Chainsaw, gas, two-cycle oil, 30-weight oil for chain, sturdy boots, gloves, fire extinguisher and shovel are mandatory. If your chainsaw gets jammed in a tree, a maul and a few wedges can get you free. If you flood the engine, a spark- plug wrench can come in handy.

Law of the land: Cut only trees that are dead and down.

the path of the chain. Instead, always keep your head out of the plane of the chainsaw. This is where a companion, watching for any errors, can keep the cutter out of trouble. Alone, you may not even be aware of the mistake.

Kickback, which occurs when a dull saw hits a tough spot or knot, is the most dangerous element of woodcutting. The best prevention for that accident is to keep your chainsaw razor sharp.

Your logs should be split either with a maul, or a sledge and wedge, so the wood will dry and make a perfect-sized package for your

WHERE TO FIND FIREWOOD AND GOOD MEMORIES

El Dorado National Forest, east of Placerville:
Write 100 Forni Road, Placerville, CA 95667, or phone (916) 622-5061.
Inyo National Forest, in the eastern Sierra Nevada, north of Bishop:
Write 873 North Main Street, Bishop, CA 93514, or phone (714) 873-5841.
Klamath National Forest, northeast of Eureka:
Write 1215 South Main Street, Yreka, CA 96097, or phone (916) 842-2741.
Lassen National Forest, east of Redding:
Write 707 Nevada Street, Susanville, CA 96130, or phone (916) 257-2151.
Los Padres National Forest, south of Monterey:
Write 406 S. Mildred, King City, CA 93930, or phone (408) 385-5434.
Mendocino National Forest, northeast of Ukiah:
Write 420 Laurel Street, Willows, CA 95988, or phone (916) 934-3316.
Modoc National Forest, in northeast corner of state:
Write 441 N. Main Street, Alturas, CA 96101, or phone (916) 233-3521.
Plumas National Forest, northwest of Lake Tahoe:
Write P.O. Box 1500, Quincy, CA 95971, or phone (916) 283-2050.
Sequoia National Forest, south of Sequoia National Park:
Write 900 W. Grand Avenue, Porterville, CA 93257, or phone (209) 784-1500.
Shasta/Trinity National Forest, north and west of Redding:
Write 2400 Washington Avenue, Redding, CA 96001, or phone (916) 246-5222.
Sierra National Forest, south of Yosemite National Park:
Write Federal Building, 1130 O Street, Fresno, CA 93721, or phone (209) 487-5115.
Six Rivers National Forest, between Eureka and Crescent City:
Write 507 F Street, Eureka, CA 95501, or phone (707) 442-1721.
Stanislaus National Forest, east of Sonora:
Write 19777 Greenley Road, Sonora, CA 95370, or phone (209) 532-3671.
Tahoe National Forest, northwest of Lake Tahoe:
Write Highway 29, Nevada City, CA 95950.

fireplace. Cedar, pine and fir can often be split with one swing of the maul, with no wedge necessary. After being split, the wood will be cured as soon as two to four months.

It's a good project for teamwork -- with one person cutting, another splitting and another loading. In only an hour, you can have enough firewood cut, split and stacked for many nights of warm fires.

It will also simplify your trip. Instead of problems, you will have solutions. Instead of work, getting a load of firewood can be a fun diversion on a weekend camping trip.

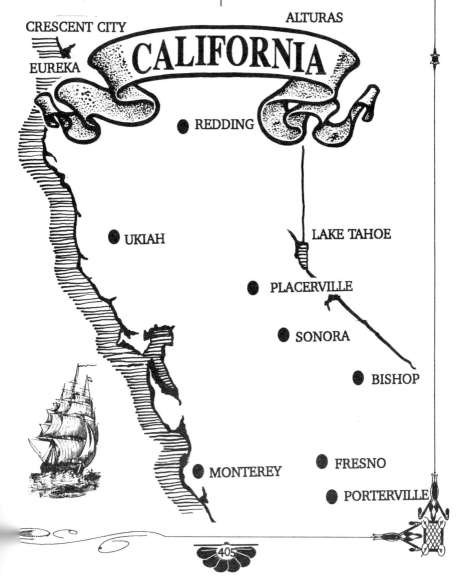

CRESCENT CITY

ALTURAS

CALIFORNIA

EUREKA

● REDDING

● UKIAH

LAKE TAHOE

● PLACERVILLE

● SONORA

● BISHOP

● MONTEREY

● FRESNO

● PORTERVILLE

BONUS TRIPS

CALIFORNIA GOLD
PANNING

GOLD FEVER IS CONTAGIOUS

M oney doesn't grow on trees, but just the same, it is sprouting like weeds in many California streams.

That doesn't mean you can take out a garden hoe and start digging up bags of $100 bills. But with a gold pan and skilled hands, you can find yourself 25 to 100 flakes of gold per hour. If you pluck a gold nugget, even a small one, you'll be laughing all the way to the bank about the minimum price you can get -- $320 per ounce.

Most people believe most of the earth's gold has been taken from nature's grasps by wily miners. But in California, gold seekers have literally only scratched the surface. Envision the earth's core as a pressurized molten mass, emerging where it can find cracks and fissures in the surface. The gold often rises to the earth's surface where it can find these weak spots -- and in California, the Mother Lode gold belt is so famous for this that we are

known worldwide as the Golden State. The gold rises out of the bowels of the earth on these veins and stringers, and the storms of winter and snowmelt of spring robs the gold from the bedrock and brings it to existing river canyons and feeder streams. From Mariposa up to Downieville, streams such as the Feather, American, Yuba, Mokelumne, Tuolumne and Stanislaus all cross the gold bearing belt.

One fellow who developed remarkable expertise in the search for gold is the late Jim Martin, a long-time panner and sluice boxer who wrote the book, "Recreational Gold Prospecting."

"You can be walking along a trout stream fishing, and suddenly see a small gold nugget and you'll be hooked on it for life," Martin told me. "Gold fever is contagious. I have been up in the mountains since the '50s; gold intrigues me. It's a lot like fishing. If you don't get anything, then it's time to try a new

spot. You never know when you're going to get the big one."

You need little equipment to get started. A gold pan (about $10), a shovel, magnifying glass, a toothpick, tweezers and a bottle to put your gold in is all that is needed.

But that doesn't make it easy. The key elements are knowing how to separate the silt and worthless fool's gold from the genuine gold -- and exactly where to ply this art. Master that, and you had better make an appointment with the assayer at Wells Fargo.

"The thing to do is to sit on the edge of a stream on a comfortable log or rock, to keep the pan underwater while swishing it from side to side," Martin had said. "You need to let the flow of water carry the lighter stuff out of the pan."

After about five minutes, you will have reduced the contents of your pan to nothing but the jet black sand and gold flecks. With a bit of water in your pan, you should swirl the pan in a circular direction, which will bring to light the flecks of gold -- those shiny little rascals you're in search of.

"If you see anything big, pick it out with your tweezers," Martin continued. "We call these 'picker outers.' Usually you just see the flecks. Take a toothpick, moisten the tip, then pick out the gold and put it in your bottle. With a magnifying glass, this is no problem."

Some gold seekers use mercury to separate the gold, but this can be quite dangerous to your health if the liquid enters your system through a nick on one of your fingers, or other cuts. "Don't fiddle with mercury," advised Martin. Others will not attempt to separate the gold from the black sand at streamside, but instead collect it, and do the fine, intensive work under a bright light at home. "A real key is processing a lot of material," Martin acknowledged.

To start your search, you need to select one of the rivers along the gold bearing belt. Rarely will you find gold above 4,500 feet. Nature makes the rules, and you have to play by them. And if you're new to the game, you might start taking your trout fishing equipment to the Sierra Nevada, and look for signs of gold as you fish.

Traces of past gold activity are usually best tipped off by piles of rocks along the stream. These are called tailing piles, where miners removed rocks as they were trying to search out a hot spot. Remains of abandoned cabins and any semblance of a man-made tunnel or cave are tipoffs as well.

"I have a spot on a tributary to the Feather River where you can pick out 100 flakes of gold per hour," Martin had said. "It's all in tiny flecks. I have another spot where you find these little nuggets. You bet they're harder to find. You have to get right down to the bedrock, get in where nobody else has been. The average person might find a pocket where you find several nuggets, then go a number of days without finding any. You just never know."

NORDIC SKIING

THE PASSION OF THE MOUNTAIN

The passion of the mountain is the reward for the cross-country skier.

The thing that stays with you is the winter quiet. There are no birds, no squirrels, no marmots. In the real high country, there is not even the sound of running streams. At first the quiet seems eerie. Then it seems to cast its own spell. Once you feel it, you'll never be the same.

The sport is inexpensive, adventurous and peaceful. For people who backpack in the summer, it offers a chance to reclaim the mountain experience. For people who downhill ski, it offers an option

without the crowds. For people who haven't done either, yet are curious, cross-country skiing is easy to learn, cheap to get into, and requires little specialized equipment.

To start, you need some skis, boots and poles. You can rent all three for less than $20.

More than 20 Nordic ski areas offer groomed trails, often just marked by ribbons tied to trees poking up through the snow. You push your way along, exploring the mountain country.

Because you just kind of glide along, you have a chance at a closer bond with your companions than when downhill skiing. The experiences are shared. After an hour or so, you can find yourself in a beautiful wilderness setting, whether it be overlooking Lake Tahoe or at the base of Mount Shasta, stopping for a picnic lunch.

To newcomers, it can be surprising how little similarity cross-country skiing has with downhill skiing. There is no stress, no competition. There are no lines. There are no hecklers daring you to try the steepest slope, or Alpine hot dogs running you down. Also, there is no ambulance waiting for you at the bottom of the hill -- it's a heck of a lot safer.

Nordic skis are longer than the skis used for downhill, and instead of strapping your boots into a harness, you are attached to the skis by the tips of your boots. You just push along in a walking motion, or for climbing slopes,

---

Nordic ski areas:

TAHOE AREA:
Aschi, South Lake Tahoe at Highway 50, (916) 544-7873; *Big Chief*, near Squaw Valley off Highway 89, (916) 587-4723; *Clair Tappaan Lodge*, near Soda Springs off Interstate 80, (916) 426-3632; *Echo Summit*, eight miles west of South Lake Tahoe on Highway 50, (916) 659-7154; *Incline*, north of Tahoe off Highway 28, (702) 831-6500; *Kirkwood*, south of Tahoe off Highway 88, (209) 258-8864; *Northstar*, north of Tahoe off Highway 267, (916) 562-1010; *Royal George*, near Soda Springs off Highway 80, (916) 426-3871; *Squaw Valley Nordic*, northwest of Tahoe off Highway 89, (916) 583-8951; *Strawberry Touring Company*, eight miles east of Kybruz off Highway 50, (916) 659-7200; *Tahoe Donner Nordic*, northwest of Lake Tahoe off Highway 80, (916) 587-9821; *Tahoe Nordic*, two miles east of Tahoe City off Highway 28, (916) 583-9858; *Telemark Country*, at South Lake Tahoe on Highway 50, (916) 577-6811.

CENTRAL SIERRA:
Bear Valley, located 55 miles east of Angels Camp on Highway 4, (209) 753-2834; *Leland Meadows*, 37 miles east of Sonora on Highway 108, (209) 965-3745; *Tamarack*, three miles west of Bear Valley on Highway 4, (209) 753-2594; *Yosemite Mountaineering*, based in Yosemite Valley, (209) 372-1244.

NORTHERN CALIFORNIA:
Childs Meadows, nine miles southeast of Lassen Park on Highway 36, (916) 595-4411; *Fifth Season*, at Mount Shasta, (916) 926-3606; *Lassen Ski Touring*, at southwest entrance to Lassen Park on Highway 36, (916) 595-3376; *Quiet Mountain*, at Nevada City on Highway 49, (916) 265-9186; *Mount Shasta Nordic Center*, at Castle Lake (916) 926-3443.

EASTERN SIERRA:
Mammoth Ski Touring, two miles outside Mammoth Lake Village, (619) 934-2442; *Sierra Meadows*, outside Mammoth Lakes, (619) 934-6161.

slightly angle the skis. That's all there is to it.

And for the ambitious, there are no boundaries. As you gain experience and become acclimated to the high altitude, you leave the groomed trails and head yonder for the mountain wildlands. Some of my friends have had 100-mile trips exploring the iced high country above 10,000 feet. This kind of trip is for experienced mountaineers only, but it gives you an idea of what is possible.

For the most part, cross-country skiing is a peaceful sport, more of a communion of nature and your friends than a race to the bottom of the hill. It seems to require little physical effort at first, but after a few days the sport will hone your body like a knife blade on a whet stone. You return feeling fit. After a good trip, some people will have a glow about them for weeks.

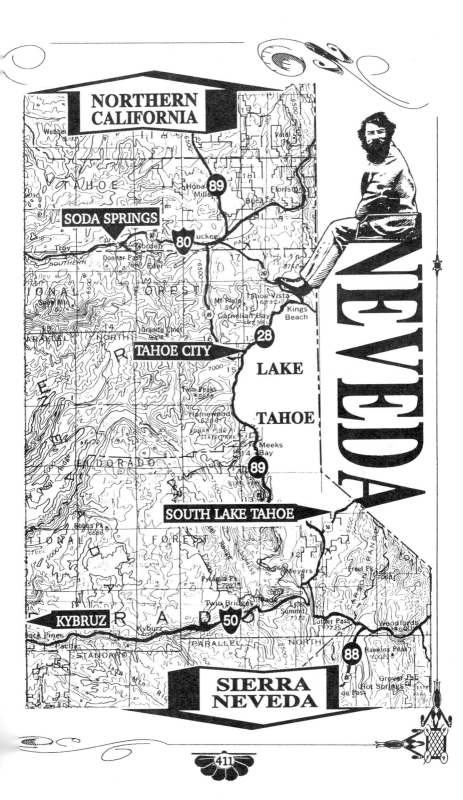

NORTHERN CALIFORNIA

NEVEDA

SODA SPRINGS

TAHOE CITY

LAKE

TAHOE

SOUTH LAKE TAHOE

KYBRUZ

SIERRA NEVEDA

A SKIING PROGRAM
FOR KIDS

SKI-WEES TRADE IN SITTERS FOR THE SLOPE

S kiing has a new look to it -- kids. They are flocking to the slopes with their parents like thousands of little snowflakes.

And we're not talking about teenagers -- they've long known the excitement of skiing. The new boom is in kids from 6 to 12 years old, new recruits to a sport that has become safer due to new equipment and better instruction.

"A lot of parents didn't know what to do with their children when they wanted to go skiing," said Devon Salter, director of skiing at Dodge Ridge. "Now they're able to enroll them in a number of programs designed to get them skiing. We make it easy and fun. A number of ski resorts are providing new kids programs."

Parents have discovered a lot of problems are quickly solved if their kids learn how to ski correctly in a fun environment. For one thing, the parents can go off for a day of skiing without worrying about junior -- the ski-wee program is all day and includes lunch. For another, junior learns how to ski right without any pressure from mom and pop.

At Dodge Ridge, the program costs $50 per day and includes ski rentals, instruction, full-time supervision, lunch and snacks. If you supply the skis, the price is $38.

Instead of handcuffing junior to a baby sitter at home, parents can now enjoy skiing as a family. Sales indicators show the program is working.

The ski class for junior starts at 10 a.m. when they are placed in groups of six, all in their own age group and skiing ability. Most of the instruc-

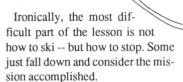

tors are young women with professional experience in child training.

The kids first are taught how to put on skis, walk on snow, and shown some basic, proper downhill techniques. Instead of a traumatic test in front of their parents, any mistakes just become good fun with a group of friends, all who are likely making the same mistakes. By the end of the day, the kids will know how to get on and off rope tows and lifts, how to make a straight downhill run, and how to fall down.

SKI INSTRUCTION

Ski resorts that feature Ski Magazine's instructional program:

Dodge Ridge Ski Area: *Located on Highway 108, 32 miles east of Sonora. For information, call (209) 965-3474. A brochure is available by writing P.O. Box 1188, Pinecrest, CA 95364.*

Heavenly Valley: *Located near Lake Tahoe on Highway 50. For information, call (916) 541-1330 or write P.O. Box 2180, Stateline, NV 89449.*

Sierra Summit: *Located just south of Yosemite National Park alond Highway 168. For information, call (209) 893-3316, or write P.O. Box 236, Lakeshore, CA 93634.*

June Mountain: *located near Bishop in East Sierra off Highway 395. For information, call (619) 934-2571 or write P.O. Box 24, Mammoth Lake, CA 93546.*

Ironically, the most difficult part of the lesson is not how to ski -- but how to stop. Some just fall down and consider the mission accomplished.

However, with a little practice, kids learn to "snow plow," where the tips of the skis are angled toward each other, and where weight is then applied toward the inside of your feet. The pressure slows down the skier.

When mom and dad return at 4 p.m., the parents are given a progress card, a bag of treats and a list of ski pointers.

The whole thing is part of a national instructional program formatted by Ski Magazine. Some 50 ski resorts are taking part in the program across the country, including four in the Sierra.

The nearest to the Bay Area is the Dodge Ridge Ski Area. Heavenly Valley, Sierra Summit and June Mountain also feature the program. A number of other ski resorts have junior programs, but they are not affiliated with the format designed by Ski Magazine.

"A lot of people think skiing is just for adults," said Salter at Dodge Ridge. "We're proving that just isn't true. It's for anybody who has the spirit for it."

BONUS TRIPS

THE THRILLS
OF RAFTING

BEING SHOT OUT OF A CANNON

If you have ever wondered what it might feel like to get shot out of a cannon, you should try rafting the Upper Klamath River and tumble through Hell's Corner Gorge. Rapids like Satan's Gate, Scarface and Ambush can make you feel like a human cannonball.

If you don't want to join the circus, consider a canoe or raft trip down the mid-Klamath, from Horse Creek on downriver. There's just enough white water to put the trip on edge, but tame enough to make a family outing of it.

If you have never taken a raft or canoe trip, you may have a small tinge of curiosity over why people get excited about the sport. On the upper Klamath, you get the full-dose answer. I recommend it, either for curiosity seekers going solo, experts looking for a test or for a family outing.

A few springs ago, when the Klamath was near flood stage, six of us in three rafts challenged the entire river from its headwaters in Oregon all the way to the Pacific Ocean. We did it in six days, covering as many as 50 miles per day, and tumbled through more than a thousand rapids in the process.

The whole idea about rafting is to get out there on the "edge," out there in no man's land. The Klamath can get you there.

The first rapid you face in the Hell's Corner Gorge is called Caldera. We were roaring downriver when the nose of the raft headed straight into a big wave, the boat completely disappearing underwater. Moments later, the raft popped up in the air, surging forward -- and right then a crosswave hit us from the right and flipped us. I went flying out of the raft like a piece of popcorn. Like I said, the human cannonball.

I went floating down the rapids, the hydraulics of the river pulling me under and then I'd pop to the surface. Your life-saving equipment makes sure of that. You just time your breathing as you go bobbing along until you eventually come to an eddy, where you can paddle over to gain safety.

A lot of people never flip, but to most, it's kind of like a badge of honor, like "Yeah, I rafted Hell's Corner Gorge and Branding Iron got us good."

River rapids are rated on a scale of I to VI, with Class I being a piece of cake, and Class VI being suicide. The Upper Klamath has Class IV and V white water, and the mid-Klamath Class II, sprinkled with some Class III.

So if you want more of a family-oriented trip, the mid-Klamath provides it. By raft or canoe, it's a heck of a fun trip.

My preference on the mid-Klamath is to go by canoe. You get more speed, faster cuts, faster decisions, and alas, faster flips.

What do these trips cost? A weekend raft trip through Hell's Corner Gorge offered by

Wilderness Adventures, for instance, costs around $200 per person, and includes food, drink, guide, life, jacket, and of course, raft. That's the going rate. On the lower Klamath, Turtle River Rafting offers a two-day trip for around $150. Canoe rentals for do-it-yourself trips starting at Horse Creek are priced at $40 per day. That gives you an idea of the cost range.

Many rivers on the slopes of the Sierra Nevada run low in the summer. The Klamath provides not only the answer, but a personal challenge.

You might even find out what it feels like to be shot out of a cannon.

☞ RAFT TRIP FACTS

Canoe rentals: Only one outfitter provides canoe rentals. That is the Bigfoot Recreation Inn, located 28 miles west of the Interstate 5 Bridge on the Klamath River Highway. They can be reached at (916) 496-3313 or by writing 30841 Walker Road, Horse Creek, CA 96045.

Who to contact: About a dozen rafting companies offer trips in the Hell's Corner Gorge. For a free list and brochures on what's available, write Shasta Cascade, 1250 Parkview, Redding, CA 96001 or call (916) 243-2643.

BONUS TRIPS

1 8 RIVERS
TO RAFT

RESOURCE FOR CALIFORNIA WHITE WATER

D espite the disappearance of white-water rivers like the once popular Stanislaus behind dams, there remains some 50 outstanding streams in the state, all varying dramatically in difficulty, dependent on what stretch of river you want to try.

The best booklet describing rivers of America is the "Canoe Trails Directory," by James Makens, (Doubleday), which details 46 of California's best.

A key aspect of white water is learning the significance of water flows. When rivers are high, brush and trees are hidden just under the surface -- and if you run into a

"snag" you can be jarred or thrown from your craft like a piece of corn flying out of a popcorn popper. Water flows are measured in cubic feet per second (cfs). The Department of Water Resources maintains a flow-phone recording service, which runs Monday through Friday. The number is (916) 322-3327.

Here's a river-by-river guide, numbered from north to south:

Easy to moderate

■ **1. Main Klamath River:** Beginners are advised to put in below Weitchpec, where the river broadens and the rapids are not as menacing. Above Weitchpec, particularly on the upper stretches of the river near Highway 5, experience is necessary to safely navigate the difficult rapids.
Who to contact: For more information, call the U.S. Forest Service at (916) 842-6131.

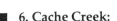

■ 2. Trinity River:

The 16-mile stretch from Lewiston to Douglas City is a good weekend trip. From Big Bar to South Fork Junction is 21 miles. It's okay for intermediates.

Who to contact: For more information, call the U.S. Forest Service at (916) 623-6106.

■ 3. Sacramento River:

With 400 miles of river to choose from, there's something for everybody. Above Shasta Dam, the river is fairly difficult, especially for canoeists. From Red Bluff there is 100 miles of easy paddling.

Who to contact: For more information, call Shasta Cascade, (916) 243-2643.

■ 4. Eel River:

Know your river! From Dos Rios to Alderpoint (50 miles) is for advanced rafters only and you should beware of the waterfall beyond the sharp turn at Island Mountain. From Alderpoint to the South Fork (32 miles) is an easy paddle and an ideal first trip.

■ 5. Middle Fork of the Eel River:

This is a beautiful run, sitting high in the mountains with picture-postcard scenery. Because of water diversions, this river is rarely in good shape past June.

■ 6. Cache Creek:

Here's a six-mile, one-day run that is ideal for the Bay Area rafter. The river is little more than 100 miles from San Francisco. One note: Please pick up your trash.

Who to contact: For more information, call MG Whitewater, (707) 255-0671.

■ 7. South Fork of the American River:

A good put-in is at the Route 193 Bridge and take-out at either the picnic area beyond the State Historical Park (six miles) or the short road off Route 49. Warning: Do not try to run from Peavine Ridge Road to El Dorado Powerhouse -- it's a death trip!

■ 8. East Fork of the Carson River:

The river has many good campsites in the 20 miles from Markleeville to to Gardnerville. There's one bad rapid about halfway through the run. The beauty of this mountain river run is one to remember. By the way, the casinos in Gardnerville are killers.

■ 9. Stanislaus River:

This was the second-most popular stretch of water in America until it was flooded by the backwaters of New Melones Reservoir. What's left is a moderate stretch of water with some small rapids from Knights Ferry to Oakdale Bridge (13 miles).

Who to contact: For more information, call (916) 985-4474.

■ 10. Kings River:

The nine miles of river from Upper Kings Campground to Kirch Flat Campground is okay for intermediates. Warning: Advanced only from Pine Flat Dam to Centerville. It's beautiful water, but lives have been lost in this stretch.

Who to contact: For more information, call (209) 855-8321 or (209) 787-2589.

Difficult

■ 1. Upper Klamath River:

The Upper Klamath starts in Oregon and tumbles its way into Copco Lake, with exciting rapids along the way. It's runnable throughout the year because flows are regulated by releases from John Boyle Reservoir in Oregon.

Who to contact: For more information, call Wilderness Adventure at (916) 243-3091.

■ 2. Salmon River:

Here's one of my favorites. There are many short, quick rapids from the forks of the Salmon on downstream to here it pours into the Klamath. The scenery is outstanding, with high canyon walls bordering the river.

■ 3. South Fork of the Eel:

A good put-in is at Richardson Grove State Park where you can float 40 miles through redwoods to Weott, a good run for three or four days. Warning: Portage around the low-level bridge before Benbow Lake.

■ 4. North Fork of the Yuba River:

The preferred stretch of water is the lower portion from Goodyear's Bar to the Route 20 Bridge, but portage around the 10-foot dropoff near Route 49. Warning: Do not try the four miles from Downieville to Goodyear's Bar; unrunnable.

■ 5. North Fork of the American:

This is a very popular run from Colfax to the North Fork Dam (18 miles), but dangerous at a few spots. It is advisable to scout rapids before attempting to run. Warning: Do not try the Giant Gap Run below the dam -- it's suicide.

■ 6. Main Tuolumne River:

Here's a real gut-thumper. From Lumsden Campground to Ward Ferry Bridge is 18 miles of wild beauty. Until flows drop in mid-summer, this stretch of water is almost continuous rapids.

Who to contact: For more information, call (916) 985-4474.

■ 7. Merced River:

The best water here is from Briceburg to Bagby, 15 miles of Class III and IV rapids. When you portage around the 20-foot waterfall, look out for poison oak. The rapids ease greatly beyond the waterfall.

Who to contact: For more information, call (916) 985-4474.

■ 8. Upper Kern River:

The prized section is from Kernville to Lake Isabella, a half-day, five-mile run for advanced paddlers only. Very scenic. Avoid the river above the bridge, a very tough run.

BONUS TRIPS

CACHE CREEK
WHITE WATER

MEET MAD MIKE & BIG MOTHER

Mad Mike is waiting for you. Regardless of where you are reading this -- at home, on a bus, on a train -- Mad Mike is waiting. And if you make a mistake, he'll get you.

And if you don't watch it, Big Mother will get you too. Mad Mike? Big Mother? That's right, these are the names of two pulse-pounding rapids on Cache Creek, which is the closest river to the Bay Area to provide a classic white water experience. For beginners and experienced paddlers alike, Mad Mike is a fellow worth tangling with.

You hear him before you see him. In your raft, you come around a turn, and the river seems to disappear. The heart starts to pump. Below you, the river suddenly takes a five foot drop into a chute, and as you tumble down, all you can see is white bubbling water all around you. Just as suddenly, the river takes an upward bend, and all you see is blue sky. Praying doesn't

seem to help.

"I've dumped three times at Mad Mike," said rafting guide Mark Gholson. "But as rafting goes, if there isn't the chance at dumping, you miss the excitement. The idea is to get out there on the edge, and sometimes, when you go over the edge, you find it's an amazing and exhilarating place to be.

Cache Creek is located north of the Bay Area, below Clear Lake. It is 110 miles from San Francisco, about a 2.5 hour drive. For north bay residents, it's only 65 miles from Napa. MG Whitewater Adventures offers a two-day trip for around $100, complete with New York steak dinner, which is priced as reasonably as any weekend rafting excursion in California.

For one-day trips, a good put-in spot is about 10 miles north of Rumsey. You can cover about eight miles of river, including shooting three Class III rapids (on a scale of I through VI), and use the adjacent

Highway 16 as your shuttle road. A beginner can take it with safety, yet get the excitement of a quality run. For two-day trips, MG Whitewater will take you on a remote four-wheel drive road off of Highway 16 that climbs to 3,000 feet. On a clear day, you can see Mount Shasta and Mount Lassen to the northeast, and to the west sits the Coast Range. You camp at stream's edge at Buck Island, where rafting techniques are reviewed, and you can also watch wildlife or go fishing. Turtles, tule elk and even eagles are common sights, and for fishermen, catfish seem to come in one size -- big. A 30-pounder was caught in 1984 and is on display in a little tackle shop in the town of Guinda.

On the two-day trip, you'll cover about 15 miles of river, spending about four hours on the river the first day, and about six hours on the second. You go through many rapids, but the highlights are Mad Mike, Big Mother, and Mario Andretti Bank.

The only thing in your boat, which looks something like an inflatable kayak, is yourself, your paddle, and your lunch and drinks in a waterproof bag. Don't worry about getting wet; it's welcome in the typical 90-degree summer temperatures.

"This trip is a particularly unique, compared to most other river runs in California, because you do not paddle with a guide, but a buddy," said Gholson of MG Adventures. "That means you can control your own destiny, as well as take a break when you want. Novices start out scared and tense, but by the end of the first day, they have a great feeling of accomplishment, because they have done it themselves. The next day, they're ready for anything."

And it's a good thing, because Mad Mike is waiting.

☞ CACHE CREEK WHITEWATER TRIP FACTS

How to get there: Take Highway 80 to Highway 505 cutoff, and 17 miles later, head northeast on Highway 16, which runs adjacent to Cache Creek.

Camping: If you own your own raft, an overnight campground is available on the river about 10 miles north of the town of Rumsey.

Trip Tip: Remember to bring a change of clothes, primary camping equipment such as a sleeping bag, and a stuff sack to pack your clothes.

Trip Cost: MG Whitewater offers two-day trips, including all meals, for $95 per person.

Who to contact: MG Whitewater Adventures can be reached by calling (707) 255-0761, or by writing P.O. Box 2472, Napa, CA 94558.

CUTTING YOUR OWN
CHRISTMAS TREE

57 TREE FARMS

Cutting your own Christmas tree can be the link to the traditions of yesteryear -- and at the same time provide a prime family outing.

Once upon a time, into the hills families would go, searching for just the right tree to brighten their homes for Christmas. Today, there are many acres of trees to provide the same purpose. In the Bay Area alone, there are 57 Christmas tree farms, and in the state, almost 250.

Instead of going to a concrete lot where your basic generic trees are propped up on wooden stands, you have the opportunity to get out, explore, search and, ultimately cut and carry your own selection. As a family decision, it can add a special, personal touch to your Christmas.

Trees on lots also tend to be smaller and a bit dried out, rather than the big, fresh-cut conifers you have a chance for at a tree farm.

Another option for Christmas is to not cut down a tree at all, but to purchase a live conifer growing in a five-gallon pot. After Christmas, you can plant the tree, and it will stand as a reminder of the year every time you look at it. I've done this the past four years and the three-footer is now a 10-footer that seems to stretch out a few more inches every month.

If you choose to cut down your own tree, you can expect to pay $20 to $25, which is an industry standard. At Santa's Tree Farm east of Half Moon Bay, for instance, a Monterey pine goes for $22, a Douglas fir for $25, with no size limit on your choice. The tree farms all provide saws. Expect an increase in cost each year.

Living trees in five-gallon pots generally cost $15 and up, depend-

ing on size. At Bongard's
Christmas Trees in Half Moon Bay,
a two-footer goes for $18 and a
six-footer for $47.50. That is also a
Bay Area standard.

The larger choose-and-cut
Christmas tree farms are filled with
thousands of conifers, most of them
Monterey pines. That is because
Monterey pines are the fastest-
growing conifer and can be
trimmed in the fall to fit the classic
Christmas tree shape. The needles
are long, the color a rich green and
they bring a rich pine scent into your
home.

Douglas fir and blue spruce are
also popular, and tend to cost a bit
more than Monterey pines. Fir and
spruce have shorter needles than
pines, tend not to fill in quite as
heavily as pines when trimmed, and
are sturdier than pines.

The latter goes double when purchasing a live tree that will be
planted after Christmas. Monterey
pines grow so fast that they can be
too tall for their root structure to
hold when stiff winter winds follow
heavy rains. When planting pines, a
good idea is to plant more than one
and plant them close together. They
will act as a windbreak for each
other, rather than each tree having
to take the brunt of wind on its own,
and eventually toppling over.

Other varieties of pine
trees can make good Christmas
trees, such as Bishop, Scotch, and
Stone pine. At some tree farms,
Sierra redwood can be available.

Some tree farms are located in
areas that offer the chance to parlay
your Christmas tree expedition into
a good hike as well. The best example is the Skyline Ranch Tree
Farm, located on the mountain ridge
of the San Francisco Peninsula
above Palo Alto. It borders Skyline
Ridge Preserve, which is managed
by the Midpeninsula Regional
Open Space District.

You can drive right up to the tree
farm on Skyline Boulevard, and
after choosing a tree, you can continue your day by exploring the adjacent preserve. In fact, a hidden
lake can be quickly reached by
taking a trail that starts at the
Skyline Ranch Tree Farm.

Another hike here can take you to
a great lookout at 2,493 feet. From
here, a deep canyon plunges below
you, and on clear December days
you get a great view. For information and free map, call the Midpeninsula Open Space District at
(415) 965-4717.

A few other tree farms with nearby recreational opportunities include the Olema Preserve in Marin County (located near the Point Reyes National Seashore), Sunol Christmas Tree Farm in Alameda County (located near Sunol Regional Preserve) and San Gregorio Tree Farm in San Mateo County (located near Memorial County Park).

If you have a family, cutting down your own tree can really add some spice to Christmas. In fact, after the December dust has cleared, it can be the most memorable event of the holiday season.

I was a maniacal 10-year-old the first time my dad took our family into the Santa Cruz mountains to cut our own tree. Seven of us, five kids and the two parents, fanned out like the turning spokes of a bicycle wheel across a huge tree farm, in search of the perfect tree.

So what happens? Wouldn't you know it that every one of us found the perfect tree? Seven people, seven trees. After 20 minutes' worth of comparison, it was narrowed to four. Then, my dad, eager to take us to Big Basin State Park for an adventure, and by virtue of having the saw, settled the dispute with a few quick strokes with the blade.

A lot of Christmas seasons have gone by since then, but it still remains as one of my special memories.

You see, he picked my tree.

Alameda County

■ **1. Castro Valley Christmas Tree Farm:**
Three miles north of Castro Valley on Redwood Road. (415) 376-1044.

■ **2. Mission Peak Ranch Christmas Trees:**
In Fremont at Mission Boulevard and Vineyard Road. (415) 657-1011.

■ **3. Moraga Christmas Tree Farm:**
One mile southeast of Moraga at the end of Camino Pablo Road. (415) 376-1044.

■ **4. Sunol Christmas Tree Farm:**
In Sunol Valley. (415) 278-2261.

■ **5. Volkman's Valley Ranch:**
Near Livermore near the Wente Winery. (415) 447-0076.

Contra Costa County

■ **6. Alhambra Valley Tree Farm:**
Two miles south of Martinez. (415) 228-5324.

■ **7. Bear Creek Tree Farm:**
Two miles east of Clayton. (415) 672-4569.

■ **9. Dayley's Choose & Cut:**
In Martinez. (415) 372-7755.

■ 10. San Ramon Christmas Tree Farm:
In San Ramon on Pine Valley Road. (415) 376-1044.

■ 11. Shelter Green Tree Farm:
In Pittsburg. (415) 452-1815.

Marin County

■ 12. Olema Preserve:
Just east of Olema on Sir Francis Drake.

Napa County

■ 13. Bruderer's Christmas Tree Farm:
In Napa on Solano Ave. (707) 226-3502.

■ 14. Evergreen Christmas Tree Farm:
In Napa on Hagen Road.

■ 15. J.B.'s Christmas Trees:
In Napa on Big Ranch Road. (707) 224-5354.

■ 16. Mount George Tree Farm:
In Napa on Big Ranch Road. (707) 224-3729.

■ 17. Napa Valley Christmas Tree Farm:
In Napa on Big Ranch Road. (707) 252-1000.

San Mateo County

■ 18. Bongard's Christmas Trees:
In Half Moon Bay on Highway 92. (415) 726-4568.

■ 19. Coastways Ranch:
In Pescadero on Highway 1. (415) 897-0414.

■ 20. Rancho Siempre Verde:
South of Half Moon Bay on Highway 1. (415) 326-9103.

■ 21. Sand Hill Christmas Tree Farm:
East of Menlo Park on Sand Hill Road.

■ 22. San Gregorio Tree Farm:
West of La Honda on Highway 84. (415) 747-0357.

■ 23. Santa's Tree Farm:
East of Half Moon Bay on Highway 92. (415) 726-2246.

■ 24. Skyline Ranch Tree Farm:
At the intersection of Skyline and Page Mill.

Santa Clara County

■ **25. Battaglia Ranch:**
In San Jose at 1410 Four Oaks Road. (408) 272-0666.

■ **26. Buena Vista Christmas Tree Ranch:**
In Gilroy. (408) 842-8092.

■ **27. Casa de Fruta:**
East of Gilroy on Highway 152. (408) 637-0051.

■ **28. Christmas Carol Trees:**
In Coyote. (408) 463-0238.

■ **29. Cocco's Monta Vista Tree Farm:**
In Monta Vista. (415) 369-3665.

■ **30. Liagas Creek Christmas Tree Farm:**
Southwest corner of Watsonville Road and Santa Terea Boulevard. (408) 779-2847.

■ **31. Montecito Christmas Tree Farm:**
In Morgan Hill. (408) 779-2847.

■ **32. Mountain View Christmas Tree Farm:**
In Mountain View near the Shoreline Amphitheater. (415) 376-1044.

■ **33. Nichols Christmas Tree Farm:**
Between Morgan Hill and Gilroy. (408) 842-4783.

■ **34. Patchen California:**
South of Los Gatos. (408) 353-1615.

■ **35. Peacock Tree Farm:**
Near intersection of Highway 17 and Summit Road. (408) 353-3501.

■ **36. San Martin Christmas Tree Farm:**
Just north of San Martin. (408) 683-2368.

■ **37. Sunshine Christmas Tree Farm:**
In Morgan Hill. (408) 779-3451.

Solano County

■ **38. American Canyon Tree Farms:**
A mile north of Vallejo. (415) 228-5324.

■ **39. Davis Christmas Tree Farm:**
Near Dixon. (415) 228-5324.

40. Grandad's Christmas Tree Farm:
Two miles east of Vacaville. (707) 448-4264.

41. Pleasant Valley Tree Farm:
In Vacaville. (707) 448-3250.

42. Silveyville Christmas Tree Farm:
Near Dixon. (916) 678- 1823.

Sonoma County

43. The Christmas Tree:
Three miles west of Sebastopol. (707) 823-3605.

44. Evergreen Farm:
In Santa Rosa. (415) 433-0691.

45. Family Christmas Tree:
In Santa Rosa. (707) 546-3877.

46. Garlock Tree Farm:
In Sebastopol. (707) 823-4307.

47. Green Valley Tree Farm:
Four miles north of Sebastopol. (707) 823-1544.

48. Kenwood Tree Farm:
Four miles north of Sebastopol. (707) 833-5856.

49. Kitchen Ranch:
In Healdsburg. (707) 433-4085.

50. Larsen Christmas Tree Farm:
In Petaluma. (707) 762-3617.

51. Moon Mountain Christmas Tree Farm:
In Boyes Hot Springs off Highway 12. (707) 996-6454.

52. Petaluma Tree Farm:
In Petaluma. (707) 762-2143.

53. Randy's Christmas Tree Farm:
Between Sonoma and Napa. (707) 938-4420.

54. Santa's Trees:
Five miles west of Sebastopol. (707) 823- 6635.

55. Schieth's Tree Farm:
In Petaluma. (707) 762-6293.

56. Sorensen's Christmas Tree Farm:
In Sebastopol. (707) 823-6657.

57. Starcross Trees & Wreaths:
In Annapolis, seven miles east of Highway 1 at Sea Ranch. (707) 886-5330.

BONUS TRIPS

SCIENTIFIC
BAY CRUISE

TOUR BOAT AS MARINE LAB

W hat might start as nothing more than curiosity and a boat ride can end by changing your perspective on life.

Providing, that is, the name of the boat is the Inland Seas and your ride is a four-hour tour of San Francisco Bay -- with the chance to see, touch and experience all the little critters that make the Bay environment click.

It is called Discovery Voyages and it is one of the unique adventures available anywhere in the West. From the outside, it appears to be a fun, four-hour cruise exploring the south Bay. From the inside, it is like a Jacques Cousteau expedi-

tion with a chance to view the Bay in a way you may have never considered.

The Inland Seas, an 85-foot cruiser, departs from Chesapeake Drive in Redwood City and heads out to the Bay between the San Mateo and Dumbarton bridges. You don't need seasickness pills. In fact, the Bay is often so calm out here that the skipper calls it "San Francisco Lake."

Out on the water, the crew takes charge -- with a net trawl for fish, and samples of plankton water and mud from the Bay bottom. You see, this boat is a floating marine laboratory and the public is invited along for a special science lesson.

By itself, the boat ride is lots of fun, but the chance to explore, question and observe the inner workings of San Francisco Bay will make you feel different about the area as your home.

"Five million people live and work around the Bay," said Bob

Rutherford, president of Discovery Voyages. "Few of them realize their quality of life is greatly influenced by the Bay.

"We don't pull any punches and we're not pointing any fingers. We are analyzing the Bay with students. It doesn't matter who is aboard, whether it is an oil company or the Leslie Salt Co., we do the same thing."

Since the first voyage 18 years ago, Rutherford estimates 135,000 people have taken the trip. Some go for the boat ride, some to supplement their science education, others to get in touch with the vast body of water that is the center of the Bay Area metroplex.

There are many questions, and on this trip, many answers.

You start with a simple water-plankton sample. It is like looking into a crystal ball, because it can tell you the future. In that water you will find plankton, the basis of the marine food chain. A net with tiny openings just 80 microns across is dragged through the water, and after being retrieved, you follow a scientist to a room inside the boat. Using a specially designed microscope/projector, an image of the plankton is projected on a screen, where everyone can view it at once.

You see tiny copepods, dyatoms, dyno flagellate, a small protozoa, all of them squiggling around. Without them, there would be no other life in the Bay.

"This is the beginning of the marine food chain," said Peter Olds, one of the scientists aboard. "We explain how everything starts with plankton on the bottom of the food chain. And we emphasize the possible effects that man might have on it.

"If there's too much sewage going into the bay, for instance, there can be an algae bloom. The plankton and algae will rot, and then the decomposition of the plant matter uses up the oxygen in the water. Without enough oxygen, fish cannot survive."

The mud samples are especially fascinating to kids. They seem to like the idea of a scientist getting all mucked up.

But then you discover that all kinds of little critters are living in the mud as the scientist finds and identifies them: tubeworms, oysters, mussels, clams, sponges, little crustaceans, snails. You find out that there is more to the muck than just muck.

The fish trawl is often the most exciting. The small net is called an Otter Trawl, and it is dragged behind the boat allowing a wide sampling.

Perch -- seen in many species -- are the most abundant. You are also likely to see leopard sharks, brown smoothhound sharks and bay rays. Anchovies, sole, halibut, and sometimes, although rarely, striped bass and sturgeon also are captured. After inspection, the fish are returned unharmed.

You end up with a unique look at the Bay in the process of a fun adventure. You also begin to understand the chain of life in Bay waters, and how man can affect it.

"We conserve only what we love," Rutherford said. "We love only what we understand. We understand only what we have learned."

☞ BAY TOUR TRIP FACTS

How to get there: From Highway 101, take the Port of Redwood City exit. Continue past the harbor, eastward. The Discovery Voyage headquarters is located across from the giant salt pile of the Leslie Salt Co.

Tour Schedule: Charters are available year around. Public trips are scheduled, but individuals can often join private charters too.

Trip Cost: Boarding pass is $30 for adults, $20 for students age 10 to 18.

Who to contact: For a brochure or information, write Discovery Voyages, 1200 Chesapeake Drive, Redwood City 94063, or call 364-2760.

WE CONSERVE ONLY WHAT WE LOVE.

WE LOVE ONLY WHAT WE UNDERSTAND.

WE UNDERSTAND ONLY WHAT WE
    HAVE LEARNED.

- RUTHERFORD

CALISTOGA
MUD BATHS

OOZING STREES FROM YOUR BODY

The first time you imagine taking a mud bath, you are apt to get all kinds of crazy ideas of what it's like. Then when you do it, you will find out that most of them are true.

As you slowly sink into the hot black ooze, you feel like you are being enveloped by a giant sponge. Your body submerges deeper, and an attendant then covers you right up to your Adam's apple. There are immediate, multiple sensations: 100-degree heat, the weight of a 100 pounds of muck, the smell of peat and a general sort of strange euphoria.

After five minutes, your body has a strange glow from the heat and you might start to feel lightheaded, tipsy. Two minutes later, you might become a little short of breath as the toxins begin leaving your body, and sweat pours from your forehead. Ten minutes in, you start thinking you can't take it anymore, you need escape, your breathing is short, the heat is all encompassing.

Finally you surrender.

Then you find out this strange journey has only begun.

After the mud bath, "The Works" comes with 10 minutes in a tub full of 106 to 108-degree mineral water, steam room treatment, towel wrap, and massage. At that point, what you will probably need is somebody to cart you away in a wheelbarrow, because after all this, you will feel like a happy, amorphous blob.

This is the treatment at Dr. Wilkinson's Hot Springs, one of the oldest mineral spas in Calistoga. Your first visit here might be out of

curiosity, relief for stress, or a search for a cure for rheumatism. Regardless of what gets you here, you leave feeling like you are starting a whole new life, and the glow stays with you for days.

"People used to originally come here looking for relief from rheumatic ailments," said Dr. John Wilkinson, founder and owner of the spa. "Nowadays the main reason they come here is because of stress." They come back because they find the treatment works pretty well.

Calistoga, located in the north end of the Napa wine valley, is the nation's headquarters for mud baths and hot springs. Why here? Because submerged in the earth under this small town are several boiling cauldrons of mineral water. The mineral spas tap it, and in turn, are able to offer its unique powers to the public.

"It's like a giant tea kettle under this building," Wilkinson said. "Imagine a boiling pool of 250-degree water. That's what it's like down there. Our biggest problem is cooling it down before we use it."

A large mineral spa with bubbling 103 or 104-degree mineral water is available. But when you sign up for "The Works," the water goes into the tub much hotter, like 107 or 108 degrees. Two larger pools are also available at Wilkinson's, one that feels like soaking in a big bathtub, the other set at swimming pool temperature.

At the least, just soaking in mineral water will take all the fight out of you. At the most, it will make you feel like a new person. Most folks walk out somewhere in between.

According to Wilkinson, soaking in hot mineral water helps rid your skin of toxins. The effect is compounded in the mud bath treatment, which is actually a combination of Canadian peat and Calistoga volcanic ash mixed wit the hot mineral water. Topping it off with the steam room seems to flush and clean your entire body.

Though your sweat out fluids profusely during the experience, cold, carbonated mineral water is provided so you do not get dehydrated.

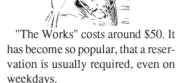

"The Works" costs around $50. It has become so popular, that a reservation is usually required, even on weekdays.

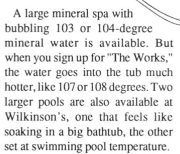

Ironically, it sometimes is not the mud bath or mineral spa that ends up as the most memorable moment. It is the towel wrap. What happens is you are wrapped in a towel and blankets, with an ice cold towel on your forehead -- just after having finished the mud bath, mineral spa and steam room consecutively. As you lie there, you might feel you are the center of some great phenomenon of sensory experience. It's because you are.

The mud bath itself is a relatively small, square tub filled with dark, bubbling goo. As you first start sinking into the stuff, it feels kind of like wallowing in warm, shallow quick sand. Then when submerged to your neck, there is a sense of weightlessness, as if there is no bottom, no sides, and you are floating in space, suspended in hot mud.

If you think it might be a strange experience, to find yourself sitting in the stuff, well, you are right.

But if you want to feel like a "whole new person," this is one of the best ways to do it.

☞ BOX 1 HOT SPRINGS

Where to go: Follow Highway 29 past Saint Helena to Calistoga, located 70 miles north of San Francisco at the northern end of the Napa Valley.

Trip Cost: An individual mud bath, mineral whirlpool bath, mineral steam room and blanket wrap runs about $31. "The Works" which includes a half-hour massage costs about $50.

Who to contact: Call the Calistoga Chamber of Commerce at (707) 942-6333. They will be able to tell you about the seven full spas in town and direct you to lodging as well. If you have time (allow three weeks), ask for the free visitor's guide to Calistoga.

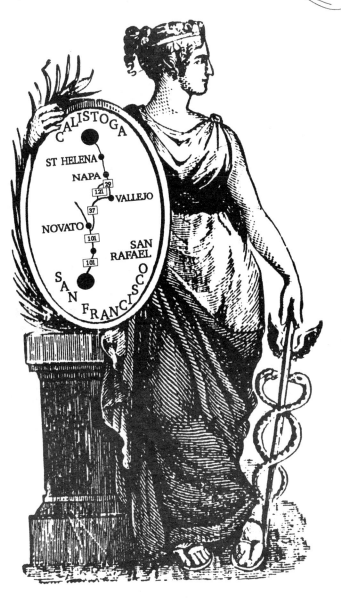

CALISTOGA

ST HELENA

NAPA

29

121

VALLEJO

37

NOVATO

101

SAN
RAFAEL

101

SAN

FRANCISCO

BONUS TRIPS

10 NATURE
PRESERVES

THE QUIET AMERICA

T he Quiet America -- It is a land unencumbered by concrete, stop lights and miles of cars and people. It is a delicate place, where one can retain the belief that you, one person in a vast world, are still important.

It is a retreat where one can slink away from mass society and instead focus on the life immediately around you, whether it be a trout rolling in a stream or just a piece of moss clinging to a tree.

But rapidly, places like this are vanishing.

Environmental stability is a thing of the past. One by one, at the rate of one thousand species per year, extinction is being assured by the destruction of key habitats. Few areas remain in this state in their natural primitive form, unchanged by man.

But because of an organization called the Nature Conservancy, unique areas are being preserved in their natural state. In Northern California, 10 areas have been bought by or donated to the Conservancy -- which offers free access to all.

Each preserve offers something special, from fishing for Dolly Varden trout on the McCloud River Preserve to experiencing the mystical attraction of Bishop Pine Preserve near Inverness.

The number of people allowed on a preserve varies from as low as two people per day to as many as 30, depending on the fragility of the area. Access is free, but by reservation only -- which is easily arranged by calling The Conservancy at (415) 777-0487. Camping is not allowed on the preserves themselves, but campgrounds are situated nearby every area.

The goal of the Nature Conservancy is to preserve rare and threatened areas. The McCloud River, for instance, is the only remaining home in the state for the Dolly Varden trout.

The Conservancy does not take political stands like other environmental organizations, but works by acquiring lands and offering a special and quiet place to be enjoyed by all. A reservation is your only requirement.

Does this mean long waiting lists? Not by a long shot.

"I've been here three years and I have not even once turned someone away," said Tom Hesseldenz, who helps manage the McCloud Trout Preserve.

The Conservancy is a nationwide organization that owns more than 1.5 million acres, operates 670 preserves and has projects in all 50 states.

Exploring remote areas has become so popular in this state that it's often difficult not to come upon a party of hikers with high regularity. On a preserve, your solitude is guaranteed.

Call it The Quiet America.

Here's a breakdown of the preserves available in Northern California.

■ 1. Spindrift Point Preserve:

Spindrift serves as a sea mark for the migrating California gray whales that breach as they pass by the rocks at the tip of the point. The preserve is graced with meadows that provide an elaborate wildflower displays and is home for a variety of wildlife.

It's a summer haven for kingfishers, hawks, gulls and the California brown pelican, among many other birds.

It's located along the Marin coast near the community of Muir Beach just a short drive from San Francisco. Camping is available at the Point Reyes National Seashore. Access is limited to five people per day.

■ 2. Bishop Pine Preserve:

Bishop Pine is a 400-acre area in Marin County about 35 miles north of San Francisco. It sits on the Point Reyes peninsula, overlooking Tomales Bay near Inverness. The Samuel P. Taylor State Park and the Point Reyes National Seashore offer nearby camping.

The preserve is named after its stand of Bishop Pines, which exists with dense growths of a mixed evergreen forest. This is home for deer, coyote, squirrels, chipmunks and bobcats. A spring-fed stream flows through the center of the preserve and empties into Tomales Bay at Willow Point.

3. Fairfield Osborn Preserve:

Fairfield Osborn consists of 150 acres of oak, evergreen forest, fresh water marsh, ponds and streams high on the slopes of the Sonoma Mountains, 60 miles north of San Francisco.

Copeland Creek crosses the preserve which helps support deer, fox, weasel, quail and owl. As many as 20 people per day are allowed on the preserve. Camping is allowed at Sugar Loaf Ridge and Sonoma Coast State Beach.

4. Boggs Lake Preserve:

Boggs Lake is nestled in the mountains between Kelseyville and Cobb Valley in Lake County, just eight miles south of Clear Lake, where camping sites are plentiful.

It offers an unusual combination of vernal pool and pond that sit in a basin of volcanic rock. As the lake dries in the summer, wildflowers bloom in concentric rings in the shallow water.

The animal life consists of the common natives of the area: deer, raccoons, skunks and an occasional bobcat, mountain lion or fox. Five to 10 people per day are allowed access to this area.

5. Northern California Coast Range Preserve:

This is the oldest and largest preserve in Northern California, some 8,000 acres were protected in 1958. Black bear, deer, mountain lion and other mammals are still found in a wild state here, unaccustomed to the presence of man.

Virgin Douglas fir forests have been reduced to a few remaining stands in Northern California after being cut extensively for wood products. But here, a tranquil life, unchanged for centuries, can still be experienced.

It is situated between Laytonville on Highway 101 and Westport on Highway 1. Camping is offered on the coast at Russian Gulch and Van Damme State Park.

6. Lanphere-Christensen Dunes Preserve:

Just a few people per day are allowed in this fragile area, which is situated along the Pacific Coast just north of Humboldt Bay near Eureka.

The dunes were formed by the accumulation of sand washed onshore by waves, then blown inland by sea winds. A beach pine forest is found farther inland, where dense stands of tree stand over ferns and mosses and offer an undisturbed home to the wild.

Camping is allowed at Patrick's Point Prairie Creek and Redwood State Park, where trails are like tunnels through lush vegetation.

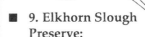

7. The McCloud River Preserve:

Here's your chance fishermen. Rainbow, brown and Dolly Varden trout are native to this river, where catch and release with flies and lures is the rule. Joe Montgomery of Dunsmuir caught 36 trout in one evening, the biggest measuring 21 inches.

Up river of the preserve, two fish per day may be kept, should you want to catch dinner. Ten rods per day are allowed on the preserve's 6.5 miles of river.

The McCloud sits in a steep canyon that is lined with a forest that's home for ringtail cats, black bears, mountain lions and blacktail deer. More than 85 species of birds, including bald eagles, have been seen on the preserve.

8. Sacramento River Oxbow Preserve:

John Muir described these woodlands as "forests of tropical luxuriance." The dense foliage of oaks, cottonwoods, ash and willows provide habitat for a wide variety of wildlife, such as beaver, muledeer, river otter, ringtail cat, mink and wildcat. No other terrestrial habitat in the state supports so large a number of bird species, including the very rare yellow-billed cuckoo.

The preserve is located near the Sacramento River southwest of Chico and nearby camping is available at Woodson Bridge State Recreation Area and Colusa Sacramento River State Recreation Area.

9. Elkhorn Slough Preserve:

Elkhorn Slough is the second largest salt marsh in California, and is one of the last major undisturbed estuaries on the coast.

It opens into Moss Landing, between Santa Cruz and Monterey, and contains a seven-mile tidal channel. The preserve contains 441 acres.

Some excellent clamming is available on low tides (in the minus one-foot range) just west of the preserve. Camping is available at Fremont Peak State Park.

10. Big Creek Preserve:

Big Creek is located about 45 miles south of Carmel and, at sea level, includes nearly four miles of rock coast centered in the California Sea Otter Refuge. The reserve land rises from the ocean to an elevation of 4,000 feet at its eastern boundary in the Santa Lucia Mountain.

The preserve is home to mountain lions, blacktailed deer, bobcats and endangered sea otters. Plus 125 bird species have been observed, including hawks, owls and myriad number of shorebirds.

Big Creek is also one of the last central coastal areas that supports a vigorous run of steelhead.

Camping is available at Pfeiffer Big Sur State Park and Andrew Molera State Park. The preserve will allow 20 people access per day.

APPENDIX

ADVENTURES
OF THE WEST

❧ BEYOND ❧

NO. CALIFORNIA

CONTENTS:—

PUBLISHED BY FOGHORN PRESS
SAN FRANCISCO
QUALITY OUTDOOR BOOKS

EXPLORING AMERICA'S UNTAMED WILDERNESS

RELIVING THE PAST

Exploring America's untamed wilderness is the one way left to relive the great fishing and hunting adventures that greeted the West's first trailblazers.

Jedediah Smith, Joe Walker, Jim Bridger ...the wilderness is much as they found it 150 years ago. "Wild America is still protected from Machine America," a ranger once remarked. You travel by foot or horseback, going your way quietly as you sense freedom and a tremendous release. Great things are still possible in this world, and a wilderness trip proves it.

Show me a place that can't be reached by car, boat or airplane, and I'll show you a place that can provide an abundance of fishing and hunting. All you have to do is strap on your boots or saddle up a horse and find the trail. Secret, untouched areas are out there, places where few have ever cast a fishing line or stalked game with a rifle or camera. You have 50 million acres of wilderness to choose from in nine western states.

Even in some of the more well-known wilderness territories, you can still have a trip that is inexpensive, healthy -- and provides an outstanding experience. My first trip into the Bob Marshall Wilderness of northwest Montana was like this. It is the best of the wilderness system, known for its superb cutthroat trout fishing on the forks of the Flathead River and in back country lakes.

"The Bob" also attract heavy visitor use. Yet by taking an obscure trailhead, we saw only two other persons in a week and caught plenty of big cutthroats, not one under 18 inches. Moose were more numerous than other campers.

The possibilities can bring vivid daydreams. In the wilderness of the Wallowa Mountains in northeast Oregon, you can spot and stalk magnificent bighorn sheep. In the Marble Mountain Wilderness of California's northwestern corner, you can camp at a different lake each night, arriving in time to catch a limit of trout in less than 30 minutes. In Colorado's Weminuchi Wilderness, set in the San Juan Mountains, you leave the crowd behind, fishing and hiking in solitude, and in the process find your own retreat in the rugged, primitive setting.

As you get deeper into the interior of a wilderness, the longer you stay, you will notice that you will begin to shed the cares of civilization like layers of unneeded clothing. After awhile, it feels pretty good.

What sets apart designated wilderness areas from anywhere else is a few clear precepts. First, wilderness is an area where man is a visitor only. He does not remain, and neither does any sign of his presence. The only indications of man are hiking trails and primitive camps along lakes and streams. No mechanized form of transport is permitted, including mountain bicycles -- and even the Forest Service is prohibited from using helicopters or power tools, except in emergency rescues. For instance, if

workers must clear trails of fallen trees, the use of a chainsaw is not permitted; they use hand tools.

To start your trip, write to the appropriate Forest Service office for the area you would like to visit and ask for information regarding wilderness areas in their region. (An accompanying list provides addresses and phone numbers for Forest Service offices in the Western United States). After reviewing the wilderness material, you should then send for a map of the wilderness you intend to visit, which will cost $1 or $2 depending on the map.

More detailed topographic maps are available from the U.S. Geologic Survey for $2.50, plus a small handling charge. For a list of maps available, write Topo Maps, USGS, Western Distribution Branch, Box 25286, Federal Center, Denver, CO 80225 -- or Topo Maps, USGS, 345 Middlefield Road, Menlo Park, CA 94045. Many sporting goods dealers and outdoor equipment stores also carry USGS topographic maps.

The next step is to call the district Forest Service office that manages the area you wish to visit. You should ask rangers the following

INFORMATION SOURCES

California
Office of Information, U.S. Forest Service, Pacific Southwest Region, 630 Sansome Street, San Francisco, CA 94111. Phone (415) 556-0122.

Washington/Oregon
Office of Information, P.O. Box 3623, Portland OR 97208. Phone (503) 221-2877.

Montana/Northern Idaho
Office of Information, Forest Service, P.O. Box 7669, Missoula, MT 59807. Phone (406) 329-3511.

Colorado/Wyoming
Office of Information, U.S. Frest Service, 11177 W. Eighth Avenue, Box 25127, Lakewood, CO 80225. Phone (303) 236-9645.

Arizona/New Mexico
Office of Information, U.S. Forest Service, Federal Buiding, 6th Floor, 517 Gold Avenue SW, Albuquerque, NM 87102. Phone (505) 842-3292.

Utah/Nevada (also southern Idaho and northwestern Wyoming)
Office of Information, U.S. Forest Service, Inner Mountain Region, 324 25th Street, Odgen, UT 84401. Phone (801) 625-5352.

questions: **1.** Do I need a wilderness or fire permit? **2.** Are there any special restrictions I need to be aware of? **3.** Are the trailheads crowded, and what alternatives are available? **4.** Are there any unusual natural hazards?

District Forest Service rangers are often the most helpful of any of the public agencies, and are happy to provide the information you need.

Whether the number of people in an area is too high is a matter of perspective. Newcomers often prefer higher-use areas because if they need help, they know they can get it. Others want solitude, and are satisfied if they don't see another person for a week.

There are many examples of both. In California near Lake Tahoe, Desolation Wilderness is one of the most popular and crowded hiking areas in the West. Other crowded wilderness areas are in Colorado near Denver, Vail and Aspen, and in Utah near Salt Lake City. Yet both states have alternative destinations that can provide pure solitude. For instance, Warner Wilderness in northeastern California is a remote, mysterious land that is rarely traveled and has good fishing in small lakes and streams. In Colorado, the Raggeds Wilderness in the central Rockies also gets few visitors, yet can provide superb high-mountain trout fishing.

"The closer you get to a major urban center or popular mountain resort town, the heavier the use," says Matt Mathes of the Forest Service. "If you want to be alone in the wilderness, just give us a call and we'll suggest some of the lesser-used areas."

There are many to pick from. The biggest single concentration of wilderness is clustered in central Idaho. It is called the River Of No Return Wilderness, which is comprised of parts of six national forests covering 2.4 million acres. It is best known for a remarkable network of rivers and streams, which attract rafters/fishermen from all over the country. This area is very steep, and most of the travel is by raft, not by foot.

Alaska has the most wilderness, with 5.45 million acres, much of it unexplored, other than by bush plane. California and Idaho have the highest ratio of acres of wilderness to national forest, almost 20 percent.

To people who live on the East Coast, the West still resembles the great frontier. For the most part, wilderness areas in eastern states are more like small preserves. In comparison, Idaho has the most wilderness of any state in the Lower 48, with 3.96 million acres. Idaho is followed by California (3.9 million acres), Montana (3.3 million acres), Wyoming (3.1 million), Colorado (2.6 million), Washington (2.5 million), Oregon (2.1 million), New Mexico (1.4 million), Arizona (1.3 million), Utah (775,000 acres), and Nevada (64,000 acres).

With that much territory, you can choose your adventure, self-styling it to fit your exact desires.

Wilderness areas include the highest (20,320 feet at Mount McKinley) and lowest (282 feet below sea level at Death Valley) points in North America. They span enchanted forests, hard deserts and hidden lakes and streams -- and each is a living portrait of an America that was.

You might find the best fishing and hunting of your life. You also will be open to a more subtle world where you become aware of the pure taste of the breeze blowing across a snow-covered mountain pass, a coyote howling at the moon, a trout rising to a caddis hatch.

Some of you might get the feeling that your experiences match those of the great pioneers of the West. After awhile, you might even believe the spirits of Kit Carson or Liver-Eating Johnson are guiding your way.

No amount of words and pictures can get you there. It is something you f el, not see. To do it, you have to make your own footprints.

OVERLOOKED ADVENTURES
OF THE WEST

THE TOP 10

Most world-class vacations have three things in common: They're expensive, overcrowded, and despite as much fun as they sound, you rarely take them.

In contrast, there is the adventure that is cheap, remote and as easy to take as providing the time and spirit for it. Qualifications? Great natural beauty, not too many people, not too expensive and an element of excitement that gives the whole trip some genuine sizzle.

That's what it takes to be considered for my Top 10 Overlooked Adventures in the West. Peace and excitement, these places provide them both:

■ **1. Grand Teton Wilderness, Wyoming:**

This is a huge chunk of raw nature with superb hiking, trout fishing and wildlife populations -- with the magnificent Tetons towering above you every step of the way. It is the perfect alternative to nearby and crowded Yellowstone National Park.

Summer afternoons bring with them short but thrilling thunderstorms where heavy clouds will suddenly roll over, then send lightning bolts and thunderclaps rattling off the Tetons. It's a dramatic event that you will never forget.

The cutthroat trout are wild and big, averaging 14 to 17 inches. The best of it comes for those hiking in to lakes.

An option is visiting the nearby Grosventre Wilderness, located northeast of Jackson in Bridger-Teton National Forest. This is one of the best wildlife areas of the West, with great populations of deer, elk and moose.

Who to contact: Office of Information,

U.S. Forest Service, 11177 W. 8th Avenue, Box 25127, Lakewood, CO 80225; (303) 236-9645. Maps are available for $1.

■ 2. Mount Saint Helens, Washington:

This is the number one hike in America, a trail that takes you right to the rim of the volcano. You actually have to be careful not to fall in -- there are no guard rails.

From the rim, you look down into the flume of the volcano, a u-shaped crater, crater, and scan the devastation, a moonscape for miles. In the crater, there are wisps of smoke rising, and still bits of lava spewing up as the old volcano builds a new peak. This is a living mountain, where you can watch the birth of a new mountain peak taking place.

From where you park, the trail is five miles long, with a 5,000- foot gain. It is a one-day trip, but some hikers do it in less. It is best when there is plenty of snow and when you can fit crampons on your hiking boots, and carry a ski pole or ice axe to make the ascent.

As you drive to the trailhead, the sight of the big volcano will send a mercurial bolt of energy through you. It's all the energy you need to reach the volcano rim.

Who to contact: A trail permit is required through the Forest Service. Write Mount Saint Helens Visitor Center, 3029 Spirit Lake Highway, Castle Rock, WA 98611. Or call (206) 247-5473 or 247-5800 (climbing info only).

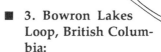

■ 3. Bowron Lakes Loop, British Columbia:

This is one of the top canoe circuits in the world, a one-of-a- kind 75-mile trip that takes paddlers across 13 lakes, six rivers and requires seven portages. Unlike other canoe or kayak trips, this adventure ends just a few hundred yards from the starting point. You never have to double back, but instead press on, ever forward. As you go, you will explore the magnificent Canadian wilderness in central British Columbia, east of Quesnel.

The trout fishing is good, particularly at the first three lakes: Kibbee Lake, Indian Point Lake, and giant Isaac Lake. The best technique is to let a woolly worm fly, no weight, drag behind the boat as you paddle along.

This is a one-in-a-million adventure. In a week here, we met people of all ages, from all parts of the world. Glaciers and moose, woods and water, canoe strokes and friendly mates, this place is something special.

Who to contact: Write Bowron Lakes, Ministry of Environment and Parks, 540 Borland Avenue, Williams Lake, BC Canada, V2G-1R8 and Beckers Canoe Outfitters, Box 129, Wells, BC Canada, V0K-2RO.

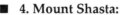

■ 4. Mount Shasta:

Giant Shasta is the centerpiece of Northern California, rising to 14,162 feet above the lowlands that surround it. It is a mountain of fire and ice, a place that presents both a challenge and a mystery.

The challenge is to climb it and the reality is that you can. Anyone in decent physical shape, equipped with crampons, ice ax, and dressed for the 35 degrees on top, can make the ascent.

The mystery is that the old volcano seems to have a living spirit, and the mountain's legends of Lemurians and Yaktavians enhance that. As you climb, you will feel a special sense of power, and when you claim the peak, exhilaration and victory.

The most common route is from Horse Camp. From there, it is a six-mile climb with an elevation gain of 6,000 feet. In addition to being properly equipped, one key is drinking enough water along the way to prevent dehydration.

Who to contact: Write Shasta Cascade, 1250 Parkview, Redding, CA 96001. Or call (916) 243-2643. The brochure is free.

■ 5. Baja Camping, Mexico:

Mexico has hundreds of miles of unspoiled coast, with quiet beaches, protected bays, and outstanding swimming, snorkeling and fishing by boat or surf.

The best way to see it is to avoid populated areas, where litter is always a problem, and instead strike off on your own and camp along the beaches on Baja's Pacific coast. The trip can be perfected if you have a four-wheel drive and your own boat, either a rubber Zodiac, car-topper or small trailered skiff. But it is not a necessity.

If you don't have a boat, shorefishing can be very good, particularly for big barred perch, spotfin croaker and many varieties of rockfish. In addition, the Mexican fishermen with pangas (pronounced pongas), a 20-foot open boat with an outboard motor, can be convinced with a little American green to take you fishing for many other species.

The way to get there is to drive off the paved road and instead follow the dirt routes to the coast. Have all your meals, drinks and gear already packed. Some of the better fishing spots include San Isidro, San Quintin and Puerto Santo Domingo.

Who to contact: Write for the Angler's Guide to Baja, Baja Trail Publications, P.O. Box 6088, Huntington Beach, CA 92615, $10 including postage.

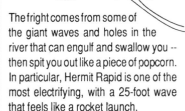

■ 6. Bob Marshall Wilderness, Montana:

This is the crown jewel of the nation's wilderness system -- over a million acres of forest and rivers -- yet is missed by thousands of tourists who instead visit nearby Glacier National Park.

It is the kind of place for the rugged few who don't mind the chance of meeting up with moose, black bear and maybe even a grizzly.

It is also the place for people who want solitude and a chance to catch big trout. The more obscure hikes will take you deep into the interior of Montana's Rockies. In a week, you might see somebody else, you might not. The easy-to-reach trailheads get heavier use, of course.

The lakes and streams of the Flathead River system provide excellent fishing for cutthroat trout. A 15 or 16-inch is about the average, good prospects for anglers using fly or spinning gear.

Who to contact: Write the Office of Information, Forest Service, P.O. Box 7669, Missoula, MT 59807 or call (406) 329-3511. A map is available for $1.

■ 7. Rafting the Grand Canyon:

Shooting the giant waves at the bottom of America's biggest canyon is an untamed, sometimes frightening, experience.

The excitement comes from the countless miles of white water, and the awesome scenic beauty of the deep, gold canyon. All of it is worth filming. The sunsets are among the prettiest in the world. There's not a bad seat in the house.

The fright comes from some of the giant waves and holes in the river that can engulf and swallow you -- then spit you out like a piece of popcorn. In particular, Hermit Rapid is one of the most electrifying, with a 25-foot wave that feels like a rocket launch.

Trips vary from five days to two weeks, with the cost about $125 per day, including guide, food and shuttle. Many people raft the Grand Canyon, but start-ups are staggered so you see few people.

Who to contact: Call Oars at 800-446-7238 or Grand Canyon National Park, P.O. Box 129, Grand Canyon, AZ 86023 at 602-638-2411, Ext. 248.

■ 8. Deschutes River, Oregon:

The Deschutes is one of America's top trout streams, and it is the perfect place to combine a multiday raft or drift-boat trip.

The river is set along the eastern side of the Cascade Range, with the best

fishing along a 45-mile stretch from the Warm Springs Indian Reservation north to Maupin.

One reason fishing is so good here is because access by shore is a problem. It is best to go by raft or drift boat, then stop to fish and camp along the way downstream. You can buy a permit at the Warm Springs Indian Reservation, where access is permitted.

The trout are native rainbows, beautiful fish that average 14 inches. They take dry flies and nymphs, and from the end of May through to mid-June, there is a sensational salmon fly hatch. As the weather warms in summer, smaller flies and lures become necessary.

A few notes: No bait is allowed, camp only on the east side of the river, and boaters will get added thrills from Class III rapids.

Who to contact: Call or write Guide Ray Baker, P.O. Box 5586, Eugene, OR 97405, 503-343-7514 or Warm Springs Indian Reservation at (503) 343-7514.

■ 9. River of No Return Wilderness, Idaho:

Idaho is known best for "famous potatoes," but if more people visited the River of No Return, Idaho would be better known as a sportsman's paradise.

There are runs of steelhead, salmon on the main rivers, with good trout fishing on the feeder streams. In addition, the wilderness has abundant populations of moose, bear, deer, elk, mountain goat, sheep and mountain lion. The land is virtually untouched.

It is located in central Idaho, covering some two million acres of land and thousands of miles of waterways. Much of the terrain is quite steep, and as a result, the most popular way to explore it is by raft, combining a multiday rafting/fishing adventure.

By foot, it is rugged, steep, primitive country with dramatic elevation gains and losses. It is too steep for most hikers. It is recommended to go by horseback, or bring a donkey along to carry your gear. Your rewards are quiet camps and superb fishing and hunting in idyllic settings.

Who to contact: Echo, The Wilderness Company, 6529 Telegraph, Oakland 94609, (415) 652-1600 or Office of Information, U.S. Forest Service, P.O. Box 7669, Missoula, MT 59807, (406) 329-3511. Maps are $1.

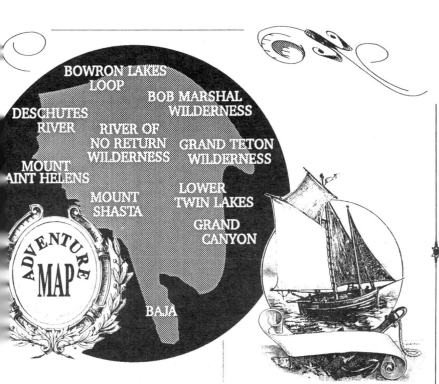

ADVENTURE MAP

BOWRON LAKES LOOP

BOB MARSHAL WILDERNESS

DESCHUTES RIVER

RIVER OF NO RETURN WILDERNESS

GRAND TETON WILDERNESS

MOUNT SAINT HELENS

MOUNT SHASTA

LOWER TWIN LAKES

GRAND CANYON

BAJA

■ 10. Lower Twin Lakes/ Bridgeport:

Much of California's mountain country has very small trout, but there is one area where you need a scale to measure the fish, not a ruler.

It is the Bridgeport area on the eastern Sierra, more specifically, Lower Twin Lakes, Bridgeport Reservoir, the East Walker River, and more than a dozen hike-in lakes within a half-day's walk.

This is where brown trout grow to huge sizes, 10 pounds and up. Lower Twin Lakes even has a special club of fishermen who have caught 10-pounders. Last year, a brown trout weighing 26 pounds, eight ounces was caught at Upper Twin, and a 26-pounder was caught the previous year at Lower Twin. In addition, there is a good fishing for rainbow trout in the two-pound class.

Much of the eastern Sierra is craggy, dry country, but this area is quite pretty, and accessible for anyone. Both Upper and Lower Twin Lakes are nearly full of water. The East Walker River below Bridgeport Reservoir is one of California's best wild trout waters .

Who to contact: Call Ken's Sporting Goods at (619) 932-7707; Mono Village, Upper Twin Lake at (619) 932-7071; Lower Twin Lake at (619) 932-7751; Falling Rock Marina, Bridgeport Reservoir at (619) 932-7001; Toiyabe National Forest at (619) 932-7070, or send $2 for map to Office of Information, U.S. Forest Service, 630 Sansome Street, San Francisco, CA 94111.

FISHING HOLE

APPENDIX

GREAT HIKE-IN FISHING
OF THE WEST

16 WILDERNESS AREAS

When you spend a few hours on a wilderness trail, it provides a chance for your mind to wander and be free. But if you like to fish, thoughts of that evening's camp and adventures always spring to the forefront.

Each step seems easier when you start daydreaming about the fishing or hunting to come. Many wilderness areas in the Western U.S. provide superb hike-in fishing, especially for trout.

Westerners have 50 million acres of wilderness to pick from, which include thousands of lakes and streams that you can explore. The opportunity is diverse and spectacular.

In the Colorado Rockies and California's High Sierra, you can catch golden trout, the rare and most brilliant colored of the trout. In western Montana and Wyoming, big cutthroat range 15 to 22 inches, some bigger. Many are measured in pounds, not inches. In small mountain streams of Oregon and Washington, rainbow trout hide in pocket water behind boulders and logs, waiting for their next meal to drift by.

But if you are not accustomed to fishing wilderness lakes and streams, you will have to adjust your perspective. The one element synonymous with most wilderness areas is "small water fishing." Large lakes and rivers are relatively rare. For many anglers, it demands a completely new approach.

For example, the time period can be relatively narrow for first-class angling, confined to early-morning and late-evening when direct sunlight is off the water. Furthermore,

your approach to the lake or stream must be accomplished with the care of a burglar sneaking through an unlocked window.

On our wilderness trips, my brother Rambob and I have developed a system some may choose to pattern. We fish at daybreak for about an hour, then eat breakfast, break camp and spend the morning hiking to the next destination. We try to time the arrival for early afternoon, so we avoid hiking during the heat of the afternoon. That time is spent setting up another camp, getting a bear-proof food hang, and eating a small meal. By 5 p.m., we're rested, hunger satisfied, our fishing rods are rigged, and we are both eager and ready to fish the prime evening period through sunset.

You don't just walk up to a spot and start pulling huge fish out, not even in areas where the trout have never seen a lure. They're too wary for that.

You must, instead, creep up on a spot, crouching to keep your shadow off the water. Your footprints must be light, making certain the trout do not detect your presence. Your casting motion must also be low and short -- this goes for fly or spinning gear -- because any high, waving motion can tip off the fish.

You identify likely spots that will hold fish, then work them. Rather than just casting away hoping a trout grabs the bait, you fish a spot, working it like a hawk circling over an unsuspecting rabbit. It is more like hunting than fishing.

The water can be clear, especially in the high mountain country. This causes extreme sunlight penetration. In turn, the fish become spooked and elusive. After a careful approach, we often catch a fish on our first or second cast. Then, we might make another cast or two, but soon leave, getting ready to sneak up on the next spot. Cast and move is the strategy. In an evening you might cover a mile or two and catch a stringer of the most beautiful fish you can imagine.

With the right outlook, you can share in some of the best fishing and hunting in the country. You will no longer wonder what people mean when they talk about a "oneness with nature." Because you will have it.

Here's a guide to 16 wilderness areas:

1. Six Rivers National Forest:

These mountains are filled with big cedars and pines and are cut by trails that can take you to many remote fishing areas and lookouts. Out of Gasquet, near Oregon, you can drive to Doe Gap, then hike in to Buck Lake (good fishing) or Devil's Punchbowl. The latter requires a gut-buster of a hike for a few hours, but you are rewarded with a seat next to a remarkable lake, the Punchbowl, actually a rock bowl carved by glacial action and filled with water. With a longer hike, you can detour to Preston Peak, a great vista, then head down the Clear Creek drainage and beyond to Wilderness Falls.

Who to contact: Call forest headquarters at (707) 457-3131, or (707) 442-1721.

2. Caribou Wilderness Area in the Lassen National Forest:

Exploring natural volcanic activity and good one-day in-and-out hikes highlight the Caribou Wilderness. Longer trips involve tying in trails that connect the Caribou Wilderness to Lassen Park. The trout fishing is best here in Black Lake and Turnaround Lake, and both provide fairly easy access for hikers. On a week-long trip, you could tie in Snag Lake or Juniper Lake. Elevations range from 5,000 to 7,000 feet.

Who to contact: For more information, call (916) 257-2151.

3. Marble Mountain Wilderness in Klamath National Forest:

A 1,000-mile network of trails, most of it in the 230,000-acre Marble Mountain Wilderness, offers an outstanding area for backpackers. Trails range as high as 9,000 feet, but most are at about 4,500 to 6,000 feet elevation levels. A prime fishing lake is Ukonom Lake, which is best reached out of the Happy Camp side of the Marbles, but many lakes here can provide good fishing. Upper and Lower Right Lakes and Deep Lake are favorites. Bigfoot is reputed to stalk these mountains.

Who to contact: For more information, call (916) 842-6131.

4. Thousand Lake Wilderness in Lassen National Forest:

Cypress Trailhead is the way to get to Eiler Lake. Eiler Lake is a good trout lake nestled at 6,000 feet elevation. This is an easy in-and-outer and a one-day hike. If you're staying longer, a good option is to hit nearby Box Lake, and Barrett Lake as well, making it a five-mile loop hike. Trout fishing can be okay at McGee and Everett lakes, reachable on the McGee Peak Trail, five miles in. For a week-long trip, you can connect to Tamarack Swale, Bunchgrass, and the adjacent Caribou Wilderness for an imaginative trek.

Who to contact: Call the national forest at (916) 257-2152.

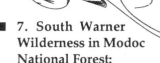

5. Salmon/Trinity Alps Wilderness:

This country is rugged and steep, and most of the lakes are difficult to reach. The highlights here are the Caribou Lakes (out of the Big Flat area), providing a good multi-day hike with good trout fishing. Josephine Lake is a good option. In the summer, temperatures often range between the 80s and 90s, which can make early starts a key to enjoying your trip. Keep your eyes open for giant footprints.

Who to contact: For entry from the north contact Klamath National Forest at (916) 467-5757. For entry from the south contact Shasta/Trinity National Forest at (916) 246-5222.

6. Yolla Bolly Wilderness:

The best fishing is in the very remote areas, where skilled woodsmanship, and rugged multi-day trips are required. If you're not scared off, try Little Fork of Stony Creek (very steep canyon) and Cottonwood Creek. There are almost no one-day hikes, but you can drive in to lakes such as Letts, Pillsbury, Hammerhorn, Plaskett -- and then use those areas as jumpoff points. Many rarely used trails are in this area and range from 3,000 to 6,000 feet.

Who to contact: For entry from the south, contact Mendocino National Forest at (916) 934-3316. For entry from the north contact Shasta/Trinity National Forest at (916) 352-4211.

7. South Warner Wilderness in Modoc National Forest:

The Warner Mountains is a lonely area overlooked by many. It has a genuine mystique highlighted by a remote and extensive trail system. You should take a week and hike the Summit Trail Loop, a 23-miler that traverses both sides of the ridgeline. The west side of the Warner Mountains are like the Sierra, with pine trees, meadows, and streams; the east side is high desert, sagebrush, juniper, and quite rugged. The contrast is stunning. The streams on the western slopes are small, at high altitude, but provide good trout fishing. In particular, East Creek is good, and for a lake, try Clear Lake, Patterson Lake, or North and South Emerson Lakes.

Who to contact: For more information, call (916) 279-6116.

8. Desolation Wilderness:

This is one of the most popular of all hiking areas in the world. It's a take-your-pick situation: The trails out of Emerald Bay are quite steep -- but take you to stunning lookouts. In contrast, the trails out of Echo Lake are quite flat. You could hike for a day, or hike for two weeks. It's a real diverse trail system. There are more than 120 lakes, so if you don't connect with the trout at one, just keep walking. Entry into Desolation Wilderness is on a permit system, which allows no more than 700 overnight visitors at any one time. That makes reservations a necessity. Elevation levels range from 6,300 feet to 9,900 feet.

Who to contact: For entry from the east contact Tahoe Basin management at (916) 544-6420. For entry from the west contact El Dorado National Forest at (916) 622-5061.

■ 9. Immigrant Basin Wilderness in Stanislaus National Forest:

One of the centerpieces of this range is the Kennedy Meadows trailhead, which can lead you to Kennedy Lake, Immigrant Lake areas. These are primarily multi-day backpack trips. For the adventurous, you can connect to the Pacific Crest Trail and ultimately even hike all the way to Yosemite Valley. Some of the best fishing lakes include Immigrant Lake, and in the southern end, Huckleberry Lake and Cherry Lake -- but there are more than a hundred lakes to choose from. Elevations range from 4,500 (Cherry Lake) to peaks above 9,000 feet. Be wary of stream crossings, especially in the afternoon, when snowmelt can raise rivers to dangerous levels.

Who to contact: For more information, call the Stanislaus National Forest at (209) 965-3434.

■ 10. High Sierra Wilderness in Sequoia National Forest:

This is the high country, with mountain passes varying from 9,000 to 12,000 feet, with snow almost always at those levels. With 26 trails on the western slope, hikers have a lot to choose from -- and many of those trail connect to other systems. Good fishing can often be discovered in Kern Canyon, up Copper Creek in Cedar Grove, and from Tyndall Creek. Stream crossings on trails are quite common.

Who to contact: Call Sequoia National Forest at (209) 565- 3307.

■ 11. John Muir Wilderness:

You could begin your trip at Florence Lake or Edison Lake -- reachable by car -- and from there, hike to Evolution Valley in Kings Canyon National Park. Bear Creek is a good fishing spot, but often crowded. Edison Lake is a good jumpoff point (actually at Mono Hot Springs). Trails reach as high as 12,000 feet -- one of which is the classic John Muir Trail.

Who to contact: For entry from the west contact Sierra National Forest at (209) 841-3311 and for entry from the east contact Inyo National Forest at (619) 873-5841.

12. Kaiser Wilderness in the Sierra National Forest:

A trip here was marred by an incredible mosquito attack above the 9,000 foot level, swarms of them feasting on human blood. Upper and Lower Twin Lakes are popular jumpoff points. Trails can be steep, and lead to high country, often buried in snow in early season.

Who to contact: Call the national forest at (209) 893- 6611.

13. Ansel Adams Wilderness:

This is one of the prettiest backpack areas in the world. The trail system is extensive, with some 250 miles in the Minarets alone -- and connects to even more on the Inyo side. Most of the trails are moderate hikes, and elevations in the wilderness range from 7,200 to the top of Mount Ritter at 13,157 feet. After that you start floating. If you want good fishing, a good destination is the Lillian Lake Loop. Several lakes are worth trying, including Stanford, Vandenberg and Lillian Lake itself. The fish are not big, but they are abundant.

Who to contact: For entry from the west contact Sierra National Forest at (209) 877-2218). For entry from east, contact Inyo National Forest at (619) 873-5841.

14. Mokelumne Wilderness:

The more remote areas are in the 8,000 to 9,400 foot levels. Backpackers have a network of trails to choose from, with the Horse Canyon Trail, east of Silver Lakes, a good boot thumper. You could start a trip here by driving to Silver Lakes, Caples Lakes, Bear River Reservoir, camping at night, then taking off on a trail the next morning.

Who to contact: Call El Dorado National Forest at (209) 295-4251. For entry from the south contact Stanislaus National Forest at (209) 532-3671.

15. Ventana Wilderness in Los Padres National Forest:

Hundreds of miles of hiking trails are available, but as you progress inland, the weather can be quite hot in the summer, and fire danger often extreme. When the Sierra is locked up with snow in the spring, this is a good choice. Lost Valley Trail, Arroyo Seco Trail, South Fork Trail, and Big Sur Trail are all good choices.

Who to contact: Call the national forest at (408) 385-5434.

16. Hoover Wilderness:

Nine trailheads offer access to the remote interior areas. The best of these is the Sawtooth Ridge and Matterhorn Peak, which look like the swiss alps; jagged rocks, snow-covered in parts. Most of the back country lakes provide good fishing early in the season; Green, East, Barney, Crown and Peeler lakes can all be good.

Many lakes are within range for one day hikes.

Who to contact: For entry from the east, contact Toiyable National Forest at (619) 932-7070. For entry from the south contact Inyo National Forest at (619) 873-5841.

RULES OF CONDUCT

It takes little time in the backcountry to realize that wilderness is a great cathedral of nature. To many visitors, it is an outdoor church. In turn, it should be treated as a sacred place. We can all follow a code to keep it that way.

Wilderness Permit:
Permits are required for entry into some western wilderness areas, primarily in popular spots in California and near Denver, Aspen and Salt Lake City. This allows rangers the opportunity to assess use, and in popular areas to establish quotas and make certain than no one region is impacted by too much foot or horse traffic.

Campfire Permit:
Permits are required in order to build campfires in most California wilderness areas. During the late summer, some rangers will not issue campfire permits because of forest fire danger.

Pack Out Litter:
Paper can be burned in a campfire, but all other litter must be packed out. Use ziplock bags as small trash containers. A common error is trying to burn the foil packages that contain freeze-dried dinners, because they won't burn -- and the well meaning but mistaken campers will leave trash in the fire ring.

Bury Your Waste:
To prevent the spread of Giardia, a harmful bacteria, bury your waste products at least eight inches deep and at least 100 feet from natural waters.

No Mechanization:
No travel by mountain bicycle or the use of any power equipment is permitted in wilderness areas.

Size Of Party:
The number of people or horses can be restricted in some areas. Check with the district office prior to arranging your trip.

Leave No Trace:
In some wilderness areas, rangers ask that before you leave, you cover your fire pit with dirt and pine needles, scatter the rocks you used for a fire ring, and also toss a few pine needles over your sleeping site.

INDEX

A to Z REFERENCE
TO THE
GREAT OUTDOORS

PUBLISHED BY FOGHORN PRESS
SAN FRANCISCO
QUALITY OUTDOOR BOOKS

A

A.W. Way County Park: 314
AC Transit: 59
Ackerman Campground: 268
Acorn Trail: 213
Adams Reef: 373
Addimando, Tony: 332
Agate Beach: 180-181
Ah-Di-Na Campground: 121, 294
Aikens Campground: 314
Alambique Creek: 42
Alameda County: 2, 5, 8, 14, 224, 424
Alameda Creek: 9, 77, 336
Alaska: 302-304, 445
Albacore: 362-363
Albuquerque: 444
Alcatraz: 346, 354, 347
Alderpoint: 417
Alhambra Creek Valley Staging Area: 15
Alhambra Valley Tree Farm: 424
Almanor Ranger District: 94
Alpine Lake: 33, 188-89
Alpine Meadows: 252
Alturas: 404
Alviso Boat Dock: 370
Amador County: 226
Amador Lake: 242-243, 248
Amador Lodge: 247-248
Ambush: 414
American Canyon Tree Farms: 426
American River: 322, 326-327, 406, 417
Ancil Hoffman Golf Course: 328
Anderson: 210, 302
Anderson Lake: 193

Andretti, Mario: 58
Andrew Molera State Park: 441
Angel Island: 3, 36-37, 348, 355, 371
Angels Camp: 409
Angels Creek: 251
Angler's Guide to Baja (book): 448
Annadel State Park: 130-131
Annapolis: 427
Ano Nuevo Lookout: 342-343
Ano Nuevo State Reserve: 71-72, 99, 148-149, 158-160, 390-391
Ansel Adams Wilderness: 458

Antioch: 34, 185, 335, 353, 364
Antioch Bridge: 335
Antioch Chamber of Commerce: 335
Arastradero Lake: 212-214
-Hiking Trails: 213
-Arastradero Preserve: 214
Arcata: 321
Archery Fire Trail: 51
Arizona: 446-447, 449
Armstrong Redwoods State Reserve: 134-136, 324-325
Armstrong, James: 134
Arroyo Seco Trail: 458
Aschi: 409
Asilomar State Beach: 173-174
Aspen: 446, 459
Austin Creek Recreation Area: 134-135, 320, 324
Ayala Cove: 37

B

Bagby: 419
Bait Shops - See Tackle
Baja: 448
Baja Trail Publications: 448
Baker, Ray: 450
Balconies Cave: 138
Balls Ferry Resort: 302
Bamboo Reef: 174
Barge Hole: 303
Barney Lake: 458
Barrett Lake: 454
BART: 46, 48
Barth's Retreat: 29
Basalt Area: 274

Bass:
-American River: 326
-Anderson Lake: 210
-Annadel State Park: 130
-Arastradero Lake: 213
-Bay Area Lakes: 184
-Berkeley Pier: 387
-Berryessa: 232
-Clear Lake: 238
-Delta, The: 334
-Del Valle Reservoir: 218
-Henry W. Coe State Park: 194
-Lake Amador: 246
-Lake Chabot: 80-83
-Lake Siskiyou: 270
-Lake Sonoma: 234
-Marin Lakes: 188
-New Melones Reservoir: 250
-Northern California Lakes: 224
-San Francisco Bay: 346
-San Luis Reservoir: 272
-San Mateo Coastline: 366-367

-San Pablo Reservoir: 216
-Santa Clara Lakes: 192
-Shasta Lake: 264
-Suisun Bay: 364
-Trinity Lake: 282
Bass Cove: 81
Bass Pond: 197
Bass-Tub: 348
Battaglia Ranch: 426
Battlin, Harry: 198
Baum Lake: 296, 299
Bay Area coast: 358
Bay Bridge: 36, 337, 371
Bay Shark Derby: 354
Baylands:
-Baylands Interpretive Center: 18-19
-Baylands Trail: 56-57
-Bicycle Trail: 56-57
Bear Creek: 421, 456
Bear Creek Tree Farm: 424
Bear Gulch Cave: 138, 140
Bear River Reservoir: 458
Bear Valley: 409
Bear Valley Trail: 6, 23
Bear Valley Visitor Center: 24
Beardsley Reservoir: 256-258
Beaver Creek Campground: 314
Beckers Canoe Outfitters: 447
Beckey, Fred: 395
Beegum Creek: 94
Beegum Gorge: 94
Belmont Lake: 212
Benbow Lake: 418
Benicia: 365
Berkeley: 34, 84, 346, 349, 353, 370
Berkeley Hills: 15
Berkeley Marina: 347, 370-371, 387
Berkeley Pier: 371, 380, 386-387
Berry Creek: 100

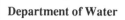

D

E

F

G

Giardia: 195, 459
Gilliam Creek: 135
Gilroy: 74-75, 97, 272, 274, 426
Glacier National Park: 449
Glacier Point: 106
Glenburn: 300
Goethe Park: 328
Gold: See panning
Gold Bluff Beach: 115
Gold Lakes Basin: 113
Golden Gate Bridge: 136, 146, 341, 346-347, 379, 386
Golden Gate National Recreation Area: 3, 5, 27-28, 39
Goodyear's Bar: 418
Gracia, Dan: 306
Grand Canyon National Park: 394, 449
Grand Teton Wilderness: 446
Grandad's Christmas Tree Farm: 427
Grassy Flat Campground: 314
Gray's Falls Campground: 314
Gray, Frank: 231-233
Great Escape, The: 365
Green Lake: 458
Green Valley Tree Farm: 427
Greenwood Road Bridge: 320
Grismill: 328
Grizzly Creek Redwoods Campground: 314
Grosventre Wilderness: 446
Gualala River: 177, 320
Guerneville: 135, 324-325
Guide Seamount: 362
Guinda: 421
Gulf of the Farallones: 340, 343
Gumboot Lake: 121, 270

H

Half Dome: 11, 13, 76, 102, 105-106, 136, 287, 394
Half Moon Bay: 9-10, 19, 45, 64, 66, 69-70, 72, 147-149, 156, 163, 165-169, 170-171, 319, 343, 360, 362-363, 367, 389-391, 422-423, 425
Half Moon Bay State Beach Parks: 20, 148, 152, 169
Halibut: 346, 387
Hamack, Ed: 203
Hammerhorn Lake: 455
Hap's Bait: 335
Happy Camp: 454
Happy Hooker: 349
Happy Isles: 106
Harding Golf Course: 201
Harris Harbor: 365
Harris, Luther: 334
Hartman Reservoir: 197
Hat Creek: 296-299
Hat Creek Anglers: 298
Hawkins Peaks: 139
Hayden Flat Campground: 314
Hayward: 64, 168, 185, 218
Healdsburg: 324-326, 427
Heart's Desire Beach: 376
Heavenly Valley: 413
Helen Lake: 111, 397-398
Hell Ho e Reservoir: 228
Hell's Corner Gorge: 414-415
Henry Cowell State Park: 3, 100
Henry W. Coe State Park: 194-199
-Camping: 199
-Fishing: 194-199
Hermit Rapid: 449
Hesseldenz, Tom: 437
Hi's Tackle Box: 370, 380

I

J

J.B.'s Christmas Trees: 425
Jackass Springs Camp: 93
Jacksmelt: 378-381, 387
Jackson: 446
Jackson County: 225
Jackson Creek: 243, 247
Jackson Meadows Reservoir: 227
Jacobs Valley: 8
Jamestown: 251
Jedediah Smith Redwoods State Park: 118-120, 313-314
Jenner: 152
Jennings, Waylon: 170
Jepson Trail: 376
John Boyle Reservoir: 418
John from Princeton, Capt.: 360
John Muir Trail: 13, 102, 106, 287, 395, 421, 456
John Muir Wilderness: 456
Johnson Park: 298
Johnson, Bill: 201
Johnson, Liver-Eating: 445
Johnsville: 113
Jones Valley Resort: 265
Josephine Lake: 455
Junction City Campground: 314
June Mountain: 413
Juniper Lake: 109-110, 454

K

K. Marauder, Capt: 365
Kaiser Wilderness: 458
Kelly Lake: 195, 197
Kelsey Creek Campground: 238-239
Kelseyville: 438

Ken's Sporting Goods: 451
Kennedy Lake: 456
Kennedy Meadows trailhead: 456
Kent Lake: 33, 190
Kentfield: 238
Kenwood Tree Farm: 427
Kern Canyon: 456
Kern River: 419
Kernville: 419
Keswick Lake: 229
Kibbee Lake: 447
Kids (specific programs):
-Skiing Program: 412
-Trout Fishing: 75
Kimsey, Joe: 123, 293-295
King City: 277, 404
King Island: 335
King Mountain Range: 320
King's Creek Falls: 110
King's Creek Trail: 110
King's Tackle: 325
King, Bob: 335
Kings Canyon National Park: 421, 456
Kings River: 333, 418
Kirch Flat Campground: 418
Kirkwood: 409
Kitchen Ranch: 427
Klamath: 321
Klamath National Forest: 93, 121, 401, 404, 454-455
Klamath River: 122, 177, 180, 308, 310, 314, 317-319, 321, 395, 414-416, 418
Klamath/Trinity system: 307
Knights Ferry: 417
Kopta Slough: 132-133
Kourth's Pirate Lair: 335
Kutzkey, Al: 318
Kutzkey, Tim: 318-319
Kyburz: 409

L

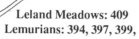

M

O

P

Q

R

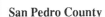

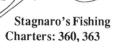

T

U

V

W

Y

Z

■ Photo credits:

R. Valentine Atkinson: 269. Abe Cuanang: 361. Mark Gholson: 419. Paul Glines: 161. John Gorman: 67, 141. Kim Komenich: 157. Ned MacKay, East Bay Regional Park District: 17, 83. Dick Pool: 205. Kurt Rogers: 349. Lee Romero: 357. Paul Sakuma: 49. San Francisco Examiner: 137. State Department of Parks and Recreation: 29, 493. Tom Stienstra: 35, 98, 117, 122, 153, 237, 240, 249, 259, 262, 275, 284, 381, 457.

■ About the Author

Tom Stienstra is recognized as one of California's premier outdoors writers. He is outdoors editor for the San Francisco Examiner, Camping Editor for Western Outdoors, and the founding president of the Outdoor Writers of California.

More importantly, Tom is an avid adventurer. As a full-time outdoors writer, he has traveled throughout the state in search of prime fishing, hiking and camping areas. Among his many adventures are a month-long hunt for Bigfoot, hiking the John Muir Trail and climbing California's highest mountains.

A graduate of San Jose State, Tom joined the San Francisco Examiner in 1980 where he has won many writing awards. In 1989, he won first and second place for "Pride in America" writing awards from the Outdoor Writers Association of America. In 1988, he was awarded first place for the nation's best feature outdoors column. His articles appear regularly in Western Outdoor News, and Field & Stream. His other books include California Camping, which ranks among the top selling outdoor books in the state, Pacific Northwest Camping (named the number one bestseller by the Portland Oregonian) and Rocky Mountain Camping, all published by Foghorn Press, as well as California Salmon Magic.

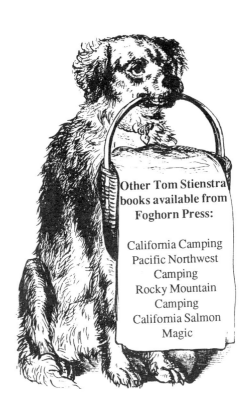

Other Tom Stienstra
books available from
Foghorn Press:

California Camping
Pacific Northwest
Camping
Rocky Mountain
Camping
California Salmon
Magic